Black Messiahs and Uncle Toms

Black Messiahs
and Uncle Toms:

Social and Literary Manipulations of a Religious Myth

Wilson Jeremiah Moses

The Pennsylvania State University Press
University Park and London

Library of Congress Cataloging in Publication Data

Moses, Wilson Jeremiah, 1942–
  Black Messiahs and Uncle Toms.

  Includes bibliography and index.
  1. Messianism, Afro–American. 2. Afro–Americans
—Race identity. 3. Black nationalism—United
States. 4. Afro–Americans—Religion. I. Title.
E185.625.M67   305.8'96073   81–9645
ISBN 0–271–00294–8   AACR2

Designed by Dolly Carr

Printed in the United States of America

For Maureen

Contents

	Preface	ix
	Acknowledgements	xiii
1	The Concept of Messianism, Sacred and Secular	1
2	A Search for African Roots of the Tradition	17
3	The Black Jeremiad and American Messianic Traditions	30
4	The Myth of Uncle Tom and the Messianic Mission of the Black Race	49
5	Faith, Fatalism, and Racial Christianity: The Slavery Crisis and Reconstruction	67
6	Booker T. Washington: A Black Moses and the Covenant Revealed to Him	86
7	The New Negro and America's Changing World Mission	107
8	Marcus Garvey: The Resurrection of the Negro, and the Redemption of Africa	124
9	Du Bois' *Dark Princess* and the Heroic Uncle Tom	142
10	Waiting for the Messiah: From Joe Louis to Martin Luther King, Jr.	155
11	Chosen Peoples of the Metropolis: Black Muslims, Black Jews, and Others	183
12	Messianic Oratory and the Theme of "Ethiopianism" in Ralph Ellison's *Invisible Man*	196
13	Racial Messianism and Political Revivalism in the 1960s	207
14	Black Messianism and American Destiny	226
	Notes	235
	Selected Bibliography	261
	Index	271

Preface

The most convincing proof of an ethnic group's cultural health is its ability to sustain a myth of its history and destiny. As black messianic myths die out, new ones spring up to take their places. Martin Luther King is dead and the millenarian integrationism that he symbolized sleeps with him—at least for the present. Malcolm X and Elijah Muhammad are dead; the Black Muslims have splintered into numerous impoverished groups. Minister Farrakhan, one-time spokesman for Mr. Muhammad, has split from the departed Messenger's sons to organize his own masjid.[1]

Meanwhile in the East, a new leader has arisen. He is Al Hajj Imam Isa Abd'Allah Muhammad Al Mahdi, usually referred to as Imam Isa. Encountering two of his white-robed followers on the subway in Manhattan, I asked if they had any association with Minister Farrakhan. My informant stiffened almost imperceptibly. "Farrakhan is still under the five-point star," he said, and I noticed that he was wearing a small pendant—a six-point star surmounting a crescent with the horns pointing upward—the symbol of the Ansaru Allah Community, led by the mysterious Imam.

The prophets are not all dead. Imam Isa, as his followers believe, is the great-grandson of Al Imam Muhammad Ahmad Al Mahdi, who led the jihad (or holy war) against the British in the Sudan during the 1880s. But Imam Isa does not promise us a jihad, although he displays the Mahdi's battle flag. "HE IS THE LAMB, the sacrificial victim or offering to ALLAH for the sins of the 144,000," reads the Ansar literature. "You persecute him. . . . YOU ARE CRUCIFYING HIM!!!"[2]

This blending of Jewish, Christian, and Islamic symbolism that one observes among the Ansars is no less striking than the merging of the images of the avenging messiah and the suffering servant. These motifs, so interwoven in the Hebraic tradition and its derivatives, are mingled to no less an extent in black leadership myths.

No study of myth and symbol can ignore the methodological contributions of Henry Nash Smith in *Virgin Land: The American West as Symbol and Myth*. In this signal exposition of the American Studies method, Smith used the words "myth" and "symbol" "to designate larger or smaller units of the same kind of thing, namely an intellectual construction that fuses concept and emotion into an image." Borrowing from Bergson, Levy–Bruhl, and Vaihinger, he formulated a theory on the nature of fictions in which myth was seen as a statement of the truth but expressed in metaphorical terms. In *Virgin Land*, he developed what has since become one of the characteristic concerns of American Studies methodology—"protest against the common usage of the term 'myth' to mean simply an erroneous belief."[3]

By means of a series of thematically related essays on a number of historical and literary topics, Smith described the growth of three important myths: the search for a Northwest Passage and its relationship to expansionism and the doctrine of Manifest Destiny; the symbol and the myth of the Frontier Hero and Heroine; and "the myth of the Great American Desert, [which] was partially supplanted by a competing version of the myth of the Garden. . . ." Smith showed how all these myths were important—either because they motivated people to productive action, or because they came to incite "behavior grossly inappropriate to the given historical situation."[4]

My approach to black messianism is similar. Like Smith, I am concerned with both social and literary manifestations of the phenomena I describe. I view black messianism as a powerful and, in many respects, a beautiful myth, permeating the thinking of both white and black Americans since the late eighteenth century. It has served a motivating function in both black nationalist and integrationist efforts for black advancement. In the past, it has undoubtedly been of use; but, like all myths, it has the potential to incite "behavior grossly inappropriate to the given historical situation" (see note 4).

For my definition of black messianism, I am indebted to an insight inadvertently provided by Martin Kilson at the Yale University symposium on Black Studies in the University.[5] Kilson observed that much of the rhetoric of black movements was based on the traditional Western religious belief in the redemptive power of suffering. This has led to the idea that black America has a special redemptive message for humanity. Kilson interprets this as racism; others, notably Martin Luther King, Jr., do not. King once wrote:

> Arnold Toynbee says in *A Study of History* that it may be the Negro who will give the new spiritual dynamic to Western civilization that it so desperate-

ly needs to survive. I hope this is possible. The spiritual power that the Negro can radiate to the world comes from love, understanding, good will, and non-violence. . . . The Negro may be God's appeal to this age—an age drifting rapidly to its doom.[6]

Thus I use messianism to refer to a group phenomenon. This is consistent with the way in which the concept is understood today by many Reform Jews who no longer await the coming of a personal messiah but see the entire Jewish community as having a redemptive message to offer the world.[7] As I have documented in the notes to Chapter 1, many twentieth-century scholars use "messianism" in this way. My usage of the term is consistent with that of Martin Buber and Bertrand Russell, who even apply it to secular movements.[8]

However, black messianism is not only a way of perceiving the group; it is a way of perceiving individuals. Here I must acknowledge my methodological debt to John William Ward and his celebrated study, *Andrew Jackson: Symbol for an Age*.[9] The influence of Ward will be most apparent in my treatment of Joe Louis. I have been more concerned with Joe Louis, the myth, than with Joe Louis Barrow, the ex-factory worker from Detroit, who was at the core of the myth. I was not aware of Lawrence Levine's brilliant treatment of the Joe Louis myth in *Black Culture and Black Consciousness* until I had finished Chapter 10.[10] While my discussion of Joe Louis is not influenced by Levine's, it is consistent with his. It is also significantly different. I have made use of an important archival source that Levine does not mention, the Joe Louis Scrapbook in the Schomburg Collection of the New York Public Library. I was also able to benefit from Louis's recently published second autobiography.

The reader will notice that I have put considerable emphasis on the myth of Uncle Tom. I have found this myth singularly difficult to untangle, because it is an old myth by American standards and has meant so many different things during the seven score years of its existence. Mrs. Stowe, of course, meant for Uncle Tom to symbolize the black race's innate propensity for Christian heroism. It was because the African race possessed the traits of patience, long suffering, and forgivingness that they would ultimately become a messianic redeemer race.[11]

But black people naturally recoiled from such an interpretation of their historical mission. They did not wish to hang on the cross for the rest of mankind. Thus, Uncle Tom soon became a symbol of misguided altruism. By the early twentieth century, the myth of "Uncle Tom" was on the way to becoming entirely distorted. Mrs. Stowe's Uncle Tom was a selfless, stoical, fatalistic martyr, who died for his fellow slaves, and whose provocation of Simon Legree presaged the cries of ghetto rioters advancing towards armed police officers taunting, "Kill me! Kill me!" Uncle Tom's martyrdom foreshadowed the "revolutionary suicide" of Huey Newton and his professed desire "to die for the people."[12] It is ironic that the humble heroism of old Uncle Tom has been transmuted into racial treason by the subtle alchemy of social amnesia.

My final methodological debt is to the American Studies methodology in literary criticism. Like Roy Harvey Pearce, F. O. Matthiessen, and R. W. B. Lewis, I believe that poets and novelists are at the center of a culture.[13] I recognize some of the problems that spring from discussing nationalism or cultural traditions in literature. As Solomon Fishman has noted:

> Literary nationalism . . . converts the national category into an active principle of composition, a criterion of value. In this perspective the preliminary condition of literary activity is a distinctive national culture; the value of a work is not only derived from nationality but also judged by fidelity to the national culture.[14]

This is a difficult problem to avoid, for an author's handling of myth and symbol properly falls within the province of aesthetic judgment, and this remains true regardless of how politically charged the myths and symbols may be. In any case, I use the nationalistic tradition, not as a "criterion of value," but as a means of elucidation. The two literary artists I have treated in greatest depth are the two who best illustrate the crisis of black messianic myth in twentieth-century fiction. W. E. B. Du Bois, as Vincent Harding has observed, was instrumental in the creation of messianic myths; Ralph Ellison has satirized the messianic tradition and portrayed its shortcomings more effectively than anyone else.[15] I have discussed elsewhere Du Bois' use of the "Ethiopian theme" in his early poetry, defining the theme as a view of history that predicts a cosmic rotation of elites when Ethiopia finally stretches forth her hands.[16] In the present work, I touch on some other aspects of his messianic mythology, especially as it appeared in his two early novels where he created protagonists who embody the characteristics of the black race, as defined in Stowe's *Uncle Tom's Cabin*.

One of the advantages of the present methodology is that it allows us to look at larger patterns of a culture by focusing on a specific symbol in which its myths are crystallized. It also allows us to see unities among phenomena that are at first glance contradictory. Religion is, of course, the primary way in which the human mind has reconciled contradiction and conflict in the universe. The symbol of Mary has been used to reconcile the conflicting ideals of motherhood and virginity. The "Kingdom of Christ" has been used to reconcile American righteousness and ruthless imperialism. The myth of black messianism reconciles the sense of separateness that black people feel and their fundamental belief that they are truly American. It is the point at which their black nationalism and their American nationalism overlap.

Acknowledgements

For their encouragement at various stages of this project, I must give thanks to George Bass, Rhett Jones, Barry Karl, Bob Leach, Otey Scruggs, and Moses Williams. Cyril Griffith encouraged me to submit the manuscript to The Pennsylvania State University Press, where it was placed in the capable hands of John Pickering and Janet Shank. James Early and Hal Williams were more than cooperative in releasing me from classroom duties at Southern Methodist University. William G. McLoughlin read an early draft of the manuscript and encouraged me to refine some of my ideas. The staff of the Fondren Library, Southern Methodist University, gave me everything I desired. The staff of the Schomburg Collection of the New York Public Library were helpful, as usual. The library of the University of Cambridge graciously allowed me readers' privileges during two years that I spent in England. Grants from the National Endowment for the Humanities, the Southern Fellowships Fund, the American Council of Learned Societies, and the American Philosophical Society provided me with free time and travel expenses that immensely aided this project. Mrs. Marjorie Johnson typed several drafts of the manuscript. My wife, Maureen Connor Moses, intrepidly blue-penciled numerous versions, undaunted by the ill humor that her diligence inevitably provoked. It is to her that I dedicate this book.

1
The Concept of Messianism, Sacred and Secular

This volume is concerned with four different varieties of messianic phenomena, all of which are subsumed under the general rubric of "messianism" as it is defined in the *Encyclopedia Britannica* and the *Encyclopedia Judaica*. The major patterns which I treat include:

1. The expectation or identification of a personal savior—a messiah, a prophet, or a Mahdi. This theme has its politico-religious manifestations, appearing in David Walker's *Appeal* (1829), *The Ethiopian Manifesto* (1829), and Albert J. Cleage's *The Black Messiah* (1969). It also has literary manifestations, as in W. E. B. Du Bois' novel *Dark Princess* (1928).

2. The far more important theme of racial messianism—a concept of the redemptive mission of the black race. The best-known statement of this theme was in *Uncle Tom's Cabin*, a work that merely "concretized" views of black personality and destiny shared by many of Mrs. Stowe's white and black contemporaries.

3. Messianic symbolism—journalistic and artistic presentations of certain black individuals as symbolic messiahs. A symbolic messiah, like Joe Louis, may be created by the press or the public imagination without his conscious cooperation.

4. "Prophetism" and "prophetic movements". Some social scientists prefer the term "prophetism" to "messianism," but in general the same phenomena are treated under both terms. In early Biblical usage, the term *mashiah* (anointed) was applied to prophets, and "could denote anyone with a special mission from God."

The central idea of this study is that the Afro–American messianic myth has thrived because its rhetoric is familiar to the people of the United States, who envision themselves as a "redeemer people." But the power of the black community to conjure with messianic shibboleths is grievously weakened in an age when America's messianic self-concept has been seriously damaged. Black messianism has always been reinforced by the messianic strains in American culture. It echoes the utopianism and isolationism that have characterized so much of American life, from the founding of the Massachusetts Bay colonies, to the pilgrimage of the Mormons, to the separatism of contemporary black Jews. Black messianism is not to be understood as cult behavior— although, to be sure, some black cults are messianic. Nor is black messianism in the United States to be understood as a survival of the African background, although there are certainly some African cognates for Afro–American messianism.

I shall presently discuss the theological origins of the concept of messianism, but here at the outset I remind the reader that the term is seldom used in a purely religious sense. I define the term broadly, as does Professor R. J. Zwi Werblowski of the Department of Religion at Hebrew University in Jerusalem. In his article for *Encyclopedia Britannica*, Werblowski includes both religious and secular phenomena under the definition of messianic movements. It is, of course, well known to students of the history of religion that messianism does not necessarily imply belief in a personal savior. As Werblowski observes, "Messianic ideologies and movements are not necessarily centred on a messianic figure, though there is a tendency for such movements to personify the messianic ideal, and to have a personal messiah play the central role in its realization."[1]

In agreement with Werblowski are the scholarly rabbis, Louis Jacobs, Ph.D., and Professor Sergio Joseph Sierra, Lecturer in Hebrew Languages and Literature at the University of Turin. In their article for *Encyclopedia Judaica*, they have demonstrated that a group conception of messianism is now accepted by most Jews (see note 1). A conference of Reform rabbis meeting in Columbus, Ohio, in 1937 spoke of messianism in terms of the collective mission of the Jewish people. The conference proclaimed that it was the "messianic goal" of modern Judaism "to cooperate with all men in the establishment of the kingdom of God." Martin Buber has also argued for a group conception of messianic mission, and has interpreted the involvement of Jews in modern revolutionary movements as stemming from the Jewish messianic legacy. Bertrand Russell has even attributed Marx's conception of history to the Jewish heritage, and he speaks of Marxism (along with fascism) as a messianic movement derived from a Jewish eschatology.[2]

Within the context of American history, the group concept of messianism has been well described by E. L. Tuveson in *Redeemer Nation*. He shows how the concepts of "kingdom of God" and "American Destiny" were linked in the thinking of prominent American religious thinkers. Among the most important of those he mentions are Timothy Dwight in the 1790s, Lyman Beecher in the mid-nineteenth century, and Josiah Strong at the turn of the century. Tuveson's study should be discussed in connection with Martin Marty, *Righteous Empire*, Robert Bellah, *The Broken Covenant*, and H. Richard Niebuhr, *The Kingdom of God in America*. All these authors describe, although they do not approve, the self-righteous messianism of the American tradition, which has so often seen its mission as the salvation of the world.[3]

William G. McLoughlin, in *The American Evangelicals*, examines the rhetoric of the Civil War era and shows how America's concept of its destiny was capable of assuming messianic proportions. Christ's vengeful second coming would be acted out, at least in a metaphorical sense, by the righteous Union Army, which would crush the serpent with its heel. God had "chosen the *United* States of America to lead the way to the redemption of the world for Christian freedom." Edmund Wilson, in *Patriotic Gore*, has made similar observations. McLoughlin shows how Julia Ward Howe endowed the Union with the qualities attributed to the Biblical Messiah by means of the numerous Scriptural allusions in the "Battle Hymn of the Republic."[4] White abolitionists often viewed the Union armies as messianic; occasionally the black race, standing at the eye of the storm, was invested with messianic qualities.

George Fredrickson, in *The Black Image in the White Mind*, has shown how the qualities with which Harriet Beecher Stowe endowed her Uncle Tom were commonly held stereotypes of the black race, not necessarily intended as pejorative. Indeed, as S. P. Fullinwider has shown in *The Mind and Mood of Black America*, these qualities were usually perceived as Christlike. Tuveson has also shown how the redeemer-nation concept was adapted by such abolitionists as Theodore Parker to imply a messianic destiny for the black race. Referring to more recent phenomena, Vincent Harding and August Meier have shown how black leaders like W. E. B. Du Bois and Martin Luther King have employed messianic myths in their attempts to manipulate public consciousness.[5]

Black messianism is often discussed in connection with religious black nationalism, as defined by John H. Bracey, to include a wide range of phenomena. Religious nationalism may refer simply to a sense of racial solidarity within a predominantly white denomination, or to a desire for a black theocratic state. How one defines black nationalism will depend on how one defines the concept of nationalism in general, and there is no universally accepted definition of nationalism. For the purpose of this study, however, I find very useful Hans Kohn's history-of-ideas approach as presented in *The Idea of Nationalism*. Kohn sees nationalism as a sense of peoplehood, traceable to the Jewish conception of themselves as a group united by history, blood, and culture, and distinguished from the rest of humanity by a God-given destiny. Nationalism implies, in addition, a striving after statehood, especially republican government in the tradition of the Greek polis. Most nations conform to these patterns, and the applicability of at least the first part of the definition to the messianic view of black nationalism should be obvious.[6]

It can be seen that "messianism" as we use the term today is a complex concept. It is commonly used to refer to any phenomenon characterized by prophetic, millennial, or missionary ideology. Attempts by sociologists and anthropologists to manufacture an alternative ter- minology have been totally devoid of success. The problems have been discussed by Harold W. Turner, Director of the Project for New Religious Movements at the University of Aberdeen. He has suggested that social scientists should not even use terms such as "messianic" or "millennial."[7] His is an extreme view that may have merit for sociologists and anthropologists, but not for students of social mythologies, whose business it is to investigate the ironic contradictions and emotional implications of terms, not to avoid them. So here at the outset, I shall provide a working definition of messianism as the perception of a person or a group, by itself or by others, as having a manifest destiny or a God- given role to assert the providential goals of history and to bring about the kingdom of God on earth.

The term "messiah" derives from the Hebrew, *mashiah*, meaning anointed. In the traditions of the ancient Hebrews, it signified the belief in a future great deliverer—a priest, king, or prophet—who would come with a special mission from God. Usually this mission was seen as politically revolutionary but culturally reactionary. The belief in a messiah grew out of the Hebrews' experience of oppression at the hands of the great Middle-Eastern empires. It symbolized their hopes for an improvement in the fortunes of their nation and the restoration of their ancient ideals. The messiah would usher in a messianic age. The chosen people would revolt against their political oppressors and revitalize the conservative values advocated by the prophets. Messianic ideas were adapted by the early Christians, who saw Jesus of Nazareth as the long- awaited messiah (*Christos* in Greek means the anointed one). After the death of Jesus, the early Christians began to await his second coming, at which time he would inaugurate a messianic era of a thousand years' duration. This belief came to be known as millenarianism or chiliasm, from the Latin *millenarias* and the Greek *chilios* (a thousand).[8]

Thus the terms "millennium" and "messianic era" are interchangeable, and messianism thus implies a doctrine of perfectionism which is usually even more important than the expectation of a personal messiah. Indeed it has been shown that the term *mashiah* was applied in the Old Testa- ment, not only to sacred persons, prophets, and kings, but to sacred objects and ideals. The term came to signify the Jewish people themselves and, more recently, any other nation or religious group who see themselves as the agents of a messianic destiny. A messianic people are a chosen or anointed people who will lead the rest of the world in the direction of righteousness. The messianic people traditionally see themselves as a conscience for the rest of the human race—sometimes as a suffering servant or a sacrificial lamb, sometimes as an avenging angel.

Black messianism is a very American tradition, but it has cognates throughout Africa. Roger Bastide has suggested, indeed, that "prophetic salvationism," as in the case of Father Divine, "embodies certain undeniably African features."[9] Be that as it may, Bastide bases his conjectures on scant evidence and reveals his characteristic tendency to confuse sources and analogues. Whether or not Afro–American messianism can be seen as deriving in any direct way from African antecedents, an understanding of black messianism in the Old World will be useful to our discussion. The African's confrontation with Western civilization and colonialism produced varieties of prophetic millenarian consciousness that are similar to those experienced in the Americas.

Certain characteristics of indigenous African religions, long noted by social scientists, indicate that they are by nature hospitable to messianic doctrines. In her study of ceremonial spirit possession, Sheila S. Walker has shown how chosen individuals among various African traditional peoples utilize states of possession as occasions for acting out rebellious feelings towards authority figures. Similar observations have long been made by other scholars.[10] Divinely inspired rebellion against the social order is, of course, a traditional aspect of Judeo–Christian messianism. The traditional linkage between rebellious roles and prophetic activity can be seen in the rise of the Zulu prophet Isaiah Shembe. Shembe revived the traditional role of the prophetic witch doctor, which he combined with the Judeo–Christian messianic role to form his independent church in the early twentieth century. He was reactionary in his resurrection of tribal religious forms, but revolutionary in urging his followers on towards millenarian expectations. Thus did his pattern of leadership echo that of the Old Testament prophets.[11]

The impact of Judeo–Christian ideas on African thinking predates by many centuries the activities of Western European explorers. Ethiopia was converted to Christianity by the end of the second century, and the origins of Ethiopia's black Jews are guessed to be at least equally ancient. The black Jews of Ethiopia claim to be descended from the followers of Menelik I, the child of King Solomon and the Queen of Sheba.[12] The Ethiopian monarchs, until the dethronement of Haile Selassie, had their own version of the myth and arrogated to themselves a messianic status as descendants of the Hebrew kings. As successors to the line of David and Solomon, they fell heirs to the tradition that had venerated the Kings of the Jews as living messiahs. The Falasha Jews of Ethiopia, however, still await the coming of their messiah and the establishment of a "millennium" that will last for forty years.[13] The possibility that messianic ideas have penetrated other areas of the continent from Ethiopic sources cannot be overlooked, and perhaps future researchers will find convincing evidence of such.[14]

Muslim influences may likewise have brought messianic traditions to precolonial Africa. Although Islam is not a messianic religion, it does have room for Mahdism, the belief in a divinely guided restorer of the faith, who will establish a prophetic kingdom at the end of history. At the commencement of the slave trade to the Americas, Islamic influences were hardly unknown in most areas where the slave trade was operational. Although they were far from being universally adopted by the peoples of West Africa, Judeo–Islamic ideas were gradually trickling in from the east at the same time that Christian ideas were penetrating as a result of the slave trade. By 1700 the awareness of Christian and Muslim intrusion was touching on most African societies. One therefore feels comfortable with George Shepperson's estimation that prophetic Christianity beyond the borders of Ethiopia is traceable to at least as early as the fifteenth century.[15] Messianic religion inflamed the zeal of a sect attempting to restore the independence of the Congo during the late 1600s. The prophetess Beatrice, leader of this sect, was burned for her efforts in 1706.[16] By the mid-nineteenth century some evidence of messianic Christianity is detectable in almost every region of Africa.[17]

"Ethiopianism" is the name given to the millennial Christianity of various sects and cults arising at the end of the nineteenth century. These, despite their name, have little to do with traditional Ethiopian religion, however. Their rise has been attributed by Shepperson, Oosthuizen, and others to the messianic zeal of Afro–American missionaries.[18] The name of the movement is derived from the Biblical passage so often cited by black missionaries, "Princes shall come out of Egypt; Ethiopia shall soon stretch forth her hands unto God" (Psalms 68:31). The passage traditionally has been given a political as well as a missionary interpretation in the English-speaking world since the eighteenth century, and has been viewed as a prophecy of African glory. The redemption of Africa involved not only Christianizing the continent, but liberating it from foreign domination. "Africa for the Africans" was at once a religious and a political slogan. Although these movements were utopian and seldom showed any real understanding of the highly organized technological cultures against which they rebelled, Ethiopianism planted the seeds of modern revolutionary nationalism in Africa.[19] Because of its preoccupation with messianic chiliastic Christianity, it also prepared African minds for the acceptance of the Marxist view of history, which is derived from the Judeo–Christian eschatology.

Ethiopianism and other forms of black messianism also appear in the

Caribbean. In Haiti certain national heroes, notably Toussaint L'Ouverture and Dessalines, have been deified; and it is believed that they can possess the bodies of living persons.[20] Under the presidency of Francois Duvalier, voodooism (a form of synthesis between African and Judeo–Christian concepts) became the state religion, with a living prophet at its head in the person of the president himself. The best-known example of Ethiopianism in the Caribbean is Rastafarianism, which ironically derives from a legend concerning Marcus Garvey. On the occasion of his departure from Jamaica in 1916, Garvey is purported to have told his followers to look to Ethiopia whence a new king would come to lead them.[21] A desperate and impoverished element among the Jamaican people came to believe that this king was none other than the emperor of Ethiopia, Ras Tafari Makonnen. Garvey, of course, developed the profoundest contempt for Ras Tafari, who changed his name to Haile Selassie upon his coronation. He felt that the emperor was an irresponsible leader, and that he had betrayed his duty to the African peoples by failing to repulse Mussolini's invaders in 1936. Furthermore, Garvey had great contempt for Jamaican cult behavior, as he made clear in his editorials in *The Black Man* during the 1930s. This was apparently unknown to the Rastamen, who are still fond of displaying the red, black, and green colors of the UNIA flag and see Garvey as occupying a place only a notch below Haile Selassie in the black nationalist pantheon. The Rastafarians are out of step with Garveyism; however, they are typical Ethiopianists in their millennial view of history and their belief in the messianic destiny of the African race, who are a chosen people.

The belief of Roger Bastide, Leonard Barrett, and others, who see black messianic and millennial phenomena as deriving primarily from African sources, is difficult to support when we recall that similar behavior has been observed among the indigenous peoples of North America and the South Pacific. True, the natives of New Guinea, among whom the so-called cargo cults have developed, are a Negroid people. Conceivably there is some prehistoric missing link between the messianic cults of Melanesia and those of Old World and New World Africans. Cargo cults arose during and after World War I, when natives of the islands adopted the belief that steamship cargoes were in reality gifts from the ancestors to the islanders but which had been appropriated by the whites, who must be overthrown if the natives were to receive their due. These cults are similar to the messianic religions of the rest of the black world, because they are a response to the dogma of white supremacy and the pattern of European domination.[22]

The ghost dance movements among the Plains Indians of North America are even less likely to have derived from African sources. These movements, like the others discussed here, seemed to arise out of the crisis of confrontation with European expansionism and white supremacy. People develop a messianic view of themselves because of the historical experience of being oppressed as a group. Messianic traditions persist because the heritage of oppression persists. Ancient African roots are much less important to black messianism than is the experience of white domination in the modern world.

It would be wrong, of course, to say that messianic ideals are the exclusive property of the oppressed. Rich and powerful peoples are equally capable of viewing themselves as chosen nations. Sometimes this is so because they have not yet cast aside the myths and traditions that sustained them during their early history, when they were weaker and less imposing. In their infancy the American colonies were havens for the spiritually oppressed, fleeing from domination by the intolerant. So, at least, goes the great American myth. The growth and development of American culture has meant the inevitable expansion of libertarian ideals. For this reason, God and history have been on the nation's side. If any mistakes have ever been made, they have always been made with the purest of intentions. At least so Americans like to think.

That the United States has appropriated to itself from its earliest history a messianic role and a millennial destiny has inspired voluminous commentary.[23] The tradition is usually traced to John Winthrop's drawing up a covenant with God and declaring that the Massachusetts Bay Colony would be a citadel of social perfection. During the early years of the Republic, two varieties of American messianism seemed to evolve. There was a hard-line messianism that eventually developed into the doctrine of white racial supremacy, ruthless expansionism, religious intolerance, and economic insensitivity. There was also a soft-line messianism, growing out of the unrealized ideals of the Jeffersonian tradition and the American enlightenment, which came to emphasize America's mission to preserve the inalienable rights of man. According to the latter set of beliefs, the American mission was not to dominate the rest of the world, forcing it into the paths of righteousness, but to serve as an example of the spiritual perfection that human nature could aspire to in an atmosphere of political freedom.

The values of both hard-line and soft-line messianism were detachable and transferable. They could be appropriated at random from the American ideological smorgasbord by liberals and conservatives alike. For example, during the ante-bellum years neither abolitionists nor pro-slavery advocates had a monopoly on white racial supremacy or religious intolerance. And during the Gilded Age, a social gospeler like Josiah Strong could be sensitive to the economic woes of the American working class, while giving encouragement to the most ruthless advocates of imperialism and Manifest Destiny.

Within the United States, members of numerous ethnic and religious groups have taken on messianic beliefs akin to, but distinct from, those of the larger society. Examples include the Mormons, the Shakers, the Oneida Community, the Amish, the Jehovah's Witnesses, and, in some rare instances, Jewish utopian communalists.[24] No group of Americans have had a more deeply rooted or more stubbornly maintained messianic tradition than black Americans, however. This is singular because, unlike the other subgroups in society who have seen themselves as messianic, black Americans have not had a common religion. They have nonetheless been able to maintain a distinct messianic tradition despite differences in class, culture, and regional background. With the possible exception of Jewish Americans, no other group is seen as constituting a permanently separate entity within the American nation. While black Americans may no longer fit the image of a nation in bondage as they did at the time of the Dred Scott decision, they are still something other than just another ethnic group.

The essence of the black messianic tradition has been described by Martin Kilson, who perhaps overstresses its ties to "the black racialist or black nationalist view":

> In this view of the black experience, the slave trade . . . endowed the black man with a special aura of righteousness, indeed that same righteousness that has been applied to the oppressed and wretched of the earth since the birth of Christianity. . . . Of course the typical black nationalist would not today attribute to Christian doctrine his view of the special aura of righteousness accruing to the oppressed and despised black man.[25]

Now, Kilson is correct when he identifies this strain in the consciousness of many black people. I take issue, however, with his assertion that black messianism is peculiar to black nationalists or black racists. He is demonstrably wrong when he goes on to suggest that most black nationalists would reject the Christian origins of their messianic self-conception. As we shall see, integrationists and prophets of Christian *agape* have identified themselves with the doctrine of black messianism. Since the nineteenth century, even white writers as diverse as Harriet Beecher Stowe and Arnold Toynbee have attributed a messianic role to black people. Finally, the tendencies of various social and racial groups to think of themselves as chosen peoples certainly did not begin with Christianity. While Kilson is correct in recognizing that the essence of black nationalism is in the Judeo–Christian messianic tradition, he fails to observe that the entire heritage of black people is suffused with that tradition precisely because they are American.

The crucial period in the formation of the Afro–American messianic consciousness was in the decades preceding the Civil War, a period during which messianic, millennial, and apocalyptic ideas were raging throughout America. That such a conception of the crusade against slavery was characteristic of abolitionist rhetoric is a point so often made that it scarcely needs to be repeated here.[26] With the ante-bellum years dominated so strongly by the rhetoric of militant Christian soldierism, black Americans came to think of their struggle as a moral crusade. The holy war against slavery and their ultimate deliverance from it was associated in the minds of black people and in the minds of some other Americans with the sacred mission of the United States to extend freedom to all persons within its boundaries. Thus the struggle for black freedom came widely to be viewed as the central issue in American moral life.

Concurrently with the growth of the abolitionist movement, the aforementioned black nationalism developed. It was expressed mainly by black writers, who were influenced by the hard-line American messianism. The soft-line black messianists came to think of the Afro–American destiny in terms of the nation's mission as a land of freedom, in which all races might participate on a basis of equality. The hard-liners developed ideologies of black supremacy that found ultimate expression in the stridency of Garvey's pseudo-militarism and Du Bois' adaptation of Anglo–Saxon diffusion myths to create the equivalent of a black Aryanism.

The messianic self-conception that dominated the Afro–American struggle against slavery was carried over into the desegregation struggle. From the age of Alexis de Tocqueville to the age of Gunnar Myrdal, the second-class status of black Americans was seen as the central contradiction in American democracy. Black people were clearly not just another ethnic group but, in the terminology of Allison Davis, Lloyd Warner, John Dollard, and Oliver Cox, analogous to a caste.[27] It is because the condition of black Americans has historically contradicted the moral stance of the United States and the peculiar nature of its divinely inspired mission that the status of black Americans has traditionally been viewed as a moral issue.[28] Michael Novak comments on this moralistic strain:

> In the evangelical tradition, blacks seem to take up this politics of morality by second nature. Many describe racism as a moral failing, about which people should feel guilty and change their ways. (A different tactic would be to treat racism as an unconscious way of perceiving, and work on issues where coalition is possible and mutual loyalties can be built. Guilt divides; shared goals unite.)[29]

Novak has correctly perceived the difference between race relations and ethnic politics, albeit inadvertently, for the American race problem has indeed been perceived as a moral problem since the early nineteenth century. But attempts by Novak and other theorists to reduce the American moral dilemma to the mundane level of ethnic politics is radically ahistorical. Furthermore, racism cannot be dismissed simply as "an unconscious way of perceiving." The merits of Novak's approach will be more readily obvious on the day when Americans (black and white alike) come to think of Negroes as just another ethnic group and race is no longer recognized. Until that time, the struggle for racial equality in America is likely to be perceived in religious and moral terms; and so long as that is true, some varieties of black messianism are likely to persist.

Black messianism in the United States has manifested itself in a variety of ways. Sometimes it has been no more than charismatic charlatanry. In his *Black Gods of the Metropolis*, Arthur H. Fauset discusses the activities of several prophets or messianic figures; the most clearly opportunistic among them is one Bishop Charles Emanual Grace.[30] A man of mixed parentage (Negro and Portuguese), Grace was known for his flowing hair and his carefully cultivated, mandarin-length fingernails. He dressed his followers in colorful costumes and in uniforms reminiscent of those affected by the Garveyites. Doctrine consisted of little more than a play on words. Since salvation was by grace alone, "Grace" was more important to salvation than was God. Every Scriptural reference to grace was interpreted as if it referred specifically to "Sweet Daddy" himself. Cult members were expected to genuflect before Daddy Grace's portrait, to contribute generously, and to consume his numerous commercial products including *Grace Magazine*.

Grace styled himself a divine messiah, who, according to Fauset, pointed out to his followers "that when he took on earthly form he chose to lead Negroes, lowly in state though they are, rather than the members of some more privileged racial group."[31] However, like many black messiahs, he refused to speak of himself as a Negro. As Joseph Washington has argued, Grace sought to deify himself, rather than to stir up the political passions of black people. The adoration of Daddy Grace was "not turned into assets for the good of individuals or the good of the black community."[32] Daddy Grace did not conform to the ideal picture of messianism, because he had no social program. His own financial success appears to have been the sole purpose of this cult. Similar in style and purpose was Detroit's Prophet Jones, who rose to prominence during the 1950s. He was known for his white mink coat, his chauffeur-driven cars, and his garishly decorated mansion called the "French Castle." Like Daddy Grace, Prophet Jones lacked many of the traditional characteristics of a messiah, for he had no intention of improving the worldly status of his followers.

Somewhat more legitimate as a millenarian figure, if not as a black nationalist, was Father Divine, who is discussed in a later chapter. Divine was concerned with the material welfare of his followers, although in a peculiar way. He seemed to have the ability to manage the financial affairs of an apparently large group of persons who lacked the ability to cope with the mundanities of economic life in modern urban society. But all of the foregoing figures—Father Divine, Daddy Grace, and Prophet Jones—were opportunistic, egotistical charlatans, who elevated themselves for purposes of self-aggrandizement. They revealed no abiding concern with ushering in a black messianic era.

By contrast, many black messiahs have conveyed an impression of altruism, an important impression for any leader to convey to his followers. The altruism displayed in the program of Martin Luther King, who advised his followers to walk the pathway of nonviolence and to redeem not only themselves but their oppressors by their travail, was certainly consistent with the Christian tradition of suffering servanthood, as S. P. Fullinwider has noted.[33] The charges of black-power advocates, who blundered upon the description of King as an "Uncle Tom," had a certain unpremeditated validity, if one bears in mind that Mrs. Stowe's creation was not a racial traitor but a Christian martyr. Even a Christian black moderate, like Joseph Washington—not to mention a radical Christian black nationalist, like the Rev. Albert Cleage— found this extreme altruism a bit difficult to swallow, however. With apologies to Emile Durkheim, one must wonder if altruistic suicide is not sometimes the most extreme form of egotism.[34]

Some varieties of black messianism have been neither purely altruistic nor purely opportunistic. During the slavery crisis and the segregation era, bourgeois leadership was increasingly secular, but it nonetheless advanced the Christian perfectionism traditionally associated with social millenarianism. Both the clergy and the laity among the middle classes realized that the prospects of their own advancement on an individual basis were limited, so long as American society remained segregated. "Lifting as we climb," the motto of the National Association of Colored Women, might easily have encapsulated the philosophy of the entire leadership class. It represented a theory that was at once selfishly motivated and altruistic. It was the idea that the limitation on social mobility for the more cultivated black Americans was a consequence of the social, economic, and educational backwardness of the masses. Naturally, the attempts of the leaders to uplift the masses implied inculcating the values of bourgeois Protestant morality. This was especially true because of the disproportionate representation of clergymen in the black leadership class during the nineteenth century. The messianic mission of the black leadership class is exemplified in such documents as W. E. B. Du Bois' 1938 commencement speech to the graduating class of Fisk University, "The Revelation of St. Orgne, the Damned," which is discussed in Chapter 10.

Messianism has had many secular manifestations, and it is interesting to note how even dialectical materialists have made use of Christian rhetoric and preacherly style in their efforts to mobilize popular support. W. E. B. Du Bois' ties to the messianic tradition have already been mentioned. Stokely Carmichael, Eldridge Cleaver, and the numerous Marxist-inspired black leaders who appeared during the 1960s, were likewise indebted to the patterns of charismatic leadership that had evolved in the Negro Church. E. Franklin Frazier once observed the tendency of all black leadership institutions to pattern themselves after the churches.[35] The similarities of black Marxists to the religious leadership that predates them reminds one of the parallels drawn by Bertrand Russell between Marxist and Christian eschatologies.[36] The Marxist conception of history is similar to the Christian concept of providence. Both envision a millennium in which the righteous, clean-living faithful will triumph over the sybaritic denizens of Babylon.

Some black messiahs have established their prophetic credentials in the white world, where their legitimacy as symbols of white American dreams has been recognized. It is interesting to note that some personalities are simultaneously perceived as black Mosaic figures leading the fight against white oppression, and yet as representatives of all Americans. Good examples of such versatile symbols are Joe Louis, Martin Luther King, and Andrew Young. Joe Louis represented to black people the triumph of black muscles over white, but most Americans saw his victories over Primo Carnera and Max Schmeling as victories for America. Martin Luther King came to prominence as a rebellious young race leader; but since his death, highways and schools have been named for him and he has been elevated, ironically, into the pantheon of American establishment heroes. Andrew Young, with his evangelical ability to function as an apostle for capitalism, achieved a fleeting recognition as a spokesman for America's messianic foreign policy.

The acceptance of black messiahs by white America leads me to consider white leaders who have intentionally or unintentionally become "black messiahs." There was an element of messianism in the crusade of John Brown, who was a left-wing radical Anabaptist. But Brown was not able to kindle in the breasts of the American slaves that spirit of revolt which his European antecedents had inflamed during the peasant wars of the sixteenth century. B. A. Botkin, in his collection of American Negro folktales, presents us with the figure of Abraham Lincoln, inflated by some of the freedmen to messianic proportions.[37] Other white messiahs are hard to identify. It is often assumed that W. D. Fard, who inspired Elijah Muhammad to found the Black Muslims, was white; but his racial identity remains hazy.[38] White persons normally have not been able to assume leadership roles in black messianic movements, or even to participate in them. The tradition of black chauvinism is far too strong, even at times when anti-white feeling is not rampant.

A recent figure of interest in this glance at white "black messiahs" is the Reverend James Warren Jones, the "Messiah from the Midwest," as he was dubbed by *Time* magazine.[39] Jones was founder of the People's Temple, based in San Francisco with an 80 percent black membership. During the late 1970s, Jones and over 900 followers founded a utopian community in Guyana, and in November of 1978 they committed mass suicide. The People's Temple conforms to the black messianic pattern in that its membership was largely black. It was outside the main current of black messianism because it centered on the personality of a white man, but he employed rhetoric that endowed black people with a special aura of righteousness. The People's Temple may appear to be a bizarre, one-of-a-kind aberration because of its white leadership and atypical suicidalism, but its linkage to black messianic phenomena has not been overlooked. James Lampley, writing in one of the more widely circulated African news magazines, has observed:

> Its [the People's Temple's] similarity to other religious cults that preceded it within the Black community is part of an all too familiar pattern. . . .
> Were two simple juxtapositions made that (1) the game of selling hope doesn't turn into something more than that, and (2) if Jim Jones had been Black instead of White, then there would be little other than magnitude to distinguish the People's Temple, or the charade of socialism practiced in Jonestown, from the kinds of unattainable promises many interpreted Marcus Garvey's back to Africa movement to mean.[40]

Despite his confusing diction and sentence structure, Lampley's observations are astute, for he accurately discerns that black sects, cults, and movements in America are often pathologically escapist. The events at Jonestown are not without precedent in world religious history. Jonestown falls as much within the province of the anthropology of religion as that of abnormal psychology or criminal law. The current fashionability of irrational cult behavior in America is a revival of one of our least charming utopian traditions.

But not all black messianism is cult behavior, nor is it all to be associated with escapism, utopianism, and megalomania. The black messianic tradition grows out of two seemingly contradictory experiences—oppression by American social institutions, and immersion in the mainstream of American messianic culture. Ironically, it represents both a rejection of white America and a participation in one of its most sacred traditions. This provides a partial explanation for the obvious sympathy with which white liberals have sometimes greeted black moral crusades. In the wake of two world wars, the world's darker peoples began to aspire to greater freedom and self-determination. At the same time, the United States was adjusting to a new position of world leadership and attempting to assume a missionary role, asserting its national mission as a moral exemplar. This was clearly inconsistent with domestic policies of segregation and racial discrimination. The successes of Martin Luther King and Malcolm X cannot be attributed entirely to their manipulation of white liberal guilt. They appealed to self-interest as well by reminding Americans of their messianic pretensions. Reverend Andrew Young, the civil-rights activist turned human-rights ambassador, represents the universal significance of the black messianic tradition and its interaction with American mainstream messianism.

Since black messianism has always been profoundly affected by American social history and indeed derives its very essence from American Christianity, it is to be expected that it will be profoundly affected by the pattern of conflict between increasing secularism and increasing religious fanaticism in contemporary America. While black messianic movements are clearly destined to continue well into the twenty-first century—and probably long after that—certain factors seem to threaten the persistence of traditional forms. The success of Martin Luther King's crusade has, ironically, facilitated the diversification of black leadership roles. It has provided Negro leaders with new opportunities in American institutional life. No longer are educated black people confined to careers in education and the ministry. The secularization of black leadership has led to a de-emphasizing of the church and church-related colleges as centers of black artistic and intellectual life. In the process of modifying its religious character, black artistic and intellectual behavior has lost much of its distinctively black quality. Black politics, too, are losing their traditional missionary and moral character and fast becoming a mere variety of American ethnic politics. The old prophetic traditions no longer occupy a central position in Afro–American life. Like other twentieth-century peoples, the blacks of the United States are being inundated by post-industrial culture, losing their folk traditions, being deprived of their illusions and, ultimately, of their values as well.

The erosion of traditional black messianism is parallel, of course, to the disintegration of the myth of destiny that once flourished at the center of American consciousness. The loss of direction experienced by black America since the deaths of Malcolm X and Martin Luther King is symptomatic of the loss of purpose experienced by the entire society since the debacle of Vietnam. In one of the closing scenes of Ralph Ellison's *Invisible Man*, the narrator experiences a nightmare in which he is castrated by his two-faced friend and former benefactor, Brother Jack:

> "Now you're free of your illusions," Jack said, pointing to my seed wasting upon the air. "How does it feel to be free of one's illusions?"
> And I looked up through a pain so intense now that the air seemed to

roar with the clanging of metal, hearing, HOW DOES IT FEEL TO BE
FREE OF ILLUSION . . .
    And now I answered, "Painful and empty." . . .[41]

I do not seek to glorify the black messianic tradition, nor to romanticize
the conditions that gave it birth. Indeed, I am somewhat embarrassed by
the idealism of those who persist in seeing black Americans as "suffering
servants" or as "God's humanizing agents."[42] But, at the same time, I
dread the loss of black America's special sense of mission, for like Ralph
Ellison I have some misgivings about the future of any society that has
been freed entirely of its illusions.

2
A Search for African Roots of the Tradition

Much of the scholarly attention that has focused on "messianic" and "prophetic" movements has developed in the field of African studies. Learned definitions of messianism and prophetism are much informed by studies of so-called "tribal religious movements" in Africa. It is sometimes argued that indigenous African religions were by nature hospitable to "Ethiopianism" and the prophetic movements that accompanied nationalism around 1900. This would seem to suggest that the African backgrounds of black American religious movements likewise contained elements that made for the ready occurrence of messianic religion in the New World setting. Did the power of the African priest remain, as Du Bois once asserted, "largely unaffected by the plantation system in many important particulars"? And did this power of the plantation priesthood in any way contribute to the growth of messianic and prophetic traditions?[1]

A current of thought, common in recent scholarship, is based on the observation that there is a transcendent unity among precolonial West African religions. A Pan–West African religion was carried to the Americas by African slaves, who were converted to Christianity but maintained many of their traditional ideas within the fabric of the new religion. This process of maintaining old cultural patterns beneath the exterior forms and rituals of the new is called syncretism. It is sometimes argued that the new religion was so uniform as to justify speaking of "the Negro Church." Finally, it is argued that black American religion has been so uniformly constituted, so homogeneous in character, and so strongly controlling of thought and feeling that, regardless of whether its characteristics are imported from Africa or native to American soil, the Negro Church may be spoken of as a "nation within a nation." I consider all of these points to be interesting, but still problematical. Succeeding generations will continue to debate their veracity.[2]

The controversy was begun by Du Bois' asserting with unbridled exuberance at the beginning of this century the "historic fact" that the black church was "the sole surviving institution of the African Fatherland."[3] He went on to proclaim that the church "naturally assumed many functions which the other harshly suppressed social organs had to surrender; the Church became the center of amusements, of what little spontaneous economic activity remained, of education, and of all social intercourse" (p. 5). He also asserted, both in his sociological and in his creative writing, a belief in the survival of the African priesthood in the Americas. Two of Du Bois' assertions: 1) that the black church was a surviving African institution, and 2) that it was the central institution around which all social intercourse revolved, have had profound influences on the writing of black social history. The validity of Du Bois' beliefs are not fully susceptible to proof or disproof by scientific method, although we may expect that axes will be ground and lances broken by future generations. I know of no writer who has refused to see Du Bois' statements as, at the very least, mythically true. In various intangible ways, one senses on entering a black church, especially among the masses of the working poor, that one is back in Africa. The mode of worship in a black middle-class church contains less that is reminiscent of African culture, it is true; but among the leadership of these churches, there has always been a profound concern for African missionary work and the redemption of Africa in a political sense. With respect to Du Bois' second contention, it cannot be denied that even in the late twentieth century, the black church continues to exert tremendous power of good and evil over the minds of the Negroes, especially in the South.

Du Bois' third contention, that the crucial element in the survival of African religions in the New World was the importation of a priestly elite, is neither demonstrable nor essential to his argument, and perhaps this is why it has attracted so little attention. Du Bois was strongly enough committed to this idea, however, that he gave it a prominent place within his theory, almost as if it were an obvious and incontestable matter of course. In describing African religion, he gave primary importance to the power of the priesthood:

> The power of religion was represented by the priest or medicine man. Aided by an unfaltering faith, natural sharpness and some rude knowledge of medicine, and supported by the vague sanctions of a half-seen world peopled by spirits, good and evil, the African priest wielded a power second only to that of the chief, and often superior to it (p. 3).

Let us suspend, temporarily, our judgments of Du Bois' patronizing tone and continue with his next reference to the priesthood a page or two later.

> It is usually assumed by historians and sociologists that every vestige of internal development disappeared, leaving the slaves no means of expression for their common life, thought, and striving. This is not strictly true; the vast power of the priest in the African state has already been noted; his realm alone—the province of religion and medicine—remained largely unaffected by the plantation system in many important particulars (p. 5).

Du Bois argued that "the Negro priest, therefore, early became an important figure on the plantation" (p. 5), and it was from the leadership provided by the "Negro priest" that the black church arose. Du Bois, so far as I know, is the only major historian to have focused his theory of the black church on a belief in the importation of the African priesthood: "Some actual priests were transported and others assumed the functions of priests, and soon a degraded form of the African religion and witchcraft appeared in the West Indies, which was known as Obi, or sorcery" (p. 5).

In attempting to explain the continuity of Afro–American religion, Du Bois almost instinctively gravitated to a theory implying a talented tenth, an African priestly elite, capable of reasserting themselves in the New World. The priesthood performed important social functions, as its members were comforters of the afflicted, and spokesmen "who expressed rudely, but picturesquely, the longing and disappointment of a stolen people" (p. 5).

Where did Du Bois gain his impressions of the role of the "Negro priest"? Indirectly, and by inference. He assumed that what he could see in rural Tennessee during the summers he spent there as a youthful schoolteacher were remnants of slave religion. He described three things that he interpreted as essentially African in the religion of the Black Belt twenty years after slavery—"the Preacher, the Music, and the Frenzy"— all of them admittedly developed on American soil, but having their roots in the fatherland.

On the one hand, Du Bois seemed to want to demonstrate the continuity between African religion and the forceful religious institutions of black America. On the other, he felt that African religious life was limited and provincial. He attributed a large part of the historical sufferings of black people to the failure of African life "to integrate—to unite and systematize in *some conquering whole* which should *dominate the wayward parts*" (p. 3; emphasis supplied). While Du Bois accepted the idea of a fundamental unity of African religious expression, he contended that insufficient "power in religion" or unity in cultural authority had been achieved to prevent the occurrence of the slave trade.

The problem of authority in the communities of slaves and freedmen was one that intrigued Du Bois. Both as a young Negro academician and as an elderly Stalinist, he felt that authority should always work towards "consolidation of power." He greatly respected the power, for good or evil, of black American religion. Its power to stifle growth and development was portrayed in the fictional works, "Of the Coming of John" and *The Quest of the Silver Fleece*, where white-controlled preachers stand in the way of education and progress. His fiction also portrayed the power of ancient African religious forces, as in *The Quest of the Silver Fleece, Dark Princess*, and *The Black Flame*. He reveals a semi-mystical respect for the black preacher, wizard, and conjure woman, who are always commanding figures of power, wielding tremendous authority either to preserve or to destroy those who fall within their power.

Although little has surfaced to support Du Bois' contentions concerning the continuity of the priesthood, scholars have flocked to his standard eager to advance his other arguments. Eugene Genovese has supported his contention that religion is at the basis of black community feeling. E. Franklin Frazier picked up on the theme of ministerial authoritarianism, although he scrupulously avoided tracing this or anything else to African roots. It is not necessary to argue for sacerdotal continuity to sustain the main thrust of Du Bois' argument.

The opinions of Du Bois were rejected by Robert E. Park, who asserted in 1919 that black Americans had brought nothing with them from Africa but their dark complexions and their "tropical temperament." This opinion remained fashionable even after Melville Herskovits argued that a humane and progressive policy towards black Americans could be achieved only if public-policy makers in the United States could overcome their ignorance of the African origins of black American culture. Herskovits marshalled convincing evidence that African culture had been preserved in the islands of the Caribbean and, as did Lorenzo Turner, attempted to demonstrate the persistence of some African religious patterns in the more remote areas of the United States as well.[4] He argued, along with Bronislaw Malinowski, for a Pan–African methodology, a holistic approach to African and Afro–American experience. One could not understand the society and politics of either the Old World or the New World Negro without understanding the cultures of both.[5] E. Franklin Frazier, Guy B. Johnson, and Gunnar Myrdal had little tolerance for such ideas. Afro–American religion was, in their view, essentially American and was to be seen as only an imperfect imitation or a pathological manifestation of middle-class American religion.[6] The current tendency in scholarship related to black American culture is to reject the pathological interpretation, and numerous scholars including John Blassingame, Eugene Genovese, Herbert Gutman, and Lawrence Levine have viewed black slave culture in the Americas as a blend of

African and American traits leading to the creation of a culture that is an alternative structure rather than an imperfect imitation.[7]

An underlying premise for those who have put great emphasis upon the retention of African characteristics in black religion is the assumption that there is extraordinary continuity in the religious belief of most West African cultures. Prominently identified with this school of thought is Basil Davidson. Davidson is committed to demonstrating the existence of something that he refers to as "the African genius." He is also determined to prove that the mental conceptions of the universe and its laws created by Africans are just as rational as those created by Europeans. This leads Davidson to develop a curious second argument, namely, that there are similarities of culture and belief existing between Africans and Europeans, especially southern Europeans.[8] There is an immediate appeal in Davidson's argument that common patterns of human behavior bridge cultural gaps between disparate races. Implicit in his approach is the belief that modern societies are not necessarily more efficient than "primitive" societies at confronting the anxieties of life. But in order to support his second argument, Davidson finds it necessary to undercut his first. If, in fact, the folk beliefs and world view of Africans are similar to those of Europeans, then it is less meaningful to speak of a distinctly African world view.

Davidson offers no explanation for the similarity of patterns that he perceives among the various religions of Africa. He does, however, caution against too hasty an acceptance of diffusionist theories that assume a common origin for all similarities among various African religious expressions. Likewise, he warns the reader against attributing a common source to similar customs shared by Africans and Europeans.[9] Regardless of the sources of the similarities that Davidson sees, he does believe that they are present. His view is shared by other authorities, including John Mbiti, who admits that his knowledge is incomplete and that his generalizations concerning African philosophy and religion are based for the most part on East Africa.[10] Geoffrey Parrinder, who bases his generalizations on studies of West African religion, seems committed, along with Mbiti and Davidson, to the idea that there is an underlying similarity to African religious beliefs.[11]

Once one accepts the idea of the unity of African religious culture, or at least of West African religious culture, it becomes easier to accept the idea of the unity of Afro–American religious expression. For if black Americans, despite their having originated among numerous diverse regions and cultures, all shared a common Old World religion, then it becomes more reasonable to speak of the commonality of their religious experience in the Americas. The historian is released from the responsibility of tracing specific religious expressions back to their myriad

African origins. The only problem with this approach is that scholars tend to overstress similarities among "primitive" cultures, especially in Africa, and to forget that many of the similarities among those cultures are shared among "advanced" societies as well. That there are similarities underlying the various cultures of West Africa cannot be denied. It would be downright astonishing if no such similarities existed; but one wonders if demonstrating the existence of these admitted similarities is as crucial to the argument as some have maintained.

Forty years ago, Melville Herskovits defined the parameters for all subsequent discussions of black religion, and there has been remarkably little deviation from his line of argument for black religious survivals based on the idea of "underlying similarities between the cultures of the area where slaving was carried on."[12] Recent scholars are sympathetic to his belief that Africanisms have persisted in the religious life of the New World Negro. They look with less favor upon his statement that black folk, "in contrast to other underprivileged groups elsewhere in the world . . . turn to religion rather than political action or other outlets for their frustration."[13] Such a view implies that Afro–American religion is essentially escapist and would seem to undermine the argument that the presence of Africanisms in black religion is evidence of black nationalism. Herskovits places much emphasis upon emotional expression, "shouting" sects, and ritualized worship "that expresses itself in song and dance."[14] In this regard he is reminiscent of Gobineau and other nineteenth-century racists, and he reveals a typical bias of the Western mind with respect to "primitive" peoples, especially Africans. One must ask whether religious mysticism among the African peoples is any more emotional than the mysticism of Roman Catholic flagellants or Chassidic Jews. The tendency to attribute emotionalism to the African personality is a bias that commonly accompanies the tendency to see a uniformity among African religious cultures.

Albert J. Raboteau, in an excellent work of synthesis and interpretation, provides a good overview of the current state of our knowledge on slave religion and its connections with African life. He acknowledges the "many significant differences among the religions of various West African peoples . . . ," but reminds us that "beneath the diversity, enough fundamental similarity did exist to allow a general description of the religious heritage of African slaves." Unlike many historians of his persuasion, he does not overstate these similarities. The characteristics of African religion identified by Raboteau include "belief in a High God or Supreme Creator of the world," although this High God is seldom approached in ritual or prayer. He also identifies the worship of "lesser divinities or secondary gods," who control natural phenomena and must be pacified, propitiated, or appealed to. Africans often make fetishes, charms, and amulets to represent their gods, and the gods are often identified with particular localities or shrines. There are numerous cults and priesthoods that serve these cults. There are also numerous spirits who are able to affect the lives of people. African religions put great emphasis on ritual, dance ceremonies, and trance-like states in which spirits sometimes take possession of human beings. There is a universal pattern of ancestor veneration in which dead kindred act as mediators between the mundane and the supernatural.[15]

Raboteau's is perhaps the best evaluation we have of the debate between E. Franklin Frazier and Melville Herskovits. He recognizes that both positions have been caricatured and that each of the contestants made a significant contribution to our understanding. Herskovits was able successfully to demonstrate the survival of some African behavioral patterns in the United States. Frazier exposed Herskovits' excesses, and demonstrated the Americanness of black culture in the United States. However, Raboteau seems to come down squarely on the side of Frazier; his summary statement is, "In the United States the gods of Africa died."[16] Within the context of the fact that he entitled his chapter on African survivals "The Death of the Gods," it becomes clear that Raboteau considers North American retentionism to be relatively unimpressive. This is true, at least, when we compare it to retentionism in Latin America and the Caribbean. Even those cultural survivals that do exist in North America are difficult to identify as purely African. Some of the "survivals" might just as easily be traced to Europe—for example, the belief that "crossroads are places of peculiar power for the exercise of evil magic."[17] In fact, Raboteau does point out that

> Many Afro–American witchcraft beliefs are European in origin. As such, they are a prime example of an area where there is a fusion of African and European folklore. The capacity of folk beliefs from different peoples to parallel and mutually influence one another makes the enterprise of separating one from another not only difficult, but also artificial and speculative. Here perhaps is a fitting place to end the search for Africanisms in black religion in the United States.[18]

Raboteau's *Slave Religion* takes us a long way towards the elimination of sectarianism, hero worship, and mysticism from the study of Afro–American culture. I doubt, however, the accuracy of one reviewer's comment that, in his book, Raboteau lays the Frazier–Herskovits debate to rest.

The strongest evidence for the survival of African religious traits in the New World has been collected in the Caribbean as opposed to North America. This was certainly the case with Herskovits, and it has been true with respect to more recent students as well. Roger Bastide has alluded to elements of Fanti—Ashanti culture among the Bush Negroes of the Guianas, persisting in the form of rites connected with birth:

> The child receives the name of the week-day on which it was born, but is also baptised in church. Sometimes, in order to avoid the "evil eye" which might otherwise be put on it, we find the parents taking it also to the rabbi, who gives it a biblical name.[19]

Students of the problem rarely see Africanisms surviving in pure forms, but rather in syncretic or amalgamative forms. The Ashanti custom of naming the child after the day of the week exists in easy harmony with the baptism rite and the Hebraic naming ceremony. Bastide also observes the retention of a pantheon of chthonic deities who are preserved in Guiana under names similar to or reminiscent of their West African names. Minor deities are preserved in Catholic societies, as well, where they become identified with various saints of the church.[20] It is interesting to note in this regard that many of the Catholic saints have been identified with pre-Christian deities of barbarian Europe, and many Catholic holy days with pagan feasts.

Orlando Patterson, like Herskovits and Bastide, finds strong evidence for the retention of African religious traits by black people in the Caribbean. Patterson focuses his study on Jamaica, where he identifies African origins for beliefs relating to the spirit world, ancestor worship, and the burial of the dead. He accepts from Herskovits and Parrinder the thesis that there is remarkable uniformity in religious beliefs all along the Guinea coast.[21] The myal man (good enchanter) and the obeah man (worker of evil spells) in Jamaica utilized a system of charms and incantations reminiscent of their counterparts in West Africa. They seemed at times to possess a knowledge of herbs and medicines unknown to white physicians. "Obeah functioned largely in the numerous rebellions of the slaves," states Patterson.[22] This would seem to place him in the camp with those who argue that black religion in the Americas was not an alternative to protest nor an escape from worldly concerns, but an instrumentality through which chiliastic pre-revolutionary consciousness may have found expression. Furthermore, if slave revolts are to be seen as a sign of incipient black nationalism, then the argument of Patterson would seem to support the view that black religion constitutes a support for the black nationalist spirit.

Herskovits and his followers have admittedly found fewer examples of African religious survivals in North America than in the Caribbean. Nonetheless, *The Myth of the Negro Past* is concerned with identifying some Africanisms in the religion of the Negroes of the United States. Herskovits argues that black Americans were attracted to the Baptist and Methodist churches because of the preference of the former for baptism by total immersion and the tendency of both to encourage ritualized emotionalism. Herskovits viewed patterned emotionalism as an African survival, and he viewed baptism by total immersion as a survival of West African river cults.[23] E. Franklin Frazier attacked Herskovits's thesis, arguing that Africans became Baptists and Methodists because those were the denominations that proselytized among the black population.[24] Herskovits's argument is weakened by his own observation that there are far more black Catholics in the New World than black Baptists and Methodists combined.[25] Geography was the prime factor determining whether a black population would become Catholic or Protestant. Both Catholic and Protestant denominations show African traits, because black people irrepressibly Africanize their institutions.

Roman Catholicism had many characteristics that must have seemed familiar to newly imported Africans. Its elaborate ceremonialism, its intonation and response chanting, its prayers to saints and angels, and its veneration of icons must have had an immediate appeal to those blacks who were exposed to them. Yet there has been little impact of Catholicism on the blacks of the United States, except in those areas where the white population is also Catholic. Roman Catholics in the United States were not powerful enough to have much effect on blacks at the time they were undergoing mass conversion by Baptist and Methodist preachers. This would seem to support Frazier's contention that the proselytizing activities of the latter denominations were the prime determinant of slave religion.

Scholars like George Rawick, however, are using contemporary documents, including interviews with former slaves taken during the 1920s and 1930s, to argue that "what contemporaries referred to as the 'African cult' not only did not disappear, it continued to flourish with great creativity and strength and was clearly the mainspring of black religion in the United States."[26] He makes much of the slave's practice of turning an iron pot upside down in the middle of the room in the belief that this would deaden the sound of their rites and so prevent discovery. Rawick quoted numerous instances of this practice; the following is representative of the testimony offered in the slave narratives:

> They'd have prayer meetings at times at home, but they had to get permission, and if they didn't I've known them to have to turn down a pot to keep the sound in. No'm, I have never known them to get caught while the pot was turned down at my home; but I have heard of them getting caught.[27]

Rawick follows after Herskovits and William Bascom in remarking on the importance of the iron pot as a West African religious artifact. He also cites Harold Courlander and Sidney Mintz, who have seen ritual similarities between the pot and the drum (another important religious artifact) and suggest that the pot may have functioned as a symbolic drum surrogate, especially in those parts of the New World where slaves were forbidden to keep drums. Rawick also notes similarities between Afro–American conversion experiences and certain West African myths.[28]

The recent studies of Lawrence Levine, John Blassingame, Nathan Huggins, and Leslie Owens likewise give credence to the contention of Herskovits that African religious customs were preserved among the slaves. Levine argues that the sacred music of the slaves was syncretic, a hybrid of European and African forms "with a strong African base." Furthermore, slave songs demonstrate that elements of the "African heritage remained alive not just as quaint cultural vestiges but as vitally creative elements of slave culture." He also argues that the survival of a tradition in folk medicine was a variety of religious retentionism.[29] Blassingame makes mention of voodoo practices in Louisiana and refers to the survival of the snake god cult (the worship of Damballa) which permeated some segments of the white community as well. The blending of Catholicism with West African religious practices is reminiscent of Haitian voodoo, in which Damballa also plays an important role.[30] Nathan Huggins summarizes, in a lively and interesting manner, the customary arguments for the unity of African culture and its survival in the Americas.[31] Owens, too, provides the usual tales of hoodoo, voodoo, obeah, and Gullah conjuring, mentions the "Hushharbor" (church in the woods) where slave religion was practiced clandestinely, and adds a few new tales based on his voluminous archival research.[32] While none of the foregoing have substantially advanced our knowledge of African survivals, each has made a small contribution to the store of evidence that seems to vindicate the Herskovits thesis.[33]

Eugene Genovese's treatment of the relationship between African religious survivals and black messianism is very interesting. His discussion of slave religion, although informed and detailed, adds little to our specific knowledge of African survivals; but a major contribution is the creative way in which he summarizes prior research. He also offers speculative observations on the nationalistic element in the "black variant of Christianity."[34] Like Rawick, he avoids the trap of equating violent rebelliousness with nationalism, and he is sensitive to the fact that the determination of the slaves to preserve elements of their African culture was in itself a form of rebellion to cultural repression, suggestively similar to typical forms of nationalistic resistance. Genovese perceptively notes "the contradictory nature of the slave's religion as part of American Christianity and yet . . . as a faith apart."[35] While the message of black American religion has been particular and nationalistic, it has also been universal.

The universal quality of black religion is indeed one of the problems that make it difficult for us to trace African survivals or influences. We may accept the thesis of Parrinder and Davidson that West African religions are remarkably alike, or we may even speak of a Pan–African religion. We must then, however, be willing to follow the implications of Davidson's suggestion that there are certain elements common to all religious behavior, whether in West Africa or elsewhere. Several important thinkers, including Franz Boas, Levy-Bruhl, Evans-Pritchard, and Levi-Strauss, have discussed the religious and magical cosmologies of the "primitive mind" and the "savage mind." Such scholars have observed a remarkable unity among all expressions of "primitive religion" and, in the case of Levi-Strauss, an underlying unity among all human world views, whether "savage" and "mystical" or "civilized" and "scientific."[36]

Early black-nationalist statements on African religious expression made observations that anticipated the views of modern anthropology. J. E. Casely Hayford, a Gold Coast nationalist, argued in 1903 that West African life and customs could not be viewed as the grotesque eccentricities of unenlightened peoples in the world's cultural backwaters. Many of their life modes were analogous to the customs of European peoples whose contributions to Western civilization were universally acknowledged. He found parallels between the descriptions of life in Homeric Greece and his own observations on folk customs among Gold Coast ethnics.[37] Orishatukeh Fadumah, also a Gold Coast intellectual, a participant in Alexander Crummell's American Negro Academy, and an organizer in Alfred C. Sam's Back-to-Africa movement, made similar observations in 1904:

> There is nothing new in the religion of the Negro. He is by no means a peculiar man from a religious standpoint. The physical contortions and gyrations noticed in his Christian worship are as old as the history of religion itself, if not older than it. In his worship we may see things which are found in the heathen rites of the native African, in the Bacchanalia of the Greeks, among the Sali or dancing priests of the Romans, and among the Corybantes. The same effect which is produced on the feelings of the Negro has been produced on the feelings of the American Indian, as well as on the ancient bards of Scotland, Ireland, Wales, and Germany.[38]

Such observations can be extended to post-industrial, electronic societies. American senators still assert that the United States Constitution is a divinely inspired document. Do they mean by this that when the Congress drafts a constitutional amendment it is possessed by the Holy Spirit? Basil Davidson reports that the Christian leaders of Rhodesia, that outpost of rational Western civilization, instructed its people to pray for rain as late as 1968.[39] The rise of the charismatic movement and the intrusion of "born again" Christianity into high levels of government lead one to suspect that religious interpretations of American destiny have not yet died out in the United States.

It is probably correct to say that there is a Pan—African religion, but it is no more correct than to say that religiosity seems to be a universal human experience and that there are similarities in the way that it manifests itself among all peoples. The religion of black slaves in the United States was similar to both that of West Africans and that of Europeans. These similarities may be attributed to African retentions, syncretic tendencies, and spontaneous parallel evolution. That connections between revolutionary nationalism and African religious survivals may have existed has been suggested by George Rawick and others. One recalls the story of Gullah Jack, a co-conspirator of Denmark Vesey, who apparently made use of his status as a conjure man to exhort the slaves to violence. But one also remembers that Nat Turner claimed to have utilized traditional Christianity as the basis for his religious rebellion and to have eschewed the employment of African religious leadership techniques.[40]

It has been suggested by scholars as diverse as Du Bois, Frazier, and Genovese that black religion constitutes the foundation of the black nation. This seems reasonable enough, although there has never been any systematic demonstration of ties between black religion and black nationalism. Even Genovese provides no more than some tantalizing suggestions as to ties between *slave* religion and black nationalism. The roots of American black nationalism have not been identified in any of the African cultural traits that were unquestionably retained in nineteenth-century slave communities.

Black nationalism was the creation of the Northern free-black community. Its ideology revealed no influence of an African priesthood, although it was clearly influenced by the "redeemer nationalist" rhetoric of the Northeastern clergy. Unlike their European nationalist counterparts, black nationalists were not obsessed with the search for cultural inspiration among the masses. It was more to their purposes to argue that the masses were deprived of all culture, including true religion, because of the ravages of slavery. Alexander Crummell's attitude was typical:

> Their religion, both of preachers and people, was a religion without the Bible—a crude medley of scraps of Scripture, fervid imaginations, dreams, and superstitions. . . . The Ten Commandments were as foreign from their minds and memories as the Vedas of India or the moral precepts of Confucius. Ignorance of the MORAL LAW was the main characteristic of "PLANTATION RELIGION!"[41]

Thus, the influences on black nationalism derived, not from slave religion, but from American "civil religion." The messianic American civil religion, as it is described by Robert Bellah, was the main influence on black nationalism. This was the myth of Americans as a chosen people with a message for the world and a covenantal duty to respect the enlightenment doctrines of political and economic freedom. This mythic perception supported black nationalism, racial integration, and mainstream American nationalism.[42] The rhetoric of American messianism could be adapted to these three apparently conflicting purposes, because of the complexity of Christian symbolism. The messiah is both a suffering servant and a King of Glory; both a protector of *chosen* peoples and a redeemer of *all* mankind. The rhetoric of American messianism could be modified by blacks to assert black militancy, to support racial harmony, and at the same time to instruct self-righteous white Americans, a chosen people, as to their convenantal responsibilities. The rhetorical device for accomplishing this was the "jeremiad," the earliest expression of black messianism in America.

3
The Black Jeremiad
and American Messianic
Traditions

American historians have paid considerable attention to a phenomenon known as "the jeremiad." Perry Miller is ultimately responsible for the current great awakening of interest in the tradition. In *The New England Mind: The Seventeenth Century*, he noted that lamentations over waning zeal increased during the 1640s and "by 1680, there seems to have been hardly any other theme for discourse and the pulpits rang week after week with lengthening jeremiads." But jeremiads, in the broader sense, may deal with other things besides waning zeal, as Sacvan Bercovitch has recently argued in *The American Jeremiad*. James H. Moorhead, writing on the Civil War period in *American Apocalypse*, sees a jeremiad as a "theological rationale for the sufferings of a chosen people."[1]

The term takes its name, of course, from the prophet, Jeremiah, who is believed to have lived around 650–570 B.C., and who predicted the conquest of Judah by the Babylonians and the destruction of the temple in Jerusalem. He saw these events as punishments for departing from the Mosaic covenant. Jeremiah advised his countrymen to accept the Babylonian yoke as a punishment from God, but to adhere to their own cultural and religious traditions. He is believed to be the author of the book of Lamentations, which describes the humiliation of Israel, prostrate at the feet of Babylon. Hence, in the words of the *Oxford English Dictionary*, a jeremiad is a "lamentation" or "doleful complaint."

Perry Miller used the term in its broader, more biblically correct sense in *The New England Mind: From Colony to Province*, where he described the jeremiad as a response to some present tragedy and a warning of greater tribulations to come.[2] I use the term "jeremiad" to describe the constant warnings issued by blacks to whites, concerning the judgment that was to come for the sin of slavery. Blacks ingeniously adapted their rhetoric to the jeremiadic tradition, which was one of the dominant forms of cultural expression in revivalistic ante-bellum America. Their use of the jeremiad revealed a conception of themselves as a chosen people, but it also showed a clever ability to play on the belief that America as a whole was a chosen nation with a covenantal duty to deal justly with the blacks.

The black jeremiad was not characteristically concerned with explaining the dismal status of the African people during the slavery period. Both Alexander Crummell and Marcus Garvey offered theological explanations for slavery, but that was some time later and their statements were not truly jeremiadic. The black jeremiad was mainly a pre-Civil War phenomenon and showed the traditional preoccupation with impending doom. It was often directed at a white audience, and it bemoaned the sinfulness of slaveholders—fellow Americans who defied the natural and divine law that they were covenantally bound to uphold—and predicted God's punishment that was to come.

From colonial times, Americans had conceived themselves a chosen people.[3] They had entered into a covenant with God, who had delivered them from the "Egyptian bondage" of Old World vice and tyranny.[4] Providence had opened up a new Canaan for them, where they were to build a new Jerusalem. As God's new Israel, they were entrusted with a sacred mission—the creation of a model society.[5] Perry Miller has illustrated how this belief became increasingly strong as Puritan pessimism gradually gave way before Enlightenment optimism.[6] The winning of the American revolution fortified the belief of Americans in their destiny.[7] They came to interpret their covenant as obliging them not only to preserve Christian ideals, but to uphold the natural rights of man. Enlightenment ideology was well in accord with Protestant doctrine on the subject of national purpose.

And, yet, there were certain nagging questions in the backs of American minds. If the bondage of the Colonies to England was similar to the enslavement of Israel in Egypt, was not the bondage of blacks in America an even more perfect analogy? If Americans, by virtue of the ideals of their revolution, were in fact a covenanted people and entrusted with the mission to safeguard the divine and natural laws of human rights, was there not a danger to the covenant in perpetuating slavery? Thomas Jefferson made dire predictions based on such unsettling speculations:

> And can the liberties of a nation be thought secure when we have removed their only firm basis, a conviction in the minds of the people that these liberties are the gift of God? That they are not to be violated but with his wrath? Indeed I tremble for my country when I reflect that God is just; that his justice cannot sleep forever; that considering numbers, nature and

natural means only, a revolution of the wheel of fortune, an exchange of situation is among possible events; that it may become probable by super-natural interference! The Almighty has no attribute which can take side with us in such a contest.[8]

If white Americans were given to such speculations, literate black Americans were even more so inclined. They were not tempted in quite the same way as were the Anglo–Americans to view the American revolution as an apocalyptic act of deliverance. The moment of deliverance was still to come. God would yet reveal whose side he was truly on. Black writers in the early republic were to repeat the themes of the Jeffersonian jeremiad with enthusiasm for the next several decades. Sometimes these writers employed a black nationalist rhetoric, for the black literary tradition in English arose simultaneously with the rise of European and American nationalism, from which it borrowed many of its themes. Afro–American nationalism, like European and Anglo–American nationalism, attempted to link together a particularism and a universalism. Its spokesmen envisioned themselves as the scribes of a chosen people who were working out an independent destiny, but this did not imply hostility to the rest of the world. Indeed, like their Anglo–American counterparts, black Americans hoped to lead by example in the direction of Christian progress. It was hoped that the millennium could be achieved by peaceful means. For obvious reasons most black writers did not wish to be identified as inflammatory pamphleteers. But this did not mean that early black writers consistently eschewed the rhetoric of violence, confrontation, or racial chauvinism.

Early black writers in America often referred to themselves as a chosen people. Their enslavement did not necessarily symbolize a curse or a mark of God's disfavor; it boded rather that He had some great plan in store for them. Scripture could be cited to show that those whom God would exalt He first prepared by tempering in the fires of oppression. Slavery was therefore to be understood as a "Providence," a seeming disaster, from which God would draw forth some greater good. Since black American slaves were a chosen people, it followed that those who oppressed them were soon to be chastized themselves by a just God. There can be no question that much of this was an attempt to play on the fears that Jefferson had revealed, as well as to expose his hypocrisy.

The Christian black writers came to make thinly veiled references to slave rebellions as means whereby God might effect his justice, and this was especially true after the Santo Domingo revolt. Generally, however, one feels that the rhetorical threat of violence was not based on any real desire for a racial Armageddon. Black jeremiads were warnings of evils to be avoided, not prescriptions for revolution. When Ethiopia stretched forth her hands, it would not be to take up a sword but to embrace her erstwhile enemies.

In November and December 1788, there appeared a two-part "Essay on Negro Slavery" in the *American Museum*. Its author identified himself as "Othello," claiming to be a free Negro from Maryland. Some scholars have suggested that his essay reveals an acquaintanceship with Jefferson's *Notes on the State of Virginia*.[9] Certainly he addresses one of the central points of Jefferson's essay when he contrasts the professed goals of the revolution with the new republic's tolerance of slavery, and warns of the possible consequences: "So flagitious a violation can never escape the notice of a just Creator, whose vengeance may even now be on the wing." He seemed aware of the tradition that claimed a special covenant between America and the Creator, and that which claimed God as the friend of the oppressed. God had shown his favor to America by blessing her revolution, which was fought in defense of divine principle and natural law. "Beware Americans!" he warned, "Pause—and consider the difference between the mild effulgence of approving Providence and the angry countenance of incensed divinity."

Othello made two suggestions as to what should be done with the slaves: either they should be emancipated immediately and colonized in the Western Territory, or liberated gradually, presumably so that they could take up their rights and responsibilities as American citizens. Othello was more concerned with warning of the dire consequences of continued racial oppression than with developing his vision of a less sanguinary future. He believed that black Americans were under the special protection of Providence. He saw the United States as a nation watched over by Providence, as well, by virtue of its implied contract with the God of natural rights. Americans would demonstrate their loyalty to the covenant by extending its provisions to the blacks.

This was the central idea of Benjamin Banneker's letter to Thomas Jefferson in 1791. Human beings had a set of natural rights which were a gift from God. This was true in a personal sense, and it was also true for American society as a whole, for one could not deny that the success of the American revolution was due to forces both "miraculous and providential." Likewise, the present "freedom and tranquility" enjoyed by the new republic was clearly "the peculiar blessing of heaven." The reason for America's enjoyment of this peculiar blessing was obvious— she was in accord with the laws of God and nature. Thus it was a matter not only of conscience, but of self-interest, to mend any imperfections in this country's compliance with natural and divine law. Banneker's argument proceeds from the idea that one self-evident implication of the national covenant is the Christian obligation "to extend . . . the rights of human nature . . . to the relief of every part of the human race."[10]

Banneker's letter was thus more than an appeal to Jefferson's sincerity and sense of justice; it was almost a legalistic argument, attempting to manipulate fears of violating the covenant. Banneker was appealing to a very real belief in America's divine mission and providential destiny. He was also appealing to the Enlightenment view that a glorious future could be expected only if the nation conformed to universal natural law. American nationalism must by implication be committed to universalism. It therefore did not matter whether the blacks were perceived as part of the American people or as a nation apart. Americans must extend the provisions of their natural rights covenant to include the blacks, or deny the covenant itself.

In Richard Allen and Absolom Jones's "Address to those who keep Slaves, and approve the Practice" (1794), the jeremiadic themes are more pronounced. The authors draw a direct analogy between the Africans in America and the ancient Hebrews in Egypt:

> We do not wish to make you angry, but excite your attention to consider, how hateful slavery is in the sight of that God, who hath destroyed kings and princes, for their oppression of the poor slaves; Pharaoh and his princes with the posterity of king Saul, were destroyed by the protector and avenger of slaves.[11]

They provoked the imaginations of their readers by pointing—not too subtly—at the form divine retribution might take. God had pleaded the cause of the slave by raising up "instruments . . . sometimes mean and contemptible in your sight" and at other times "such as it hath pleased him, with whom you have not thought it beneath your dignity to contend." The "dreadful insurrections" that the slaves had made were a proof not only of their discontent, but of God's displeasure at a crime against nature.

Lest their bloody warning be interpreted as an incitement to violence, they expressed their sorrow at "the late bloodshed of the oppressors as well as the oppressed." Both were guilty in the sight of God and both would be punished, for "he that sheddeth man's blood, by man shall his blood be shed." Allen and Jones appended an epistle "To the People of Color" at the end of this warning to slaveholders, urging them to be patient, to trust in God for their deliverance, and "to feel an affectionate regard towards your masters and mistresses."[12] But this only served to soften, not to obliterate, the threatening tone of their message.

More subtle, if equally dismal, was Prince Hall in his *Charge Delivered to the African Lodge at Menotomy* (1797). Like Allen and Jones, Hall leavened his address with the rhetoric of racial reconciliation. Taking seriously his role as a Masonic leader, he felt it his duty to encourage brotherly love. It was on this note of "love to all mankind" that he began his speech, but he quickly turned to a description of the "chequered world we live in," where good fortune may suddenly turn to ill. He lamented for the "numerous sons and daughters of distress . . . dragg'd from their native country by the iron hand of tyranny and oppression." He spoke of "the bloody wars which are now in the world . . . and cities burnt and destroy'd," and of "states and kingdoms . . . rich today, and poor tomorrow." In a world of violence and mutability, he encouraged his brethren to "seek those things which are above, which are sure, and stedfast and unchangeable." He counseled them to bear with strength and patience "the daily insults you meet with in the streets of Boston."[13]

But there was one paragraph of Hall's address that led to some uneasiness and charges of "insolence," when circulated outside the community of black Masons.[14] He made some passing references to the recent history of the French Antilles:

> My brethren, let us not be cast down under these and many other abuses we at present labour under: for the darkest hour is before the break of day. My brethren, let us remember what a dark day it was with our African brethren six years ago, in the French West Indies. Nothing but the snap of the whip was heard from morning to evening; hanging, breaking on the wheel, burning, and all manner of tortures inflicted on those unhappy people for nothing else but to gratify their masters' pride, wantonness, and cruelty. But blessed be God, the scene is changed. They now confess that God hath no respect of persons, and therefore receive them as their friends, and treat them as brothers. Thus doth Ethiopia begin to stretch forth her hand, from a sink of slavery to freedom and equality.[15]

This passage raises some interesting questions. Was Hall really so blissfully unaware concerning events in the West Indies? Did he think that his audience was? Did he speculate on how his indirect reference to the bloodiest and most successful of all the slave revolts would be received by white Americans? The impact on America of the Haitian revolution has been summarized in detail by Philip Foner, who shows that reports of the revolution contributed both to white apprehension and black self-esteem.[16] Reports of slave conspiracies proliferated, according to Herbert Aptheker, and along with them legislation calculated to thwart the possibility. Jefferson warned that what had occurred in Haiti could happen in the Southern states, and in a letter to John Drayton, Governor of South Carolina, he reported having overheard a plot by the French to carry the St. Domingo revolution into North America.[17] John Randolph of Virginia reported having eavesdropped on a conversation between two of his slaves in which they alluded to the killing of whites in "the French island."[18] Newspapers exploited the sensational events for their shock value and published sentimental accounts of impoverished planters forced to leave their homes. Refugees soon arrived to tell their own stories, bringing with them their presumably faithful slaves. But the slaves of refugees were, at best, a source of dangerous rumor among the indigenous blacks; at worst, they became rebels themselves.[19]

One must assume that Prince Hall was well aware of the threatening aspect the Haitian revolution presented to whites, for reports were circulated that Northern blacks were sometimes boisterous in their celebration of the rebellion. He knew full well that events in the West Indies represented something other than interracial brotherhood to Bostonians. After Toussaint L'Ouverture signed his treaty with the French in 1794, there were constant rumors that the slave states were soon to be invaded. That black and white Jacobins were now in league was hardly a comforting thought for every member of Hall's wider audience. For a black man to publish a pamphlet making references to the Haitian revolution at a time when Massachusetts Federalists were advocating passage of the Sedition Act required considerable courage.[20]

Federalists sometimes even blamed Jefferson for the revolt in Haiti, or at least attempted to show how passages in *Notes on the State of Virginia* might be encouraging to Jacobins and Emancipationists. Gabriel's conspiracy in 1822 was likewise exploited as anti-Jeffersonian propaganda.[21] Gabriel did, as a matter of fact, represent that class of literate, assimilated blacks who were likely to have been familiar with the Jeffersonian jeremiad. Gerald Mullin has strangely suggested that a major reason for the failure of Gabriel's revolt was his failure to exploit the religiosity of the ordinary field hand or the messianic traditions that figured so prominently in the revolts of Denmark Vesey and Nat Turner.[22] Like Lawrence Levine, I am puzzled by Mullin's statement that the rebellion was "lacking a sacred dimension."[23] Mullin himself has written a very fine interpretation of the Young Spring meeting, at which the revolt was planned and where religion seems to have played an important part. Ben Woolfolk's confession at his conspiracy trial reveals this dimension of the plot, as well as the role of Gabriel's brother Martin as a religious exhorter:

> Martin said there was this expression in the Bible, delays breed danger. . . . I told them that I had heard in the days of old, when the Israelites were in service to King Pharaoh, they were taken from him by the power of God, and were carried away by Moses. God had blessed him with an angel to go with him, but that I could see nothing of that kind in these days. Martin said in reply: I read in my Bible where God says if we will worship Him we should have peace in all our land; five of you shall conquer an hundred, and a hundred a thousand of our enemies.[24]

This same religious dimension was even more pronounced in Denmark Vesey's conspiracy of 1822. Robert Starobin has commented on the "extraordinarily rich ideology" of the Vesey plot. Its theological base was recorded by contemporary observers at the trials of the conspirators. The court, in passing sentence on several of the conspirators, took time to produce Biblical arguments sanctioning slavery and counseling "servants" to obey their masters. The Baptist Convention of South Carolina asserted that the deliverance of Charleston was due to special intervention of Providence, and urged the Governor to set aside a day of Thanksgiving.[25]

Observations on the state of mind of the white population have led to some doubts being expressed as to the actual existence of a plot. Richard C. Wade suggests that the white citizens of Charleston, driven by a combination of guilt and hostility, over-reacted to what was "never more than loose talk by aggrieved and embittered men."[26] The majority of scholars are agreed that a conspiracy did, in fact, exist; and contemporary documents suggest that the fears of the whites were inspired by more than "loose talk." There is no doubt, however, that the conspiracy provided an excuse to stamp out independent black religion. When an African Methodist church was closed down in the months following the conspiracy, authorities claimed that all leaders of the planned insurrection had been members. This church was intimately connected with the African Methodist church in Philadelphia, established by Richard Allen and Absolom Jones. A report to the Governor of South Carolina described it as an "irregular Association . . . , whose Principles are formed on the Scheme of General Emancipation, for which they are zealous Advocates; & they endeavor to support, by a Misconstruction, or Perversion of the Scriptures."[27]

Despite the hostility with which black oratory and pamphleteering were met during the first half of the nineteenth century, the black jeremiad flourished. Sometimes its warnings were militant and direct— as was Maria Stewart's, which compared America to the fabled city of Babylon:

> She is indeed a seller of slaves and the souls of men; she has made the Africans drunk with the wine of her fornication. . . . God will surely raise up those among us who will plead the cause of virtue and the pure principles of morality more eloquently than I am able to do. . . . They will have their rights; and if refused, I am afraid they will spread horror and destruction.[28]

At other times, as we have seen in the case of Richard Allen, the tone was that of a friendly warning, couched in the rhetoric of Christian conciliation. It is thus likely that much of the black messianic oratory and most of the pamphlets that spoke of divine retribution were produced for the benefit of whites, although ostensibly directed towards black audiences. The attempts of the slave states to ban black writing and preaching were aimed mainly at curbing the flow of seditious ideas, but they also represented the characteristic attempt by racists to close their own eyes and ears.

Black jeremiads were often admittedly directed at whites. In 1808, a member of the African Society of Boston issued a pamphlet clearly addressed to whites as well as blacks, filled with references to the fates of the Egyptians and the Babylonians. But the pamphleteer's object was not to call down a curse upon the whites; it was to issue a warning to all Americans, lest through waywardness they lose their favored position in the sight of God:

> . . . if freedom, that inestimable blessing, which many of complexion are deprived of, is our lot, then let us be careful, lest we incur the displeasure of God by our ingratitude, as many have done, and by the means of which they have had the blessings removed from them.[29]

These particular remarks were specifically addressed to "Africans who inhabit Massachusetts," but clearly the warning was just as applicable to whites in Virginia.

Black sermons and pamphlets continued to play upon the Jeffersonian theme, that slavery was a violation of natural and divine law. Their authors may be interpreted as loyal informers, in a sense, issuing a warning to whites, revealing the hostility and resentment that pervaded black communities North and South, slave and free. But the purpose of the black jeremiad was not simply to provide a verbal outlet for hostilities; it was a means of demonstrating loyalty—both to the principles of egalitarian liberalism and to the Anglo–Christian code of values.

A document that illustrates all the themes so far introduced is [David] Walker's *Appeal* (1829). It is a direct response to Thomas Jefferson's racial theories and apocalyptic prophecies. It mingles the conciliatory and the strident tones of the black messianic tradition; and although it is addressed to blacks, it obviously has a message for whites. Like earlier jeremiads and other examples of black creativity in the use of Scripture, Walker's *Appeal* was viewed by contemporaries as seditious. It is now often seen as an early instance of revolutionary black nationalism. There can be no doubt of the pamphlet's nationalistic and revolutionary elements, but some of its other interesting features have been almost completely ignored.[30]

Walker began with the conviction that American slavery, because of its racial character, was the worst the world had ever known. Jefferson had written several paragraphs of pedantic nonsense attempting to demonstrate that slavery in America was benevolent in comparison to that of ancient Rome. Walker would show how slavery in America was really far worse. The "heathen nations of antiquity had little more among them than the name and the form of slavery, while wretchedness and miseries were reserved apparently in a phial, to be poured out upon our fathers, ourselves, and our children by *christian* Americans" (p. 11). By Jefferson's own reckoning, the chief difference between Roman and American slavery—aside from the comparative mildness of the latter—was the obstacle to emancipation, which was racial. "Among the Romans," observed Jefferson, "emancipation required but one effort. But with us a second is necessary, unknown to history. When freed, he is to be removed beyond the reach of mixture."[31]

William Hamilton, in an earlier response to *Notes on the State of Virginia*, had already stood Jefferson's argument on its head by showing that it was the very ease with which emancipation could be effected in the Empire that demonstrated its comparative mildness. Furthermore, once emancipated, the Roman freedman was "eligible to all the offices of state."[32] Walker likewise refused to accept Jefferson's arguments, and for the same reasons. American slavery was racial, justified by a theory of racial inferiority to which Jefferson himself subscribed. Anyone who could suspend "prejudice long enough to see that we are men, notwithstanding our *improminent noses* and *woolly heads*," would have to admit that American slavery was worse than the Roman form. For the Romans had created no rationalizations for condemning their slaves to "the most abject ignorance and degradation." Slavery in the United States was at least as wicked as the most heinous crimes of pagan Rome, and it would just as certainly be punished.

Walker was influenced by contemporary cyclical theories of history. Like Jefferson he viewed destiny as a revolving wheel on which various peoples rose and fell relative to one another. In addition it was becoming increasingly fashionable to view civilizations as progressing in accordance with the life cycle of birth, maturation, and demise.[33] Every civilization contained the seeds of its own destruction. In a world of mutability, nothing could endure forever, of course; but societies, like living organisms, could ensure their longevity by a strict obedience to the dictates of nature and of reason. History had shown the demise of various civilizations—the Egyptian, the Greek, the Roman, and the Byzantine, each "in consequence of the oppression and consequent groans of the oppressed." Even as he wrote, Walker could easily "recognize the judgements of God among the Spaniards" for having instituted the slave trade in the New World. Slavery was "*the principal cause*" of the "fierceness with which they cut each other's throats" (p. 15).

The *Appeal* was divided into four articles, the first of which was "Our Wretchedness in Consequence of Slavery." This began with the premise that all human beings "ought to be free." The fact that Americans considered slavery the natural state of black people was demonstration that whites thought of blacks as animals. American slavery, because it was based on dehumanization, was therefore worse than the slavery of the Egyptians. Pharaoh had freed his slave Joseph, then exalted him to the highest office in the land; but one would search in vain for any black public officials in America. Pharaoh had given Moses an Egyptian wife, the daughter of a noble priest, but Americans made laws forbidding blacks and whites to intermarry. It was not that Walker would give so much as "a pinch of snuff" for a white wife, but he was sensitive to the insult of anti-miscegenation laws.

> It is not that I care about intermarriage with the whites . . . , for the Lord knows there is a day coming when they will be glad enough to get into the company of the blacks, notwithstanding we are in this generation levelled by them almost on a level with the brute creation. . . . I only made this extract to show how much lower we are held, and how much more cruel we are treated by the Americans than were the children of Jacob by the Egyptians. . . . Have they not held us up as descending originally from the tribes of Monkeys or Orang-Outangs (p. 19)?

This was, of course, all inspired by Jefferson's declaration that there was a black preference for white mates "as uniformly as in the preference of the Oranootan for the black woman over those of his own species."[34]

It is clear that what Walker meant by slavery was more than the economic institution of the South, where most blacks were owned as property. He spoke rather of the national customs that rendered all black people slaves—even if they had no masters. He referred to the widespread institutionalization of the canons of black inferiority as expressed in "Mr. Jefferson's very severe remarks on us." Slavery derived its nefarious and dehumanizing character from the very nature of the arguments that Jefferson had used to justify its existence. His arguments had been based neither on moral nor on scientific grounds, but purely on a racist aesthetic. Emancipation could not be accomplished without the additional expense of colonization, for despite their singular physical repulsiveness to whites, blacks would inevitably intermarry with them unless removed. "The circumstance of superior beauty, is thought worthy of attention in the propagation of our horses, dogs, and other domestic animals; why not in that of man?" That slavery was the only viable alternative to colonization seemed almost self-evident. "But," asked Walker, "is Mr. Jefferson's assertion true? viz. 'that it is unfortunate for us that our Creator has been pleased to make us black.' We will not take his say so, for the fact. The world will have an opportunity to see whether it is unfortunate for us, that our Creator has made us darker than the *whites*."[35]

Walker's jeremiadic prophecy was a conscious and deliberate response to Jefferson's ominous predictions. He called upon "each of [his] brethren, who has the spirit of a man to buy a copy of Mr. Jefferson's 'Notes on Virginia,' and put it in the hand of his son" (p. 25). Knowledge of the document would not only help black folk to discover the doctrine of white supremacy which made even free blacks "slaves of the community" and "slaves without masters," it would also help blacks to discover the strength of their moral position in a Christian America, presumably watched over by a just God.[36]

The title of Article II is "Our Wretchedness in Consequence of Ignorance." Just as Walker attaches a special definition to "slavery" in Article I, he attaches a special definition to "ignorance" in Article II. He has already given an indication of how he will use the term in the "Preamble," where he refers to the "many of my brethren" who are "ignorantly in league with slave holders" (p. 12). He uses the term to mean the failure of black people to know and act in accordance with their best interests. He also uses the term to indicate the inability of black people to take a cosmic view of their history and their contemporary political state. Ignorance of their past has led blacks to believe "that they are an *inferior* and *distinct race* of beings" (p. 29). History shows that the comparative superiority and inferiority of peoples is not static. He makes another passing reference to Jefferson's *Notes* and the author's brooding on the grim but inexorable turning of the wheel of fate: "Fortune and misfortune, two inseparable companions, lay rolled up in the wheel of events, which have from the creation of the world, and will continue to take place among Men until God shall dash worlds together" (p. 29).

Walker proceeds to take "a retrospective view" of the historical accomplishments of the "sons of Africa or of Ham." In his survey are included the building of the pyramids and the triumphs of Hannibal, that "mighty son of Africa . . . , who defeated and cut off so many thousands of the white Romans or murderers" (p. 30). It was Walker's "candid opinion" that Hannibal would have "taken that cruel and barbarous city by storm," if the Negroes of Carthage had united behind him and given their full support. Perhaps this epitomized the sin for which black people were being punished, the failure to support the leaders that God sent. The Haitian revolt in more recent times had shown some signs of promise. Haiti's future was uncertain, of course, because she was "plagued with that scourge of nations, the Catholic religion" (p. 31). Nonetheless, the Haitians had revealed an ability to stand united and follow their leaders. Walker prophesied that God would soon be sending black Americans a great leader, a prediction also made by Robert Alexander Young in his *Ethiopian Manifesto* of 1829. Walker charged his readers "before my God to lay no obstacle in [the] way" of this coming messiah (p. 30).[37]

Ignorance and treachery were almost synonymous in Walker's vocabulary. He did not believe that a truly intelligent and knowledgeable person could work against the interests of his or her race, for this would violate self-interest. Servility could result only from the acceptance of inferiority, which was a mark of ignorance. Had Jefferson maintained that blacks were intellectually inferior to whites? Well, how were we to contradict him "when we [were] confirming him every day by our *groveling submissions* and *treachery*" (p. 39)? Free blacks thus had an obligation to educate themselves and labor for the enlightenment of their brethren; they must "go to work and *prepare the way* of the Lord" (p. 42).

Walker reprinted with manifest disgust a story from a local newspaper which described "the force of degraded ignorance and deceit among us." This was the report of an abortive slave revolt in Ohio during 1829 in which some sixty blacks slipped their chains, beat and killed two of their drivers, and, leaving a third one for dead, almost made their escape. This third driver, however, regained consciousness and with the aid of a Negro woman was able to mount his horse and flee. The neighborhood was rallied and as a result the whole gang was recaptured.

> Brethren what do you think of this? Was it the natural *fine feelings* of this woman to save such a wretch alive? . . . Natural observations have taught me these things; there is a solemn awe in the hearts of the blacks, as it respects *murdering* men. . . . But I declare, the actions of this black woman are really insupportable. For my own part, I cannot think it was any thing but servile deceit, combined with the most gross ignorance: for we must remember that *humanity, kindness* and the *fear of the Lord*, does not consist in protecting *devils* (p. 35).

The only cure for such behavior was a knowledge of letters, of grammar, of geography, "and a taste for reading." The prospect of Africans acquiring learning "makes tyrants quake and tremble on their sandy foundation." A person of "good sense and learning," with a knowledge of the Bible and of history, could surely never submit to racial slavery (p. 44).

Walker's belief that knowledge was the cure for subservience may have been too optimistic, but he did perceive accurately the ignorance and servility of many black Christians. The distorted conception of religion that led many blacks to submissive behavior had been observed by others. Frederick Douglass, while appalled by such religion, did not deny that it sometimes took hold: "I have met, at the South, many good, religious colored people who were under the delusion that God required them to submit to slavery and to wear their chains with meekness and humility."[38]

Another former slave, Josiah Henson, confessed that a life of bondage had so misformed his moral sense that he thought of resisting the will of his master as rebellion against God. On one occasion, he inadvertently crossed the Ohio River into the free state of Ohio while travelling with a group of slaves under his supervision. When he was informed by local citizens that he and the others were free, Henson faithfully carried his charges back into slave territory, and not a single person was lost. On another occasion Henson, learning of his master's plans to sell him, contemplated murdering him in his sleep, but Christian teaching prevailed and his heart was softened. Mrs. Stowe later claimed that Henson's tenderness of heart was a real-life instance of the black altruism she had mythologized in Uncle Tom. Unlike Uncle Tom, Henson was finally able to escape. He fled to Canada, became an agent of the Underground Railroad, and claimed responsibility for the escape of hundreds of slaves. The betrayal of his charges never ceased to trouble him, and he said: "My infatuation has seemed to me the unpardonable sin. But I console myself with the thought that I acted according to my best light, though the light that was in me was darkness."[39]

Walker's awareness of such a distorted and "ignorant" religious consciousness led him naturally to Article III, "Our Wretchedness in Consequence of the Preachers of the Religion of Jesus Christ." This was not an attack on Christianity, but on the churches and their officials for their perversion of the Christian doctrine. The chapter began on a transcendental note as Walker recognized underlying similarities in the religious consciousness of all nations—Pagans, "as well as Mahometans, the Jews, and the Christians." Every faith had some inkling of the truth, "but pure and undefiled religion, such as was preached by Jesus Christ and his apostles, is hard to be found in all the earth" (p. 47). The history of true religion, like the history of civilization, was perceived as cyclical. God handed down his divine will first to the children of Israel, "who through hypocrisy, oppression and unbelief, departed from the faith." A new covenant was formed, this time with Europe, but the Europeans had in their turn also proven unfaithful. Rather than proselytizing the blacks and making them true Christians, they had delivered them a perversion of the Scriptures in order to bind them more securely in ignorance.

Had not the slave trade been initiated by a Catholic priest, the "very notoriously avaricious" Bartolomé de Las Casas in 1503? Since that time the Christian churches of all denominations had given it their blessings. Pagans, Jews, and "Mahometans" all extended the protection of their religions to those who embraced them, observed Walker. Christians, on the other hand, had wielded their faith as a weapon against all who accepted it. While the Americans were proud of their so-called missionary societies, they feared the growth of religion among the slaves. The freedom to preach, to pray, and to interpret the Bible were severely abridged among them. Rather than taking the faith to Africa, the Christians had taken the weapons of war to encourage feuding among the natives and the trading in slaves that warfare produced. Despite their constant hammering away at real and imagined issues of moral reform (for example, anti-Masonry), American preachers overlooked the moral issue of slavery.

> They have newspapers and monthly periodicals which they receive in continual succession, but on the pages of which you will scarcely ever find a paragraph respecting slavery, which is ten thousand times more injurious to this country than all the other evils put together and which will be the ruination of this country. . . . Americans, unless you speedily alter your course, you and your *Country are gone!!!!!!* . . . I call God—I call angels— I call men, to witness that your DESTRUCTION *is at hand*, and will be speedily consummated unless you REPENT (pp. 51, 56).

Article IV, "Our Wretchedness in Consequence of the Colonizing Plan," is the most confusing section of Walker's *Appeal* for those who look on it as a black nationalist tract. It is an attack on the American Colonization Society, which was the most important institution advocating the resettling of American blacks in West Africa. Walker was not alone in his hostility to Liberia; other black writers were equally unimpressed and would continue to express their misgivings long after emancipation.[40] But while some persons attacked only the Colonization Society and not every expression of emigrationism, Walker was opposed to any sort of expatriation scheme. This was because of his sense of commitment to America and his underlying faith in her principles, and it was, no doubt, the main reason for his extreme bitterness.

Walker turned his attention in this article away from Jefferson to launch an attack on Henry Clay, who had argued that free-black people "neither enjoyed the immunities of freemen, nor were they subjected to the incapacities of slaves, but partook in some degree, of the qualities of both." Since it was self-evident that "they never could amalgamate with the free whites of this country," he felt it best to "drain them off." Clay made it quite plain that the colonization plan should only apply to free Negroes and disassociated himself from Robert Finley and the gradual abolitionists, who had seen deportation as a means of encouraging general abolition.[41] Walker warned Americans that Clay was a Jonah in their midst, and likely to "bring down the vengeance of God" upon the republic.

In Walker's view, Clay's intention was simply to be rid of the free-black population, who, aside from having an annoyingly anomalous status, were the source of discontent among the slaves. The Society and its officers seemed agreed that, the more cultivated and prosperous the free-black population became, the less satisfied they would be. They would continue to increasingly desire "those privileges which they cannot attain." Walker cited the attitudes of Clay as proof that the Society had as one of its aims making certain that the American black population would be uniformly degraded and ignorant: "For if the free are allowed to stay among the slaves, they will have intercourse together, and, of course, the free will learn the slaves *bad habits*, by teaching them that they are MEN, as well as other people, and certainly *ought*, and must be FREE." Walker counseled the free Negroes to ignore the colonization lure and to "stand still and see the salvation of God and the miracle he will work for our deliverance from the wretchedness of the Christians!!!!!!"

At this point Walker quoted at length from one of Richard Allen's published statements on the Colonization Society, a passage interesting for its possible allusion to Jefferson's remarks on the inherent virtue in agricultural pursuits:

> We have *tilled* the ground and made fortunes for thousands, and still they are not weary of our services. *But they who stay to till the ground must be slaves.* Is there not land enough in America, or "corn enough in Egypt"? Why should they send us into a far country to die? See the thousands of foreigners emigrating to America every year: and if there be ground sufficient for them to cultivate, and bread for them to eat; why would they wish to send the *first tillers* of the land away (p. 68).

It is likely that both Allen and Walker were familiar with Jefferson's belief that "those who labor in the earth are the chosen people of God."[42] Both were certainly of the opinion that, purely on the basis of their contribution to the agrarian economy, Africans were entitled to remain in the land "which we have watered with our tears and our blood."

Walker agreed with Allen that America was now the "mother country" of his people. That the black majority was in agreement with Allen's and Walker's reasoning on this is a point often observed. To advocate the anti-emigrationist position led to considerable emotional conflict, however, because the affection that black people felt for the United States was unrequited. To feel an intense commitment to the United States, its culture, and its people, while experiencing the pain of rejection, was humiliating and difficult. There was a desire for acceptance that prompted Gabriel Prosser to plan a victory dinner party with the white officials of Richmond at the completion of his rebellion.[43] There was a clear assimilationist desire on the part of "A Colored Female of Philadelphia," who wrote to *The Liberator*: "I would not be taken to Africa, were the Society to make me queen of that country; and were I to move to Canada, I would not settle in the colony, but take up my abode in one of the cities where a distinction is not known; for I do not approve of our drawing off into a body anywhere."[44] Even Walker, despite his professed bloodthirsty feelings for whites, urged his black readers that if they must emigrate they should as a first choice prefer England, for the English were "our greatest earthly friends and benefactors" (p. 66).

Walker concluded his *Appeal*, not with the hope that his dreadful prophecies would be fulfilled, but with the hope that Americans could be persuaded to adhere to the covenant:

> I say let us reason . . . I speak Americans for your good. . . . And wo, wo, to you if we have to obtain our freedom by fighting. Throw away your fears and prejudices then, and enlighten us and treat us like men, and we will like you more than we now hate you. Treat us like men . . . , and we yet, under God, will become a united and happy people (pp. 80–81).

Although Walker's *Appeal* purported to be directed "to the Coloured Citizens of the World, but in particular and very Expressly to Those of the United States . . . ," its most striking passages are its warnings, specifically addressed to whites. It was an extreme example of the jeremiadic tradition, written by a man who thought of himself as an American speaking to other Americans. It was conceived with American interests at heart. Walker was a black nationalist in the sense that the term has been employed by Henry F. Sweet, who observed: "Black nationalism provided the creative thrust for black demands of American nationality."[45]

The jeremiadic themes of David Walker were constantly reiterated in instances both rhetorical and actual in the decades preceding the Civil War. One thinks immediately of the Nat Turner revolt, so often mentioned within this context, and of John Brown's crusade. Henry Highland Garnet and other militant abolitionists began to depict slavery as the Antichrist, a theme in antislavery thought which is brilliantly illustrated by David Brion Davis.[46] Slavery was the last remaining obstacle to the American millenium; it represented the armies of Babylon threatening the City of God. It symbolized the chariots of Pharaoh soon to be engulfed in the tide of America's sacred history.[47]

It was at this point that black messianism began to have an effect on American foreign policy. During the three decades preceding the American Civil War, a sizable number of fugitive slaves and free blacks made tours of Europe, especially the British Isles, where they denounced the evils of slavery. They were usually sponsored by church groups or at least by abolitionist societies having a strong religious base. Black abolitionists, whether at home or abroad, tended to use the methods of religious revivalism, often speaking in churches where they preached in the evangelical style, convincing their audiences by vivid descriptions and emotional appeals. They treated slavery as a moral issue and dragged the United States before the court of British public opinion, pointing out the hypocrisy of slaveholders in the land of the free.

Since their audiences were composed of Victorian Protestants, they made it a point to demonstrate that slavery in the South led to violations of every code of the Protestant ethic. Slaveholders were poor Christians, because they were too slothful to do their own work. Slaveholders sinned against chastity, because they made their female slaves into concubines. They sinned against the sacrament of matrimony, because they broke up slave families. They stole the fruits of the slaves' labor, and therefore they were thieves. Throughout the slaveholding South, one witnessed dueling, bearbaiting, gambling, drinking, adultery, and other signs that the strenuous and forthright Protestant virtues were incompatible with slaveholding.

By the beginning of the war, much had been done to plant the idea that it was in the North that the truest values of Anglo–Saxon Protestantism were preserved. The Civil War was the long-expected judgment of God upon the South. American diplomacy during the war clearly profited from thirty years of Afro–American "ambassadorship" and from the idea that those who fought against the slave power fought on the side of God.[48]

The Civil War marked a period when Northern intellectuals linked the militant, chauvinistic, hard-line view of American destiny to the values of egalitarian liberalism. In his second inaugural address, Lincoln indeed spoke of binding up the nation's wounds "with malice toward none, and charity for all," but he left no doubt of his feelings concerning the cause of the war. The cause was slavery, the nation's collective sin. The war was God's judgment on the South for having committed the sin and a punishment to the North for having tolerated it so long.

> Fondly do we hope, fervently do we pray, that this mighty scourge of war may speedily pass away. Yet if God wills that it continue until all the wealth piled by the bondsman's two hundred and fifty years of unrequited toil shall be sunk, and until every drop of blood drawn with the lash shall be paid by another drawn with the sword, as was said three thousand years ago, so still it must be said, "The judgements of the Lord are true and righteous altogether."[49]

A point often made is that this and other statements made by Lincoln during the course of the war were inspired by the Jeffersonian jeremiad.[50] Within a year, Lincoln was to become the final propitiatory offering to a wrathful deity. And if the martyred John Brown was to become the white counterpart of Nat Turner in the black messianic pantheon, so was Lincoln to become the counterpart of Uncle Tom. Indeed, Mrs. Stowe was one of many contributors to the myth of Lincoln as a patient, long-suffering, Christlike martyr for the sins of the nation. It was fortunate for America that his strength was "not aggressive so much as passive," she reasoned. "A reckless, bold, theorizing, dashing man of genius," she said, "might have wrecked our Constitution and ended us in a splendid military despotism."[51]

Stowe was not the only one to attribute to Lincoln these traits of passive heroism. The fallen president was continually portrayed as a patient sufferer, who prognosticated his own martyrdom and went to meet his destiny with a spirit of resignation.[52] He was sentimentalized as a man of sorrows by the same romantic racialists who created the myth of Negro suffering-servanthood. Even during his presidency, Lincoln had been portrayed as a blackamoor by his political enemies, who insinuated that his sympathy for the blacks might be due to a strain of Negro blood.[53] After his assassination he was not infrequently sentimentalized in terms of traits associated with the personality of Uncle Tom. His former law partner wrote:

> For fifty years God rolled Abraham Lincoln through his fiery furnace. He did it to try Abraham and to purify him for his purposes. This made Mr. Lincoln humble, tender, forbearing, sympathetic to suffering, kind, sensitive, tolerant; broadening and widening his whole nature; making him the noblest and loveliest character since Jesus Christ.[54]

Thus it was that the theme of American redemptionism was personified in its martyred president. The myth of Abraham Lincoln, the martyr, became an aspect of America's messianic myth as E. L. Tuveson has argued in *Redeemer Nation*. Suffering-servanthood and the image of the man of sorrows are, of course, essential ingredients of the Christian messianic myth. The idea of the patient, suffering servant could be applied to presidents as well as to slaves. The Uncle Tom myth, a variation on the suffering-servant theme, was more complex than is generally assumed—a point made by S. P. Fullinwider. The traditional attributes assigned to Uncle Tom amounted to more than a pious preachment of idealized slave morality, although they were certainly that, too. The Uncle Tom myth had wider implications, as we shall presently see.

4
The Myth of Uncle Tom
and the Messianic Mission
of the Black Race

The racial symbolism personified in the character of Uncle Tom was not originally intended to be pejorative. The conception of the black personality that Harriet Beecher Stowe illustrated in *Uncle Tom's Cabin* was a messianic one. It bore an ironic resemblance to conceptions of African racial traits acceded to by principal spokespersons for black nationalism, from Delany to Garvey. The qualities of kindliness, patience, humility, and great-hearted altruism, even in the face of abuse, were the very Christian virtues that were needed to redeem the world. Just as Christ had died for the sins of his tormentors, so had Uncle Tom been portrayed as dying for the sins of the South. But it was obviously not for his Christlike martyrdom alone that Uncle Tom represented a messianic ideal.

Mrs. Stowe believed in African colonization; and she—like many of her contemporaries, both black and white—had a mystical vision of the destiny of the black nation that was to be constructed in Africa. To her mind, African colonization embodied more than establishing a haven for troublesome, unwanted, free Negroes. Liberia was to be a land of promise, and she assigned it a redeeming mission similar to that which her father, Lyman Beecher, and her brother, Henry Ward Beecher, had assigned to Anglo–America. The Anglo–American conception of world mission was softened and made suitable to a black context in *Uncle Tom's Cabin*. Mrs. Stowe put the following words into the mouth of her creation, George Harris, announcing his decision to set sail for Liberia:

"To the Anglo–Saxon race has been intrusted the destinies of the world during its pioneer period of struggle and conflict. To that mission its stern, inflexible, energetic elements, were well adapted; but as a Christian, I look for another era to arise. On its borders I trust we stand and the throes that now convulse the nations are, to my hope, but the birth pangs of an hour of peace and brotherhood."

Here, Mrs. Stowe is clearly directing George to speak in terms of a messianic era or a millennium, which is to be ushered in by the establishment of a black nation. This nation is to be characterized by the same traits that have been delineated in the Christlike martyr, Uncle Tom. George continues:

"I think that the African race has peculiarities yet to be unfolded in the light of civilization and Christianity, which, if not the same with those of the Anglo–Saxon, may prove to be, morally, of even a higher type. . . . If not a dominant and commanding race, they are, at least an affectionate, magnanimous, and forgiving one. . . ."[1]

Stowe was not the first white author to assign a messianic mission to the Back-to-Africa movement. In 1838, Robert Breckinridge had spoken to the American Colonization Society in terms reminiscent of John Winthrop's at the founding of the Massachusetts Bay Colony. Winthrop envisioned a "City on a Hill," a shining example to the world of what a Christian and covenanted people might become. Breckinridge's adaptation of this to the African context was equally lofty, for on the moment that "one single city of free civilized Christian blacks [was] placed near the equator on the western coast of Africa," the black race would be redeemed. More strikingly and in a broader millennial vein, "the human race itself [would be] launched into a new and glorious career, of which all the triumphs of the past afford no parallel.[2]

Breckinridge saw black Americans as having a redemptive destiny, not only with respect to Africa, but for the entirety of humanity. Stowe and Breckinridge were not alone in assigning Christlike redemptive qualities to the Negro race. George Fredrickson, in *The Black Image in the White Mind*, has shown that this "romantic racialism" was typical of the attitudes of mid-century abolitionists. Whether they were gradual abolitionists, believing in colonization, or immediate abolitionists, believing that the destiny of the black race was in America, they all were appealed to by the Christlike stereotype. E. L. Tuveson, in *Redeemer Nation*, has shown how Theodore Parker assigned to the black Americans the qualities of a "redemptive people." I would add to the observations of Tuveson and Fredrickson that such views often went hand in hand with a patronizing claim for black superiority that was perhaps only half sincere. The attitude was similar to Kipling's "You're a better man than I am, Gunga Din."

As one might expect, black Americans were ambivalent concerning such stereotypes. If white colonizationists really believed that black Americans were such a desirable stock, why were they so anxious to be rid of them? As early as 1852, the year in which *Uncle Tom's Cabin* appeared, the Reverend J. B. Smith, a black minister, protested against Uncle Tom's conception of Christian virtue because it made him submit to tyranny. It was tempting to think of oneself as belonging to a noble, long-suffering, Christlike people, with a mission to redeem the world, but should not Christianity also imply militancy? The Christlike conception of the black mission would persist into the twentieth century, but there would always be some doubts. Sometimes the allusions to Christian resignation and passivity became bitter in tone. Marcus Garvey gave a sarcastic twist to the myth in a 1937 statement that drew laughter and applause:

> The black man has a kind heart and no one knows it more than the white man of the North American continent. We withstood slavery and yet we still smile. It is because our hearts are tuned to righteousness and love. . . . We can always be regarded as a peace-loving people. I feel sure if there is any trouble in any district, it isn't the Negro. The only trouble the Negro will make is to get drunk.[3]

Garvey's sarcasm points up what was a central paradox in the thinking of classical black nationalists—a desire to cling to the myth of moral superiority with which the romantic racialists of the nineteenth century had endowed them, but counterpoised by the recognition that there was something degrading about drawing one's self-image from a slavery experience in which one was forced to play submissive roles.

As a rule, black nationalists of the ante-bellum period had no high opinion of the slave personality or the slave community; a tone of dull outrage and brooding disgust is recurrent in their writings. Martin Delany bitterly observed that "wherever there is one white person, that one rules and governs two colored persons."[4] Robert Alexander Young saw the slaves as "a people rendered disobedient to the great dictates of nature, by the barbarity that hath been practiced upon them."[5] Alexander Crummell attributed the manifold problems of Liberia to the lingering effects of slavery upon black people, which rendered the colonists, "with rare and individual exceptions, ignorant, benighted, besotted and filthy, both in the inner and the outer man."[6] "It cannot be denied," wrote Edward Wilmot Blyden, "that some very important advantages have accrued to the black man from his deportation to this land, but it has been at the expense of his manhood. . . . We have been taught a cringing servility. We have been drilled into contentment with the most undignified circumstances."[7]

"Where else among black people," asks Sterling Stuckey, the Afro–American historian, "can one find such gloomy and devastating, such stereotypical portraits of black humanity as among nationalists?" Commenting on the writing of David Walker, the vitriolic nineteenth-century pamphleteer, Stuckey sees Walker's black nationalism as illustrating "almost perfectly a black nationalist tendency to exaggerate the degree of acquiescence to oppression by the masses of black people." David Walker's *Appeal*, in Stuckey's interpretation, "brooded over the degradation of his people."[8] The observation seems accurate, especially with respect to Article II of the *Appeal*, "Our Wretchedness in Consequence of Ignorance," where Walker describes slave society as permeated by the basest forms of treachery. He asserts that a son may be seen to beat his mother, or a husband his pregnant wife.[9] Servile Negroes, claims Walker, all too frequently betray those who are inclined to resist. The scenes that he conjures loom disquietingly in the shadows, a somber background to the images of robust, earthy peasantry painted by John Blassingame in *The Slave Community* and by several other scholars in derivative works.[10]

There is a myth of slave servility and a myth of slave resistance. In most discussions of these myths, we sooner or later encounter some passing reference to the contrasting but related symbols of Nat Turner and Uncle Tom. We know them both primarily as symbols, although there was a real historical Nat Turner and a man named Josiah Henson who claimed to be the model for Uncle Tom. It is very doubtful that the historical Josiah Henson really was the model for Uncle Tom. As for the historical Nat Turner, we know almost nothing of him or his motivations. We know them both mainly as literary creations. Both of them are surrounded by obscuring legends. Both of them live for us as symbols transcending the reality of their once actual existence. Vincent Harding reminds us that a mythical Nat Turner has long existed side by side with the historical person, that there has been a "vital tradition concerning Nat Turner . . . in poetry and fiction . . . Sunday School and Lodge pageants and plays. . . ."[11] Who is to say whether the personality of the historical Nat Turner was more accurately recorded by such literary productions or by the report of Thomas R. Gray, a county court attorney, of Southampton, Virginia.[12]

With regard to Uncle Tom, he is much maligned by many persons who have never read Mrs. Stowe's novel. This is ironic, for Uncle Tom ought to be a sympathetic figure for sentimental ethnic chauvinists who are obsessed with demonstrating that a spirit of "caring and sharing" was characteristic of slave-community life. Loyal and steadfast in his dealings with the other slaves, heroic and unflinching in matters of principle, the literary Uncle Tom was in no way symbolic of the racial treason with which his name has more recently become associated. Indeed, it was not Uncle Tom but his historical cognate, Josiah Henson, who was guilty of cooperating with the slaveholder by returning a cargo of slaves to Kentucky soil after inadvertently freeing them in Ohio. The literary character has been made to bear the burden of guilt for his historical counterpart's misdirected sense of loyalty.[13]

In order to understand the persistence of Uncle Tom and Nat Turner as symbolic representations of the slave personality, we must, of course, utilize insights provided by the sociological approach to the history of slavery. At the same time, we must be aware that we are attempting to analyze myth and symbol and that the tools of literary analysis may at times assist us in finding insights that social science alone cannot provide. Despite the objections raised by Robert Berkhofer, Jr., and the historical behaviorists, there is much merit in the attempt by Henry Nash Smith and the "so-called, 'image' school of American Studies" to understand non-rationalistic conceptions of life that play such an important part in the motivation of human behavior. The Nat Turner and Uncle Tom myths, like the myths that Smith describes, may or may not "accurately reflect empirical fact," although they have sometimes exerted "a decided influence on practical affairs."[14]

Black Americans have found both the Uncle Tom and the Nat Turner myths useful. During the forty-year period of repression following the end of reconstruction, even such fiery militants as Frederick Douglass and Ida B. Wells would play on the image of the faithful, long-suffering, honest slave. In an address entitled "The Lesson of the Hour," Douglass appealed to the myth of the slave who guarded the virtue of the plantation mistress during the Civil War. Ida B. Wells did the same, as she reveals in her *Autobiography*. Joel Chandler Harris provided a melodramatic version of this myth when he described Uncle Remus standing guard behind his plantation mistress with an axe, in the face of Union soldiers. Sutton Griggs, a black Baptist minister, similarly appealed to the myth of the loyal slave who was willing to die protecting the virtue of his mistress.[15]

These were myths directed at white audiences, for reasons that must be understood in historical context. When a man like Frederick Douglass, who had done so much to build the myth of the heroic slave, turned to celebrating the loyalty of slaves to their masters, there must have been some provocation. Black writers chose to emphasize slave loyalty because lynching was on the rise and the supposed black propensity to rape was the most commonly supplied excuse for mob violence.

The emphasis on the myth of a black male who put the welfare of his master's family above his own and who defended his mistress while his own loved ones remained in bondage was obviously not a flattering one. It contributed to a desexualized image of the black male and to the myth of the ignorant, stupid darky, contented to remain in bondage. In late-Victorian America, the usefulness (despite the unattractiveness) of the myth can readily be seen. But the myth was one that obviously had negative potential, for it could also be used to buttress the argument that black people were naturally servile.

The myth of the vengeful Nat Turner, on the other hand, was rightly kept alive by black militants. Ministers like John W. Cromwell and Alexander Crummell held him up as a symbol of manly resistance to tyranny. The Turner myth became especially appealing during the 1960s to black Christians like James H. Cone and Joseph Washington, who craved a more virile image of the Christian soldier than that provided by Uncle Tom.[16]

S. P. Fullinwider, in his discussions of the impact of Christianity upon black American thought, has made some sharp observations on the nature of messianic symbolism in the minds of nineteenth-century black Americans. Inspired, no doubt, by the tradition of Edward Gibbon, who viewed Christianity as a slave religion, Fullinwider has recognized that the faith tends at times to encourage submissive behavior—that is, turning the other cheek. The religion of Afro–American slaves, in Fullinwider's interpretation, provided a rationalization for the submissive attitude that the slave necessarily adopted in order to survive. And, in fact, by meditating on the bruised and battered Jesus of traditional Christianity, some slaves were able not only to redeem their self-respect, but to share in the divinity of a masochistic God. One could actually embrace one's degraded status by rationalizing that it made one Christlike: "They crucified my lord, / And he never said a mumblin' word"[17] Throughout the nineteenth century, black nationalist intellectuals continued to identify the dispersed African peoples as a mystical body of Christ whose sufferings would lead in the long run to the redemption of Africa and, ultimately, to the uplifting of all humanity.

Fullinwider's approach, while imaginative, sensitive, and essentially sound, was disappointing in one respect. It failed to note the unity of opposites that characterizes Christian doctrine, as it does so much human behavior, for Christian rhetoric encourages assertiveness as well as submission. To be sure, the Christian Messiah is often depicted as sallow, lacerated, crowned with thorns, and seeking suffering, not only for himself but for his followers, who are commanded to turn the other cheek. At the same time, of course, the Christian Messiah is a warlike God. This is true in the apocalyptic tradition of the New Testament, developed by the Puritan poets John Milton and Edward Taylor, and by the evangelical Julia Ward Howe. The two faces of Christianity are reflected in American culture—in the strident Christian soldierism of "The Battle Hymn of the Republic," as well as in "The Peaceable Kingdom" of Edward Hicks. These are not necessarily conflicting traditions; they seem to coexist with little difficulty in the minds of many sincere Christians.[18]

The folklore of slavery provides a variant model of this seeming conflict, symbolized in the monumental personalities of Nat Turner, the holy warrior, and Uncle Tom, the long-suffering, sacrificial victim. Despite apparent dissimilarities, these two messianic figures are much the same; and I will argue that, no less than Nat Turner, Uncle Tom represents the intrinsically Christian black nationalism of the nineteenth century. Black Christianity, with its mingled elements of submission and potential violence, was no less complex than its white counterpart. It allowed its adherents to rationalize a broad spectrum of human behaviors. It allowed revolutionary Christians like David Walker to hope—appeals to violence notwithstanding—that black and white Americans would some day become a "united and happy people."[19] Christianity provided a framework within which black Christians could reconcile peacefully the warring ideals of resistance and accommodation that they so forcefully experienced.

Uncle Tom's Cabin is a novel, of course, but a novel with experiential cognates, as Harriet Beecher Stowe maintained.[20] Contemporary sources from the period covered in *Uncle Tom's Cabin*, including slave testimony, travelers' accounts, and reports of slaveholders and abolitionists alike, bear witness to the fact that religion of the ante-bellum blacks was often otherworldly and escapist. These tendencies have long been recognized by such scholars as Benjamin Mays, who commented on their appearance in early Afro–American writing.[21] W. E. B. Du Bois and E. Franklin Frazier were often critical of other-worldly elements in black religion and of the tendencies of black religious leaders to discourage political activism and social consciousness among the masses.[22] Recent historians have correctly tried to compensate for the tendencies of earlier generations to ignore the religious basis of atti-tudes of resistance among the slaves.[23] It cannot be overlooked, how-ever, that Christianity was usually encouraged to promote submissive behavior among American slave populations.[24] Although historians have rightly emphasized African cultural survivals as mechanisms for the support of resistance,[25] future researchers should be successful in iden-tifying African cultural traits that provided mechanisms for adjusting to slavery and submission. The "Uncle Tom" personality cannot be attrib-uted solely to the internalization of Christian values.

Mrs. Stowe portrays Uncle Tom as a highly civilized man, "sym-pathetic and assimilative," having acquired "refined . . . tastes and feelings."[26] His acculturation is symbolized by his ability and desire to read the Bible. He does not actively rebel against his enslavement and seems to be a perfect characterization of the type of slaves, commented upon by Frederick Douglass, who accepted their status as the will of God and hoped for deliverance in the life to come.[27] Even when Tom learns that he is to be sold away from his wife and children, he refuses to flee to the North partly in order to prevent forcing his master to the alternative of breaking up the plantation and selling everyone. But Tom also feels a sense of loyalty, "Mas'r always found me on the spot—he always will. I never broke trust, nor used my pass no ways contrary to my work, and I never will."[28]

Although Tom is always loyal to his master, he refuses to betray his fellow slaves. He acknowledges Eliza's right to flee with little Harry and does not betray her trust. His first beating at the hands of Simon Legree occurs because he is unwilling to administer a beating to the hapless Cassy at his master's orders. Tom stands firm saying, "I'm willin' to work, night and day, and work while there's life and breath in me; but this yer thing I can't feel it right to do;—and, Mas'r I *never* shall do it,— *never!*"[29]

As the days pass, Tom continues to invite Legree's anger by openly professing his Christianity, singing hymns in the field, and assuming a manner of cheerfulness and spiritual joy. It is almost as if he intends to be provocative, and indeed Mrs. Stowe notes that Legree is "provoked beyond measure."[30] Tom increasingly assumes an identification with the martyr Jesus. In thinking of death, his heart has begun to throb with "joy and desire," and he says to Legree, "Ye may whip me, starve me, burn me,—it'll only send me sooner where I want to go."[31] As the two characters continue to interact, Legree develops a semiconscious suspicion that perhaps he has waded beyond his depth. The years of habitual sadism have actually been a form of self-inflicted personality destruction. The passive rebellion of Uncle Tom, combined with the manipulations of Cassy, has penetrated a vulnerable spot of his weakened ego; and Legree has begun to tremble with "superstitious dread." In one epiphanic confrontation, a mental role reversal actually occurs in which Legree sees himself as a demon suffering in hell, while Uncle Tom becomes at once both sacrificial victim and retributive messiah.

> He understood that it was GOD who was standing between him and his victim, and he blasphemed him. That submissive and silent man, whom taunts, nor threats, nor stripes, nor cruelties, could disturb, roused a voice within him, such as of old his Master roused in the demoniac soul saying, "What have we to do with thee, thou Jesus of Nazareth?—art thou come to torment us before the time?"[32]

Legree becomes increasingly obsessed with Tom's passive defiance and with silencing his verbal torture, even if this means destroying his valuable human property. Tom, for his part, so thoroughly assumes the masochistic personality of the suffering Christ that he desires only to be a servant of servants, regardless of the wrath of Simon Legree.

> Tom's whole soul overflowed with compassion and sympathy for the poor wretches by whom he was surrounded. . . . He longed to pour out

something for the relief of their woes. . . . Gradually and imperceptibly the strange silent patient man, who was ready to bear everyone's burden, and sought help from none,—who stood aside for all, and came last, and took least, yet was foremost to share his little all with any who needed . . . this man at last began to have a strange power over them. . . .[33]

At the climax of the novel, Tom is beaten to death for refusing to reveal the whereabouts of the escaped Cassy and Emmeline; but before he expires he calls Legree a "poor miserable critter" to his face, and his martyrdom so impresses the brutal drivers Quimbo and Sambo that they bawl like babies and embrace the faith, wailing "Lord Jesus, have mercy on us!"[34]

The retributive and masochistic elements of the Christian ideology run parallel to the elements of sadism and masochism present in every human personality.[35] In any relationship between two persons, there is both dominance and submission; and occasionally the two individuals involved will experience a reversal of roles. Simon Legree is dependent to an infantile extent upon the voluntary submission of Uncle Tom, who is a formidable physical adversary, "a large, broad-chested, powerfully made man."[36] What is more, he must surely live in constant dread that Uncle Tom will suddenly press the role reversal to its logical extreme and reveal a Nat Turner at the core of his being. Legree's dependency upon his slaves for his own self-definition and his unacknowledged fear of them becomes obvious not only in his attempts to break Tom, but in his relationship with his old mistress, the mulatress Cassy. Even after being cast aside, she is able to arouse his superstitious fears and, as she reminds Sambo, the slave driver, she retains a certain influence over Legree.

> "Dog!" she said, "touch *me*, if you dare! I've power enough, yet, to have you torn by the dogs, burnt alive, cut to inches! I've only to say the word."[37]

The driver is obviously impressed by this display and withdraws from the confrontation. It is difficult to believe that Mrs. Stowe and other observers of the slavery system simply dreamed up the idea that slave mistresses occasionally exerted influence over plantation masters.

The role reversal that occurred between Legree and his slaves was not without analogues in the real world. Josiah Henson, described by Mrs. Stowe as an "instance parallel with that of Uncle Tom," tells us of such a role reversal in his autobiography.[38] He says that he felt morally and physically superior to his master and, indeed, contemptuous of him. On occasions when his master would become involved in drunken brawls, Henson would drag him from the local tavern.

> I was young, remarkably athletic and self relying, and in such affrays carried it with a high hand, and would elbow my way among the whites—

whom it would have been almost death for me to strike—seize my master and drag him out, mount him on his horse, or crowd him into his buggy, with the ease with which I would handle a bag of corn. I knew that I was doing for him what he could not do for himself, showing my superiority to others, and acquiring their respect in some degree, at the same time.[39]

As in the relationship between Tom and Legree, the master is totally dependent upon the loyalty of the slave, and the slave—irony of ironies— derives his sense of superiority over the master by serving him faithfully. Harriet Beecher Stowe seems to have intuitively grasped this aspect of the master–slave relationship in creating the plantation world of Simon Legree and his slaves. Subordinate individuals and dominated classes often rationalize their status by asserting that their position in society is proof of their superiority to those above them.[40]

The patterns of adjustment to inferior status are not peculiar to black American slavery, nor are they in any way attributable to characteristic traits of the African personality. Comparisons between the behavior of American slaves and other oppressed peoples date back to the sixteenth century, when Bartolomew Las Casas noted the readiness with which Africans, as opposed to American Indian tribes, adjusted to slavery. In one sense, blacks came off the worse in such comparisons, since their ability to adjust to slavery was seen as proof of the natural suitability of their race for bondage. Those who were given to making such comparisons, usually to the disparagement of black humanity, ignored the fact that races and nations that were unable to adjust to outside domination had a way of becoming extinct.[41] They also ignored the fact that the history of Europe provided many instances of white people submitting to domination. John S. Rock, a black lawyer from Boston, observed this in his debate of 1858 with the Rev. Theodore Parker, who had once opined that "the stroke of the ax would have solved the question [of the abolition of slavery] long ago, but the black man would not strike." Rock countered with the observation that black American slaves were not the only oppressed class in world history, nor were they in any way remarkable for their failure to overthrow their oppressors by violence:

> The white man contradicts himself who says, that if he were in our situation, he would throw off the yoke. Thirty millions of white men of this proud Caucasian race are at this moment held as slaves, and bought and sold with horses and cattle. The iron heel of oppression grinds the masses of all European races to the dust. They suffer every kind of oppression, and no one dares to open his mouth to protest against it.[42]

Rock might have gone on to add that not only the serfs and peasants of Europe, but the working classes of England and America as well, willingly acquiesced in their domination by the aristocracy and the bourgeoisie, and that without their acquiescence the upper classes would have been deprived of their ostentatious, oppressive power.[43] The tendency of plebians, serfs, and slaves to identify with the grandeur of the big house—which Douglass observed in the case of his fellow slaves—seems to be as universal as human nature.[44] Despite the universality of the experience of submission, however, nineteenth-century observers tended to exaggerate the submissiveness of American Negro slaves and to attribute this submissiveness to inherent traits of the African personality.[45]

As late as 1918, Ulrich Bonnell Phillips saw subservience as an inborn racial trait of black people (in the preface to his still highly regarded *American Negro Slavery*).[46] Writing at the Army base of Camp Gordon, Georgia, Phillips observed all around him what he identified as "a plantation atmosphere." The persistence of this plantation atmosphere a full generation after slavery strangely did not convince him of the effectiveness of slavery in modifying the social behavior of Africans. In fact, it convinced him of just the opposite:

> It may be that the change of African nature by plantation slavery has been exaggerated. At any rate a generation of freedom has wrought less transformation in the bulk of the blacks than might casually be supposed.[47]

Phillips' reasoning is curious here, as it is at other points throughout the book. His most significant contribution to our conceptualization of slave society was his comparison of a slave plantation to an army camp:

> The negroes themselves show the same easy-going, amiable, serio-comic obedience and the same personal attachments to white men as well as the same sturdy light-heartedness and the same love of laughter and of rhythm which distinguished their ancestors. The non-commissioned officers among them show a punctilious pride of place which matches that of the plantation foremen of old; and the white officers who succeed best in the command of these companies reflect the planter's admixture of tact and firmness of control, the planter's patience of instruction and his crisp though cordial reciprocation of sentiment. The negroes are not enslaved but drafted; they dwell not in cabins but in barracks; they shoulder the rifle, not the hoe; but the visitor to their company streets in evening hours enters nevertheless a plantation atmosphere. A hilarious party dashes in pursuit of a fugitive, and gives him lashes with a belt "moderately laid on." When questioned, the explanation is given that the victim is "a awnrooly nigger" whose ways must be mended.[48]

Forty years passed before Stanley M. Elkins attempted to explain slave behavior in a similar way by drawing analogies with other types of authoritarian systems. Elkins suggested that the plantation was not infrequently a "closed system," similar to a concentration camp, and thus capable of breeding patterns of authoritarian behavior. Indeed, it would seem that authoritarian pathologies exist in all institutional life, regardless of whether the institutions are "closed systems."[49] Phillips' peremptory declaration that the behavior of black soldiers on a military base illustrated a survival of "plantation atmosphere" and was therefore proof of the African's natural subservience was hardly rational. Far more intelligent would have been an argument similar to that of Elkins that whatever submissive tendencies blacks demonstrated, whether in the army or on the plantation, had to do with their socialization into the respective institutions.[50]

Since Phillips believed that the African genius was an imitative one, he might have argued that the behavior he observed on his army base—the punctilious pride of non-commissioned officers, the ready submission to authority—was learned behavior, imitative of the behavior of whites. Was not the army an ideal environment to encourage the revival of such "plantation" behavior patterns as submission to authority? Submissiveness may more readily be viewed as a typically military than as a typically African trait. The behavior that Phillips noted could more easily have been explained in terms of universal human tendencies to observe, imitate, and adjust than in terms of some hazily conceived African racial genius. Blacks are not the only soldiers in history who have submitted with enthusiasm to officers for whom they have felt genuine feelings of adoration and doglike devotion. The black men that Phillips observed had learned the Western code of military submission, because they were absorbed into a cultural institution that had been developed specifically for inculcating such submissiveness. The "plantation atmosphere" of the army base described by Phillips was not the result of a natural tendency toward "easygoing, amicable, serio-comic obedience." This behavior was learned from the white officers and men at the training camp, who had already undergone an almost identical indoctrination in authoritarian behavior.[51] It had nothing whatever to do with ineradicable traits of the African personality.

Mrs. Stowe would have agreed with Phillips that the African was suited by nature to faithful servanthood. By a strange twist, however, she converted this assessment into proof of a variety of racial superiority. She predicted that it was the destiny of the African peoples to evolve into "an elevated and cultivated race." The coming civilization of Africa would "awake there with a gorgeousness and splendor of which our western tribes faintly have conceived." All this would come to pass, not only because of the singular richness of the African environment, "that far-off mystic land of gold, and gems, and spices, and waving palms, and wondrous flowers, and miraculous fertility"; it would result partially from the native genius of the African race itself. Black people were destined to "show forth some of the latest and most magnificent revelations of human life."[52]

Certainly they will [excel], in their gentleness, their lowly docility of heart, their aptitude to repose on a superior mind and rest on a higher power, their child-like simplicity of affection, and facility of forgiveness. In all these they will exhibit the highest form of the peculiarly *Christian* life, and, perhaps, as God chasteneth whom he loveth, he hath chosen poor Africa in the furnace of affliction, to make her the highest and noblest in that kingdom which he will set up, when every other kingdom has been tried, and failed; for the first shall be last, and the last first.[53]

Mrs. Stowe's contemporary, Hollis Read, toyed with similar ideas on African redemption, derived from his reading of the influential T. J. Bowen, a missionary to Yorubaland who had travelled extensively in the interior. Read accepted Bowen's testimony as to the "sterling honesty, kindness, and affection, as well as . . . the qualities constituting force, stability, and endurance of character."[54] Read hailed the redemptionist spirit that seemed to be pervading Africa and agreed with Stowe that "under civilizing and Christianizing influence [Africans] would develop powers that would astonish the world." Indeed, he expected "in the future of the Negro a higher type of Christianity and a better order of civilization than the world has heretofore witnessed." Read based this inference on "the peculiar religious instincts" of the people and the "facility with which they receive religious teachings." He asserted as a self-evident truth that the "religious instinct of the Negro is everywhere noticeable." The Negro was genetically predisposed to faith and morality, and he seized the Word of God "with an avidity common to no other race." The African race was naturally inclined to the Christian virtues of humble reverence and unselfish loyalty and possessed a "susceptibility . . . for a higher order of the spiritual life." Read's enthusiastic prediction "that coming generations shall witness in Africa nationalities of a higher order than have heretofore existed [was] predicated chiefly on the fact of the religious susceptibilities of her people. . . ."[55]

Similar attitudes were accepted by the major philosophers of black nationalism during the mid-nineteenth century. The tendency to think of blacks as dreamy, sensitive, genial, humble, unselfish, loyal, and long suffering, is present in major black writers during the nineteenth and early-twentieth centuries.[56] Such racial stereotyping appears in the writings of David Walker, who dramatizes and overstates the tendencies towards conciliation and forgiveness, typical ideals of "Uncle Tom" Christianity, among the masses of the slaves. And Walker, we must remember, came close to personifying the stereotype when, with touching idealism, he expressed the hope that blacks and whites would someday become "a united and happy people." The tendency towards stereotyping is also present in the writings of Alexander Crummell, who agreed with Mrs. Stowe and Hollis Read as to the religious instincts of black people: "As a people we like religion—we like religious services.

Our people like to go to church, to prayer meetings, to revivals. . . . We like to be made happy by sermons, singing, and pious talk."[57] Martin Delany, as well, accepted the myth of the instinctive religiosity of black people. "The colored races are highly susceptible of religion," he wrote, "it is a constituent principle of their nature, and an excellent trait in their character. But unfortunately they carry it too far."[58] Blyden became increasingly ambivalent about Christianity as his career progressed, but during the 1860s he felt the appropriateness of phrasing his appeals to black Americans in the rhetoric of Christian redemptionism.[59] During the 1890s he admitted a conscious parallel between his Pan–Africanism and the messianic consciousness of Zionism. Marcus Garvey, recognizing the importance of a religious appeal to his followers, attempted to encourage a militant Christianity in place of the all too prevalent "otherworldly" religion noted by contemporary students of black religion.[60]

Booker T. Washington, cunning and slippery, played upon the Uncle Tom stereotype in his Atlanta Exposition Address, where he characterized Afro–Americans as ideal workers and model citizens, highly preferable to emigrants from southern and eastern Europe. "Cast down your bucket," he advised his audience, "among the 8,000,000 you have tested in days when to have proved treacherous meant the ruin of your firesides." He then went on to assign to black Americans the dubious proofs of superiority associated with the Uncle Tom tradition:

> You can be sure in the future, as in the past, that you and your families will be surrounded by the most patient, faithful, law abiding, and unresentful people that the world has seen. As we have proved our loyalty to you in the past, in nursing your children, watching by the sick-bed of your mothers and fathers, and often following them with tear dimmed eyes to their graves, so in the future, in our humble way, we shall stand by you with a devotion that no foreigner can approach, ready to lay down our lives, if need be, in defense of yours. . . .[61]

W. E. B. Du Bois commented on "the slow, steady disappearance of a certain type of Negro,—the faithful, courteous slave of other days, with his incorruptible honesty and dignified humility."[62] He also alluded to the "deep religious fatalism, painted so beautifully in 'Uncle Tom.' "[63] Du Bois, with his concept of the nobility of servitude, which he revealed in *Darkwater*, harkened back to the romantic racialism of the nineteenth century and to the stereotypical conception of black racial genius to which Stowe had clung.[64] From the mid-nineteenth to the early-twentieth century, black nationalists accepted the "Uncle Tom" stereotype as representing at least a portion of reality. Indeed the philosophers of black nationalism, despite their commitment to political self-assertiveness and economic independence, were almost slavish in their commitment to Victorian civilization and Protestant Christianity.[65] They often revealed a deeply felt patriotism towards the United States despite the ill treatment they had received from white Americans. They tended to identify with the established religious bodies despite the occasional ambivalence and usual hostility of those bodies towards the Negro race. While militant spokesmen like David Walker and Henry Highland Garnet might call for universal revolt among the slaves, they would both betray a desire for premature conciliation and an unreciprocated longing for amity and fellowship with their oppressors.[66]

So far, the fact has been stressed that elements of accommodationism were present in the religion of the enslaved masses, the educated urban elite, and other blacks in ante-bellum America. However, it must be reemphasized that potential revolt, as well as submission, was ever present among the Old South's slave population.[67] Of course, the violent behavior that occasionally flared up did not necessarily imply nationalistic sentiments. Marion D. Kilson has argued that only a small number of slave revolts were characterized by the careful planning and clear perception of goals usually associated with nationalism. In her study of sixty-five selected "major" slave revolts and conspiracies before 1861, she has identified only four as having the aim of establishing a Negro state. Nat Turner's uprising is not listed among these four, and there seems to be no evidence that Turner had any nationalistic aspirations whatever. The conspiracies of Denmark Vesey and Gabriel Prosser both aimed at the establishment of independent black states but neither reached the point of actual full-scale violence.[68]

The most successful slave revolt in the Western Hemisphere—led by Toussaint L'Ouverture in Haiti—was demonstrably nationalistic. Interestingly, the little we know of the life of Toussaint L'Ouverture indicates that he conformed in some striking respects to the "Uncle Tom" stereotype. He was a devout Christian and was loyal to his master. Not until the revolution was a month old did he join the insurrectionists, and then only after providing for the safety of his white folks. While we know a considerable amount concerning his actions as a general and a statesman, his military genius and diplomatic brilliance, we can only speculate about the first fifty years of his life during which he seems to have been a model of the trusted, dependable slave.[69]

There are those who will consider it shocking and blasphemous to think of Nat Turner, the slave hero, as having a personality consistent with that of Uncle Tom. During the late 1960s, William Styron, a white author, was rightly criticized by black writers for having concocted a history of homosexuality in his depiction of Turner; but Styron was on more solid ground when he suggested that Turner was in an advanced stage of acculturation, and that in many respects he was committed to

European values.[70] There is some evidence in the original confessions of Nat Turner to support such an interpretation.[71] Turner was a solitary man, more thoroughly Christianized than his fellow slaves, from whom he held himself aloof. He viewed with disdain those African religious survivals that persisted as an element of slave culture. He maintained a control over the minds of the other slaves, "not by means of conjuring and such like tricks—for to them I always spoke of such things with contempt."[72] The basis of Turner's control over the other blacks was his understanding of the dominant culture, his mastery of the white man's language and religion, symbolized by his ability to read and interpret the Bible. In his narrative, Turner conveys the impression that much of his power over the other slaves derived from the extent to which he had impressed whites with his high intelligence and charismatic personality.

Around 1825 Turner had escaped from his plantation and hidden in the woods for thirty days, but he returned to his master because of a sense of Christian duty. This had surprised and even angered the other slaves, but Turner explained his behavior in the following way:

> . . . the reason of my return was, that the Spirit appeared to me and said I had my wishes directed to the things of this world, and not to the kingdom of Heaven, and that I should return to the service of my earthly master— "For he who knoweth his Master's will, and doeth it not, shall be beaten with many stripes, and thus have I chastened you." And the negroes found fault, and murmured against me, saying that if they had my sense they would not serve any master in the world.

At this point, Turner withdrew even more "from the intercourse of my fellow servants," but continued to remonstrate with whites on religious subjects. He apparently gained some sort of psychic control over one white man (Etheldred T. Brantley), who experienced a religious conversion accompanied by psychosomatic disorders—"a cutaneous eruption, and blood oozed from the pores of his skin." The psychic power that Mrs. Stowe gives the slaves over the superstitious Simon Legree is reminiscent of this part of the confession.

The question of the validity of the *Confessions* is, of course, a serious one. I am inclined to accept their validity. Nat Turner is portrayed as a man of conviction, strength, and intelligence, convinced of the rightness of his actions. It is difficult to imagine why (assuming that the *Confessions* are a hoax) a white man and an officer of the court would have concocted such a strangely respectful and, at times, almost sympathetic portrait of a slave insurrectionist. There is also the question of Turner's truthfulness. Did he manipulate Gray; did he play with his mind? This is indeed possible. The closest thing to a primary account that we have of the happenings in Southampton County, Virginia, in August of 1831 is Gray's record of his interview with Turner. In this interview Gray seems to be quite ingenuous—self-revealing in ways of which he was not aware, deeply impressed by Turner's personality in spite of himself.

In Nat Turner's confession (assuming that it was accurately recorded), there is little of hostility, wrath, or vengefulness. Despite the fact that his *Confessions* were recorded by pro-slavery racists, he is not portrayed according to the usual stereotype of the ignorant, emotional Negro. His revolt, says Gray, "was not instigated by motives of revenge or sudden anger, but the results of long deliberation and a settled purpose of mind. The offspring of a gloomy fanaticism." This is a far cry from the sort of racial stereotype that appears in most contemporary documents. Turner killed his master with some reluctance, admitting that he had "no cause of complaint of his treatment," and saying, "I could not give a death blow, the hatchet glanced from his head. . . . Will laid him dead, with a blow of his axe." He was also unable to kill Mrs. Newsome: "I struck her several blows over the head, but not being able to kill her, as the sword was dull. Will turning around and discovering it dispatched her also." Only on his third attempt was Turner able to shed blood, clumsily killing Miss Margaret "after repeated blows with a sword," and then finally "by a blow on the head with a fence rail." When asked by his inquisitors if his apprehension and trial had not convinced him that he was wrong, Turner replied, "Was not Christ crucified?" Turner clearly identified with the Christian God of suffering and saw the threat of punishment only as a vindication of his moral rightness. While Turner was superficially reminiscent of the wrathful, retributive messiah, he had actually merged this identity with that of the sacrificial, long-suffering Jesus.

The Christian Savior is both masochistic martyr and retributive messiah. Black Christians during the ante-bellum decades identified with both images of the Christ. The "Uncle Tom," whether in life or in literature, is not to be seen as a peculiarly black personality but, as Fullinwider argued, a typical representative of a human tendency to rationalize in religious terms a forced pattern of submissive behavior. The Nat Turner image provided an equally convenient role for those blacks who rejected the model of the submissive Christ but remained loyal to the more militant traditions of Christianity.

For black nationalists, both the Uncle Tom and the Nat Turner models persisted as functional myths. Uncle Tom images were constantly present in the writings of black nationalists and in the rhapsodies of white pro-colonizationists, as well, who argued that Africans were natural Christians endowed by nature with inborn traits of Christian civilization. These traits included the qualities of natural gentility, forgiveness, charitableness, cooperativeness, and social instinct. Uncle Tom represented a variety of racial superiority. To be sure, the inherently Christian nature associated with Uncle Tom could be interpreted as an impediment to racial elevation, as Delany argued. As he saw it, blacks were too much inclined to trust in divine deliverance, too readily disposed to submit to the dictates of a hazily conceived providence. Still, the Uncle Tom myth was important as a means of impressing white and black alike with the ineradicable humanity of the slave. It reemphasized the idea of the essential nobility of the human personality, which could not be destroyed even under the brutal conditions of slavery. The myth contributed to the messianic vision of a millennial African civilization that would serve as a shining example of human fulfillment in an ideal nation state.

Nat Turner also captured the imagination of black nationalists and their white supporters. It has been observed that Turner's confession paralleled attitudes reflected by militant black nationalists. He represented the current of militant millennialism that appeared in the writings of Henry Highland Garnet and David Walker. William Lloyd Garrison compared the rebellion to nationalistic uprisings among Poles, Turks, Greeks, and Americans.[73] Even the pro-slavery legislative and judicial system of Virginia took Nat Turner seriously, treating his ideas with a strangely awed respect. His *Confessions*, as recorded by Thomas Gray, convey the image of a dignified, articulate, and intelligent man.[74] The people of Virginia did not find it impossible to believe in the serious, brooding African who disdained to participate in the plantation revelries of his fellow slaves but meditated constantly upon the fact that he was miserable, abject, and degraded. For there have always been black people who could never allow themselves to forget their condition and have seethed constantly with resentment. It was, no doubt, a source of pride to serious-minded black abolitionists that there were certain slaves who did not wear a mask, who did not laugh to keep from crying, and whose identification with the long-suffering Jesus did not lead them to adopt, then rationalize, submissive behavior.

Nonetheless, the conception of the black personality that informed Mrs. Stowe's creation of Uncle Tom revealed a common perception of black racial traits. Her view of the black personality and of its importance to the messianic mission of the African race was part of a tradition shared by numerous white clergymen in the colonization movement. Among the most prominent were Samuel Hopkins, Samuel Mills, Ebeneezer Burgess, Frederick Freeman, and, especially, Hollis Read. Black contemporaries also accepted certain aspects of the stereotype, among them Edward Wilmot Blyden, Martin R. Delany, Alexander Crummell, James Dennis Harris, and James T. Holly. Even by the early twentieth century, the Uncle Tom myth had not been fully rejected. It was resurrected for political purposes by Booker T. Washington, and for artistic purposes by Du Bois. It was parodied—and yet half-believed—by Marcus Garvey. Various revitalizations of the myth will be among the concerns of the following chapters.

5

Faith, Fatalism, and Racial Christianity: The Slavery Crisis and Reconstruction

Late nineteenth-century religion among educated black people in the North moved in the direction of Christian nationalism and the social gospel. Among the masses of the South, black religion continued to be otherworldly. The mission of the Northern-based, black-controlled churches as they established themselves in the South was often perceived as one of replacing the planter's preachments and the slave's escapism with a creed of greater social and personal responsibility. Not all of the new missionaries who came into the South were religious reformers in the strictest sense. But it is widely acknowledged that the Reconstruction South received an influx of black and white Northerners concerned with reshaping its moral and social life.[1] The purpose of this chapter is to recognize the differences and the similarities between the racial Christianity of the Southern black masses and that of the Northern black leadership elite. Du Bois once wrote of the "deep religious fatalism, painted so beautifully in 'Uncle Tom,' [which] came to breed, as all fatalistic faiths will, the sensualist side by side with the martyr." He offered these observations in the midst of reflections on the complexities of black Christianity in the United States, where the lines between an activist sense of racial mission, an otherworldly escapism, and an orgiastic emotional abandon are so often blurred. Du Bois' chapter on "The Faith of the Fathers" dealt well with the ambiguity present in the religious songs of slavery times.[2] He recognized that more than one interpretation can be attached to such a verse as the following:

> Children, we shall all be free
> When the Lord shall appear!

As Du Bois noted, such a verse may indicate despair at realizing freedom in this world and an eager grasping at "the offered conceptions of the next." However, it may just as likely refer to the "avenging Spirit of the Lord" in temporal affairs. Although it enjoins patience until the day of deliverance arrives, it does not preclude the possibility that deliverance from slavery will come about in this world when God asserts his power. Conversely, when the black bards sang in obviously militant tones, they were not totally divorced from the elements of fatalism and otherworldliness that pervaded their religious consciousness. Even the famed "Freedom Spiritual" contains a note of ambiguity, which adds to its interest both as poetry and religious myth:

> O Freedom, O Freedom, O Freedom over me!
> Before I'll be a slave
> I'll be buried in my grave,
> And go home to my Lord
> And be free.

The martyr-like spirit that finds death preferable to slavery resembles the philosophy of "death rather than sin." It may be interpreted as eminently idealistic and otherworldly, as totally lacking in accommodative pragmatism. Or it may be seen as representing the ultimate in social responsibility, the consummate practical statement whereby the individual expresses an ethical commitment, superseding even the demands of his personal welfare. As Emile Durkheim observed, discussions of acts of self-sacrifice must deal with the question of whether they are acts of courage and responsibility or of cowardice and escapism. This question makes all discussions of religious and political martyrdom problematic.[3]

The religion of the black masses was thus both pragmatic and escapist, in Du Bois' view. It was typically millenarian in its blending of temporal and otherworldly attitudes. During the fifty years preceding the Civil War, black religion had "transformed itself and identified itself with the dream of Abolition, until that which was a radical fad in the white North and an anarchistic plot in the white South had become a religion to the black world." When emancipation came, as it did, amid the social catastrophe of civil war, it seemed "a literal Coming of the Lord." The freedmen stood "joyed and bewildered . . . awaiting new wonders," totally unprepared for the grim realities of an "Age of Reaction."[4]

During the Civil War years, the slaves sang "Go Down Moses, tell ole Pharaoh to let my people go." A note of revenge crept into at least one of the recorded stanzas:

> Thus spake the Lord, bold Moses said
> Let my people go!

> If not I'll strike your first born dead
> Let my people go!

But although it contains some political allusions, "Go Down Moses" is not uniformly political. In complete early editions of the spiritual, one finds that the chief concerns of the singers were with the spectacular sensationalism of the plagues of Egypt; and among the verses of the first standard printed edition, one finds the following:

> I do believe without a doubt
> Let my people go
> That a Christian has a right to shout
> Let my people go.

> I'll tell you what I likes the best
> Let my people go
> It is the shouting Methodist
> Let my people go.[5]

Here, in what is perhaps the best known of all the black spirituals and the one that is most often cited as evidence of social concern among the slaves, one finds again the blending of this-worldly and otherworldly religious elements. One may imagine that early performances of "Go Down Moses" were occasionally followed by wild orgies of emotionalism, choruses of shrieks and shouts, and dancing. In the black church, not only did the sensualist dwell side by side with the martyr, the escapist made harmony with the activist. One could experience· the presence of the Lord by dancing in church, or by raging against one's oppressors. The Christianity to which black people had been exposed, through their contact with whites, had acquainted them with both roads to glory.

The conflicts and contradictions that have so often been noted in the religious expression of Afro–Americans are inherent in the American evangelical tradition from which it is derived. It is difficult to pin down what the essential qualities of evangelical religion are, but the most important of its qualities seems to be the need for individual regeneration, which usually comes about in the form of a conversion experience. This conversion experience is most often described in terms of an emotional response to a sudden infusion of God's grace. Beyond this there is little agreement as to what evangelicals believe, but several patterns seem to characterize such religion as it has expressed itself in America. These include a softening of the extreme predestinationism of seventeenth-century puritanism; an increased emphasis on free will, individualism, and voluntarism; a renewed interest in missionary and benevolent societies; and the growth of camp-meeting revivalism.[6]

The emphasis placed by the American evangelicals on an emotionally based conversion experience made salvation equally accessible to everyone. The evangelicals assumed that a true conversion experience must manifest itself in some visible way. At one level, this led to frenzied behavior on the part of the convert at the moment of conversion; on another level, it led to a search for ways of demonstrating that one's life had come under the influence of God. The convert felt an obligation to become a witness for Christ in some demonstrable way; and the most obvious way in which to do this was through missionary work of some sort. As early as the 1740s, American preachers had begun to charge their congregations with the duty of sharing the gospel with their slaves. By the early nineteenth century, it was generally regarded as no less than common sense to provide for the religious instruction of the black population. It was better to instruct them in their religious rights and obligations than to allow an independent religious institution to grow up.[7]

The planters who hoped to exert control over the development of slave religion were unsuccessful in some respects, but successful in others. They were unable to completely eradicate independent religious institutions among the slaves. They were not able to exert complete control over the slaves' religious experiences, even when they did control the slave churches. They were, however, successful in controlling certain aspects of black social life. Slaveholders could, for example, validate and sanctify marriages when and if they chose to use their power in this way. They could encourage a high standard of honesty, sexual morality, and work ethic—when they were so inclined. Slave testimony on this score leads one to believe that cases did occur in which the bondsperson absorbed and internalized conventional American morality from the master's household. The position that argues that slaveowners were universally hypocritical in their efforts to proselytize the slaves is not supported by the evidence.[8]

Equally insupportable is the idea that slaves always regarded the Christianity of their masters with cynicism. Accounts of slave religion published by the abolitionists tended, and with good cause, to emphasize the unscrupulous use of religion by the planter class. Undoubtedly there was a good deal of religion preached in the slave quarters that amounted to little more than elaboration on the text "servants obey your masters." This brand of religion was, according to most accounts, rightly rejected by the majority of slaves. Still there can be no doubt that Christianity took hold among the slave population, and that somehow the slaves were able to reconcile their acceptance of the masters' religion and their rejection of the masters' attempts to manipulate them through that religion. The reason for this occurrence was that slaves learned their

Christianity not only through what was preached to them, but by exposure to those beliefs that the masters themselves held.[9]

All available evidence indicates that the overwhelming majority of white preachers and many black preachers encouraged the slaves to wait patiently for deliverance in the world to come. It should not be surprising that many blacks accepted this doctrine, since many whites accepted it as well. By the early 1800s, however, egalitarianism was making itself felt in American religion to such an extent that some Christians even began to doubt that God ever intended for social rankings and class distinctions to exist in society. The doctrine of social perfectionism that steadily gained strength throughout the nineteenth century looked upon inequality as a social evil. As Christian social perfectionists began to conceive of a secular millennium as the fulfillment of the Kingdom of Christ, churches became increasingly involved in social reform.[10] In the North, this took the form of various movements for the improvement of society. In the South, where reform causes were less fashionable, the Christian message was never secularized in quite the same way. Religion in the South was pietistic and placed more emphasis on the act of worship than on establishing a code of behavior for daily life.[11]

This is not to suggest that pietism existed wholly independently of morality in the American South. However, the evangelical tradition of the South differed from that of the North in several important respects: It did not lead to the doctrine that social reform was the duty of Christ's Kingdom-builders; it did not regard religion as a system of rules whereby one climbed the rocky road to heaven; and it did not come to regard religion as a covenantal relationship between God and the United States of America. The relationship between pietism and morality in the Southern evangelical tradition has been explained by David Kucharsky in his campaign biography of Jimmy Carter. "In the evangelical view," says Kucharsky, "salvation is by God's grace and not through works, that is, good deeds. Evangelicals contend that their central message of making peace with God provides a person with what is sometimes described as the 'power source' for ethical conduct."[12] This is certainly the view of Christianity that thrived in the South during the nineteenth century and remains predominant today. It should therefore not surprise us that the religion of the black population was not obsessed with an ethic of achievement.

The black population of the South may have been indoctrinated in a somewhat distinctive form of Christianity, especially tailored by the master to suit his conception of their needs, but that was not the source of their otherworldliness. Directly and indirectly, they were exposed to the main currents of Southern Christianity, which was hardly preoccupied with social concerns. Still, the religion of the slaves—like the religion of the whites that it imitated—was a large enough vehicle to reconcile such apparently contradictory doctrines as vicarious atonement and the commendability of good works, common-sense philosophy and conversion through the emotions, and ritual escapism and temporal perfectionism. Each of these phenomena, as they existed in the minds of the black masses, deserves some discussion here.

Booker T. Washington believed that a lack of concern for practical matters was one of the principal defects of Afro–American religion.[13] Black peasants' obsession with a redeeming and forgiving Savior, who had already paid the ransom for their souls, led to an attitude of dependency, fatalism, and irresponsibility. Washington felt that it also led to immorality, for as students of the black South have noted, religious fervor often coexisted with a freewheeling interpretation of Christian ethics. Not without a certain degree of cynicism, the opinion was sometimes expressed that there could be no such thing as sexual misconduct between two Christians, since both were saints and thus incapable of sin.[14] Such attitudes were clearly not confined to the world of sexual behavior but, as many black reformers have noted, extended into economic and political life as well. The fatalistic perception of salvation through grace alone and by virtue of divine agencies outside the power of the individual to control corresponded to fatalism in all areas of life.

Why this essentially Calvinistic creed should have led to fatalism in the case of the black masses of the South and not in the case of New England Puritans is a difficult question to answer. A possible reason is that Southern blacks, during both slavery and reconstruction, encountered a variety of experiences that impressed them with their powerlessness and encouraged escapist behavior. Furthermore, the black population of the South was ignorant and isolated from the wider world of experience. With rare and remarkable exceptions, they seem to have had little knowledge of where they stood in time and space. The rigors of black life in the nineteenth century were such that a religion that presented a tough or austere reality would hardly have attracted them. The faith that appealed to black folk, both before and after emancipation, had to be one that brought tidings of comfort and joy.

Some of the most readily available information on the religious beliefs of the black population of the South is the oral history material gathered during the Depression by the Federal Writers' Project. In using this material, it is important to bear in mind that the typical informant had been free for over seventy years at the time of his or her being interviewed. Their knowledge of slavery was thus limited to childhood recollections and obscured by the passage of time. In many cases, however, the informants were old enough at the time of emancipation to have vivid memories of slavery and of the continuity of Southern culture from the end of slavery to the Great Depression. Whatever their weaknesses as a source for the study of slavery, the slave narratives of the 1930s are eminently useful for the study of black culture during the late nineteenth and early twentieth centuries.[15]

Many of the informants displayed a fondness for what they called the "Old Time Religion." This was a faith of highly charged emotionalism that placed great emphasis on the conversion experience. It was not enough for a Christian simply to live righteously, to attend church services, and to pray; one must undergo a conversion experience and personal contact with the Lord. "You got to have something revealed to you through your soul," as one informant put it.[16] The conversion must involve the actual seeing or hearing of Jesus. One woman who was apparently already a believer experienced considerable anxiety while waiting for the charismatic experience. She felt she could not join a church until she received a message guiding her in the right direction. Finally the voice of the Lord came to her with the injunction to "go down on Pearl Street and join Murray's church." At first she had some misgivings, for Murray's on Pearl Street was that Baptist Church where they were "always having a lot of fusses and rows in the church." But the voice of the Lord told her never to mind. Since joining the Pearl Street church, she had given up dancing and other un-Christian practices. No doubt Murray's church provided all the excitement she required.[17]

The informants spoke of religious experiences in terms of actual sensory perceptions. The Lord did not always deliver a verbal message, however. "I seed the Lord," confided one informant, "but I never heard nothing." Jesus looked "just like you see him in those pictures. Long white robe and long hair and beard."[18] Another admitted that she hadn't "seed him but once, and I viewed him that one time. He was standing on a big hill" on the steps of a white pillared building that reminded her of the capitol. "Folks say you really got to see him," she explained.[19] Conversion usually involved an experience of unusual intensity even by the informant's standards. They often spoke of being "struck dead."[20] One narrator was possessed by the Spirit to strip off his clothes and run through the woods, where he prayed and prayed until finally Jesus came, at which point he lost consciousness.[21]

One must be wary of the data on black religion gathered from the slave narrative collections, for the informants were not always completely open with the interviewers. One old man would say only that he had been a Methodist for thirty years, "but I don't like to talk religion with white folks."[22] Those who were inclined to talk religion with whites conformed to the pattern of Mandy Edmundson, who impressed her interviewer as "a devout Christian [who] spends much of her time singing and shouting."[23] The attempt to spend as much time as possible singing and shouting was, in some cases, a carry-over from slavery days:

> At times big fields full would be a workin', dey would be a singin', hollerin', an' a prayin'; de overseer would ride up on his horse an' think 'nough work hadn't been done, den he would beat 'em till dey would fall in de fields, an' us would haf to tote water to 'em an' bring 'em to.[24]

This leads one to speculate that overseers may have seen a distinction between work songs that lightened the load and set the pace of labor and religious ruses that provided a very literal escape from one's worldly tasks.[25] Whites were also aware of the power of enthusiastic religion to rouse rebellious passions. One informant remembered an occasion when the slaves were in church, with white patrollers observing their worship, as was customary. The religious expression reached a high pitch as the blacks sang "Ride on King Jesus; no man can hinder Thee," and the patrollers told them to stop or they would show them whether *they* could be hindered or not.[26]

One narrator told the story of an elderly slave who was allowed to accompany his master to church if he would promise to restrain himself. To seal the bargain, he promised him a new pair of boots if he could keep quiet. But halfway through the service, the old man exclaimed "Boots er no boots, I'se gwine ter shout."[27] One old woman recalled that whites shouted just as much as the blacks. She remembered being taken by her white folks to camp meetings and asserted that whenever they shouted the most enthusiastically at meetings they were sure to give their slaves an enthusiastic beating on returning home.[28] Other informants found the worship rituals of white folks too sedate. "A white woman took me to church one day with her baby," said one old lady, "and I liked to tore them white folks church up shouting. The preacher said, 'Let her shout; she is a Christian, an' got religion.' . . . They left me home with the baby after that."[29]

People remembered the old days as being more religious: "We tried to have religion. We sung an' prayed an' shouted all us could an' sung songs in de fiels' about loving de Lord. Ole Time Religion wuz a favorite among us."[30] But the old-time religion seemed to be passing away:

> They have college preachers now. They don't have religion like they used to. I saw old man George Jones do a thing one day that I never seen before or since. Right down here in the Methodist Church on Sunday he got happy and actually flew around the altar, not a foot nor a hand was touching the floor. I believe he was really a Christian.[31]

Thus it seems that many of the complaints about the passing away of old-time religion were due to a definition of Christianity that placed great emphasis on emotional abandon. The waning of the tradition led one aged member of the Sanctified Church to complain, "Every time I go in the church, one of the sisters grab me and say, 'Sit down an behave yourself.' "[32]

The obsession with enthusiastic worship did not necessarily betoken a disregard for righteous living. The emphasis placed on the conversion experience and vicarious atonement was somehow able to coexist in the minds of many with the doctrine of justification by works. "I never will forget that morning when I was saved by His blood," reminisced one old lady; but she also believed that "every deed you done, you gotta give strict account of." She reminded her interviewer: "You young folks can't carry on yo' wicked ways without some kinda terrible fall, do you hear me?"[33] An informant from Mississippi also believed that salvation had to do with virtuous behavior: "I doan want to live no other life but a Christian life, so I'll be saved and go home to rest, fer the Bible say the wicked will be lef' here and burned up."[34] An informant from Tennessee also stressed good deeds: "I tries to do what's right, for I want to get to heaven when I die."[35] One woman felt that her conversion had come about as a result of trying to live virtuously: "I was converted by just laying off everything that looked like sin."[36] Her concept of sin included drinking, dancing, working on Sunday, belonging to lodges and clubs. So adamant was she in her commitment to righteous living that the man she was living with threw her out of the house. It is clear, then, that while some Southern blacks had a view of religion that was purely sensationalistic and preoccupied with vicarious atonement, others believed that works were important. And this was a step in the direction of a racial Christianity with room for social concerns.

The Work Projects Administration (WPA) interviewers attempted to get at questions related to racial and social issues in the religious experience indirectly. Often they attempted to discover how whites felt about their slaves becoming religious. Findings were inconclusive, for most of the interviewees interpreted the plantation attitude towards religion solely in terms of their own experiences. Some said that whites actually made them go to church: "That was the rule in slavery time—fer everybody to go in de church."[37] Others reported that their white folks were "hard on colored for being religious."[38] Some recalled that their religious meetings had been broken up by the patrollers. Some slaves went to church with their white folks and sat in the back pews. Others reported that they went to services held for blacks, either with or without the masters' knowledge. Some did both. One interviewee recalled that she had received religious education and moral instruction, but that the slaves had not had church services.[39]

Some informants saw a connection between Christianity, education, and emancipation. Occasionally one would express the belief that the Scriptures forbade slavery. One informant was certain that he had seen that famous rabble-rousing preacher named Abraham Lincoln, who had started the Civil War.[40] Another narrated a more believable reminiscence of a Kentucky slaveholder who insisted that all his slaves learn to read. The slaves on his plantation read the Bible a great deal and there was a high runaway rate among them, but this never soured the old master on educating his slaves. The result was that

> We read the Bible until the pages became dogeared and the leaves fell from the binding. My relatives were religious and never refused the privilege of serving God. We prayed and our forefathers offered prayers for 275 years in American bondage, that we might be given freedom. The Negro preachers preached freedom into our ears and our old men and women prophesied it.[41]

One informant recalled "church meetins in arbors out in de woods. De preachers would exhort us dat we was de chillun of Israel in de wilderness en de Lawd don sont us to take dis land ob milk en honey. But how us gwine take land what was already took?"[42] Others recalled hearing black preachers say, "Obey your mistress and Master."[43] Most informants could recall secret prayer meetings. "Yes mam," said one, "I've heard them pray for freedom."[44]

Occasionally in the post-bellum slave narratives one encounters attitudes that are unquestionably tied to racial Christianity and social consciousness. One of the interviews with an evangelical preacher reveals striking intelligence and social consciousness on the part of a self-educated man. Identified only as Mr. Reed, he revealed knowledge of slavery that went beyond his personal experience. This was due to the fact that he was able to read and took considerable pride in his mind.

> My grandfather was a preacher and didn't know *A* from *B*. He could preach. I had a uncle and he was a preacher and didn't know A from B. I had a cousin who was a preacher. I am no mathematician, no biologist, neither a grammarian, but when it comes to handling the Bible I knocks down verbs, break up prepositions and jumps over adjectives.[45]

"I am a God sent man," proclaimed the old preacher; and he went on to express his belief that black Americans were a messianic race. He compared them to the "children of Israel, four hundred years under bondage." He expressed a view that God lived close to the slaves and revealed the slave songs to them. Another respondent put it more colorfully, "God gave black folks wisdom to study out dem songs."[46] Mr. Reed believed this wisdom had its source in fear of the Lord—Solomon had said that. And "What nationality was Solomon? He was a black man. 'Forsake me not because I am black.' Who was it that bore the cross when Christ was dragging the cross up Calvary hill? He was a black man, Simon of Cyrean."[47]

The informant called himself "a hard working man," distinguishing between working and preaching. He owned his own home and asserted, "I have never been arrested in my life, never was drunk, never cussed but once; got scared and quit." He veiled his contempt thinly indeed when describing how "preachers used to get up and preach and call moaners up to the moaner's bench. They would all kneel down and sometimes they would lay down on the floor, and the Christians would sing

> Rassal Jacob, rassal as you did in the days of old,
> Gonna rassal all night till broad day light
> And ask God to bless my soul."

He described people walking out in the woods, and rolling and shouting and telling everybody they had "found Jesus" and then shouting some more, "and sometimes they would knock the preacher and deacon down shouting. But about a week after that they would go to a dance, and when the music would start they would get out there and dance and forget all about religion." Mr. Reed believed, obviously, that the essence of religion was not in emotionalism but in walking "upright." For the Bible said, "Be not deceived, God is not mocked, whatsoever a man soweth that shall he also reap."

He believed that "the breaking up of slavery was started some by the churches." He realized that there had been some churches who would not admit slaveholders to membership. He felt that the profession of religion had become too easy. All people had to do these days was to see a little white man—"Always a little *white* man."[48]

The religious attitudes expressed by Mr. Reed were exceptional. He was hostile to the worship of whites, or at least to the personification of divinity in the form of "a little *white* man." He had little patience with a religion that was emotionally based, and believed that the essence of religion was to "live close to the lord." He was a hard-working man, who took pride in the fact that he had been a wage earner since he had been freed. His pride in accomplishment seems consistent with his intelligence and with his philosophy. The variety of intelligence he displayed was more common among the educated ministry, who showed hostility to the excessive ritualism and emotionalism that characterized the religion of the masses. Although racial Christianity made occasional appearances among the peasants of the South, the dominant pattern of black religion in the nineteenth century is exactly what one might have expected of a people who had limited knowledge of the value of their labor or of their place in history. The religion of the masses, according to all accounts, both before and after slavery tended to be ritualistic, emotional, and escapist.

Naturally, there were attempts throughout the nineteenth century to encourage a form of worship that would be more responsive to the long-range needs of an oppressed people. These efforts were largely in the North, where it was possible to organize independent black churches and to preach political sermons in relative safety. Literacy, of course, played an important part in the creation of racial Christianity. The religion of blacks who were exposed to the world of ideas naturally reflected a wider and more sophisticated range of concerns than did the religion of those who simply reacted to emotional stimuli. Those blacks who lived in the Northern cities were influenced by the social millenarian current in the American creed, and by the nationalistic conception of religion that reached high tide during the nineteenth century.

Racial Christianity made its first appearances during the late eighteenth century among successful, urbane blacks and the clergy who ministered to them. Persons of this class, like their white counterparts, sought a variety of religion that would support their entrepreneurial ambitions, their political concerns, and their desire to serve God through institutionalized reform. Representatives of this class included Peter Williams, Paul Cuffe, James Forten, Richard Allen, and Absolom Jones, all of whom knew one another and all of whom saw religion as a means of cooperating with the divine Architect in his plans for the worldly kingdom. Paul Cuffe, a shipowner, and James Forten, a sailmaker, because of their involvement in the maritime industries, often expressed their faith that it was God's plan for black Americans to become involved in opening up the continent of Africa for trade. They were cautiously encouraged in this endeavor by Allen, Jones, and Williams, all of whom were clergymen, but were strongly urged to remember that their first Christian duty was to the antislavery cause in the United States.[49]

Allen and Jones were founders of the Free African Society in Philadelphia, which was a non-denominational Christian society that concerned itself with a number of fraternal, social, and civic functions. Eventually, the Society evolved into a church organization, affiliating with the Episcopalians by vote of the membership. Allen went on to become a Methodist minister, while Jones remained with the Episcopal group, eventually to be ordained as a priest. Meanwhile, Peter Williams, in New York, would become a priest in the Episcopal church. These three early independent black churchmen were never known for any activities that smacked of militancy or extreme black nationalism, but their commitment to religion suited to the needs of black people is beyond question. Allen later said that he was confident that "there was no religious sect, or denomination, that would suit the capacity of the colored people as well as the Methodists." However, the bulk of the membership in the Free African Society were disturbed by the "wild and noisy excitement of the Methodists of those times."[50]

One should not gather from this statement that the Methodists under Allen became involved in excessively enthusiastic religion. Indeed, the course he initiated would lead to an eminently respectable middle-class tradition. A concern with racial progress was often accompanied by a preference for comparatively sedate worship in the nineteenth-century black church. This was eventually taken to extremes, for a point was soon reached where any and all expressions of exuberance were discouraged, and this tended to isolate certain segments of the black community. It also led to a tendency on the part of some denominations to look down on the masses of black people, rather than working with them for mutual uplift. This tendency developed quite early, as we can see in the case of Bishop Daniel Alexander Payne, who was known for his social activism, his campaign for an educated ministry, and his unyielding opposition to what he believed were "Africanisms" in church worship.[51]

Why Payne should have been opposed to Africanisms is not clear, and there is some question as to whether the rituals he objected to were actually African in origin. But he was most certainly opposed to the "praying and singing bands" and the "strange delusion that many ignorant but well meaning people labor under." His description of a bush meeting that he once attended to please a local pastor reveals not only his bias, but his lack of sensitivity to the feelings of those he hoped to lead:

> After the sermon they formed a ring, and with coats off, sung, clapped their hands and stamped their feet in a most ridiculous and heathenish way. I requested the pastor to go and stop their dancing. At his request they stopped their dancing and clapping of hands, but remained singing and rocking their bodies to and fro. This they did for about fifteen minutes. I then went, and taking their leader by the arm requested him to desist and sit down and sing in a rational manner. I told him also that it was a heathenish way to worship and disgraceful to themselves, the race, and the Christian name. In that instance they broke up their ring; but would not sit down, and walked sullenly away.[52]

What Payne was observing may have been African in origin, but it was consistent with typically American forms of revivalistic behavior and probably quite harmless. His way of handling it certainly showed little sympathy for the emotional needs of his people. Granted, black people in nineteenth-century America did need to be instructed in a more rational and socially conscious form of religion, but one doubts if Payne made any converts that day.

Payne was clearly more at home with socially oriented Christianity that responded to black concerns. This becomes apparent to anyone who reflects on his institutional commitments. He founded Wilberforce University. He served on the board of the African Civilization Society, but was an opponent of the American Colonization Society. He identified with immediate abolitionism, and contributed to the messianic view of the Afro–American people and their place in history. This was pronounced in his celebrated speech during the Civil War, when he likened the Confederate armies to the legions of Pharaoh and the Union armies to the chariots of the Messiah in *Paradise Lost*.[53] Payne was not a racial chauvinist, and his messianic view of black Americans did not exclude white Americans. He saw both groups sharing in the blessings of a God who had great things in store for the American people. Blacks had been "redeemed" by the sacrifice of the Union and the martyrdom of its soldiers. Thus, he remarked on the signal providences affecting black history in 1862, when he addressed freedmen in the District of Columbia:

> . . . As he blessed the chosen seed, by the ministry of men and angels, so in our case, the angels of mercy, justice and liberty, hovering over the towering Capitol, inspired the heads and hearts of the noble men who have plead the cause of the poor, the needy and enslaved, in the Senate and House of Representatives.
>
> For the oppressed and enslaved of all peoples, God has raised up, and will continue to raise up, his Moses and Aaron. Sometimes the hand of the Lord is so signally displayed that Moses and Aaron are not recognized. Seldom do they recognize themselves.
>
> Thou, O Lord, and thou alone couldst have moved the heart of this Nation to have done so great a deed for this weak, despised and needy people![54]

The struggle against slavery showed not only that God was on the side of the black people, not only that he was on the Union side—it showed that he was guiding the entire nation. Payne utilized the fashionable Hebraic imagery of American civil religion to appeal to the popular idea of the nation as a chosen people. The black population was analogous to Israel within this schema, as one might expect, but the American people were not likened to the Egyptian oppressors. Through their Senators and Representatives, they became Moses and Aaron; and their destiny was thus linked to that of God's oppressed, enslaved, and, therefore, chosen people. Although Payne showed some sporadic interest in black nationalism throughout the war, he aligned his rhetoric on this occasion with the broader messianism of American destiny.

Many black Christian spokesmen resembled Payne during the late nineteenth and early twentieth centuries in that their black nationalism was vacillating while their racial Christianity was constant. For racial Christianity could be used to support more than one conception of black destiny. It could support the idea of separate development and black nationalism, as it did in the cases of James T. Holly, Alexander Crummell, and Edward Wilmot Blyden; or it could support the idea of a Negro mission in America. This was an idea that found some prominence in the writings of Henry Highland Garnet, an active black nationalist during the 1850s and a founder of the African Civilization Society, who nonetheless frequently revealed his faith in an American social millennium that would be characterized by racial justice.[55]

Garnet was born in slavery in 1815, but his family escaped to New York when he was nine years old. His father was a shoemaker, a skilled tradesman, and was thus able to provide the boy with an education at the African Free School, organized by the Rev. Peter Williams and other abolitionists. Along with his fellow pupil, Alexander Crummell, Garnet was immersed in a racially conscious, social Christianity from about the age of eleven. When he took up his career as an evangelical preacher, he combined the emotional appeal of his profession with the social concern that was becoming influential in American evangelical circles during the 1840s. He became a part of the movement that used the techniques of the revival meeting to urge the renunciation of sinfulness—in this case, the sin of slaveholding.[56]

Racial Christianity rather than black nationalism is the most accurate description of the philosophy of Garnet, although he revealed a commitment to black nationalism and Pan–Africanism on several occasions. But Garnet, like David Walker (whose *Appeal* he reissued, bound in the same pamphlet with his own *Address to the Slaves of the United States*), never completely abandoned faith in the coming messianic era of American democracy. Garnet's *Address* was not bitter, vindictive, or fanatical in its attitude to the United States, nor was it separatist in tone. It has been claimed by many scholars that it represents revolutionary black nationalism, and, to be sure, there is a nationalistic strain in the speech. But the central concern of the *Address* was not with establishing black people's claims to a distinct national heritage and destiny, nor to assert the peculiar peoplehood of black Americans. Garnet's *Address*, like Walker's *Appeal*, combined particularistic and universal concerns. Along with its strong nationalistic elements, it presented a transcendental, cosmopolitan view:

> You can plead your own cause, and do the work of emancipation better than any others. The nations of the old world are moving in the great cause of universal freedom, and some of them at least will, ere long, do you justice. The combined powers of Europe have placed their broad seal of disapprobation upon the African slave trade.[57]

By calling on the slaves to plead their cause before the court of world opinion, Garnet implied a belief in universal laws of human decency that affect the collective conscience of mankind. More importantly, he implied a belief that Americans were sincere in their commitment to human rights and that they could be persuaded by moral arguments. Needless to say, the threat of a slave revolt is hardly a moral argument; but, then, the possibility that Garnet's ideas were going to have any immediate effect on the slaves was remote. The *Address* was really directed at white Americans, who were certain to be affected by its familiar evangelical style. The sermons of an evangelist are intended equally for the community of saints and the sinners he hopes to convert. Garnet knew that Americans desired a place in the forefront of the world movement for "the great cause of universal freedom." He trusted that, at least in the North, the commitment was sincere. He had faith in the desire of his white readers to maintain their prophetic leadership role in this world pilgrimage.

This is not to deny the nationalistic elements in Garnet's *Address*, for its argument followed in the tradition that viewed black Americans as a people or a nation in bondage. And Garnet certainly exploited the time-honored Judeo–Christian belief that God always sided with the underdog. Like David Walker, he implied that Christians who violated the laws of justice to one's fellow humans would be punished more severely than non-believers. While the *Address* was hardly the most systematic exposition of black nationalist ideology that Garnet or his contemporaries ever penned, it certainly contained nationalistic elements. But in the same year that he published the *Address*, Garnet produced another essay, "The Past and Present Condition and the Destiny of the Colored Race," which has been held up as representing the very epitome of assimilationism. The pamphlet began with an overview of the past glories of the African people and a summary of the history of the slave trade. It passed on to a description of the evils of slavery in the contemporary United States. All of this was perfectly consistent with the black nationalism that is usually attributed to Garnet. But in the final pages, where he turned to the future of black people, he placed in italics his belief that "*The western world is destined to be filled with a mixed race.*"[58]

The purpose of Garnet's pamphlet was not to promote miscegenation, of course, but to attack the idea that black Americans had no home and no country. While on the one hand he spoke of the glorious future of his race, which would soon "come forth and re-occupy their station of renown,"[59] he asserted that their future was in America. The black and white people "love one another too much to endure a separation,"[60] he quipped, then launched into a catalogue of famous white Americans who had either Negro ancestry or colored mistresses. He completely rejected repatriation:

> Ruth, of the Old Testament, puts the resolve of our destiny in our mouths which we will repeat to those who would expatriate us: "Entreat me not to leave thee nor return from following after thee, for whither thou goest I

will go, and where thou lodgest I will lodge; thy people shall be my people, and thy God shall be my God. Where thou diest there will I die, and there will I be buried. The Lord do so to me, and more; If aught but death part thee and me."⁶¹

It is a well-known fact that Garnet wavered from this position. In the year following publication of his manifesto on the "Destiny of the Colored Race" in America, he asserted: "I am in favor of colonization in any part of the United States, Mexico or California, or in the West Indies, or Africa, wherever it promises freedom and enfranchisement."⁶² By 1860, on the other hand, he had denied that he was a colonizationist and claimed that his African Civilization Society was concerned with the uplift of black people everywhere.⁶³ He quarrelled openly with Frederick Douglass on the question of repatriation schemes and Pan–African interest, with Douglass accusing him of truckling to white colonizationists and Garnet denying the charge furiously.⁶⁴ Ironically, they were both investigating the possibility of Haitian colonization by the start of the Civil War. However, when it became apparent that the Civil War would be a war against slavery, Garnet, Douglass, and so many others revealed their true feelings about colonization by becoming staunch supporters of the Union cause. Garnet, like Bishop Payne, was quick to take the messianic rhetoric formerly impressed into the service of black separatism and adapt it to a broader view of an American national destiny characterized by racial harmony.

In 1865, Garnet revealed his millenarian conception of the American mission in a sermon before the U.S. House of Representatives. He praised them for having "bowed with reverence to the Divine edict . . . , and thus saved succeeding generations from the guilt of oppression, and from the wrath of God."⁶⁵ He had been invited by William H. Channing, Chaplain of the Senate, to give the speech during February of that year, shortly after the Congress proposed the Thirteenth Amendment.⁶⁶ During the speech, he quoted from Chaplain Channing's uncle, William Ellery Channing, a famous preacher in his own right. W. E. Channing had denounced slavery not only as being in opposition to "every principle of our government and religion," but as violating "the spirit of our age." Garnet picked up on the themes of Channing, that American inequality had isolated the nation from "the communion of nations and the civilization of our age." But now, thanks to the Thirty-eighth Congress, the nation would have "all the moral attributes of God on our side." It would be cheered "by the voices of universal human nature [and] animated with the noble desire to furnish the nations of the earth with a worthy example."⁶⁷

It was not the black population alone, but the entire nation that had "begun its exodus from worse than Egyptian bondage." Now that Garnet's hopes for the American destiny of his race had been rekindled, the messianic prophecies of the Bible referred to all America, not only to the black people within it. Working together, black and white Americans would prove to mankind the superiority of American political institutions. "Thus before us a path of prosperity will open," predicted Garnet. "Thus shall we give to the world the form of a model Republic, founded on the principles of justice, and humanity, and Christianity. . . ."[68]

Garnet's faith in American Destiny was almost fatalistic. He was much influenced by the current of theological historicism that insinuated itself into every nook and cranny of Northern intellectual life. The traditions of social Christianity that had passed down from Jonathan Edwards to the Channings and the Beechers were antislavery, and dedicated to the formation of a model democracy. God had *destined* America to lead the rest of the world along freedom's road. The evangelical millenarianism that permeated American religion during the years of Garnet's ministry reinforced his belief that the power of God was steering the nation in the direction of increasingly perfect democratic republicanism.

Garnet's beliefs were typical of the faith of numerous other black preachers in the North, among them J. W. C. Pennington, Samuel Ringgold Ward, C. B. Ray, and Daniel A. Payne. All derived a faith in America from their faith in a God who directed the destinies of nations. The black masses of the South had a much more limited conception of racial Christianity. Their religion was predominantly concerned with the conversion experience and with periodic supplementary ecstacies. Their Christianity was no more social than that of the whites in their region. Of course, one immediately recalls the religious rhetoric of the three major slave revolts; but one should bear in mind that one of these revolts was attributed to the influences of a Northern black denomination, and the other two were led by literate blacks, whose religion, like their politics, was atypical.[69]

By the end of the nineteenth century, the black church in the cities had a tradition of social Christianity to draw on, and thereby it was able to modify the concerns of Washington Gladden, William Vaughn Moody, and Josiah Strong.[70] A later generation of black ministers, including Reverdy C. Ransom, Adam Clayton Powell, Sr., Richard Wright, Jr., and Francis J. Grimke, hardly felt outside the mainstream of Christianity when they adapted the social gospel to black concerns. In that same tradition, the philosophy of Walter Rauschenbusch continued to influence educated black clergymen like Martin Luther King, Jr.[71] The Christianity of the black masses, however, all too often reflected the influences of backwoods evangelism, where emphasis was placed on knowing Jesus rather than on doing his will.

Ultimately, black social Christianity, whether among the masses or the educated city dwellers, was based more on emotion than on mind, more on faith than on reason. As Fullinwider has observed, it represented "a step in the emancipation of the Negro mind," but it was still a mythological system. Racial Christianity in the nineteenth century was an intellectual prison, in that it was based more on the necessity of belief than on analysis of dismal facts known to be true.[72] Black Christians *needed* to believe that the black presence was a crucial factor in American moral life—that blacks were the God-appointed missioners of a model and regenerate American republic. The idea was traceable to the tradition of the Channings, the Beechers, Payne, and Garnet.

The faith of the educated urban blacks was not based on face-to-face encounters with blue-eyed Jesus nor obsessed with his personality. It was based on the psychological need for the racial covenant between the God of the oppressed and black America and in the belief that America was predestined to be an egalitarian utopia. It implied, as well as faith in God, a faith in the American people and in their commitment to keeping their covenant with God. It assumed not only the traditional covenant between God and the nation, but a special covenant involving the status of black Americans. If black and white Americans lived up to their covenantal duties to one another, they would thereby fulfill their duty to God. For whites, this implied a responsibility to deal fairly with blacks; for blacks, this implied a responsibility to make themselves model citizens of the model republic. The covenantal relationship between white America, black America, and their God was finally revealed at the end of the nineteenth century to the man who became known as the "Negro Moses." He spoke face to face with God and counseled absolute faith in a predestined racial millennium, concluding his most famous speech with the Biblical prophecy of "a new heaven and a new earth."

6
Booker T. Washington: A Black Moses and the Covenant Revealed to Him

One of Booker T. Washington's chief concerns as a black leader was to undermine the old otherworldly religion of the plantation, and to replace it with the ethic of achievement. At the turn of the century, even as Max Weber was defining the "Protestant Ethic" so precisely in terms of the preachments of Benjamin Franklin, Washington was already exploiting the Franklin myth.[1] He was teaching the students at Tuskegee a religion based on Christian principles as the road to riches. In his efforts he was supported by some of the older black social millenarians, most notably Bishop Daniel A. Payne. As his career progressed, Washington attempted to bring his philosophy of black advancement into harmony with the social gospel of the Reverend Josiah Strong, whose rhetoric was imbued with the doctrines of evangelical patriotism and Anglo–American destiny. It was recognition of Washington's deliberate and well-publicized attempts to manipulate black religion that led so many of his followers and admirers to endow his leadership with religious symbolism. "I had the pleasure of hearing your address given last spring to the students and residents at Knoxville College," wrote W. J. Cansler to Booker T. Washington a few days after the Atlanta Exposition Address. "I believed then, and know now, that you are our Moses destined to lead our race out of the difficulties and dangers which beset our pathway and surround us on all sides." Cansler, a black teacher in the Knoxville, Tennessee, public schools, was only one voice in a chorus of like exclamations from the press and from private citizens that hailed Washington as "the Negro Moses."[2]

Washington was neither the first nor the last black American public figure to be hailed with this title. Black Americans did not always approve of the Mosaic imagery applied to him. The *Cleveland Gazette* editorialized that it was "both aggravating and amusing to note the unflagging persistence with which white people of this country endeavor to make Afro–Americans accept Mr. Washington as their 'Moses' and leader, when his work and position make such a thing . . . absolutely impossible."[3] And even one of Tuskegee's staunch white supporters was forced to admit that the analogy had its limitations. The Biblical Moses had led his people out of Egypt and into the promised land; Washington was identified with the view that black Americans were already in the promised land. The original Moses had been fiery and authoritarian; Washington was conciliatory and accommodating.[4] Nonetheless, he recognized the usefulness of exploiting the Mosaic myth. He hoped to make a covenant with God and with America, according to which the blacks would gain acceptance in the land of their former bondage by learning the art of making "bricks without straw."[5]

Washington shrewdly worked to reconcile the myth of America as a chosen nation with the myth of the black population as a chosen people. The two groups, white and black, would work to redeem one another. In his vision, the Civil War and the emancipation of black Americans had placed them at the center of American destiny. This led to his repeatedly depicting them as super-Americans, whose history was watched over by Providence, and whose bloody deliverance bespoke a messianic fate.

At the Atlanta and Cotton States Exposition in 1895, Washington reminded his listeners that the black struggle up from slavery was central to American history, especially that of the South. What is more, the black American was morally and emotionally attuned to American patterns of thought and habit to a degree "that no foreigner can approach." Thus Washington urged the white South to "cast down your bucket . . . among my people [and] you and your families will be surrounded by the most patient, faithful, law-abiding and unresentful people that the world has seen."[6] Americans had long thought of themselves as a "redeemer nation," leading the rest of the world to salvation by example. The overcoming of racial animosities would set before the world a new ideal of Christian democracy.

Washington portrayed the black people of the South as quintessential Americans, a "New People," born on this soil, and having no history, language, or culture other than that which was American.[7] He did not mind slightly distorting history to prove his point. He subscribed to a belief common among his contemporaries that true Americanism implied a total isolation from Old World backgrounds, attitudes, and cultural habits.[8] As a people without a past, blacks were ideal Americans. Unlike European immigrants, they experienced no conflicts between Old World loyalties and American interests. Indeed, black people had already demonstrated that they perceived their interests as identical with those of the white people among whom they lived. He alluded to the loyalty of the slaves during the Civil War, conjuring up the myth of their "choosing" to sacrifice "four long years protecting and supporting the helpless, defenceless ones entrusted to [their] care." Black loyalty had not wavered even at the approach of invading armies, for the slaves had valued honor above personal safety or even freedom. And now, by virtue of their peculiar brand of stoical courage and their example of patience, hard work, and long suffering, they would join with the South and the rest of humanity in fashioning "a new heaven and a new earth."[9]

Washington's speech in Atlanta made use of a lopsided interpretation of American Protestant traditions. Certainly, the black American was a participant in these traditions. Unlike the bulk of immigrants to the United States during the 1890s, blacks were familiar with the evangelical rhetoric and perfectionist doctrines that are commonly recognized to be at the root of American culture.[10] But Washington's appeal to American religious sentiment was one-sided, because he scrupulously avoided the chauvinistic enthusiasm that characterized so much of the rhetoric of his contemporaries. There is a warlike strain in American religion, an occasionally blustering, supercilious tone and a moral aggressiveness. Such elements did not achieve prominence in Washington's writings and speeches. He was concerned with emphasizing the softer view of Christianity that was more in accord with his accommodationist policies.

It is not only difficult but presumptuous to interpret the sincerity of an individual's religious statements. Perhaps they are to be taken literally as expressions of supernatural belief. Perhaps they are metaphorical statements, revealing commitment to noble ideals. Or perhaps they represent only hypocrisy and opportunism. One can never know whether another individual sees the Bible as divine revelation, or as wise fables, or as silly myths to pacify children. Such questions are particularly difficult to answer with respect to Booker T. Washington, a man who was not given to disclosing his inmost feelings. On the other hand, it is not difficult to discover patterns in the public statements that Washington made concerning religion. There are four dominant elements: (1) A practical code of ethics, aimed at increasing the efficiency and affluence of Afro–Americans; (2) an accommodationist morality that included pietism as a facilitator of assimilation; (3) an interest in Christianizing and civilizing Africa; and (4) the millennial rhetoric of the "New Heaven and the New Earth," words taken from Revelations 21:1 and cited in the Atlanta address as an appeal to the American traditions of moral and material perfectionism.

Washington's practical attitude to religion developed early. In later recollections of childhood, he described encountering a this-worldly, materialistic, and utilitarian view of religion among the slaves. In *Up From Slavery*, he commented on double meanings in the lyrics of "Negro

Spirituals." Before the War, the blacks had been careful to explain to their masters that lyrical references to freedom represented only their desire to escape from sin. As the War drew near its end, references to "freedom of the body in this world" became less guarded.[11] From the beginning, there must have been planted in Washington's mind the seed of the idea that religion could have its political and social uses. It was during his youth, however, that he met the influences which led to his preferring the practical gospel of work and duty to that of comfort and complacency. Due to his training under Yankee auspices, he rejected the idea so common among his fellow Negro Baptists that the essence of religion was an ecstatic conversion experience leading to personal friendship with Jesus Christ. He was inclined to place more faith in the stern, Old Testament God of Providence, who provided mankind with a series of trials that must be successfully passed in order for individuals or groups to merit salvation.

Washington's puritan education was the major step in his developing a practical religiosity and a utilitarian ethic. Like W. E. B. Du Bois, he was influenced at an impressionable age by the austere Yankee values of work, cleanliness, and thrift. Thus, as Du Bois acknowledged, he "grasped the spirit of the age which was dominating the North . . . , the speech and thought of triumphant commercialism, and the ideals of material prosperity."[12] Washington came under the New England influence at around ten years of age, when he went to work for Viola Ruffner, transplanted New Hampshire bride of a West Virginia pro-Unionist, who had been a major general in the militia during the Civil War. Subsequently, he encountered the strict but helpful head teacher of Hampton Institute, Miss Mary F. Mackie, and the institution's founder, General Samuel C. Armstrong. The influences of these two puritanical personalities are recounted elsewhere by Washington himself and by each of his biographers. Washington idolized Armstrong, who became for him a symbol of practical Christianity and a "type of that Christlike body of men and women who went into the Negro schools at the close of the war by the hundreds to assist in lifting up my race."[13]

Washington represented what Robert Bellah has called the doctrine of "Salvation and Success in America." The two ideas are admittedly contradictory at first appearance, for eternal salvation is not reputedly attainable by means that lead to worldly riches. God and Mammon are not in league. Bellah argues, of course, that mythic truth is frequently engendered by a mingling of opposites—stern pietistic values may lurk beneath the appearance of affable worldliness in a personality like that of Benjamin Franklin, who was influenced by such Puritan writers as Cotton Mather and John Bunyan. The "scheme of moral perfection" represented by Franklin is a secularization of the Protestant ethic, and, as Bellah observes, "we cannot tell for sure whether virtue is pursued for its own good or for the public seeming of good ('Honesty is the best policy' clearly illustrates the problem)."[14]

The problem that is present in Franklin is also present in Washington. Neither of these self-proclaimed prophets of the American success myth seems interested in convincing his readers that virtue is its own reward. Franklin refused to have beer with his midday meal so that he could be more alert and productive in the afternoon. He preached against the pleasures of night life with the slogan, "Early to bed, early to rise, makes a man healthy wealthy and wise." Washington spelled out in detail the material benefits of abstaining from wine, women, and song:

> Quite a number of our young men in the cities stay up until twelve, one, and two o'clock each night. Sometimes at the gambling table, or in some brothel, or drinking in some saloon. As a result they go late to their work, and in a short time you hear them complaining about having lost their position. They will tell you they have lost their jobs on account of race prejudice, or because their former employers are not going to hire colored help any longer. But you will find, if you learn the real circumstances, that it is much more likely they lost their jobs because they were not punctual or on account of carelessness. . . . There is nothing worse for a young man or a young woman than to get into the habit of thinking that he or she must spend every night on the street or in some public place.[15]

Such statements, no doubt, gave rise to the opinion that Washington was "the Benjamin Franklin of his race."[16] Like Franklin, Washington could point to himself as evidence of the practical validity of his personal ethic.

It is almost impossible to discuss Washington's personal morality without being reminded of the works of the Reverend Horatio Alger. The son of a Unitarian minister and a product of the Harvard Divinity School, Alger edified at least three generations of American youth with his stories of bootblacks and matchboys who, through hard work, honesty, and luck, were able to elevate themselves to the pinnacle of American business life. Alger, who resigned his pulpit to become a full-time novelist, symbolizes, as does Franklin, the almost complete conversion of American religious idealism into a materialistic formula for success. But the Puritan basis of the American success myth always remains visible in the writings of Franklin, Alger, and Washington.[17]

Washington's investment theory of practical morality is crystallized in a sermon entitled "Will it Pay?" delivered in the Tuskegee Chapel. Its central theme is that "regard for truth and honest dealing" causes money to flow into one's pockets. "Character is power. If you want to be powerful in the world, if you want to be strong, influential and useful, you can do so in no better way than by having a strong character." Whenever faced with the temptation to dishonesty, one should ask oneself the question, "Will it pay me in this world? Will it pay me in the

world to come?"[18] This philosophy came to be called "Christian Industrial
Education."[19] Every Tuskegee student was to be trained in "Christian
character, ideas of thrift, economy, push, and a spirit of independence,
[then] sent out to become a centre of influence and light in showing the
masses of our people in the Black Belt of the South how to lift themselves
up."[20] Accepting the role of a "black Moses" in which the press readily
cast him, Washington hoped to set his people on an errand through the
racial wilderness, fortified by Puritan self-discipline. In *The Future of the
American Negro*, he predicted that there was but one way out of the present
difficulty "and that is for the Negro in every part of America to resolve
from henceforth that he will throw aside every non-essential and cling
only to the essential,—that his pillar of fire by night and pillar of cloud by
day shall be property, economy, education, and Christian character."[21]

But for all his commitment to asceticism, Washington was hardly of a
temperament to show patience with otherworldly anchorites. Sacrifice
was to be thought of as a mere investment that would be repaid ultimately in tangible returns. Indeed, he believed that it was downright impossible for an impoverished person to make a good Christian. He preached
constantly that "the industrial and material condition of the masses of
our people must be improved . . . before there can be any change in
their moral and religious life. . . . We find it a pretty hard thing to make
a good Christian of a hungry man. Anyone leaving the exuberant rites of
a Black Belt prayer meeting with an empty stomach would be tempted to
find something to eat before morning."[22]

Like the slave morality that led to stealing chickens and pilfering at the
back door, the emotional, otherworldly religion was viewed as a remnant
of the slave heritage.

> From the nature of things, all through slavery it was life in the future
> world that was emphasised in religious teaching rather than life in this
> world. In his religious meetings in *ante-bellum* days the Negro was
> prevented from discussing many points of practical religion which related
> to this world; and the white minister, who was his spiritual guide, found it
> more convenient to talk about heaven than earth, so very naturally that
> to-day in his religious meeting it is the Negro's feelings which are worked
> upon mostly, and it is description of the glories of heaven that occupy most
> of the time of his sermon.[23]

What the church would require in the twentieth century was emphasis
on a code of morals. Religion had to be brought home from the prayer
meeting and made a part of daily life. The man who owned a home and
had the means to make an honest living would find it much easier to
adhere to a moral code. The forces of pietism and morality ought ideally
to reinforce the ethic of work, cleanliness, and thrift; and this, in turn,
should strengthen the individual's capacity for Christian perseverance.

The final result would be increased usefulness of black people as they justified their presence in America by the services they rendered.[24]

A constant theme in Washington's public statements was "The Gospel of Service." He spoke on that theme at the Dexter Avenue Baptist Church in Montgomery, Alabama, in 1901:

> Christ said he who would become greatest of all must become the servant of all; that is, he meant that in proportion as one renders service he becomes great. The President of the United States is a servant of the people because he serves them. . . . The greatest merchant in Montgomery is a servant because he renders to his customers. . . . The only man or woman who is not a servant is the one who accomplishes nothing.[25]

Washington's conception of the dignity of service derived from Yankee influence and from the inspiration provided by his teachers at Hampton. Many of them came from backgrounds of unassailable respectability, but, of course, they represented the traditional humility of the missionary ideal. Like Du Bois, who wrote an extended essay on the subject, Washington felt that performing menial tasks was good for the soul.[26] Black people should not turn up their noses at domestic service, but should see it as an opportunity to cultivate the habits of purity, cleanliness, and honesty: "In proportion as we do this we will lay a foundation upon which our children and grandchildren are to rise to higher things."[27]

There is, of course, no real dichotomy between pietism and morality, no irreconcilable opposition between spirituality and a practical ethic. Washington felt that it was important for black people to cultivate an image of "simple faith and reverence" (it was actually Du Bois who employed *that* phrase)[28] in order to make themselves more acceptable to whites. Washington felt it necessary that Tuskegee be associated in the public mind with nothing but the most strait-laced morality. He once fired a young woman teacher for keeping company with a male student, although, as he assured her father, there was "not the slightest suspicion of immorality in this matter, no one feels that there is the least ground for any such thought."[29]

One of Tuskegee's most impressive buildings was its chapel, where Washington gave Sunday evening addresses to the student body. Attendance was compulsory, as was attendance at nightly prayer meetings and Tuesday and Thursday services.[30] Tuskegee established a Bible Department in 1893 under the headship of Edgar James Penney. Washington described its functions as follows:

> This department was established for the express purpose of giving colored hearts a knowledge of the English Bible; implanting in their hearts a noble

ambition to go out into the dark and benighted districts of the South and give their lives for the elevation and Christianizing of the South.[31]

Washington claimed to be a daily Bible reader,[32] and he urged Tuskegee students not to miss attending church and Sunday school while they were away from campus.[33] When he commissioned Paul Laurence Dunbar to write the lyrics for the Tuskegee Song, he urged the poet, on the advice of the Rev. Penney, to include something in the way of Biblical allusion. Dunbar responded, however, that "the exigencies of verse" would "hardly allow" it.[34] Although Washington, unlike many of his fellow school administrators, was not a minister, he did assume some ministerial functions. In addition to delivering sermons in the Tuskegee chapel, he addressed the National Baptist Convention.[35] Similarities between the views of Washington and those of various black clergymen have been discussed by August Meier, who tentatively generalizes that large segments of their numbers supported Tuskegee policies. He argues that "most of the powerful figures in the mass churches [Methodist and Baptist] were of a conservative turn of mind," although he notes scattered evidence of militancy among the more educated Northern-based leaders. It was among the elite denominations, he argues, "the Presbyterian, Congregationalist, and Episcopalian churches of the Northern and border states that the protest point of view found its chief strength."[36] Meier's interpretation seems valid enough, but a review of the position papers of religious leaders leads one to believe that intellectual ambition was probably the most important factor in determining militancy among the clergy. Every denomination and every region had its militants, but one finds very few examples of accommodationist opinion among those ministers who were intellectually enterprising enough to publicize their views. By and large, those clergymen who could be described as men of letters were given to protest, regardless of denominational affiliation. They also displayed tendencies toward black nationalism, Pan–Africanism, and, occasionally, even socialism.[37]

The most important of Washington's agents among the black clergy was Bishop Alexander Walters of the A. M. E. Zion Church. Bishop Walters became President of the National Negro Business League, founded by Washington as a rival to the activities on behalf of black business in the Afro–American League.[38] The Afro–American Council had been founded by T. Thomas Fortune, with Du Bois taking an active role as head of the Negro Business Bureau. Walters blew hot and cold as a supporter of Washington but generally seemed intent on preserving good relations. He is perhaps best remembered for his involvement in the London Conference of 1900, where he worked along with W. E. B. Du Bois and Henry Sylvester Williams to found the Pan–African movement.[39] Walters was more militant than Washington in attacking Jim Crow and lynch law. A rift developed between the two when, in 1908, the

Bishop criticized Roosevelt's handling of the Brownsville riot.[40] Walters never rejected the Washingtonian belief in racial self-improvement, although he was increasingly identified with anti-Tuskegee forces after 1906.[41]

As has been noted elsewhere, Washington got along well enough with the Reverend Francis Grimke, until around 1903.[42] Grimke was pastor of the Fifteenth Street Presbyterian Church in Washington and a graduate of Princeton Seminary. At the time of the Atlanta Exposition address, Grimke wrote to congratulate Washington, saying that he had not read the entire address, but that he was "greatly delighted with the extracts" that he had seen.[43] Washington also received congratulations from Du Bois upon his "phenomenal success," and praise for his "word fitly spoken."[44] Grimke shared Washington's belief in the importance of stern puritanical values, sexual morality, and the work ethic. Like Washington, he was committed to emphasizing self-help, racial solidarity, and making the best of things as they are. Like Washington, he recognized similarities between the black and the Jewish situations. He saw black people remaining, like the Jews, a separate people for the foreseeable future.[45]

Grimke began to express some misgivings concerning Tuskegee policy only a few weeks after sending Washington his words of praise for the Atlanta address. A meeting at the Bethel Literary and Historical Association had been called to discuss the speech, and much criticism of Washington had been expressed in connection with a report that he had refused assistance at the Tuskegee campus to a man who had been wounded by a lynch mob. Washington responded by detailing the steps he had quietly taken to play the Good Samaritan, but asked that Grimke not reveal his efforts.[46] As the years passed, Grimke became increasingly impatient with Washington's denials of claims to "social equality" and eventually became thoroughly disgusted with him.[47] For some time, however, Grimke had represented well the tendency of even militant clergy to avoid open criticism of Tuskegee because of Washington's commitment to Christian principles and a philosophy of moral uplift.

It cannot be denied that there was considerable Christian opinion of a more militant variety than that embraced by Washington. The Rev. Charles S. Morris, a black preacher from Wilmington, North Carolina, issued a leaflet in 1899, protesting against violent intimidation of black voters in his city. America cannot afford "to go eight thousand miles from home to set up a republican government in the Philippines," he said, "while the blood of citizens whose ancestors came here before the Mayflower is crying out to God against her from the gutters of Washington." The Rev. C. S. Smith of Tennessee delivered a speech in Nashville, criticizing Washington's brand of industrial education. He argued that regardless of how well trained, the black worker would find no sphere in which to ply his trade so long as he was the object of hostility from the white trade unions. He also felt that agricultural training could have little effect so long as black farmers could not own their land.[48]

Militants occasionally gained moral support from white Christians as, for example, in the speech of Albion W. Tourgee at the First Mohonk Conference on the Negro Question in June 1890. Tourgee's address dealt with the duty of Christians to remedy the effects of injustices done to black people during the slavery period. More representative, however, was the conservative opinion of Bishop Atticus Haygood, agent of the Slater Fund and author of a volume entitled, *Our Brother in Black*. Haygood provided an optimistic description of the present and future status of the black American.[49] Washington, to his credit, was unimpressed by the lily-white character of the Conference, and wrote to George Washington Cable criticizing the "disposition of many of our friends to consult *about* the Negro instead of *with*—to work *for* him instead of *with* him."[50] The Mohonk Conference represented the moderately benevolent consensus view on American race relations from a Christian standpoint. The consensus was that the black race should be educated for freedom gradually through "evolution by a simple natural process."[51] Slavery was a "step in the hands of Providence in the progress of the race."[52] Christian industrial education was seen as the next phase in the evolution of the Negro people. Given the nature of the support that Washington was receiving for his efforts, it is not surprising that Tuskegee placed great emphasis on the inculcation of pious habits.

Washington once described his daily bath as a kind of "ritual baptism," words significantly chosen.[53] It is obvious that he saw personal cleanliness as a form of righteousness. Bathing had a "value, not only in keeping the body healthy, but in inspiring self-respect and promoting virtue."[54] The ritual cleansing of the body symbolized not only a spiritual but a social purification, and perhaps a washing away of that fancied peculiarity of odor to which Thomas Jefferson had alluded.[55] Cleanliness was valued not only for its practical effects upon health, but for its metaphysical benefits. Purification of body and purification of soul—the Protestant values of cleanliness, thrift, and hard work—were not only a means of making blacks a more efficient work force, they were a means of symbolically whitening them.

Tuskegee students were urged to keep the Sabbath holy, but this did not mean that idleness was encouraged on Sundays:

> We should never suffer a Sunday to go by without reading some helpful book. We never feel so miserably as at the end of a Sunday that is idly spent, or frittered away in some trifling conversation. Get into the habit of saying "I am going to put in my Sabbaths to the best advantage and gain something through the medium of some good book."[56]

Washington was disgusted by the tendency to use religion as an excuse for laziness. He ridiculed the ignorance and immorality of those ministers who conveniently received "calls to preach" as soon as the cotton was high and the sun hot. He described with amused contempt the way in which a call was received. The chosen one was usually sitting in church, when suddenly he would "fall upon the floor as if struck by a bullet." Sometimes he would lie on the floor for hours, and frequently, "if he were inclined to resist the summons, he would fall or be made to fall a second or third time." This form of ceremonial spirit possession was viewed with skepticism by Washington. The question of whether it was a survival of African religious behavior or a remnant of the otherworldly religion encouraged by the slaveholders was of little importance to him. While such religion may have benefited the short-term, selfish interests of individuals, it did nothing for the collective advancement of the black race as a whole.[57]

In 1890 he published an article in the *Christian Union*, "The Colored Ministry: Its Defects and Needs"; it was one of the most scathing attacks on a black institution that Washington ever delivered publicly. He asserted that "three-fourths of the Baptist ministers and two-thirds of the Methodists [were] unfit, either mentally or morally, or both, to preach the Gospel to any one or to attempt to lead any one." He conceded that the Congregationalists, Presbyterians, and Episcopalians were "as a rule, intelligent and earnest," but they were so "cramped by denominational lines" that their influence was negligible. He recognized the need for training more and better ministers, not only for the South, but for African missions as well. The answer to this need was to change the nature of black ministerial education. Black theological seminaries in the South all too often modeled their courses on those of Andover, Hartford, and Union. Only a very small proportion of those who entered were able to successfully complete the syllabus. "The smattering of Greek and Hebrew and other difficult branches they [were] dragged through merely serve[d] to muddle." He called for the establishment of a non-denominational training school where a student could gain a knowledge of the Bible and "how to prepare a sermon, how to read a hymn, how to study, and most important, how to reach and help the people outside the pulpit in an unselfish Christian way."[58]

Shortly thereafter, Washington received a letter from the Rev. Daniel Alexander Payne, venerable Senior Bishop of the African Methodist Episcopal Church, requesting a copy of the speech. Then, on November 3, 1890, Bishop Payne wrote again saying that he had wished to read for himself what Washington had said to "incense the grumblers." Payne found that, "in regard to the moral qualifications of the Methodist and Baptist ministers," Washington's article had not "overstated, but rather understated the facts."[59] Payne had long held a reputation for opposition to excessively enthusiastic religion and for the crusade against what he called "Africanisms" in the ritual of the masses. While Payne was politically sympathetic to Pan–Africanism, as displayed by his interest in the African Civilization Society before the Civil War, he was opposed to the retention of African traits, which he interpreted as anti-rational.[60] He was not alone in this. Martin Delany, Edward Wilmot Blyden, and Alexander Crummell had all gone on record as critics of the excessive emotionalism of black religion and its preoccupation with otherworldly things. Christian Pan–Africanists of the nineteenth century had little patience with enthusiastic religion, regardless of whether it could be traced to the culture of the fatherland or to European antecedents.[61]

An exception to this rule, of course, was Orishatukeh Fadumah, whose observations on similarities between the mass religion of the Black Belt and the ecstatic religious experiences of other peoples, ancient and modern, have already been noted.[62] But arguments of the sort that Fadumah marshalled in his bid for greater tolerance were of the very sort that Washington would have found irrelevant to the problem at hand, namely, the providing of stern moral leadership for the black peasantry of the American South. Washington continued to receive the support of eminent, educated clergymen; and he sent a letter defending his position to the *Indianapolis Freeman*, with Bishop Payne's statement appended.[63]

Washington's relations with the educated black clergy were not always so felicitous, however. His feud with William H. Ferris, a product of Harvard Divinity School, has drawn the attention of recent scholars. Ferris was, as has been observed by others, an erratic personality. He was also a dyed-in-the-wool race man who, in his early career, opposed Washington vigorously and, in middle age, supported Marcus Garvey. Washington is believed to have referred to Ferris in one of his descriptions of an impoverished intellectual who had once lectured on "The Mistakes of Booker T. Washington," then later attempted to ingratiate himself in hopes of finding a sinecure.[64]

The criticism of Alexander Crummell had to be taken more seriously. Crummell was an Episcopalian clergyman, educated at Queen's College of the University of Cambridge, where he was awarded the B. A. in 1853. Crummell had been a missionary to Liberia for twenty years before returning to the United States and accepting the rectorship of St. Luke's Church in Washington, D. C. Crummell was a stern, puritanical, authoritarian figure, but an intensely emotional man. He believed strongly in industrial education and had publicized his belief in a celebrated essay, "Common Sense in Common Schooling."[65] Here and elsewhere he had argued that too much emphasis in the education of black youngsters had been placed on languages and the classics. Crummell spoke with the bitter wisdom of hindsight, his attempts to bestow a liberal education on his own "poor sinful son" having failed abysmally. But he insisted uncompromisingly on liberal education for the sufficiently talented and motivated.

It was in 1897, only a year before his death, that Crummell launched what was not so much an attack on Tuskegee policy as a criticism of the philosophy underlying it. Crummell, like all the old black nationalists of his generation, believed in baptism by sweat. Labor was in and of itself a good thing, and it was a law of God and of nature that man should live by mental and physical exertion. He distinguished between labor and drudgery, however, and rejected the view that slavery organized the daily life of the black American around the principle of work. So far as Crummell was concerned, there was "no dispute as to the need for industrialism. That is a universal condition of life everywhere; but there is no need of an undue or overshadowing exaggeration of it in the case of the Negro."[66]

Later that autumn, Crummell wrote from Liverpool to his friend, the Rev. John W. Cromwell, reporting a conversation with "a noted and somewhat famous English clergyman." The unidentified divine had expressed much sympathy and indignation on the question of lynching, especially when this occurred at the "incitation of white women."

> A still stranger utterance followed this. He remarked, you have a tremendous fight before you, but one great difficulty in your way is the "white man's nigger." Some of your own men will betray and sell you. There is that Booker Washington who constantly betrays your cause to please the South!!![67]

Although Crummell never seems to have publicly identified himself with such vituperative attacks on Washington, there was little doubt as to what school of thought he was criticizing in an article he wrote for the *Independent*. The Rev. Robert Charles Bedford, a Tuskegee supporter, wrote Washington to express concern about the article and the *Independent*'s editorial endorsement of it. He said, "Only those who cannot or will not for some selfish reason understand your position are even secretly against you. No one dare openly oppose you."[68]

Later that year, Crummell gave his inaugural address as first president of the American Negro Academy. Its title was *Civilization: The Primal Need of the Race*. The title, like the contents, was an adaptation of the article which appeared in the *Independent*, "The Primal Need of the Negro Race." This need was seen by Crummell as the attainment of higher culture, "letters, literature, science, and philosophy." The address was an attack on those shortsighted race leaders who were "constantly dogmatizing theories of sense and matter," especially those "blind men" who held forth for the acquisition of property and money as panaceas. The address was shortly published in pamphlet form with another of Crummell's essays, "The

Attitude of the American Mind Toward the Negro Intellect." Here he continued on the theme that black people, like all peoples, would be uplifted by the better minds in their midst: "The struggle of a degraded people for elevation [was], in its very nature, a warfare, and . . . its main weapon is the cultivated and scientific mind." The excessive emphasis on industrial education was only a scheme by the whites to keep the minds of black youth fixed on menial things.[69]

Crummell's criticisms drew a response from Washington in the *Independent*, which published his article in two parts during January and February 1898. Here he took occasion to comment on what he considered the overly educated minister, his opinions on the undereducated clergyman already being well known:

> Only a few days ago I saw a colored minister preparing his Sunday sermon just as the New England minister prepares his sermon. But this colored minister was in a broken-down, leaky, rented log cabin, with weeds in the yard, surrounded by evidences of poverty, filth and want of thrift. This minister had spent some time in school studying theology. How much better would it have been to have had this minister taught the dignity of labor, theoretical and practical farming in connection with his theology, so that he could have added to his meager salary, and set an example to his people in the matter of living in a decent house, and correct farming—in a word, this minister should have been taught that his condition, and that of his people, was not that of a New England community, and he should have been so trained as to meet the actual needs and condition of the colored people in this community.[70]

There can be no doubt that many of the *Independent*'s readers would have seen this as an indirect attack on Crummell, just as they had seen Crummell's article as an indirect attack on Washington. Washington was a materialist, while Crummell was an idealist. Crummell saw Washington as a "Gradgrind," obsessed with the tedious, the mundane. He was a potentially great and good man, pitiably befuddled by a half-truth. Washington saw Crummell as an impractical dreamer, incapable of coming to grips with reality. Crummell was a Platonist, for whom truth existed in the world of ideas; it was an abstract, timeless, unchanging emanation from the mind of God. Washington believed that truth was circumstantial. Although he believed in natural law and in immutable standards of morality, he was not the absolutist that Alexander Crummell was. Behavior must be determined by situations; and in the present situation, an obsessive concern with mental development was foolish. Crummell worshipped a God of "large, majestic and abiding things," whose truth could be approached at any time by a sufficiently enlightened mind. Washington believed in a God who worked through dim providences, and whose ultimate purposes would be perceived only after many years of "severe and constant struggle" in the wilderness. Yet he exploited the suggestion of his ardent supporters that he was a Moses, who knew the mind of God. And he exploited Mosaic imagery, identifying the "pillar of fire by night and cloud by day" that all other black people were to follow.[71]

Washington's missionary interest in Africa has been documented in a brilliant exploratory essay by Louis Harlan.[72] African involvement before the First World War almost necessarily involved some interaction with missionaries. Tuskegee sent her own missionaries to Liberia and to Togoland to establish centers of Christian industry and agricultural education. Washington worked with Robert E. Park and Mark Twain in the Congo Reform Movement. He came into contact with Joseph Booth, a white missionary to Nyasaland, whose influences on early African radicalism have been charted by George Shepperson.[73] Washington's work was known and, with some reservations, admired by West African proto-nationalists like the Rev. Mark Hayford and his brother, J. E. Casely Hayford. Although the latter, a celebrated journalist and pioneer anthropologist, once characterized the work of both Washington and Du Bois as "exclusive and provincial,"[74] apparently he later modified his view that their work had little applicability to the mother continent.[75]

Other Africans emulated Booker T. Washington; for example, the Rev. John Langalibalele Dubé, a South African, educated in Natal, and a student at Oberlin College from 1887 to 1892. He was ordained a Congregationalist minister in New York before returning to South Africa, where he founded the Zulu Christian Industrial School in 1901. Dubé (who, like Washington, gained the support of white philanthropists in the Northern states of the U.S.) was often compared with the sage of Tuskegee, whose work he openly imitated.[76]

Tuskegee's ties to missionary Pan–Africanism became apparent around the time of the Atlanta Exposition in 1895. The contact was mostly indirect, through Washington's agents I. Garland Penn and J. W. E. Bowen. Then, in December 1895, a missionary conference on "Africa and the American Negro" was held at Gannon Theological Seminary of Atlanta. The Rev. Bowen (the Seminary's president after 1906) was a loyal Bookerite who wrote to Washington expressing his unqualified support for the Tuskegee program, which he understood as encouraging "a love of work not so much as an end to a means [sic] but as an end in itself."[77] The Gannon missionary conference featured among its speakers the Swiss missionary, Heli Chatelain, who encouraged Washington to give his work a Pan–African dimension. He urged Washington to accept his destiny as a universal race leader, advising him that his real "sphere of influence" ought to embrace the whole continent of Africa, "and even the millions of negroes in Brazil and other South

American States, who have not yet come in touch with our Evangelical civilization."[78]

Edward Wilmot Blyden, the Liberian Pan–Africanist (who was influenced by the Zionism of Theodore Herzl and whose black internationalism had been contrasted by Casely Hayford with the "provincialism" of Washington), was likewise impressed by the cosmopolitan significance of Washington's work. Blyden was unable to attend the missionary conference, but he wrote to express his support:

> The "Congress on Africa" at this time is most opportune when the world is looking to that continent as a field for political, commercial and philanthropic effort. I hope that the results of the Congress upon the Negro population of your country will be such as to lead them to take a greater practical interest in the land of their fathers.[79]

Blyden, who had been ordained a Presbyterian minister, wrote to "congratulate" Washington on having been "made by Providence an instrument" of a work greater than that of George Washington. For, while Washington had "freed one race from foreign domination, leaving another chained and manacled," Booker T. was destined "to free two races from prejudices and false views of life."[80]

Not all Pan–Africanists took such a view of the Atlanta compromise. A. M. E. Bishop, Henry McNeal Turner, expressed strong reservations. Because of his belief in separate development and racial independence, Turner had no quarrel with certain aspects of the Atlanta Exposition speech, but he thought it unfortunate that Washington had addressed himself to the question of social equality. If indeed it was impolitic to agitate the question of social equality, it was just as impolitic to deny aspirations along those lines. "Social equality," as the Bishop observed, "carries with it civil equality, political equality, financial equality, judicial equality, business equality."[81]

Turner visited the Atlanta Exposition and stumped around the grounds in fine fettle. Interviewed by the *Chicago Inter-Ocean*, he expressed little patience with "those who talk about the new negro." The exhibits in the Negro Building represented simply the artistry and skill that had always characterized black labor. The men who had owned slaves had given the best testimony to their skill; the very fact that they had fought a war over slavery was a tribute to their value as a work force. Coming out of the Negro Building and turning up the midway, the Bishop came across an exhibit purporting to be a Dahomey village and stopped to exchange barbs with a white barker who was urging visitors not to miss seeing the wild cannibals from the West Coast of Africa. When the white man asked him what he knew about Africa, he answered: "I know all about it sir, . . . I am a negro, and I live in Africa a good part of the time.

There are not, and never have been any cannibals on the west coast of Africa. . . . Stop your lying about the negro!"[82]

Two months later Bishop Turner addressed the Congress on Africa. His theme was similar to one that had occurred in some of the speeches of Blyden during the nineteenth century. It was Providence that had brought black people to the United States. Slavery was "a heaven-permitted if not a divinely sanctioned manual laboring school." This was so that the Negro might have contact with "the mightiest race that ever trod the globe."[83]

Washington, agreed with Turner that the effects of slavery on black labor had not been all negative. The evil of slavery was in its day-to-day degradation and insult, not in its insistence that the black population must work. In his grudging admiration for the might of the Anglo–Saxon race, Turner was not alone either. Throughout the nineteenth century, black writers like William Cooper Nell, J. Dennis Harris, and James T. Holly had sought to identify black Americans as bearers of the English-speaking culture. Occasionally they had referred to themselves by such names as Anglo–African or Black Saxon.[84] Blyden and Crummell had, of course, maintained that Providence had allowed slavery so that the benefits of Anglo–Saxon culture could be brought back to Africa. Even William H. Ferris, usually at odds with Booker T. Washington, agreed with him on the cultural superiority of the English-speaking peoples.[85]

Alexander Crummell, one of the speakers at the Atlanta Congress on Africa, used the platform both to reveal his continuing admiration for Anglo–Saxon high culture and to continue his implicit criticisms of the Tuskegee program. Washington had argued, in his response to Crummell's earlier attack, that it was impossible to make a Christian of a hungry man. Crummell argued that Christian principles of morality came not from full bellies but from enlightened minds, and that Africa would never be Christianized without the indispensable aid of civiliza-tion. By civilization, Crummell meant the high culture of the English-speaking peoples, not only in technology and commerce, but in literature and philosophy. Crummell had long expressed his admiration for British missionary activities in Africa—both cultural and religious.[86]

To his credit, Booker T. Washington had no inclination to ignore the more sordid aspects of British expansionism and missionary work. In December 1896, he gave vent to one of his rare expressions of indigna-tion over the ways of white folk as he described the slaughter of Matabele warriors by British troops armed with rapid-fire Maxim guns:

> With such an object lesson before us, why need Christians wonder that Africa is not Christianized faster. What is the crime of these heathen? Why are they thus shot down—mowed down by the acre. Simply because

God has given them land that some one else wants to possess—simply because they are ignorant and weak.

On the very day, perhaps at the very hour that the British troops were mowing down those Africans simply because they tried to defend their homes, their wives and their children, hundreds of prayers were being offered up in as many English churches that God might convert the heathen in Africa and bring them to our way of thinking and acting. What mockery!

Have not these Matabele warriors as much right to lay claim to the streets of London, as the English have to claim the native land of these Africans? What England has done every Christian (?) nation in Europe has done.

On one ship a half dozen missionaries go to use the Bible and prayer book—in the next ship go a thousand soldiers to use the rifle.

Can we wonder that the Africans hesitate about exchanging their religion for that of the Anglo–Saxon race?[87]

This public statement of hostility was so uncharacteristic of Washington that one might question its authenticity had it not been published during his lifetime and under his name in a reputable journal. Washington was not usually given to public displays of anger or impatience where white people were concerned. He was certainly not known for condemning the hypocrisy of Christian missionaries. The fact that those policies he decided to criticize were not American, but British, provides a partial explanation for his giving free play to a sense of outrage that he was prevented from voicing on most occasions. Perhaps he also wished to express his disregard for the limitless Anglophilia of many of his contemporaries. He was a great admirer of the German spirit, and he praised their African colonial policy.[88]

This is not to suggest that Washington did not admire the Anglo–Saxon tradition. He viewed the British as representatives of the indomitable Aryan spirit that had demonstrated its cultural supremacy over the rest of the world by means of industry, democratic institutionalism, and Protestant faith. Washington obviously did not come up with all these ideas on his own. He derived them from numerous sources and, over a period of years, blended them into his own philosophy. Such thinking had been passed down from Henry Ward and Lyman Beecher to Josiah Strong, a Congregationalist minister, supporter of the Philafrican Liberator's League (founded by the missionary Heli Chatelain), and noted advocate of American expansionism.[89]

Washington was familiar with, and he quoted from, Strong's immensely popular book *Our Country* (1886), which had already sold 130,000 copies at the time of the second edition in 1891. Strong believed in the providential role of Anglo–Saxon culture to shape the destiny of a future world utopia. He defined Anglo–Saxon "broadly to include all English

speaking peoples." Washington saw it as providential that black
Americans had gone "into slavery without a language," and emerged
"speaking the proud Anglo–Saxon tongue."[90] But it is doubtful whether
Josiah Strong would have accepted Washington as an Anglo–Saxon. He
did not, in fact, give much thought to black Americans in *Our Country,*
although his attitudes were clearly stated in a later work:

> Only those races which have produced machinery seem capable of using
> it with the best results. It is the most advanced races which are its masters.
> Those races which, like the African and the Malay, are many centuries
> behind the Anglo–Saxon in development seem as incapable of operating
> complicated machinery as they are of adopting and successfully ad-
> ministering representative government.[91]

This would certainly seem to be in direct contradiction to the Tuskegee
faith, but Tuskegeans were skillful at rephrasing unsympathetic ideas in
ways that might be useful to the Tuskegee program. The institution
existed for the express purpose of teaching black people to feel more
comfortable with complicated machinery. Washington was capable of
exploiting myths concerning black people in order to encourage support
for his efforts. If blacks were reputed to be unskillful with machines,
Washington would not deny it; he would simply continue to extol the
merits of industrial education.

> Without industrial education, when the black woman washes a shirt, she
> washes with both hands, both feet, and her whole body. An individual with
> industrial education will use a machine that washes ten times as many
> shirts in a given time with almost no expenditure of physical force; steam,
> electricity, or water doing the work.[92]

Strong had no faith in this approach to racial advancement:

> It is interesting and important to note that the advanced and the belated
> races are not travelling the same path. . . . Nor must we imagine that the
> belated race will some day reach the *same* development as that of the
> advanced race at the present time. . . .
> The negro, for instance, on emancipation in the United States, was
> thrown into the midst of an advanced industrial system, and of matured
> political and religious institutions. He cannot by developing them develop
> himself. All he can do is to accept them and adjust himself to them in a
> passive spirit.[93]

Washington recognized that the Anglo–Saxon race had not lifted
themselves by their bootstraps out of barbarism, but that they had built
on the accomplishments of prior civilizations. Blacks in America were

simply traveling "the old, old road that all races have had to travel which have got upon their feet."[94] The laws of human development applied equally to all races; and if black people could avoid being dazzled by exposure to Euro–American high culture, contenting themselves to start at the bottom, they would eventually be able to struggle upward. Washington was willing to slip through any loopholes provided by Strong's linguistic imprecision and ethnological sloppiness. The Tuskegee emphasis on the use of machinery and mastering the rudiments of standard English was clearly aimed at bringing the black American into the Anglo–Saxon fold as demarcated by Strong.

Washington was not alone. His bitterest opponent, William H. Ferris, who once wrote to remind him that a black man always remained "a nigger" no matter how refined, still hoped that the race could attain Germanic status. He came to advocate that black people should insist on being called the "Negrosaxon race."[95] Sutton Griggs was perhaps influenced by Strong when he predicted the coming conflict between the Anglo–Saxon and Slavic races. He urged the Anglo–Saxon to nurture the Negro's fundamental loyalty to the English-speaking culture.[96] Washington was thus not alone among black Americans when he hoped that the cultural, as opposed to the purely genetic, interpretation of Anglo–Saxonism would ultimately triumph.

It was basic to the faith of Booker T. Washington that Providence had placed black Americans in the plantation school. There they had learned to labor under modern industrial conditions, to speak English, and to value Christianity. In the Atlanta Exposition Address, he subtly implied that blacks were more Anglo–Saxon, and thus more assimilable, than many of the white ethnic groups.[97] He exploited fears engendered by Josiah Strong and others which associated European ethnics with "Rum, Romanism, and Rebellion." Black Americans were not only loyal by nature, but, under the influences of the Tuskegee brand of education, they were being schooled in "the duties of Christian citizenship . . . to contribute their full quota of virtue, thrift, and intelligence to the prosperity of our beloved country." Thus would the black population "knit our civil and commercial interests into yours in a way that shall make us all realize anew that 'of one blood hath God made all men to dwell and prosper on the face of the earth.' "[98]

Washington was, to be sure, cautious in his opinions. He admitted that "to state in detail just what place the black man will occupy in the South as a citizen when he has developed in the direction named is above the wisdom of anyone."[99] Then, he said on another occasion, "I believe that God in His own way will work out this problem to please all."[100] Did Washington simply dodge difficult questions by commending them to the hands of Providence? Or did he really believe, as did so many of his contemporaries, in the inevitability of progress as a law of nature? It seems likely that the semi-religious mysticism of popularly distorted social Darwinism indicated to him that the black American must inevitably evolve upward. "Progress, progress is the law of nature," he maintained. "Under God it shall be our guiding star."[101]

Blacks would assure their progress by adhering to the laws of Christian citizenship; thus would they earn their place in the American nation and participate in all the benefits of the Kingdom of God in America. As Washington once put it before a white audience: "Never since the days that we left Africa's shores have we lost faith in you or in God. We are a patient people. There is plenty in this country for us to do. We can afford to work and wait."[102]

Washington accepted and contributed to the "chosen people" doctrine of American history as advanced by Timothy Dwight, the Beechers, and Josiah Strong. If America was "God's new Israel," black Americans were, by virtue of both their blackness and their Americanness, a specially covenanted people within the American race:

> In the Bible . . . , reference is made to the Jews as "a peculiar people. . . ." The Jews because they were different . . . were able to give the world the doctrine of the unity of the Fatherhood of God and Christianity. . . . It is, I think, not too much to hope that the very qualities which make the Negro different from the peoples by whom he is surrounded will enable him, in the fulness of time, to make a peculiar contribution to the nation of which he forms a part.[103]

The Anglo–Saxon Protestants were a chosen race; Americans, a chosen nation within that race; and black Americans, a chosen people within that nation, having a prophetic mission within the nation's messianic destiny.

7
The New Negro and America's Changing World Mission

"And now the world turns with anxious hearts and eager eyes towards America. In the providence of God there has been started on these shores the great experiment of the ages." The speaker was Robert Russa Moton, Booker T. Washington's successor at Tuskegee. He spoke at the dedication of the Lincoln Memorial in Washington, D. C., in 1922, and he referred to race relations, but his concern symbolized larger issues. He argued, as an earlier generation of black leaders had been fond of arguing, that the ability to cope with the issue of black equality would validate America's claim to a moral mission in the modern world. The two races were "charged under God with the responsibility of showing the world how individuals, as well as races, may differ most widely in color and inheritance and at the same time make themselves helpful and even indispensable to each other's progress and prosperity."[1]

Moton's rhetoric, like the occasion of its delivery, harked back to the previous century. The traditional themes of racial Christianity, whether in nationalist or integrationist forms, persisted in black thought. Some leaders and movements followed in the tradition of Harriet Beecher Stowe, with the view that black racial traits endowed Africans with a variety of superiority. They argued that black people should be encouraged in their own separate sphere. Others, like Washington and later Moton, accepted Stowe's view that blacks possessed special racial traits, but with the modification that these very characteristics would ultimately prove Afro–Americans indispensable to America's well-being.[2]

Although the idea that the Negro was indispensable to American life had come to be identified with Booker T. Washington, it was widely accepted even by those who were critical of the Tuskegee program. They accepted, as well, the idea that black and white Americans could best adhere to their covenant with God by clinging to one another, for the covenant between black and white America was a reflection of the national covenant with God. By fairness to the colored population, white America would prove its fitness for the destiny outlined by John Winthrop and Timothy Dwight. And it would thus forestall the jeremiadic predictions of Thomas Jefferson. By meeting the standards set by whites, black America would really be adhering to the Protestant ethic which was an expression of God's natural law. Any people who adhered to this law would find progress and prosperity inevitable.

Robert Russa Moton and his post-World War I contemporaries revived one aspect of mainstream American missionary rhetoric that had not preponderated in the statements of Washington. In the years following the First World War, despite the putative isolationism of the period, the United States was reappraising its relationship to the rest of the world and trying to come to grips with the new leadership role that had been thrust upon it.[3] Black leaders were quick to recognize this, and so during the 1920s we see repeated attempts on their part to manipulate the new self-consciousness of a nation uncomfortably adjusting to the fact that the entire world was scrutinizing it as never before. Black Americans realized that the United States was susceptible to arguments based on the premise that America must assume the God-given duties of a world leader. For despite the undeniable isolationism of the period, the United States had become, in Reinhold Niebuhr's words, "the real empire of modern civilization."[4]

Moton's speech at the Lincoln Memorial was thus no mere echoing of nineteenth-century themes; it prophesied the interrelationship between American race relations and American foreign policy that would emerge in the new age. Black Americans, along with the rest of the society in which they lived, were undergoing changes in self-image. As Moton and numerous others observed, the black population had rapidly become more affluent, cosmopolitan, self-assertive, and better-educated than would have seemed possible in the short span of years from the death of Booker T. Washington in 1915 to the imprisonment of Marcus Garvey in 1925. The transformation of living modes and values that occurred is referred to as the Harlem Renaissance or, more accurately, as the New Negro Movement.[5] Its spokesmen were concerned with presenting a view of themselves as a worldly-wise people, as urban sophisticates and savants of a jazz-age culture. This contrasted sharply with the tendency to present the race as a repository of the quaint peasant virtues sentimentalized by Harriet Beecher Stowe, Booker T. Washington, and W. E. B. Du Bois. All these changes, occurring as they did with a suddenness both traumatic and exhilarating, are usually attributed to the effects of the First World War.

The turmoil on the continent and the disruption of Atlantic shipping caused a decline in the supply of cheap factory labor on which Northern industrialists had become dependent during periods of rapid growth. Black workers in the South were the only available source of labor for wartime industries, and conditions in the South were just as responsible as the lure of opportunities in the North for drawing them in large numbers to New York, Chicago, Philadelphia, Cleveland, and Detroit. A series of natural disasters, including a boll weevil epidemic and heavy flooding in Mississippi, combined with the exploitative labor system of Southern peonage and terrorism to drive black farmers into the arms of industrial labor recruiters. As masses of black rural Southerners fled to the cities, they were followed by members of the professional classes.[6] "In a real sense," observed Alain Locke, "it is the rank and file who are leading, and the leaders who are following."[7] He also noted that in the process of being transplanted the black masses were being transformed. They had more money in their pockets and were caught up in the spiral of rising expectations; their experiences became more diversified, and they became involved more intimately with whites and competed with them more directly. Through exposure to urban educational and political institutions, they became involved in processes of assimilation that paralleled those of white ethnic groups. Leadership in the new urban centers was shared by ministers, professionals, well-paid servants, and artisans, increasingly joined by small businessmen, civil servants, racketeers, politicians, and colorful charlatans.[8]

A prime factor in increasing the confidence of black Americans was participation by black troops and officers in military action. The use of black troops in combat had met with marked resistance in the early days of the war, because white supremacists had rightly anticipated that military experience would inflame egalitarian expectations. When black troops returned from Europe, they brought with them not only a heightened sense of their personal worth but a sense of having earned a right to the privileges and responsibilities of first-class citizenship. Ironically, the summer after the armistice, black Americans found themselves in the midst of a new wave of lynching, burning, and urban terrorism. Segregation in government offices had been increased during the Wilson administration. Race riots flared up in numerous cities of the North and the Midwest. Reorganization of the Ku Klux Klan and a revival of lynching were characteristics of the 1920s.[9]

The conditions confronting black soldiers on their return to the United States were a bitter contrast to the rhetoric with which the nation had entered the war. Wilson had spoken of making the world safe for democracy. He depicted the war as a moral struggle and entered it with a righteous, crusading zeal. Indeed, it was Wilson's messianic foreign policy (albeit eclipsed during the 1920s) that set the stage for the nation's later adoption of its world savior image.[10] American perfectionism had traditionally been isolationist and based on the assumption that the nation must remain remote and uncontaminated in order to present a worthy example to Europe.[11] By the late nineteenth century, however, American foreign policy was becoming increasingly missionary. The chauvinistic doctrines of Josiah Strong, John Fiske, and Alfred T. Mahan were achieving popularity.[12] Their philosophy prepared the way for the messianism that would burgeon with the First World War and, after lying dormant between the wars, burst forth in the 1940s.

During the 1920s, of course, most Americans were eager to return to "normalcy" in foreign and domestic policy. They were uneasy with the premonition that involvement in the war had permanently altered America's world role. Black Americans, for their part, were quick to recognize that the wartime departure from normalcy had led to a welcome departure from normalcy in race relations. It would be to the advantage of the American Negro to encourage the nation's view of itself as a champion of democracy; for if the United States should embark on a career as savior of the world and hold itself up as an exemplar of a future world order, it must first perfect itself. This was to become a theme in the writings of black Americans during the 1920s as they retooled their rhetoric, attempting to take advantage of the dawning awareness of America's world leadership role.

The post-war view was thus linked both to the old Washingtonian covenant and to a new conception of the Negro's place in the modern world. Afro–Americans retained, in Mordecai Johnson's words, "the optimism of Booker T. Washington that in proportion as they grew in intelligence, wealth, and self-respect they should win the confidence and esteem of their fellow white Americans, and should gradually acquire the responsibilities of full American citizenship." This was what Johnson described as "The Faith of the American Negro." Unfortunately, as Johnson observed, events since the war had been of such a nature as to erode that faith. The post-war quest for normalcy had meant, in the case of black people, an attempt to reduce them once again to a state of peonage. As a result of post-war disillusionment, Johnson wrote, "the Negro's faith in the righteous purpose of the Federal Government has sagged. . . . All the colored people, in every section of the United States, believe that there is something wrong, and not accidentally wrong, at the very heart of the Government."[13]

Faith in America was related to faith in God, and Johnson spoke with the evangelist's usual concern for a waning of piety. "Some of our young men," he lamented, "are giving up the Christian religion, thinking that their fathers were fools to have believed it so long." These were being attracted to the radicalism of the left, with its denunciations of capitalism and revolutionary proletarian shibboleths. He noted the appearance of a second and larger group that had retained its belief in religion and democracy, "but not in the white man's religion, and not in the white man's democracy." He referred, of course, to the appearance of Garveyism, which aimed at laying "the foundations of a black empire, a black religion, and a black culture." True, the larger masses of the colored people did not accept these radical movements, retaining their belief in traditional religion and clinging to their patriotic sentiments. But they, too, were disillusioned and were "no longer able to believe with Dr. Booker T. Washington, or with any other man, that their own efforts after intelligence, wealth, and self-respect can in any wise avail to deliver them. . . ." At least, not without the support of a public policy grounded in "the faith and will of the whole American people." In an allusion to Washington's Atlanta Exposition address, he reminded a Harvard audience that black Americans had "cut our forests, tilled our fields, built our railroads," all with a simple faith and virtue. But they had reached a point where their faith could "no longer feed on the bread of repression and violence."[14]

In a vein reminiscent of the phrases of Garvey and Du Bois and prophetic of themes to arise in much twentieth-century black protest, he gave his message an international flavor. He reminded his audience that "the darker peoples of the earth [were] rising from their long sleep." What sort of message were we sending to them? Through Christian missionaries, we were exporting humanitarian platitudes. But how were the Christian nations demonstrating, by their actions, the power of Christianity to unite mankind in bonds of brotherhood?

America, of all nations, was "best prepared" to answer that question and to be a "moral inspiration," especially to the colored world, "for we have the world's problem of race relations here in crucible, and by strength of our American faith, we have made some encouraging progress in its solution." By solving its own racial problems, the United States would point the way to salvation for the larger world. The ultimate result of the struggle for racial equality would, hopefully, "place these United States in the spiritual leadership of all humanity."[15]

Another leader whose public statements implied a modification of the Washingtonian covenant was James Weldon Johnson. The following verses were a rephrasing, though slightly more assertive, of well-known lines from the Atlanta Exposition Address:

> This land is ours by right of birth,
>   This land is ours by right of toil;
> We helped to turn its virgin earth,
>   Our sweat is in its fruitful soil.[16]

When Washington reminded his audiences of the contributions his people had made to American life, he was simply calling on whites to exercise a spirit of fair play and a sense of appreciation. Johnson, on the other hand, was demanding justice based on rights that had been earned. From Johnson's perspective in the 1920s, it seemed that blacks had fulfilled their contract with white America. They had been true to the covenant delivered by Washington and applauded universally in the sight of God. Johnson retained the old faith in America's ability to fulfill its historic mission. True, there were some temporary obstacles to the perfection of American democracy, but these were not due to any basic flaws in the American system. The attitude of the South towards the black citizenry was an aberration—a betrayal of the constitution and the national will. Johnson believed "that the spirit in which American democracy was founded, though often turned aside and often thwarted, can never be defeated or destroyed but that ultimately it will triumph."[17]

Thus it was that the black American's role in the national culture was crucial. The ability of America to assimilate the Negro would stand as the ultimate proof of its manifest commitment to Christian democracy, for, as he said, "if democracy cannot stand the test of giving to any citizen who measures up to the qualifications required of others the full rights and privileges of American citizenship, then we had just as well abandon that democracy in name as in deed." According to the logic that tested America's fitness for world leadership based on her ability to deal fairly with the Negro, black Americans had a unique position in the modern world. For they were the touchstone of that democracy that was platitudinously regarded as "the most free and glorious . . . the world has ever seen." For Johnson, as for most of his peers, the black American stood "as the supreme test of the civilization, the Christianity and the common decency of the American people."[18]

Some black spokespersons—like Reverdy C. Ransom, a Christian socialist—adhered to the melting-pot ideal of Israel Zangwill. Black Americans were, in Ransom's view, to be only one of many components of an evolving American type. "Once the tides of immigration have ceased to flow to our shores," he wrote, "this nation will evolve a people who shall be one in purpose, one in spirit, one in destiny—a composite American by the commingling of blood."[19] Amalgamationism was a minority opinion; most leaders saw the mission of black America as a separate historical force at the core of American destiny. This had become the prevailing hope at the time of the Civil War, for in freeing the slaves, as William H. Lewis recalled, Americans had ensured the freedom of the entire nation. The special relationship of the Negro to the nation's mission had been noted by George Bancroft, observed Lewis. Bancroft had said, "It is in part to the aid of the Negro in freedom that the country owes its success, in its movement to regeneration—that the world of mankind owes the continuance of the United States as an example of a republic."[20]

Lewis observed that the American people, even in that period of supposed longing for isolationism, were "fast losing their provincial character." They were becoming "a great world power with interests and possessions upon every part of the globe." This had resulted in a certain obligation being settled upon them—the obligation of the self-proclaimed most-democratic government on earth to provide leadership to the rest of the world. And so Lewis prayed, "God grant to the American people this larger view of humanity, this greater conception of human duty."[21]

No one, of course, showed greater alacrity than Du Bois in recognizing the centrality of American race relations to the nation's mission and destiny. In *The Souls of Black Folk* (1903), he wrote of the black American:

> He would not Africanize America, for America has too much to teach the world and Africa. He would not bleach his Negro soul in a flood of white Americanism, for he knows that Negro blood has a message for the world. . . . Will America be poorer if she replace her brutal dyspeptic blundering with light-hearted but determined Negro humility? or her coarse and cruel wit with loving jovial good-humor? or her vulgar music with the soul of the Sorrow Songs? Merely a concrete test of the underlying principles of the great republic is the Negro Problem. . . .[22]

Also in that volume, he made his celebrated statement, "The problem of the Twentieth Century is the problem of the color-line."[23] He repeated the phrase twenty years later in his essay "Worlds of Color," where he argued that the greatest challenge facing the modern world was to remove from the darker nations the shadow of European colonialism.[24] Du Bois was among the first to recognize that, as the African and Asian nations arose and began to flex their muscles, they would demand a resolution of the color question, perhaps to the discomfort of America. But it seemed to Du Bois that the United States had a unique opportunity to lead in setting the pattern for ideal race relations, rather than being forced to accept reality at some future date. Unfortunately, conditions in the United States were of such a nature as to diminish, with the passage of years, his optimism concerning America's world mission. But at the peak of his career, during and immediately following World War I, Du Bois believed strongly in the power of black Americans to redeem the United States.

The relationship between America's sense of mission and the role of black people in the nation's moral and spiritual life was the chief concern of Du Bois' *The Gift of Black Folk* (1924). Here he presented the now familiar argument that American destiny was bound up with the color question. But the black presence in America had a more important function than to test the sincerity of American democratic ideals. The black population had actually contributed a leavening agent to the collective personality of the nation, keeping before it certain ideals that it sorely needed. He expressed these in effusively sentimental terms, reminiscent of Washington's Atlanta Exposition Address:

> They have nursed the sick and closed the staring eyes of the dead. They have given friendship to the friendless, they have shared the pittance of their poverty with the outcast and nameless; they have been good and true and pitiful to the bad and false and pitiless and in this lies the real grandeur of their simple religion, the mightiest gift of black to white America.[25]

America tended "to look upon position, self-assertion, determination to go forward at all odds as typifying the American spirit." Black people, on the other hand, had "brought to America a sense of humility which America never has recognized and perhaps never will." Descending deeper into a mood of bitterness that bordered on cynicism, Du Bois reverted again to the rhetoric of Booker T. Washington, describing "four million black slaves . . . dumbly but faithfully and not wholly unconsciously, protecting the mothers, wives, and children of the very white man who fought to make their slavery perpetual." Thus, in its final paragraphs, the book was to portray the black man as an Uncle Tom. The black woman was typified in the figure of "the Black Mammy, one of the most pitiful of the world's Christs." *The Gift of Black Folk* cast the black masses in the role of suffering servant, a counterbalance to the cocksure, unhesitating, self-righteous spirit of mainstream American messianism.[26]

Du Bois made frequent use of Christian myth throughout his early works. If this did not signify a faith in Christianity, it showed a belief in the power of its imagery to produce the desired response. It also implied a lingering faith in the Washingtonian covenant, the belief that an adherence to the Protestant ethic would solve the black American's problems. Although Du Bois became increasingly hostile to organized religion from his thirtieth year on, he continued to compose his own prayers and meditations. One example, "The Prayers of God," is a dramatic monologue in which a speaker, personifying the oppressive spirit of white supremacy, ponders his crimes, only half-perceiving that they are crimes. He embarks impulsively on crusade after crusade, without pausing to consider that his very crusading spirit has nearly destroyed the world. Flushed with enthusiasm and undiminished zeal, he hurries off to serve Christ once again and to carry on his self-appropriated destiny as savior of the universe.[27]

In the "Credo" of 1919, Du Bois professed in his fifty-first year at least an artistic, and perhaps an emotional, dependency on the religion of the New Testament:

> I believe in God, who made of one blood all nations that on earth do dwell. . . .
> I believe in Service—humble, reverent service, from the blackening of boots to the whitening of souls; for Work is Heaven, Idleness Hell, and Wage is the "Well done" of the Master. . . .
> I believe in the Devil and his angels. . . .
> I believe in the Prince of Peace. . . .
> Finally, I believe in Patience. . . .[28]

There was a general impatience with the Uncle Tom myth by the 1920s, but black spokesmen like W. E. B. Du Bois and James Weldon Johnson continued to utilize it whenever it seemed advantageous to do so. Even Marcus Garvey, despite his rejection of the variety of leadership represented by Du Bois and Johnson, found himself in company with them in utilizing the myth, for Garvey referred implicitly to the promise of Christ that the meek would inherit the earth. "The man lowest down will rotate to the top position," he once said; "it is the will of God because the black man is not vindictive, but benevolent and kind, the world will be a better place to live in and enjoy."[29] It was ironic that he should play on the myths so carefully cultivated by Stowe, Washington, and Du Bois, while denouncing "Uncle Toms." But Garvey, along with the traditional leadership, was still clinging to the myth of the old, suffering, Christlike Negro who had a mission to redeem the world.

Needless to say, such an interpretation of the usefulness of black people could not set well with everyone. Some black leaders felt that the essence of equality would be for their people to make exactly the same sort of contribution that other Americans made and to receive exactly the same sort of reward. Francis J. Grimke, a scholarly and influential Presbyterian minister of Washington, D. C., felt that black people had made and were still making valid contributions to American life and to world civilization: "We have had a part in this world-wide contest . . . our boys . . . have done their part in bringing about the great result." The condition of the entire world would be improved as a result of "this great struggle . . . because in the dominant nations a higher sense of justice, of right, of fair play, is going to be developed." He was angered by the treatment that had been dealt black America, even while her soldiers were fighting in Europe. Nonetheless, he believed that "God is getting ready for some great spiritual awakening—that He is getting ready to shake himself loose from this miserable semblance of Christianity that exists, and to set up in the earth a type of religion that will truly represent the spirit and teachings of Jesus Christ." This would lead to a millennial Kingdom of God on earth. "The super nation of the future," he called it—"The Commonwealth of Israel . . . God centered, meek and lowly, girded with strength, and arrayed in beautiful garments of righteousness." His hope was for the "better vision of things that . . . the prophets of old foresaw."[30] But Grimke's vision was perhaps more closely related to Woodrow Wilson's sense of mission than he would have cared to admit.

Grimke's increasing hostility to the Tuskegee school of race relations, coupled with a growing bitterness during the Wilson Presidency, has been interpreted by S. P. Fullinwider as approaching "the brink of racism."[31] Fullinwider's interpretation is not without validity, although perhaps he overstates his case. Grimke certainly seems to have abandoned the rhetoric of American messianism by 1922. By then, he was certainly not inclined to pander to American national chauvinism, nor was he obsessed with painting a picture of black people as super-patriots. His criticisms of America and of American Christianity were forceful, and he expressed an absolute certainty that the nation had "little or no interest in true democracy—in the rights of man as man." The United States was hardly more fit as a guardian of liberty than was Germany. "So far as making the world safe for white supremacy," said Grimke, "there is no difference, or very little, between the Central Powers and the allies." He made a very precise distinction between the nation's real reason for entering the war, which was to "save the world from the heel of the oppressor," for which it deserved credit, and its "pretended interest in making the world safe for democracy," for which it deserved no credit. Americans ought not to be insensible "of how far short as a nation we come when measured by the ideals of true democracy, and the great eternal principles of right and brotherhood."[32]

Rather than accusing Grimke of an increasing hostility to whites, I should think it more accurate to say that he was increasingly impatient with American hypocrisy. His bluntness increased with his impatience, until he referred to American Christianity as "the miserable apology that now goes under that name." In America and all the Christian nations, "the so-called Church of God has been recreant to its high trust . . . , dominated by . . . a cowardly and worldly spirit." He referred to the representative American as "the contemptible little type that we find here in America, assuming and acting upon the theory that under a white skin only is to be found anything worthy of respect."[33] Thus Grimke's position differed markedly from the attitude of conciliation adopted by Moton, who seemed to feel that he could shame the United States into fairer policies by stating a childlike faith in its benevolence.

Grimke criticized, by implication, the position Du Bois had taken during the World War, when in his essay "Close Ranks" Du Bois had seemed to say that blacks should abate their efforts to secure their rights. Du Bois' essay had indeed been ambiguous, and when readers of the *Crisis* demanded he explain his position, his response was to list the benefits that had accrued to blacks as a result of their loyalty in the present war and in four other wars. But Du Bois never re-established his reputation with radical blacks like Hubert Harrison, who could not forget his having called on them to "forget our special grievances" and remember that "our own white fellow citizens and the allied nations . . . are fighting for democracy."[34] Nor could Grimke swallow this:

> It is astounding, almost incredible, that any colored man, even to the stupidest of them, should be led into such utter folly as to counsel the cessation of the struggle for our rights, even for a moment, when nothing is ever accomplished except by struggle, by earnest, persistent effort. The colored man, if he has an ounce of brains in his head, will have but one policy in regard to his rights, and that is the policy of being always on the job. Eternal vigilance is the price of liberty, and unless we are willing to pay the price, unless we are eternally vigilant, we will never get it. Let us hear no more of this nonsense, never mind from whom it comes, about letting up for a season.[35]

As a committed integrationist, Grimke directed his hostilities not so much towards whites as towards anyone who compromised on the issue of complete and immediate social equality. Although he certainly felt some hostility to whites, he attempted to keep it in check. Grimke claims that he became more compassionate and understanding of the problems of poor whites as he advanced in age. In 1910, he wrote:

> The time was when I used to speak of the cracker element of the South, as poor white trash; it is the manner in which many persons still speak of them, but I never do it any more. We have no right to call any human being, anyone who bears the image of God, however ignorant and degraded, trash.[36]

Grimke showed little consistent interest in endowing black people with the sentimental brand of superiority associated with Stowe's Uncle Tom. He was neither a hater of white people nor a racial chauvinist. The black nationalism that one finds in his writings is of a purely practical variety, based on a grim, tough-minded commitment to making the best of things as they were. This did not imply an accommodation to segregation as it did in the case of Booker T. Washington or William Hooper Councill.[37] Grimke had nothing but contempt for their disavowal of pretensions to social equality. He faced segregation in a spirit of Christian endurance, just as he was forced to face the other sins of the world.

Segregation was a fact of life, which he forthrightly and unequivocally opposed; but at the same time, he recognized that "for years to come . . . whether the Negro wants to remain a separate and distinct people in this country or not, the simple fact is he cannot help himself":

> . . . as a race we are to sink or swim, live or die, survive or perish together. We can't get away from each other. Never mind what progress I, as an individual may make, never mind how intelligent or wealthy I may become, the social laws and customs that operate against the Negro as a class, will operate against me. His fate will be my fate. We are all classed together, and are treated alike, whatever our condition,—rich or poor, high or low, educated or uneducated. . . . Our fate is one. We rise or fall together. Such being the case, our duty is to recognize that fact, and in the light of it to pull together for the common good.[38]

Grimke saw black Americans as a nation within a nation, and like many of his contemporaries he drew comparisons between the history of the Jews and that of his own people. Now, it is a well-known fact that some of the slave songs and many of the sermons of the grass-roots preachers during the nineteenth century had made comparisons between the plight of black Americans and that of the Hebrew children in bondage. Grimke, however, with his characteristic love of order and formality, explored the analogy in great detail in his 1902 address, "A Resemblance and a Contrast Between the American Negro and the Children of Israel in Egypt, or the Duty of the Negro to Contend Earnestly for his Rights Guaranteed under the Constitution." Grimke argued that, although Afro–Americans were a nation in bondage as surely as ever the ancient Hebrews, talk of their making a mass exit was impractical. While he saw black Americans as moving inevitably towards assimilation in the distant future, for the time being he encouraged collective consciousness with an eye to independent interests.[39] For Grimke, racial feeling was almost entirely a matter of practical politics. He had little time for discussing the high-flown theories of national destiny that had dominated the thinking of his nineteenth-century contemporaries, and he was no more attuned to the newer versions of secular black messianism espoused by a younger generation of black leaders.

The new generation of intellectual leaders that arose in black America during the 1920s tended to view the black mission in somewhat more secular terms than had the leaders of the nineteenth century. True, Marcus Garvey and his coterie of journalists, literati, and ministers of the Gospel adhered to the mystical Ethiopianist tradition. But the artists and intellectuals whose names were most frequently associated with the "Harlem Renaissance" or the "New Negro Movement" tended to think in secularist terms. The contribution of black Americans was seen as cultural and artistic by the new spokespersons. Although this did not preclude the old concern with moral and spiritual contributions, it provided a new emphasis that was not so dependent on Christian tradition—or at least not consciously so. Alain Locke, while claiming to reject old stereotypes, still characterized the gifts of black folk as "a leaven of humor, sentiment, imagination and tropic nonchalance."[40] This smacked suspiciously of the exotic primitivism popularized in Vachel Lindsay's "The Congo". As Sterling Brown observed, the Harlem Renaissance stereotype of the exotic primitive was akin to that of the contented slave: "One is merely a 'jazzed-up' version of the other, with cabarets supplanting cabins, and Harlemized 'blues,' instead of the spirituals and slave reels."[41]

The cultural messianism of the Harlem Renaissance was concerned with demonstrating that the black subculture, like the lyrics of its jazz and blues songs, was straightforward, uninhibited, and reflective of life in a way that white popular culture was not. The proponents of jazz-age culture thus argued that the contribution of black people to white America would be to add a new dimension to life. The New Negro Movement attempted to exploit the sense of a religious conversion experience that many young whites felt on first hearing jazz. The movement represented an effort to capitalize on the belief of many whites that black life represented "cultural freedom—the ability to be and express themselves, the sense of being natural."[42] All of these ideas had been associated with the African personality since the heyday of the slave trade and had developed partially in justification of it. Africans were libidinous devil-apes, driven by base instincts and thus incapable of creating civilization.[43] By the late eighteenth century, however, emotional religion, the cult of sensibility, and the myth of the noble savage were beginning to contribute to a new image of the Negro.[44] By the time of Harriet Beecher Stowe, it was possible to idealize blacks for their "childlike simplicity" and "closeness to nature." In the post-Freudian climate of the 1920s, myths that had once served to demonstrate black inferiority were reinterpreted to signify cultural and mental health.[45] Whites were infatuated with an image of black folkways that they had created themselves. They now looked to their own manufactured image of the Negro to provide an antidote to the once-fashionable Victorian morality with which the white middle class had become bored.

Not all whites perceived blacks in this way, to be sure. Melville Herskovits argued in 1925 that black Americans were little different from white Americans and that the values, aspirations, and cultural norms of Harlemites were no different than those of Anglo–American

New Yorkers.[46] By the mid-1930s, of course, he had reversed his position to advocate the belief that American society could never deal justly with its black population until it recognized that African culture was a prime determinant of their behavior.[47] Albert C. Barnes, who contributed an article to Alain Locke's *The New Negro*, was more typical of whites who were fascinated by things black. He placed great importance on the "psychological complexion of the Negro as he inherited it from his primitive ancestors and which he maintains to this day." The traits to which he referred were, of course, "his tremendous emotional endowment, his luxuriant and free imagination and a truly great power of individual expression." Barnes perceived the gift of black folk, as others had, in the tradition of Stowe, Washington, and Du Bois. He had a contribution to make to "our arid, practical American life," because of his closeness to "the ideal of man's harmony with nature." Barnes' view of the black racial mission did not differ substantially from the Christian racial romanticism of *Uncle Tom's Cabin*. The Negro was still "the simple, ingenuous, forgiving, good-natured, wise and obliging person that he has been in the past, [and] he may consent to form a working alliance with us for the development of a richer American civilization to which he may contribute his full share."[48]

White musicians of the so-called "Jazz Age" probably took the idea more seriously than any other group in America. Lawrence Levine has argued convincingly that many white musicians underwent "what amounted to conversion experiences" or spoke of jazz "as if it were a new religion." Many whites saw the jazz culture as "a collective nose thumbing at all pillars of all communities, one big syncopated Bronx cheer for the righteous squares everywhere. Jazz was the only language they could find to preach their fire-eating message." Obviously, what the young whites were looking for was something quite at odds with the cultural programs of Du Bois and Garvey. Whites were making a quasi-religion of black emotionalism, while many black elders longed for the stately theological historicism of the nineteenth century. They viewed jazz with suspicion, much as they viewed the mindless emotionalism of the storefront church. They believed that art, like religion, should provide something more than orgasmic relief.[49]

For the white negrophiles, black culture was valid only insofar as it was an act of anarchy, an escape from the repression that white middle-class society seemed to represent. But many black leaders—especially Du Bois and Garvey—saw art and culture as means for inculcating heroic virtues and Spartan seriousness.[50] Du Bois' taste in music ran to Wagner, whose German operas were being used to reinforce the values of a rising nationalism.[51] Garvey liked patriotic marches, fit to stir the hearts of warriors and, more importantly, make them move in time to a martial cadence.[52] Inasmuch as these sorts of values were exactly what Negroes needed (and still need), one can readily understand the position of the two major black nationalists of the period—they were justifiably hostile towards whites who encouraged tendencies to self-indulgence and moral looseness, represented by the cabaret.

Thus the champions of a heroic black art did not limit their invective to jazz; they seethed with rage when Carl Van Vechten published *Nigger Heaven* in 1926. Du Bois denounced the book as an unbalanced treatment of black life that emphasized only its sordid and sensational aspects. The fact that Van Vechten was white may have had something to do with his bitterness; but Du Bois was almost as hostile to Claude McKay's *Home to Harlem* (1928), which he found nauseating "and after the dirtier parts of its filth I feel distinctly like taking a bath." He believed that McKay was guilty of catering to "that prurient demand on the part of white folk for a portrayal in Negroes of that utter licentiousness which conventional civilization holds white folk back from enjoying—if enjoyment it can be called." What provoked Du Bois to dismiss McKay's novel in this way remains something of a mystery, for his own novel, *Dark Princess*— published the same year—was even more irreverent with respect to bourgeois morality. One of the reasons seems to be that Du Bois saw McKay as pandering to the desire of whites to vicariously experience "drunkenness, fighting, lascivious sexual promiscuity and utter absence of restraint" through the Negro. This was hardly Du Bois' conception of the cultural mission of Afro–Americans. However, many whites were not only surprised but indignant when blacks attempted to contribute anything other than exotic primitivism to American culture.[53]

Marcus Garvey saw the attention paid to *Home to Harlem* as part of a conspiracy by white publishers to use black writers as contributors to their own racial defamation. He viewed McKay as a "literary prostitute," ironically grouping Du Bois, Walter White, James Weldon Johnson, and Eric Waldrond with him in this category. There can be no denying that white publishers, artists, and intellectuals were using black artists, but Garvey misinterpreted their motives. They were not so much concerned with the intentional denigration of black culture as with asserting their dissatisfaction with white bourgeois culture. They sincerely believed that black people were making a contribution to American life by helping to divest it of its neuroses and hypocrisies.[54]

Alain Locke attempted to synthesize the older and the newer views of the black contribution to American culture. In his introduction to *The New Negro*, Locke spoke of the black man's "social patience" and the "gift of his folk temperament." As already noted, he accepted the myths of black emotionalism, imagination, and "tropic nonchalance," traits which he asserted had "gone into the making of the South from a humble, un-acknowledged source."[55] Although he disagreed with the burden of Albert Barnes' discussion of black art in *The New Negro* and rejected his assertion that its peculiarities were African in origin, he did not deny the existence of these peculiarities.[56] He believed in the spontaneity and earthiness of black culture as it was presented in *Home to Harlem*. For Locke, the book represented "Negro peasant life transposed to the city and the modern mode, but still vibrant with a clean folkiness of the soil instead of the decadent muck of the city-gutter." As for the attitudes of the white artistic community towards black culture, this was to be seen as "a tribute to the deeper human qualities of black humanity."[57]

The idea that black Americans had a singular contribution to make to American life grew out of the myth of black emotionalism and sensuality. It was therefore not surprising that the black writer and educator Benjamin Brawley held it as self-evident that "the Negro is a thoroughgoing romanticist . . . destined to reach his greatest heights in the field of the artistic."[58] Some black Americans protested against this idea, considering it "the Negro-Art Hokum." George Schuyler considered it stereotyping of the crudest sort. In his view, "the Aframerican [was] merely a lamp-blacked Anglo–Saxon." There was no such thing as a peculiarly "Negro" contribution to American life; even the spirituals and the blues were to be understood as "American folk-songs, built around Anglo–Saxon religious concepts." Black Americans were, in Schuyler's extreme integrationist view, Americans pure and simple. The only thing that set them apart from other Americans was that they had the misfortune to be discriminated against on the basis of color. There were no particular cultural traits that set them apart, no "fundamental, eternal, [or] inescapable differences."[59]

The Harlem Renaissance spokesmen were certainly not given to denying their Americanness, and indeed there is validity in the retrospective opinion of Robert Hayden that the movement's thrust was basically integrationist.[60] The dominant tendency among black artists and intellectuals of the 1920s was, in Alain Locke's view, a "forced attempt to build . . . Americanism on race values."[61] Most of his peers would have joined him in rejecting the idea of "one way for the Negro and another way for the rest." What most of them seemed to hope for was fulfillment of the American dream. They would encourage black Americans to assert their Africanness, and thus contribute to the nation's world mission in the way that only they could. Locke judged, perhaps accurately, that black Americans stood in a particularly advantageous position to act as a bridge between the United States and the emerging power of the darker world:

> Garveyism may be a transient, if spectacular, phenomenon, but the possible role of the American Negro in the future development of Africa is one of the most constructive and universally helpful missions that any modern people can lay claim to.[62]

It is ironic that Locke should have referred to Garveyism, for Garvey was conspicuously absent from the roster of black spokesmen contributing to *The New Negro*. Locke showed a distinct preference for the Pan–Africanism of Du Bois over that of Garvey, describing the former's Pan–African conferences as "under American auspices and backing."[63] In 1924, the Pan–Africanism of Du Bois was merged, at least temporarily, with United States foreign policy when he accepted a special ambassadorship to Liberia. At this point his Pan–Africanism, like the cultural pseudo-nationalism of Alain Locke and the ethnic contributionism of Robert Russa Moton, became subsumable under integrationist doctrine.[64] They were complementary aspects of the belief that the function of black Americans was to work at the core of American consciousness and to assist the nation in fulfilling the promise of democracy. In this way they would contribute to the larger evangelical mission of America, and assist the nation in spreading its doctrine to the rest of the world.

But not all black Americans found an outlet for their evangelical impulses in the racial contributionism advocated by Du Bois, Moton, and Locke. Black nationalists could not be content with a view of the Afro–American destiny as a mere element of the larger American mission. For the extreme nationalists, there could be no compromise with Americanism. Garveyism represented an entirely different view of black American destiny. The Reverend R. R. Porter wrote in *Negro World*, the official Garvey newspaper, that its founder had "given the world a new religion," and compared Garvey to Jesus and Gautama:

> To me true Garveyism is a religion which is sane, practical, inspiring and satisfying; it is of God, hence a devout Garveyite cannot deny the existence of God, but sees God in you [me] and the world. He knows God because he is part of God, and is assisting in the making of the kingdom of God on earth.[65]

The following chapter deals with Garveyism, the Afro–American's alternative to participation in the world mission of the United States and the most important expression of the black messianic spirit in the 1920s.

8

Marcus Garvey: The Resurrection of the Negro and the Redemption of Africa*

Although he publicized his movement as the wave of the future, Marcus Garvey owed a great deal to nineteenth-century American religious traditions, and there is some merit in Randall K. Burkett's argument that Garvey's was a religious movement.[1] Although he denied ever having set himself up as a black Moses or a messiah (which is possibly true), Garvey was incapable of organizing a purely secular political movement and insisted upon a religious tie. His attacks on Father Divine in *The Black Man* issues of July 1935, December 1935, and September–October 1936, which are discussed in a later chapter, were prompted by more than jealousy towards the man who had stolen a few of his less steadfast followers. Garvey's religious sensibilities were offended.

E. Franklin Frazier once suggested that Garvey's movement was more religious than political.[2] I believe that Frazier's observation was an intelligent one, and I must confess my opposition to that uncritical adulation of Garvey that gives credence to Frazier's claim. My criticism of Garvey is not an attack on Pan–Africanism or black nationalism; but I wish to separate myself from those who seem to feel that modern Pan–Africanism can be attributed to Garvey's single-handed efforts. It is dangerous to unquestioningly accept statements made by Garvey in his attempts to discredit rivals for leadership in the black community. By the same token, one should view with suspicion the claims of Garvey rivals with respect to the motives, methods, and sincerity of Garvey. One must avoid too hastily assuming that his success in capturing the leadership of

*This chapter is based on an article published ten years ago in *The Black Scholar*. In its present form it represents a revision of my earlier views resulting from significant developments in Garvey scholarship during the past decade.

the masses was proof of his legitimacy. Indeed, the same may be said of Daddy Grace and Prophet Jones, but where did they lead them? Was Garvey really responsible for creating the black nationalist feeling of the 1920s, or did he simply mobilize the existing black nationalism that had lain dormant in the black community since Alfred C. Sam's abortive back-to-Africa scheme a few years before Garvey's arrival in the United States?[3]

The qualified success of the Garvey movement suggests that most black communities in 1919 contained substantial numbers of persons inclined to accept black nationalism as a solution to their problems. It has been suggested by W. E. B. Du Bois, John Henrik Clarke, and others that the disillusionment of the black masses after the failure of the Garvey movement led to a cynicism about Garvey that was later transferred to black nationalism in general.[4] This same sense of disillusionment affected the small businessmen and the petit bourgeois intellectuals who provided leadership in black organizations. Then, during the black-power phase of the civil rights movement, there was a revival of interest in Garvey's movement which was characterized by a blindness to his personal faults and ideological shortcomings. A messiah who has been dead for twenty-five years is more appealing than a live one.

Garvey has been mythologized as "a man of the people," by which we usually mean a leader who is justified in terms of his appeal to a representative number of the common folk or at least to a representative sampling. We also imply that he understands those people and that his experiences are similar to those of the people he claims to represent. Garvey conforms to these standards as well as most black leaders of the period, but no better. He was born into somewhat better circumstances than the average black Jamaican in 1887, the son of a fairly prosperous stonemason who "always acted as if he did not belong among the villagers."[5] The senior Marcus Garvey was a morose and solitary man, but he was not totally anti-social; he was a member of a Wesleyan congregation presided over by a white man. It was among the four children of this white minister and the five children of another white man, whose property adjoined that of the Garveys, that young Marcus found his first playmates. The early years were unmarred by any knowledge of racial prejudice, says Garvey: "The little white girl whom I liked most knew no better than I did myself. We were two innocent fools who never dreamed of a race feeling and problem." Then, around the age of fourteen, he had an experience that seems to have been typical for late nineteenth-century black youth—the little daughters of the Wesleyan minister were forbidden to play with him, and the one he liked most called him a nigger. W. E. B. Du Bois describes a similar incident in his own childhood.[6]

In later life Garvey claimed he "had no regrets," but his life-long obsession with intermarriage would seem to indicate that this experience, coming as it did at the age of sexual awakening, was a very traumatic one. Garvey continued to play with white boys until maturity, when they rejected him. Clearly, his religious and social experiences up to that point were not atypical, especially when compared to those of North American black boys, whether in the South or in the emerging ghettoes of the North.

Garvey worked for several years as a printer and a journalist, and gained experience as an orator and a union organizer. From 1912 to 1913, Garvey was in London, becoming acquainted with the Egyptian nationalist Duse Mohammed Ali, reading in the London libraries, and possibly attending college. But Garvey's education, like that of most black intellectuals, was mostly the result of independent study. Even W. E. B. Du Bois and Carter G. Woodson gained that knowledge for which they were most famous as a result of their own efforts and not in the college classroom. Garvey's attempts to discredit black intellectuals by referring to their formal education is interesting in view of his own assertion that he had far more formal education than the vast majority of New World black men.[7]

The details of Garvey's early life should make us ask just what we are talking about when we call him a man of the people. He was one only in the sense that he had many followers who were of the people; but he was very different than they, since he had experienced a great deal of social contact with white people, both in church and in his integrated school. He was born a member of the petit bourgeois class, and enjoyed cultural, economic, and educational advantages that few of his black contemporaries were privileged to know. During his childhood, his home was dominated by a strong father who was prosperous and self-educated, although there is some doubt as to what the relationship was between Garvey and his father.

If, as has been said, Garvey was the "first mass leader" (and it is true that he organized larger numbers of ordinary black people than anyone up to his time), one must ask how he accomplished this. The observations of Frazier and Burkett lead one to believe that his methods were typically American, both in their evangelical quality and in their appeal to what Robert Bellah calls "civil religion."[8] Frazier felt that Garveyism provided the sort of utopian escapism that characterizes much of the thinking in mass religious fantasies. Burkett sees Garvey as attempting to create an official religious justification for the aims and destiny of the black nation.

Garvey, although he was a West Indian, grasped with a shrewd quickness the essentially American beliefs that had lain dormant in the semiconscious reaches of the black mass imagination. He appealed to them in terms of mainstream American ideas, utilizing the methods of a Billy Sunday and preaching a black version of the doctrines of Josiah

Strong. Needless to say, he also had antecedents and counterparts among black Americans. He was neither the first nor the last in a series of leaders of his kind, and demographic circumstances provided him with followers well primed with just the sort of enthusiasm that his doctrine could ignite.

The dominant pattern of black mass behavior from 1876 to 1925 was migration (and enthusiasm for migration) out of the Old South Black Belt. The rhetoric of this migration was often reminiscent of ante-bellum black nationalism, with its talk of escape from the land of bondage and quest for a promised land. Migration and migrationist sentiment during these years usually fell into one of the three following patterns:

1. Westward migration from the South to the Southwest, which was characterized by the setting up of all-black towns in Kansas and Oklahoma. The best-known leader associated with this movement was Benjamin "Pap" Singleton, who styled himself "The Moses of the Colored Exodus." As Nell Painter has shown, the aged Singleton represented a variety of leadership much influenced by the millenarian expectations of the unlettered peasantry to whom it appealed. Singleton was associated with the most feverishly irrational and messianic strain in the Kansas exodus during its peak years, and claimed in 1878 to be responsible for the relocation of 7,432 black people in Kansas. Throughout the decade of the seventies, he traveled through Tennessee and Kentucky, urging black people to migrate to the Kansas colonies, as they were called.

Herbert Aptheker has objected to the emphasis on Singleton, whom he considers an unrepresentative and minor figure, and has stressed the role of the populist Henry Adams. Adams was one of the organizers of an investigatory committee functioning throughout the South and Southwest during the 1870s. Their purpose was to investigate living conditions among black people and to petition the federal government for aid in establishing a colony either in the territories of the United States or in Africa.[9]

Another leader, also similar to Singleton in his migrationism if not his prophetic characteristics, was Edwin P. McCabe, who was associated with the "Great Black March Westward" during the 1890s.[10] This Oklahoma migration was climaxed by the establishment of some twenty-five all-black communities. McCabe hoped to see Oklahoma become an all-black state, and his organization planned to distribute black voters in such a way as to create a majority in each congressional and senatorial district.

2. Migration in the form of a "back-to-Africa movement," which began with a Liberian exodus in 1878 when 206 people left from Charleston, South Carolina. More were apparently interested in leaving, but the company went bankrupt before a second trip could be made. The back-to-

Africa movement continued throughout the late 1800s and early 1900s and produced two great leaders, Chief Alfred C. Sam and Bishop Henry McNeal Turner, both of whom have been subjects of recent studies.[11] Both Turner and Sam were actively involved in persuading black folk to return to Africa, but neither was able to actually relocate any large number. Their organizations were responsible for the repatriation of some five hundred blacks, although their resources were more modest than Garvey's and Garvey repatriated none. Also, unlike Garvey, both Turner and Sam made trips to Africa themselves.

As has been demonstrated elsewhere, the messianic quality of Turner's movement was readily observable. Turner was an exact contemporary of Edward Wilmot Blyden, with whom he shares much of the credit for keeping the philosophy of Pan–Africanism alive during the years before Garvey. Although Blyden and Turner did not always agree on the subject of African repatriation, they respected one another. This respect existed despite the fact that Turner was a mulatto, and Blyden was not fond of mulattoes. But the two Pan-Africanists were certainly in agreement as to the messianic destiny of the black race and the need for black people in all lands to work towards fulfillment of the prophecy that Ethiopia would soon arise and spread her noble wings.[12]

As for Chief Sam, he too had ties to the Ethiopianists. One of his agents in Oklahoma was Orishatukeh Fadumah, a Yale-educated Hebrew scholar who served as spiritual adviser on board Chief Sam's ship. Fadumah had been associated with the American Negro Academy and with William H. Ferris, one of its members.[13] He shared with many black theologians of the nineteenth century a mystical historicism which predicted that the African race was soon to embark on its destined heroic mission. Thus, his migrationism must be understood within the context of black messianic traditions. One need not deny the valid assertion of Herbert Aptheker that migrationism was a realistic response to oppressive conditions to recognize the elements of mysticism that permeated its rhetoric. Migration before the First World War was caused by political and economic forces, but was not unrelated to religion.

3. Migration in the direction of the cities. This brand of migration picked up sharply during World War I and resulted in a number of large black urban ghettoes in the North for the first time in United States history. It was to these people, newly arrived from the South and not yet accustomed to urban ghetto life, that Garvey appealed. Garvey was able to exploit the fact that large numbers of Southern blacks, used to thinking in terms of traveling to a promised land, were migrating to Harlem.[14]

Never before had a black migrationist leader had such a large and yet compact community upon which to draw. Singleton, Turner, and Sam had never been able to find such a ready-made, large audience of black people; they were handicapped by the fact that black people were distributed over a broad Black Belt across the South. However, black New York in 1920 had a population of 152,467 (still rapidly growing), and Garvey discovered—did not create—a nationally minded community, accustomed to the rhetoric of black Christian nationalism. In a sense, Garvey, his followers, and W. E. B. Du Bois were very similar—all were romantic racialists in the tradition of Bishop Turner, Alexander Crummell, and Edward Wilmot Blyden. It is also interesting to note their predilection for messianic Christian rhetoric.

The romantic black racialism of the nineteenth century has been the subject of much recent discussion.[15] The romantic nationalists were Garvey's philosophical forefathers, just as the migration leaders were his political precursors. Among them were such figures as Martin R. Delany, Edward Wilmot Blyden, James T. Holly, Alexander Crummell, William H. Ferris, Booker T. Washington, and, ironically, W. E. B. Du Bois.

The scholarly Blyden, perhaps the most impressive of these figures, became involved in the Pan–African movement—some say he founded it—in the late nineteenth century. Born on St. Thomas in 1832, he was, like Garvey, a West Indian. He emigrated to the United States in 1850 and to Liberia in 1852. Blyden made several tours of the United States—one in 1862 along with Alexander Crummell, who was at the time a Liberian colonist; and another in 1889–1890, during which he preached the doctrine that God had assigned a portion of the earth to each race. He also argued that racial separation was the will of God. Blacks were not necessarily a master race, but each race was a chosen people with its own superiority and it was the duty of the blacks to find their area of excellence. While encouraging educated and talented blacks to migrate to Liberia, Blyden did not encourage a mass exodus.[16] Garvey, too, would argue that only the better class of blacks should be allowed to migrate to Africa. Blyden had been a successful orator in the southern United States, and Edwin S. Redkey has argued that he had more than a little influence on the masses of black folk in that area, who on several occasions were cruelly hoaxed by an imposter claiming to be the popular African orator.[17] This false "Blyden" traveled throughout Arkansas, taking advantage of the mass sentiment for emigration to line his pockets.[18] It should be apparent, then, that Garvey preserved and popularized a variety of black thought that had been popular with the masses since the end of Reconstruction. Garvey was really a throwback; the patterns of his black nationalism echoed nineteenth-century Ethiopian millennialism.

By the mid-1920s, the impact of urban migration was already apparent; it was leading to the so-called Harlem Renaissance and the New Negro Movement. The year 1925 would see the publication of Alain Locke's *The New Negro,* in which appeared the pronouncement that "something beyond the watch and guard of statistics [had happened] in the life of the American Negro." Black intellectuals would begin to abandon the old religious mysticism that had dominated nineteenth-century black nationalism. They would begin to interpret the black character in terms of the urban ghetto experience. The conflict between the old and the new conceptions of black nationalism can be seen in Claude McKay's *Home to Harlem*. In this novel, Jake, a good-natured army deserter who lives for the moment and chases his little brown girls, represents the new urban ghetto hero. Jake is contrasted with Ray, a Haitian nationalist in the Blyden-DuBois-Garvey tradition. Ray tells Jake stories of Haiti and of its black liberator, Toussaint, and Jake sits, "like a big eager boy," listening for a while but soon returning to his Jazz-Age pastimes.[19]

It is well-known that Garvey and W. E. B. Du Bois quarreled violently. Du Bois had been somewhat restrained in his attacks on Washington twenty years earlier, perhaps because Washington was not inclined to practice indiscreet mudslinging. But Garvey was just as capable as Du Bois of public vituperation, and the two of them descended together into a pragmatic contradiction of the very spirit of black unity to which they paid lip service. Garvey was, as Crummell and Blyden had been, hostile to mulattoes; and he attempted to inflame prejudices against lighter-complexioned Negroes. On one occasion he described a vast mulatto conspiracy that had "defeated the whites in the tropics and brought them to terms." He argued that the "Du Bois school" mulatto conspiracy was "winning out in America":

> The men of the Du Bois school have succeeded in getting the ear of the Republican government and leading Republican politicians of the country, to the extent that they can get anything done from the White House to the Department of Labor. They can get one of their group appointed an assistant attorney general, ambassador extraordinary, or demand and get the dismissal of any white government employee, . . . or they can have imprisoned anyone they desire.[20]

Garvey maintained that Du Bois and all other members of the National Association for the Advancement of Colored People (NAACP) advocated "amalgamation or general miscegenation."[21] Although his attitude toward white women bordered at times on polite contempt, Du Bois opposed anti-miscegenation laws, which he referred to as policies to "encourage prostitution and degrade women of Negro descent." In a 1925 *Crisis* editorial on "Intermarriage" he said, "Decent custom in all civilized communities compels the scoundrel who seduces a girl to marry her no matter what race she belongs to. . . . The whole South refuses to black girls any adequate protection."[22] Blacks who criticized the Southern sexual code during the years under consideration—like Sutton

Griggs and W. E. B. Du Bois—did so on humanitarian grounds or because they wished to bring black women under the protection of the law. Those who opposed reform usually did so for opportunistic reasons, because they hoped to garner white support. Intermarriage was an issue of far greater interest to whites than to blacks, who were usually inclined to conservatism on this issue which did not affect most of them directly. Concepts such as social equality and integration were often purposefully misinterpreted by whites, and black people would sometimes allow such matters to drop rather than be accused of an interest in whites as sexual partners. Black nationalists in Garvey's tradition often mask their fear of confrontation behind a rhetoric of racial chauvinism. Intermarriage is a red herring, often dragged out to confuse issues by those who are too fearful or too cynical to confront the issues of segregation and inequality.

The conflict between Du Bois and Garvey was not, in any case, a war between the forces of integration and black nationalism. Such an interpretation has prevailed despite the attempts of Harold Cruse to clarify the issue by showing Du Bois' link to the Pan–African tradition of the nineteenth century.[23] As Garvey well knew, Du Bois' hostility was partly the jealous reaction of a rival megalomaniac, for throughout the years he spent with *Crisis* Du Bois supported a similarly grandiose Ethiopianism in spite of the hostility of some factions of the NAACP to the movement. Du Bois' chief function with the Association was not to promote intermarriage, but to edit *Crisis*, the "official" organ. During the twenty-four years of his editorship, however, *Crisis* editorials were more the voice of Du Bois than the voice of the NAACP. Du Bois was able to function with such autonomy because of the tremendous popularity of *Crisis* with the masses of black Americans. The journal was self-supporting until the beginning of the Depression, which caused the journal to become dependent on the NAACP; and at this time Du Bois' enemies were able to force his resignation. By then, of course, he had quarreled with Walter White and with other members of the Association because of his support of racial separation in some instances where he felt it would be advantageous for black people. But Garvey, as will be seen in a later chapter, was unconvinced of his sincerity.

Garvey's attacks on Du Bois were generally dishonest and more emotional than Du Bois' attacks on Garvey. To be sure, Du Bois did call Garvey a "little, fat, black man; ugly, but with intelligent eyes and a big head." However, that will not support Garvey's claim that Du Bois hated black skin. Du Bois did not say that black people were ugly, and anyone who has read Chapter IV of his *Souls of Black Folk*, in which he describes the deep-brown and midnight beauty of children in an all-black schoolhouse, cannot misinterpret him in this way.[24]

Du Bois, to be sure, showed singular lack of imagination in his response to Garvey. There were several points on which the two could have agreed. Both were racial mystics with a flair for showmanship and pageantry. They recognized the need to develop a black journalism, artistic tradition, and mode of religious mythology. Both saw the need to encourage militant nationalism in Africa. But Du Bois was so tortured by jealousy that he was not able to maintain even the public semblance of solidarity with Garveyist Pan–Africanism, and so he came to contradict his own philosophy of universal racial solidarity. If Du Bois had maintained the appearance of cooperation with Garvey, he would have been one of several black intellectuals who did so. Not every Garvey sympathizer and fellow traveler endorsed his excesses. Du Bois would not have been the only mulatto to exert influence within the movement by contributing occasional articles to *Negro World*.[25]

Garvey was an African redemptionist in the missionary tradition of Alexander Crummell, a mulatto-hating Ethiopian millennialist.[26] There can be no denying that Garvey talked about Africa and the African heritage a great deal, but that was quite a different thing from encouraging respect for Africa's indigenous cultures. His proposal for a united Africa was based on the imperial model of Victorian England. We know far too little about the attitudes of ordinary black Americans toward Africa from 1863 to the present to allow us to generalize about Garvey's impact on those attitudes. By the time Garvey made his appearance, black people might indeed have become ashamed of their African background; but the fact that the masses maintained a homing impulse from the end of Reconstruction to the time of Garvey should cause one to question this proposition. I do not think that Garvey consciously attempted to make all the black people of the world exactly like Europeans, but he certainly had more affinity for the pomp and tinsel of European imperialism than he did for black African tribal life, which some earlier black nationalists had praised.

When Garvey spoke of African glories, he referred to Northeast Africa, the Egyptians and the Ethiopians; because they, having built empires and raised temples, were considered civilized. The black people south of the Sahara were seldom mentioned, except in terms of their "Redemption." Even before World War I, some cultural Pan–Africanists had begun to acknowledge that "the real African need by no means resort to the rags and tatters of bygone European splendor. He has precious ornaments of his own, of ivory and plumes, fine plaited willow ware, weapons of superior workmanship."[27] But Garvey was either unaware of such arguments or unimpressed by them when he assumed his archducal raiment.[28] Although Garvey could, on occasion, be critical of European accomplishments—the development of "submarines to destroy life" and "liquid gas to outdo in the art of killing"—this was clearly sour grapes. Garvey admired Europe with her "armies and navies and men of big affairs."[29]

William H. Ferris, contributing editor to Garvey's newspaper, *Negro World*, a graduate of Yale, and one of several bourgeois intellectuals who occupied positions of prominence in the Universal Negro Improvement Association, had written in his sprawling work *The African Abroad* that "the Anglo–Saxon ideal of manhood and womanhood is the highest the world has yet seen, the highest that will ever be evolved in the history of the world."[30] Ferris, like Garvey, was a long-time admirer of Duse Mohammed Ali and a supporter of African independence. He revealed his hopes that Africa would soon develop a "civilization."[31] His dreams were fairly Garveyish, even as early as 1912, and Chapter 24 of *The African Abroad* was illustrated with photographs of the Sierra Leoneans, resplendent in their colonial regalia—again, Garveyish. In all fairness to Garvey, however, it should be remembered that most black nationalists up to his time tended to see black nationalism in very European terms.

While Garvey and Ferris were planning to reconstruct Africa on a Victorian model, Du Bois was calling the African village a "perfect human thing." In 1919, he wrote in *Darkwater* (which Garvey read) of the exemplary family life of the African tribe.[32] By this time, Du Bois was well on the way to developing his concept of African socialism; but Garvey's attitude toward African tribal life was essentially that of the old nineteenth-century redemptionists, black men like Lott Carey, who sailed to Liberia with Bibles and bullets to civilize the tribes.[33] Among the stated "Aims and Objects of Movement for Solution of Negro Problems" was the plan to "assist in civilizing the backward tribes of Africa" and to "promote a conscientious Spiritual worship among the native tribes of Africa."[34] For the work of promoting this "conscientious Spiritual worship," Garvey favored the African Orthodox Church and its primate, George Alexander McGuire.

Garvey's noblest effort was his attempt to support a black religion. One can only praise his effort to give black people a God in whose visage they might see their own reflected. It was certainly shrewd of him to try to utilize the religiosity of black people as a revolutionary force. Unfortunately, his attempt to appeal to the religious sentiment, which was at that time such an important factor in the lives of black people, opposed black religious traditions instead of making use of them. Garvey was at a disadvantage when trying to deal with black religion. He had little exposure to the black church, since he had been raised as a member of a white congregation, was attracted to high-church ritualism, and had experienced neither the varieties of Obi worship peculiar to the Caribbean nor the enthusiastic evangelism of the Black Belt. It is not surprising, then, that the religion his Association came to support was more Orthodox than African.

Garvey was not the first black nationalist leader to assert that God was on the black man's side, or even that God was black. Before the Civil War, there had been black preachers who felt that God was on the side of the slaves. Richard Allen, founder of the African Methodist Episcopal Church, and James T. Holly, a Protestant Episcopal clergyman, had described the slave revolts as judgments of God and the leaders of revolts as instruments of divine judgment, whom God had used to smite the hypocritical Christian slaveholders. David Walker and Henry Highland Garnet had argued that submission to slavery was a form of idolatry and a mortal sin. Josiah Henson came to fear that cooperation with slaveholders was unpardonable in the eyes of God.[35] Bishop Turner, the emigrationist, began in the 1890s to popularize the idea of a black God, saying:

> Every race of people since time began who have attempted to describe their God by words, or by paintings, or by carvings, or by any other form or figure, have conveyed the idea that the God who made them and shaped their destinies was symbolized in themselves, and why should not the Negro believe that he resembles God as much so as other people? We do not believe that there is any hope for a race of people who do not believe they look like God.[36]

And this, of course, was the same logic that Garvey used:

> Whilst our God has no color, yet it is human to see everything through one's own spectacles, and since the white people have seen their God through white spectacles, we have only now started out (late though it be) to see our God through our own spectacles.[37]

This insistence on a black God was a sign of mental health. Garvey clearly recognized an important aspect of black nationalist religiosity; but he ignored another that was equally important, for he rejected the traditional patterns of evangelical black folk religion and urged an orthodox, high-church Christianity. Perhaps this was due to that affinity for Roman Catholicism that Cronon attributes to Garvey. Whatever the reason, he appointed Archbishop McGuire as chaplain of the UNIA, thereby endorsing a faith that was, in the words of the official history of the African Orthodox Church, "a branch of the ONE, HOLY, CATHOLIC, and APOSTOLIC Church."[38] Garvey reached this decision after having encouraged the Black Jews under Rabbi J. Arnold Ford for several years. Considering the fact that Garvey had substantial support from black churchmen of established denominations, it is difficult to explain his affinity with groups that had only limited followings in the community. Perhaps because he was aware of the ambivalencies of traditional black religion, he felt a need for the official church of the UNIA to have a clean slate. He wanted a religion that would be free from any "Uncle Tom" associations. He also wanted a religion that would be entirely disassociated from storefront connotations, i.e., Holy Rollerism and the Holiness sects. Both Black Judaism and African Orthodoxy were clear in their opposition to excessive exuberance. As for Garvey's supporters in the more established denominations, they too were far removed from the storefront sweatboxes that have so often incubated characteristically black expressions of religious feeling.

In his discussion of black churchmen in the Garvey movement, Randall K. Burkett has established that there was a sizeable amount of support for the UNIA among the clergy. Nearly one-third of his sampling of ministers active in the UNIA were Baptist; almost one-third were Methodist; the rest came from the AOC and other denominations. The clergymen tended to be well-educated, and mulattoes were well-represented in their ranks.[39] This demonstrates the gap between Garvey's rhetoric and his practice, for UNIA leadership included many middle-class blacks and mulattoes. It also demonstrates that many of Garvey's harangues, including those on the worthlessness of the black church, cannot be interpreted as ideological manifestoes. They were emotional outbursts rather than policy statements.

Among the educated clergymen identified by Burkett in the movement was James Robert Lincoln Diggs, who had served as an administrator in several black colleges and universities. Diggs presided over the ceremony when Garvey married his second wife, Amy Jacques. During a period when Archbishop McGuire was alienated from Garvey, Diggs was Acting Chaplain General of the UNIA. Diggs was an ordained Baptist minister and received a Ph.D. in sociology from Illinois Wesleyan University at the age of forty. Diggs clearly thought of Garveyism as a messianic movement. He revealed this belief in his defense of the Black Star Line in a speech at Liberty Hall, the UNIA convention center:

> The voice of the Messiah calls on the nations of the earth to arise. . . . He is going to set . . . judgement on the earth by raising our station. Here is a man—here are men and women whom He is going to use in this noble purpose.
>
> Brethren, the gospel under the Messiah calls you. God speaks to you. Hear him; go forward; He shall lead you to victory. . . .
>
> I was born here, but I am not afraid to die in Africa . . . it was not until this man was called to our service that we ever dreamed of having ships. . . . We must have ships, if the vision of a philosopher called to our service and appointed by Jehovah and his son, the Messiah, will lead us on to victory.[40]

William Yancy Bell, a minister of the Colored Methodist Episcopal Church, held a Ph.D. in New Testament studies from Yale. His oration in Liberty Hall was notable for its messianic vision and Ethiopian rhetoric. "When it comes to the matter of Ethiopia's awakening and of Ethiopia's organization, you've simply got to hand it to Marcus Garvey," he said. "Christianity teaches us to equip ourselves for heroic racial endeavor, even at the price of personal comfort. 'Sell your coat and buy a sword.' Remembering that while yesterday Ethiopia grinned and endured, while today she smiles and strives, tomorrow, please God, she shall exult in glorious achievement."[41]

It seems obvious that in the provisional government of Africa there was to be little separation of church and state. Once, while debating the need "to unify the religious beliefs and practices of the entire Negro race," Garvey challenged his opponent: "You don't believe that there is a literal interpretation to Ethiopia stretching forth her hands unto God?" He believed that the prophecy could not be fulfilled so long as racial "confusion and chaos," symbolized by a "multiplicity of religious methods," prevailed. But religious unity was more easily debated than achieved. The problem of unity might easily have been achieved by keeping the UNIA a purely secular organization, but such an idea was apparently unthinkable to Garvey. He therefore appointed George Alexander McGuire as his Chaplain General, giving his implied approval to McGuire's churching of the movement. McGuire was responsible for developing a *Universal Negro Catechism* and appropriately nationalistic rituals for funerals and baptisms.[42]

The exact nature of the relationship between Archbishop McGuire, the African Orthodox Church (AOC), and the UNIA has not yet been fully determined. This is probably because the relationship was intentionally kept ambiguous during the early 1920s. The church clearly was not founded by Garvey; on this point, contemporary adherents are insistent. It was "organized" by McGuire as a black nationalistic expression of the one catholic and apostolic church. Although McGuire at one point denied that his church was still concerned with the issue of apostolic succession, this remained one of its prominent concerns. Several authorities have recently suggested that McGuire himself was the main link between the AOC and the UNIA.

As for McGuire, he was an Episcopal priest of noteworthy ability, born in Antigua on March 26, 1866. His relationship with Garvey was stormy, and he was once suspended from the UNIA. Apparently, McGuire had been attempting to organize an "Independent Episcopal Church" before the rise of Garvey, who made him chaplain of the UNIA in 1920. In organizing the AOC, McGuire was confronted by the dilemma of casting off white domination but at the same time securing "the ecclesiastical authority" so much desired. For years he was obsessed with being legitimately consecrated a bishop by one of the white Christian bodies— Anglican, Catholic, Orthodox—that claimed episcopal succession from apostolic times. McGuire approached Roman Catholic Cardinal Hayes and the Rt. Rev. William T. Manning, a bishop of the Protestant Episcopal

Church, both of whom rejected his appeal. Finally, Bishop Pere Vilatte of the American Catholic Church was willing to do the job on September 28, 1921.[43] The American Catholic Church (not to be confused with the Roman Catholic Church) did not accept the primacy of the Pope; they were a branch of the Greek Orthodox Church.

The monthly magazine of the AOC, *The Negro Churchman*, was sedate and restrained. Like many expressions of Garveyism, it was concerned with maintaining an aura of respectability. It was only occasionally political. On one occasion, McGuire protested the failure of the Protestant Episcopal Church to create a black bishopric in the United States, and expressed indignation at the practice of sending white bishops to Haiti and Liberia.[44] On another occasion, there was an unsigned article tracing the episcopal succession of the AOC from the first Bishop of Antioch to Archbishop McGuire.

The AOC retained its obsession with orthodoxy until at least 1956, but the masses of black people, needless to say, cared very little about this issue. The Church's rejection of the Calvinistic process of "gettin' saved" and its de-emphasizing of militant black nationalism has reduced its appeal, although it still survives. And, although Garvey would declaim against the Reverend Adam Clayton Powell, Sr., the African Orthodox Church was never so important in the lives of Harlemites as Powell's Abyssinian Baptist Church. While organizer McGuire was traveling about the continent in a quest for "ecclesiastical authority," the Reverend Powell was preaching to prostitutes in cold-water flats and holding prayer meetings among the most depressed class of Harlem's populace. Anyone who believes that the sheer ability to "mobilize the masses" and to gain their economic support is positive proof of a black leader's validity should examine the career of the Reverend Powell, Sr., and his "Church of the Masses." The institution that he organized has served three generations as a base of social organization, but there has always been criticism of the leadership associated with it.[45]

The African Orthodox Church was hardly the most important aspect of Garveyite religion. Indeed, not every Garveyite viewed Christianity as the most appropriate form of religious expression for black Americans. J. Arnold Ford, sometime music director of the UNIA, was Rabbi of a Black Hebrew congregation, Beth B'nai Abraham. He and many of his members identified with the UNIA and were particularly supportive of its Ethiopian rhetoric, which they interpreted literally.[46] Black Muslims were attracted to Garvey, as well, and the ties of Noble Drew Ali's Moorish Science to Garveyism have been commented on by E. U. Essien–Udom.[47] Unlike the Black Hebrews, however, the Moors rejected "Ethiopian" as a term of opprobrium.[48]

Although the various exotic religious bodies that expressed sympathy with Garveyism are interesting, it is most important to understand the observation of Randall K. Burkett that Garveyism itself was a "civil religion." Burkett has shown that Garveyist religion existed independently of the various sects that affiliated with the UNIA movement. He has also demonstrated that the UNIA made use of religious ceremonies that were nonsectarian in order to impress its members with the solemnity of its mission and the seriousness of its purpose.[49] The concept of civil religion has recently been well-described by Robert Bellah as religion that is less concerned with doctrines of salvation than with legitimization of social myths.[50] The concept encompasses a wide spectrum of activity, from invocations of divine guidance during inaugural addresses to theories of racial supremacy advanced by a chauvinistic clergy. Garvey's speeches were usually homiletic and centered on the themes of Christian militancy, black resurrection, and African redemption.

The idea of institutionalizing the Kingdom of Christ within the context of a worldly empire was certainly not a new idea to black Americans. Garvey's brand of Christian imperialism made it possible for blacks, who had always felt somewhat threatened by the mainstream concept of Manifest Destiny, to participate in one of the most virile of American traditions. Every Garveyite could be a Christian soldier, assured of the righteousness of his cause and of his membership in a specially favored race.

The idea that Africans were a specially favored race had, of course, been well-developed in the writings of nineteenth-century black religious thinkers. Alexander Crummell had argued that the universally degraded status of the black race was no sign of God's disfavor. Was it not true that God often tempered his chosen peoples in the fires of adversity? This was only His way of preparing them for the grand and noble purposes that were to be their destiny.[51] Garvey's explanation of the status of black people would have angered and offended Crummell. While Crummell insisted vehemently that black slavery was not a sign of divine disfavor, Garvey reasoned that it must be punishment for some ancient sin. "We kept the Jews in bondage for 400 years," he once reasoned. "We were punished for that and Egypt fell back like Timbuktoo and Benin and we of this generation have learnt our lesson that righteousness is the password to Heaven and to God."[52]

But if the contemporary Negro was being made to bear his cross in atonement for the sins of past generations, he must now have the faith to foresee his own resurrection. In an Easter Sunday speech delivered at Edelweiss Park in Jamaica in 1929, Garvey compared his own sufferings to the passion and death of Jesus Christ. "They framed him. They said he was preaching sedition. . . . And who were his accusers? Chiefly men of His own race." Lest anyone miss the point, he went on to observe that, "If Jesus came back to the world today, He would not have years in which to teach and preach, in five minutes He would be placed in jail." Garvey reminded his audience that "the life of Jesus is typical of the life of the race of which you and I are members." The black race had a greater claim than any other race in the world to "the redeemership of Christ." Simon of Cyrene, "a black African," was the only man on earth who had helped him bear his cross. And there was a parallel between the life of Christ and the history of the black race: "Once we were dead, once we were crucified not upon the cross of Calvary, but upon the cross of gold. . . . And so we celebrate the resurrection of the risen Christ—the resurrection that inspires us with new courage and new hope." The life of Christ, Redeemer of mankind, would inspire the messianic black race to work for the redemption of Africa. "We gaze toward the goal, and steadily we move forward and upward toward our racial resurrection that will bring us new life. It is the will of God." This did not mean that all black people were to return to Africa in an army of liberation; they could remain good citizens wherever they happened to find themselves, but they must be "absolutely loyal to the Cause of Africa redeemed."[53]

Garvey's theories on the governance of the black state echo the nineteenth-century theocratic absolutism of Alexander Crummell. It appears certain that the African regime Garvey hoped to establish was to be authoritarian, elitist, collectivist, racist, and capitalistic. "We were the first Fascists," he told J. A. Rogers, the popular black-people's historian. "Mussolini copied Fascism from me, but the Negro reactionaries sabotaged it." He felt that the salvation of the black people was to be found only in "extreme nationalism."[54] Garvey disavowed any intention of setting up an alien aristocracy in Africa to exercise an overlordship over the indigenous tribes, but, in practice, he tended to be Napoleonic. After all, the tribes were "backward" and it was the duty of the UNIA to civilize and Christianize them.

We need not depend on Rogers for proof that Garvey's ideal state was to be totalitarian. Garvey proclaimed that "government should be absolute. . . . When we elect a President of a nation, he should be endowed with absolute authority to appoint all his lieutenants from cabinet ministers, governors of States and Territories, administrators and judges to minor officers."[55] Garvey had, of course, seen to it that he would be Provisional President by staffing his UNIA with persons who were not inclined to challenge his authority directly. He planned to discourage a multi-party system by using the old dictator's argument that his government would operate "for the good of all the people."[56]

Garvey's economic program was mildly progressive, but not socialistic. He said that "capitalism is necessary to the progress of the world, and those who unreasonably and wantonly oppose or fight against it are enemies to human advancement."[57] He did propose, naively, that no individual be allowed to control more than a million dollars, nor any corporation more than five million. Little more need be said of his knowledge of corporate economics. Garvey cannot be blamed for his ignorance in some matters—no one man can be expected to know everything—but he can be blamed for his arrogance which would not allow him to make compromises and call on men of ability, even if he did not agree with them on all things.

Garvey intended to control even the most private affairs in the lives of black people. Mulattoes and brown-skinned people were to think of themselves as monstrosities to be bred out of existence. The race was to be standardized by inbreeding according to "well understood and defined codes."[58] The ideal state was to honor children who reported the criminal acts of their parents.[59] If Garvey had come into power, his regime might have been very similar to that of Haiti's Duvalier, who was also known for a hatred of mulattoes and communists and who had a penchant for exploiting a self-serving brand of negritude.

It is difficult to analyze the philosophy and opinions of Marcus Garvey, for his style was that of the revivalistic harangue, not the systematic homily. Inconsistency did not bother him; he could speak in one breath of the need for unifying black religious expression, and in the next deny that he intended to give one form of religion primacy over the others. Like Martin Delany seventy years before, he criticized black religion for erecting obstacles to political activism, and yet the thought of forging a Pan–Africanism entirely independent of religion never occurred to him. Because of his intimate association with William H. Ferris, he undoubtedly had some knowledge of Alexander Crummell. Certainly the authoritarianism, the theocratic tendencies, the black chauvinism of his philosophy were consistent with the values of Crummell's generation. Garvey was not insensitive to tradition. He attempted to establish ties with Booker T. Washington and with W. E. B. Du Bois. As yet, however, there is no evidence of his having attempted to understand the movement of Chief Alfred C. Sam, who left the United States only two years before Garvey arrived. Garvey seemed doomed to repeat the ideological formulae of his predecessors, while ignoring the causes of their practical difficulties.

Much has been made of the links between Garvey and Booker T. Washington; less has been said concerning his intellectual ties to Du Bois. Garvey early abandoned the plan, that he outlined in his letter to Washington, of returning to Jamaica to establish a trade school similar to Tuskegee. He adhered consistently to the flamboyant Ethiopian millennialism that he shared with Du Bois. As for Du Bois, he clearly viewed Garveyite theatrics as a gross travesty of his own Ethiopianism; his brand of Pan–Africanism was evolving into a more secular and materialistic phase. Influenced by Marxism, Du Bois was moving away from the mystical Pan–Africanism of Crummell's generation—although he never completely abandoned it—and re-evaluating his position with respect to the materialistic philosophy of Booker T. Washington.

At the Sixth International UNIA Convention, Garvey bewailed the existence of factionalism in the black world and expressed a desire to achieve a unified religion and ideology. But one speaker at the convention respectfully submitted that, by his efforts to impose solidarity, Garvey would only be "adding another peg in the mass of confusion."[60] Most black nationalists today lament disunity among black organizations, but few of us are willing to exercise that spirit of tolerance and compromise that is necessary to bring a unified black-power movement into existence. Perhaps when Malcolm X and Martin Luther King, Jr., met on April 26, 1964, to shake hands before a photographer's camera, they meant to symbolize the setting aside of religious controversy in order to achieve common political goals.[61] On January 24, 1965, less than a month before his assassination, Malcolm X warned the American Nazi Party that, if their agitation caused harm to the Reverend King "or any other black Americans," they would be met with "maximum physical retaliation."[62] It is unfortunate that neither Garvey nor Du Bois was capable of ecumenicism. They should have been able to find common ground; but it was the very Ethiopian tradition that they shared, with its dogmatism and inflexible religious fervor, that made compromise impossible for either of them.

9
Du Bois' Dark Princess
and the Heroic Uncle Tom

"The effigy of Du Bois and his type should be placed alongside of Uncle Tom because as a matter of fact he is of the same mentality." There was some truth in this statement by Marcus Garvey in *The Black Man* of late July 1935, although in a more complex sense than Garvey probably intended. We have seen in an earlier chapter how Mrs. Stowe, in creating the character of Uncle Tom, saw herself as painting an image of heroic Christianity. We have also seen how black nationalist spokespersons reacted to the "Uncle Tom" image, which already existed independently of Mrs. Stowe's efforts. Du Bois, as I have observed elsewhere, spoke of the beauty of Mrs. Stowe's novel in *The Souls of Black Folk*, and, like the creator of Uncle Tom, he was inclined to romanticize the suffering of black folk. Despite his occasional hostility to Christianity, Du Bois was fascinated by the idea of redemption through suffering. He believed in sacrifice and self-denial. He admired the asceticism, the idealism, the long-suffering patience of the passing generation of Negro churchmen, to whom he referred as saints and martyrs. "Entbehren sollst du, sollst entbehren!" was his motto—"Thou shalt forego, shalt do without!" He believed in service, "humble reverent service, from the blackening of boots to the whitening of souls." There was something of the otherworldly in his temperament.[1]

Du Bois often assigned a messianic quality to prominent black individuals, or even to the entire black race, in his writings. This he did in his vignette of Alexander Crummell and in his parable "Jesus Christ in Texas."[2] Du Bois' messianism seldom emphasized retribution; the ordeals of his black protagonists, whether real or mythical, were conspicuously identifiable with the redemptive suffering of Jesus Christ. Like Booker T. Washington and other writers, Du Bois was appealed to by the widely held notion of black people as innately predisposed to the acceptance of such Christian virtues as patience, forgivingness, and the ability to endure pain with dignity and in silence. Du Bois seemed to feel that it was through these virtues that black people would redeem not only themselves but also the rest of America and, ultimately, mankind as a whole. This is evidenced nowhere more strongly than in his fiction. Stoical, idealistic, otherworldly, and blindly committed to duty, the heroes of Du Bois' novels and stories are Uncle Toms in the purest and most correct sense. They are potential race-martyrs, committed to a vision of truth and beauty far beyond the ability of the world to comprehend.

The prototype for Du Bois' fictional heroes is to be found in a short story, "Of the Coming of John," in *The Souls of Black Folk.* The story alludes to Wagner's myth of Lohengrin, the saintly knight and son of Parsifal, who dwells in a faraway land, bathed in the light of the Holy Grail. Lohengrin is a champion of the oppressed who ventures into mortal realms to help the defenseless. Du Bois' adaptation of the myth centers on John, who begins life as a peasant in the Black Belt, and later returns from his adventures in the wide world to establish a one-room schoolhouse in his home town. He is unsuccessful. The whites feel, and with good reason, that education and travel have spoiled him; the superstitious black folk fear his heretical ideas. In the end, John stands stoically facing a lynch mob, having killed a young white landlord who sought to despoil his sister. He makes no attempt to escape, but fatalistically embraces death while singing (in German, of course) the wedding march from Lohengrin.

Likewise, Bles Alwyn of *The Quest of the Silver Fleece* falls into the pattern of otherworldly idealism; although he is never actually martyred, he is saintly and selfless. Almost all his thoughts and actions seem to spring from a sense of racial mission, which early takes the form of an attempt to uplift Zora. Subsequently, this sense of mission finds expression in Washington politics; and, finally, it leads him back to Alabama and to the work of educating the black peasant masses. Bles seldom reveals purely personal motivations. He reveals no strong desire to improve his financial or material well-being. He has no conscious sexual needs. His love for Zora is a spiritual longing. His involvement with Carolyn Wynn grows out of his quest for respectability and it stems from his admiration for her intelligence, her sophistication, and her taste—qualities that, in Bles's view, ought to be encouraged among the mass of Afro–American women. Bles is blind to Carolyn's failings, because it is beyond his ability to perceive the worldly values that prompt her behavior. He fails in politics, despite her manipulations, for he is never strongly tempted to become a "man of the world." Bles idealistically believes that black politics is really a means to racial elevation, rather than simply a way to make money. He unrealistically believes that black women should be disembodied symbols of civilization, rather than flesh-and-blood human beings.

Critics have faulted Du Bois for the unrealistic characterizations that predominate in his fiction. There can be no doubt but that the speech of his characters is stylized and formal, as in the often-cited "Bles, almost thou persuadest me to be a fool." If realism—either social or psychological—was Du Bois' central concern, then all his novels were abject failures. If, on the other hand, he was attempting to achieve a weird and picturesque Wagnerian grandeur, then he was successful. Like Wagner, Du Bois owed a debt to naturalism, with its insistence that characters in life's drama are compelled to action by impersonal social forces and internal Darwinian drives. Realism, on the other hand, was antagonistic to the intrinsic idealism of Du Bois' temperament. His intention was to create a national heroic art—unfortunately, at a time when the dominant trends in Western fiction were to reject heroism, idealism, and nationalism. Du Bois' novels and stories were thus constructed in a mode that has been unpopular in the twentieth century, especially with the avant-garde audience that has tended to be sympathetic to black writers.

Dark Princess: A Romance is the story of Matthew Towns, an idealistic, long-suffering, black romantic, and his love for Princess Kautilya, Maharanee of Bwodpur. The novel is one of heroic proportions, and its flaws, like its strengths, are of some magnitude. With its focus upon a roving intellectual protagonist who symbolizes not only the Negroes of the United States, but the tribeless, rootless, marginal man of the twentieth century, it is the precursor of such works as Richard Wright's *The Outsider*, Ralph Ellison's *Invisible Man*, and John A. Williams' *The Man Who Cried "I Am."* Like the anti-heroes of these later novels, Matthew Towns fights to hang on to his personal identity, while caught up in the collective struggles of his race.

The story is divided into four sections. Part I, "The Exile," is based on the true story of J. E. Coleman, who was forced to leave a Philadelphia medical college for racial reasons, despite his high grades.[3] There are also suggestions of autobiographical elements, for Du Bois—like Towns—was once a resident of Berlin. In 1911 he attended a London reception given by the Ranee of Sarawak, which may have inspired the dinner party of Chapter 6. Part II, "The Pullman Porter," provided Du Bois with an opportunity to direct some passing shots at A. Philip Randolph and the failings of black unionism. It also linked him with a tradition present in the novels of James Weldon Johnson, Claude McKay, J. A. Rogers, and later writers, who made use of material based on the experiences of the black servant class on the railroads.[4] Part III, "The Chicago Politician," is reminiscent of the literary excursion into Washington politics in *The*

Quest of the Silver Fleece. In this chapter, Du Bois anticipates much that Frazier says forty years later in *Black Bourgeoisie.* He also anticipates the observations of Harold Foote Gosnell on the venal origins of black Chicago politics.[5] Part IV, "The Maharajah of Bwodpur," is the book's most self-indulgent section, consisting of several treatises on the dignity of labor but finally reaching its fantastic climax with the birth of the Black Messiah.

The story begins with Matthew Towns in a "cold white fury" on the deck of a ship at sea, brooding over his unhappy experience in the medical school at the University of Manhattan. Towns has been denied admission to an obstetrics course that is required for graduation. "Well—what did you expect?" the dean has said. "Do you think white women are going to have a nigger doctor delivering their babies?"[6] Towns is doubly irate because, as he puts it, "I've ranked my class. I took honors. . . ." But prejudice has blocked the door to further triumphs; and Matthew, in a fury, has hurled his credentials "straight into the face of the dean and stumbled out." His voyage to Europe is uneventful, a time of sleep and recuperation after hard years of study. He barely notices the few racial slights that inevitably occur aboard ship, and finally he is sitting in the Victoria Café on the Unter den Linden in Berlin.

Here we view the beginning of a new tradition in black writing—the protagonist sitting in a European café brooding over the white world with baleful eye. Scenes similar to this will appear in the writings of other black authors as the century progresses, among them Claude McKay, James Baldwin, John A. Williams, and Frank Yerby. It happens first in *Dark Princess.* The nineteenth-century black fugitive in Europe does not do much café-sitting, obsessed as he is with temperance and reform. Matthew Towns—elegant in his tasteful brown suit and dark crimson tie, carrying gloves and a cane—is the first of the black café-sitting intellectuals, a type that has since become standard in Afro–American expatriate fiction.[7]

It is here in the café that Matthew first sees the Princess. "Many, many times in after years he tried to catch and rebuild that first wildly beautiful phantasy which the girl's face stirred in him. . . . Never after that first glance was he or the world quite the same."[8] Then, to his horror, this Princess is accosted by a brash young American, who refuses to be coolly rebuffed. Matthew knocks the American down in the street and whisks the Princess off in a taxi. "*Mille remerciements, Monsier!*" she thanks him; and then realizing that he is English-speaking, and a black American, she says:

> "How singular—how very singular! I have been thinking of American Negroes all day! Please do not leave yet. Can you spare a moment? Chauffeur, drive on!" (10)

As they chat over tea in the Tiergarten, Matthew learns that the Princess belongs to a "great committee of the darker peoples; of those who suffer under the arrogance and tyranny of the white world." Some of its representatives are to convene the very next evening at her apartment. She has recently returned from Moscow where she has heard the idea—now confirmed through her conversation with Towns—that the Negroes of the United States are "a nation" and not "a mere amorphous handful." (16)

The time of this conversation is 1923; the novel was published in 1928. During the five-year period from 1923 to 1928, the Communist Parties both in the United States and in Russia were beginning to formulate a position on the Negro question. Black communist groups, the African Blood Brotherhood, and the Trade Union Educational League, came into existence; and in 1928 the black American communist Harry Haygood helped write the draft for the Communist International resolution that was to deal with the "Negro Question" as a "question of an *oppressed nation* suffering from an especially oppressive form of subjugation."[9] It is also of interest that Du Bois began to take an interest in Russia and in the Communist revolution during the 1920s. He made his first trip to the Soviet Union in 1926.[10] Like Sutton Griggs, Lothrop Stoddard, Oswald Spengler, and, of course, Lenin, Du Bois seemed to be predicting the potential role of Russia as an instigator of resentment and rebellion among the darker peoples of the world.[11]

At dinner in the Princess' apartment the following night, Towns finds himself in a situation that is not unfamiliar to American self-made men who are dropped into Old World settings. The tradition-bound dinner guests, representing ancient aristocracies, are suspicious of him and the people he represents. They are predisposed to accept the rumors that they have heard of the inferiority of the black race. The Princess believes that "Pan–Africa belongs logically with Pan–Asia." (20) But, as the Japanese delegate remarks, there is some question "of the ability, qualifications, and real possibilities of the black race in Africa or elsewhere." (21) The Princess rises to the occasion, responding that in Russia she has been able to study reports on the Negroes of America, which reveal that "they are a nation today, a modern nation worthy to stand beside any nation here." (22) The Princess is confident, but her compatriots are less than assured.

Later that night, the Japanese, two Indians, and the Arab come to Matthew's room and order him to forget all that he has seen and heard of the international conspiracy. They are particularly concerned over the Princess' plan to have Towns deliver a letter to the leader of an American black-nationalist cadre. Met with his steadfast refusal to yield up the letter and keep his mouth shut, the Pan–Asianists are on the brink of violent action when the Princess arrives and puts them to rout with a stamp of her imperial foot. She announces that Matthew is to commence with his mission, if he is still willing. For her part, the Princess will shortly be sailing to America to investigate matters personally.

Part II begins with Matthew Towns working his way back across the Atlantic in the scullery of an ocean liner. In the first scene, the character of the heroic "Uncle Tom" manifests itself. Prodded on by other members of the kitchen crew, an Italian scullery worker picks a fight with Towns; but when the Italian lands him a cuff that nearly knocks him from his stool, Matthew rises slowly to stand with folded arms—a pose that would well befit one of Paul Robeson's theatrical creations. He stands gazing stoically at the fat, lumbering Italian, who strikes him a second and then a third time:

> Matthew stood and did not lift his hand. Why? He could not have said himself. More or less consciously he sensed what a silly mess it all was. He could not soil his hands on this great idiot. He would not stoop to such a brawl. There was a strange hush in the scullery. Somebody yelled, "Scared stiff!" But they yelled weakly, for Matthew did not look scared. (39)

The kitchen steward attempts to arrange a bout for the entertainment of the first-cabin passengers, but Matthew will not fight and the Italian almost falls over himself in his haste to accept Matthew's outstretched hand. "If rats must fight," says Matthew, "they fight cats—and dogs—and hogs." The scullery cheers, the steward accuses Matthew of "planning bolshevik stuff," but the rest of the trip passes without incident. (41)

The next sequence is perhaps the most colorful and authentic in the novel. Here the author shows that he can write realistically, when it pleases him to do so. Matthew prepares to discharge the orders of the Princess by visiting a black nationalist's headquarters, located at Fifth Avenue and 135th Street in Harlem. The building is dilapidated and dirty; the air is stale; and as he ascends the stairs, Matthew can hear "loud, continuous, quarreling voices." (43) He enters a room full of "smoke, bad air, voices and gesticulations." Groups of black men, most of them West Indians, are standing about in clusters and are engaged in heated debates: "Sometimes they shouted and seemed on the point of blows, but blows never came." Asking for Perigua, he is directed to a platform at the back of the room, where a group of several men are talking and gesticulating, "if anything louder and faster than the rest."

> "May I speak with Mr. Perigua?"
> A Man whirled toward him.
> "Don't you see I'm busy, man? Where's the sergeant at arms? Why can't you protect the privacy of my office when I'm in conference?"
> A short, fat, black man reluctantly broke off in an intense declamation and hastened up. (43)

This "short, fat, black man" will perhaps remind the reader of Marcus Garvey, whom Du Bois once described in the same language. Perigua himself is, like Garvey, a West Indian, presiding over an organization that is packed with West Indians.[12] However, unlike Garvey, Perigua is a mulatto, "a thin yellow man of middle size with flaming black hair and luminous eyes." When Towns asks, "Are you Mr. Perigua?" he responds:

> "My God, man—don't you know me? Is there anybody in New York that doesn't know Perigua? Is there anybody in the world? Gentlemen"—he leaped to the rail—"am I Perigua?"
> A shout went up.
> "Perigua—Perigua forever!" And a song with some indistinguishable rhyme on "Perigua forever" began to roll until he stopped it with an impatient shout and gesture.
> "Shut up. I'm busy." (43)

Matthew is naturally convinced by this display that he has found the right man. He whispers to him, and Perigua rises to his feet "with transfigured face."

> "Le jour de gloire est arrivé! Come, man," he shouted, and dragging Matthew, he reached the door and turned dramatically:
> "Men, I have news—great news—the greatest! Salute this ambassador from the World—who brings salvation. There will be a plenary council tomorrow night. Midnight. Pass the word. Adieu." And as they passed out, Matthew heard the song swell again—"Perigua, Perigua, Per—". (45)

But Towns's spirits droop, for he suspects that the man is too theatrical.

In the course of events, the two men conspire to sabotage a special train carrying the leaders of the Ku Klux Klan. It matters little to Perigua that not all the passengers on the train are Klansmen and that many innocent people will die. It is necessary, he feels, for black people to demonstrate to the world once and for all that they cannot be lynched and insulted with impunity. Matthew, in a state of despondency at having received no communication from the Princess, and overwhelmed with guilt because he blames himself for the lynching of a friend, is prepared to go along with Perigua's plan. He will destroy himself along with the train as proof to the Princess and the Pan—Asianists that black people are not afraid to die. It is at this point that the Princess enters his life for the second time. She is a passenger on the very train that Matthew is riding to his death. Once again inspired, he reveals the plot and stops the train. It is here that the heroic "Uncle Tom" element in his personality reasserts itself.

Matthew is too noble to reveal anything of the details of the conspiracy. Irrelevant to his sense of loyalty is the fact that Perigua has been killed in his frustrated attempt to derail the train. Matthew has come to admire the man in the months of their association, and he cannot betray his memory. Prepared to suffer in silence, he is brought to trial, where the judge remarks on his "stoicism worthy of a better cause" and sentences him to ten years at hard labor in the State Prison at Joliet, Illinois. It is while serving this sentence that Matthew attracts the notice of Sara Andrews, who uses her cynical political sophistication to engineer his release.

The personality of Sara Andrews dominates Part III of this novel. She is a formidable young woman, "self made and independent." Sara is the counterpart of Carolyn Wynn, that other disconcerting mulatto woman who appears in *The Quest of the Silver Fleece*. Her "cold clean hardness and unusual efficiency" contrast with the dreamy romanticism of Matthew. She is a shrewd political realist, with a purely situational ethic. Born in Richmond, Indiana, of a colored American chambermaid and a white German cook, an orphan in her teens, she has "fought her way through school; and forced herself into the local business college." In 1922 she moves to Chicago and becomes secretary to the Honorable Sammy Scott, a "big handsome brown man" with an infectious grin, a hearty handshake, and a curved belly.

Sammy finds Sara an invaluable asset to his "business" of running a Chicago ward. She is far more than a mere clerk or typist or even a secretary; she is an extraordinary administrative assistant. He soon discovers, to his delight, that Sara has "no particular scruples," and that "lying, stealing, bribery, gambling, prostitution" are facts that she accepts casually. At the same time, she is sexually chaste and perhaps even frigid. Early in their relationship Sammy attempts to make amorous overtures, but Sara repulses him emphatically. Then for a while he half makes up his mind to marry her and is almost certain that she will accept, but he is also a little afraid of her coldness and hardness. Sammy has "no mind to embrace a cake of ice. . . ."

Sara has followed the Towns trial, and she is impressed by Matthew's idealism. She persuades Sammy to support her efforts to secure his release, advising him that his machine could profit from incorporating such an altruist into its works. She tells Sammy that he can become more than an ordinary, colored, Chicago politician by increasing his popularity among "respectable people," or, as Sammy calls them, "hypocrites and asses." Sara does not quibble over terms, but insists that such people must be brought into the machine "or some fine day they'll smash it." (115) Of course, she has ulterior motives that she does not reveal to Sammy. She intends to reconstruct Matthew to her own purposes. Shortly after arranging his release, she is cheered to discover that his speech-making skills are extraordinary. He also turns out to be an excellent grass-roots organizer due to his simple honesty, his straightforward manner, and his genuine affection for working people. Sammy is impressed and confesses to Sara that he has begun to find Matthew an invaluable lieutenant. At this point, Sara announces to Sammy that Towns must be pushed for the state legislature: "Don't you see that this is the only man we can push, because he's tied to us body and soul." (130) She is soon to be undeceived—and to her bitter chagrin.

Sara's plan is to marry Matthew, get him elected to the legislature, and then run him for Congress. Matthew goes along with this, rather passively at first. He has not heard from the Princess, and he has become spiritually listless and cynical. One day he walks down to the Chinese laundry "for his shirts and a chat." The proprietor is glad to see him, for he has a young friend who would like to speak to Matthew. This friend turns out to be the young Chinese nationalist of the Princess' dinner party. He is happy to see Matthew, and rushes forward to clasp his hand. Matthew, however, responds cooly. "But surely you have not forgotten," protests the young man, "that word of faith in opportunity for the lowest?" Matthew growls harshly, "Bosh! That was pure poppycock. Dog eat dog is all I see; I'm through with all that." And Matthew dismisses the laundryman's concerns regarding local crime, saying; "I'm not running this district as a Sunday School." (134–36)

Throughout this section of the novel, Sara is a more active figure than Matthew. It is through her eyes that most of the developments are seen, while Matthew remains brooding, discontented, sighing resignedly in the background. Eventually, he proposes to Sara, but only because he feels that "marriage is normal," that it "stops secret longings," and that once married he will be "safe, settled, quiet; with all the furies at rest, calm, satisfied; a reader of old books, a listener to sad and quiet music, a sleeper." (136) His proposal is almost apologetic, "I haven't said anything about love on your side or mine—"; but she interrupts tartly, "Don't! I've been fighting the thing men call love all my life. . . . I don't think you're the loving kind." But here Sara is wrong; Matthew is dreamy and romantic. He finds it necessary to experience love in its most idealized and passionate form. The best he can muster for Sara, however, is a strange sense of pity and a self-sacrificing principle of husbandly duty.

Of course, Matthew is uncomfortable: "The demon of unrest [is] stirring drowsily away down in the half-conscious depths of his soul." He marries Sara and is elected to the legislature. He begins his campaign for the congressional seat. Sara continues to manipulate, promising his vote without first consulting him, committing him to policies that he cannot countenance. Their relationship degenerates. Matthew is astonished by her mechanically perfect taste, which contrasts with her total indifference to moral or aesthetic matters. Also, he finds her cold and grey, metallic and passionless:

She disliked being "mauled" and disarranged, and she did not want anyone to be "mushy" about her. Her private life was entirely in public; her clothes, her limbs, her hair and complexion, her well-appointed home, her handsome, well-tailored husband and his career; her reputation for wealth. (153)

Sara is accustomed to manipulating Sammy—and, indeed, she has more native intelligence and political cunning than he. However, she is so accustomed to being in the driver's seat that she fails to appreciate Matthew's blossoming political talents, and she never acknowledges that some of his triumphs in the legislature result from his own astuteness and are accomplished in spite of her manipulations. Sara's self-interested obsession with Matthew's career leads her to the depths of genteel depravity. She consults with the valet of old Congressman Doolittle. Money changes hands. "I do hope that all will go well, for Doolittle is a deserving old man," says Sara, "but if anything *should* change in his physical condition I'd like to know about it *before* anyone else, Mr. Amos; and I'm depending on you." Doolittle's health declines suddenly and within twenty-four hours he is dead. (181)

Now the way is clear. Sara begins to put together the coalition of professional people, politicians, businessmen, clubwomen, racketeers, and do-gooders, whose support is necessary to send a congressman to Washington. Sara vows to steer clear of only one group of any importance—the unskilled workers' unions; but Matthew's reawakening conscience goes out to these people, even though he attempts to present a callous exterior. On the evening that Matthew's candidacy is to be announced, Sara learns that a labor delegation has presented itself at her door. She is annoyed, for the house is full of important people and she has planned this evening carefully. It is to be a victory celebration, for not only will it mark the successful formation of a political alliance, it will signal the day of her social triumph—it will herald her emergence as a successful hostess in the life of white, as well as black, Chicago. Sara sends Matthew into the library to meet with the labor delegation, for, as she explains, "they are not exactly—dressed for an evening function." As Matthew goes to the library, Sara opens the portiéres that conceal the dining room. The table is a goodly sight; soft music rises; wine flows; a feeling of good fellowship begins to radiate. It is time for the toast. Sara flings open the door to the library and reveals to her scandalized guests the sight of Matthew reunited with his Princess.

> The light of the greater room poured into the lesser—searching out its shadows. The ugly Chinese god grinned in the corner, and a blue rug glowed on the floor. In the center the two figures, twined as one, in close and quivering embrace, leapt, etched in startling outline on the light. (206)

Matthew's submissive marriage to Sara has been consistent with the martyr-like "Uncle Tom" personality that he displays throughout the novel. He thinks of his marriage as a sort of renunciation. He does not seek warmth or companionship, but only to seal himself off from the unsatisfied longings and unattainable dreams that were inspired in Berlin. He allows himself to be manipulated into this hopeless marriage in much the same way that he has allowed himself to be victimized earlier in the story. Matthew challenges the world to strike him, then refuses to strike back. This is true in the scullery of the ocean liner, where he almost literally invites the Italian to use him as a punching bag. It is true in his conspiracy trial, where he refuses to speak a word in his own defense. And it is true in his selection of a marriage partner, whose spiritual poverty he has had adequate opportunity to observe.

The ultimate acts of masochism on Matthew's part, however, are to be consummated after he and Sara are separated. On the evening of the Princess' return, she and Matthew leave the party singing in the rain. They live together for several months. Then the Princess announces that they must "walk the path of renunciation. . . . First comes your duty to Sara. . . . And in living death, I go to meet the Maharajah of Bwodpur." As one expects, Matthew responds like the heroic, long-suffering "Uncle Tom" that he is, agreeing to return to Sara. "She must ask divorce, not I. And beyond that, I will offer her fully and freely my whole self." (260–61)

This leads to Matthew presenting himself at Sara's front door and having it slammed in his face. As if this is not enough, he shows up at the divorce trial, confesses his infidelity, declares his hatred for the married life he has lived, but professes his resignation to reassuming connubial duties. Naturally, Sara considers this "an insult, a low insult"; and, indeed, Matthew's behavior has been provocative. According to the standards of mundane sophistication by which Sammy and Sara live, Matthew is guilty of supreme bad taste. One must suspect the motives behind the "Uncle Tommish" sense of duty that forces Matthew to return to Sara in just this way. This flaunting of sanctimonious morality in an arena where it is not appreciated is certainly reminiscent of the provocative behavior of Uncle Tom, who taunts Simon Legree by singing hymns in his presence and challenging him to strike. The behavior of the seemingly masochistic Uncle Tom is often sadistic, and Matthew's seemingly submissive relationship to Sara has provided him with a splendid opportunity for inflicting pain.

The failure of communication between Matthew and Sara is due to the moral distance between racial messianism and ethnic politics. Matthew's struggle to preserve his individuality is a part of the cosmic struggle of the human personality against dehumanizing industrial and economic processes; but it also represents the striving of the masses of black people to make their distinct contribution to world history and to serve as a leavening agent in a world gone mad in its pursuit of wealth.[13] As for Sara, perhaps Matthew's characterization of her is just:

> To her this world-tangle of the races is a lustful scramble for place and power and show. She is mad because she is handicapped in the scramble. She would gladly trample anything beneath her feet, black, white, yellow, if only she could ride in gleaming triumph at the procession's head. (260)

The final chapters of *Dark Princess* dwell on themes of redemption through suffering, renunciation, and work. During the years between the imprisonment of Matthew and the fiasco of Sara's party, Princess Kautilya has been busy. She has twice visited Matthew's aged mother in Virginia, and she has descended into the world of work—first as a servant, then as a tobacco-factory hand, then as a waitress. Matthew groans, "Mud, dirt, and servility for the education of a queen." But she responds, "Is there any field where a queen's education is more neglected?" The Princess completes her story, telling of how she drifted into a job in a paper-box-making factory, and later became a union organizer. "I was beaten and jailed for picketing, but I did not care." (221–23)

When Matthew and Kautilya decide to part so that he can do his duty to Sara, Kautilya goes to live with his mother in Virginia, for, unknown to Matthew, she is pregnant with his child. At this point the novel evolves into a series of letters between the two lovers. These are lofty disquisitions on the nobility and necessity of labor. "I grow half dead with physical weakness," Matthew writes, "but my body waxes hard and strong." He tells the Princess that he has refused a clerk's job in order to become a labor organizer. "Can we build one of this helpless, ignorant stuff?" he asks. "I do not know. But this at least I do know: Work is God." The Princess responds, "Matthew, Work is not God—Love is God and Work is his Prophet." (272–79)

The novel ends with Matthew and his Princess reunited. They are married in Virginia by Matthew's down-home preacher: "He looked like incarnate Age." Messianic allusions abound: "The babe leapt beneath your heart." (Luke, 1:41, 44) The baby is referred to as "The Son of Man." Kautilya is portrayed as a black Madonna—"I ascended into heaven with the angel of your child at my breast." Matthew's ancient mother prays, "Make him a man, Lord Jesus—a leader of his people . . . and let my heart sing Hallelujah to the Lamb when he brings my lost and stolen people home to heaven." (310)

Dark Princess has an operatic quality, with its theatricality and intentionally stylized pageantry. The characters burst into spontaneous song, as do Perigua's disciples and Perigua himself: " 'We are recognized—recognized by the great leaders of Asia and Africa. Pan–Africa stands at last beside Pan–Asia, and Europe trembles.' " (45) A similar cry swells up from the breast of a young Chinese: " 'The great day dawns . . . Freedom begins. Russia is helping. We are marching forward. The Revolution is on. To the sea with Europe and European slavery! O I am so happy.' " (135) Matthew sings numerous times during the story, as do his mother and the old preacher. The final scene of the novel is, by Du Bois' own description, "a pageant" filled wih procession, ritual, and chanting in honor of the black messiah, the infant Maharajah of Bwodpur.

> "King of the Snows of Gaurisankar!"
> "Protector of Ganga the Holy!"
> "Incarnate Son of the Buddha!"
> "Grand Mughal of Utter India!"
> "Messenger and Messiah to all the darker Worlds!" (311)

Dark Princess, with its hodgepodge of undeveloped themes—its Pan–Africanism, its Bolshevism, and its labor-movement rhetoric; its romanticism, its Wagnerian extravagance, and its flushed, breathless idealism—is probably not a novel at all. It is an opera in prose. It is certainly more important as a handbook of Du Bois' imagery than as a landmark of Afro–American literature, although it is traditional and pre-echoes themes that will appear in later writers. The messianic vision that it presents, with its combination of proletarianism, Eastern mysticism, aristocratic notions, and survivals of Uncle Tom, is perhaps bizarre, but no more incredible than the weird, picturesque expressions of black messianism that appeared in American cities during the 1920s, 1930s, and 1940s.

10
Waiting for the Messiah: From Joe Louis to Martin Luther King, Jr.

"One of the most persistent laments among Negroes in the United States is that the race has no great leader," wrote Oliver Cox in 1948. "There is a sort of vague expectation that someday he will arise. But Negroes will not have a 'great leader' because, in reality, they do not want him." The following year, Ira Reid, writing on "Negro Movements and Messiahs," found it "ironic" that the many serious crises of the past fifty years had "produced no comprehensive race movement, not one significant race leader." Racial leadership seemed to be identified "with individual achievement in spite of the group limited handicaps rather than with group activity directed toward group goals." Figures like Marian Anderson, Ralph Bunche, and Jackie Robinson were thought of as black leaders, although they were not identified with movements directed towards racial advancement. Reid ascribed the terms "race leader" and "messiah" to individuals who possessed "the quality and ability of directing and persuading socially defined groups known as races . . . , towards specific goals. . . ." Thus, it was possible for Reid to include in his definition not only figures from political and intellectual life, but persons of the "creative type" who represented "symbolic leadership."[1]

At the time that Cox and Reid were expressing their concerns, Martin Luther King, Jr., was nineteen and in his senior year at Morehouse College. Marcus Garvey, the most successful leader of a mass movement among the black population of the United States, had died in England eight years earlier. W. E. B. Du Bois, remarkably well-preserved, was nonetheless an old man of eighty and had never commanded a massive following. His ideas were profoundly influential, even among people who had never read a word of his writing, but he was ill-tempered, arrogant, and aloof.[2] Furthermore, the prospect of leading a proletarian movement would have been repugnant to Du Bois, despite his romanticization of the black working classes. As Reid observed, it was difficult to identify any "recognized leadership for the group's chronic maladjustment," during what Roger Dalfiume has called "the forgotten years" of the black struggle.[3]

The very idea of a black messiah was contradictory in any case, as Cox had noted. A great black leader would be expected to assume the mutually antagonistic roles of racial crusader and "Uncle Tom." He would have to be, at once, a symbol of aggressive militancy and social change but, simultaneously, a subtle, manipulative seeker of good will from white American society. He would have to represent assimilative goals and the ideal of full participation in American life but, at the same time, he would have to be combative and capable of inspiring black people to group solidarity and ethnic pride. Perhaps this was the reason that a silent man, unassociated with any political ideology or pretensions to leadership, came to symbolize the aspirations of black America during the 1930s and 1940s. His name was Joe Louis Barrow. In September 1941, *Time Magazine* called him "a black Moses, leading the Children of Ham out of bondage."

From the deportation of Marcus Garvey in 1927 to the rise of Martin Luther King in 1954, no individual in black America was able to inspire the racial consciousness of the masses of black Americans in the way that Joe Louis did. He first captured the imagination of the people on June 25, 1935, with his victory over Primo Carnera in New York's Yankee Stadium. Three months earlier, three thousand people had packed themselves into Adam Clayton Powell's Abyssinian Baptist Church in that same city to demonstrate their support for the Ethiopian resistance to Mussolini's imperialistic aims.[4] Roi Ottley observed that many black Americans were rooting for Joe Louis because he was fighting an Italian; others, because he was fighting a white man; "but all Negroes joined in his corner because he was a Negro!" Louis himself reports that his camp was besieged by representatives of black groups who came to tell him of Mussolini and Ethiopia and of Marcus Garvey's back-to-Africa scheme. Louis had never heard of Marcus Garvey and was somewhat astonished by the idea that he represented Ethiopia in the minds of black nationalists, but he knocked Carnera out in the sixth round and pandemonium broke loose in the streets of Harlem.[5]

A messianic role was forced upon the twenty-year-old boxer that year. When he visited his mother's church in Detroit later that summer, the Reverend J. H. Marston made him the subject of a sermon:

> He talked about how God gave certain people gifts and that these gifts were given to help other men. My gift was fighting, and through my fighting I was to uplift the spirit of my race. I must make the whole world

know that Negro people were strong, fair, and decent. Through fighting, I was also supposed to show that the Negroes were tired of being muddled around in the ground. He said I was one of the Chosen.[6]

In celebration of Joe Louis's victories as he battled his way to the world heavyweight championship, black men, women, and children streamed into the streets of Chicago, Detroit, and New York, laughing and crying, drinking and lindy-hopping, tying up traffic, and commandeering buses. "It was like a revival," commented Richard Wright. "After one fight really, there was religious feeling in the air. Well, it wasn't exactly a religious feeling, but it was *something*, and you could feel it. It was a feeling of unity, of oneness."[7]

The Harlem celebration of Louis's victory over the 260-pound giant, Carnera, was certainly different in tone from the dire predictions of Westbrook Pegler in the *New York Sun*. Pegler had referred to the scheduling of the fight as "a new high in stupid judgment," observing that the Negroes of Harlem were "especially sore at Italy just now, because of its threat against Ethiopia." Before the fight, the *Chicago Defender* chided Pegler for his inflammatory editorial and, afterwards, the *Amsterdam News* said, "The fans didn't riot! Tch Tch Mr. Pegler." Still, the *Sun* did not pass up the opportunity to contribute a political exegesis on the fight, printing a cartoon of Louis standing before a monumental boot labeled Carnera and a diminutive, chivalric figure representing Ethiopia standing before a colossal map of the Italian boot. The caption read as follows:

JOE LOUIS DID IT, CAN ETHIOPIA DO IT?
You may read on the left some observations concerning Mr. Joe Louis who gave a fairly good imitation of David handling Goliath. This picture shows Ethiopia, another "gentleman of color" facing another Italian opponent and the question is can the king of Abyssinia, descendant of King Solomon and the Queen of Sheba, do on a big scale in Africa what Joe Louis did on a small scale in Yankee Stadium?[8]

The white press rarely reported on a Louis fight without commenting on his race. The *New York Sun* of June 27, 1935, explained his victories in terms of the widely held belief that "the American Negro is a natural athlete." The *Sun* reminded its readers of legends concerning the extraordinary physical prowess of native Africans, and remarked: "The generations of toil in the cotton fields have not obliterated the strength and grace of the African native. [Louis's] Negro managers seem eager that he should take his place at the head of pugilism, but that he should be a credit to his race."

Numerous nicknames were attached to Joe Louis—many of them racially descriptive. On December 22, 1934, a black newspaper, the *Pittsburgh Courier*, called him the "New Black Hope." The *New York Daily*

Mirror of June 27, 1935, listed such nicknames as "Brown Bomber," "Alabama Assassin," "Detroit Destroyer"; it was the first of these that became most popular. He was referred to as "The Brown Panther" (*New York Post*, June 27, 1935); "The Dark Angel" (*New York World Telegram*, June 27, 1935); "Young Black Joe" (*New York Daily News*, May 14, 1935); "Immutable Brown Sphinx" (*Daily News*, August 19, 1936). His features were imposed upon the head of a sphinx in an editorial cartoon (*New York World*, September 11, 1935) that must have warmed the cockles of J. A. Rogers' heart. He was referred to as "The Tan Terror" by the *New York Post* in June 1938.

Louis was usually portrayed as a mulatto in the press cartoons, and often without the customary blackening. His colored sparring partners were often grossly stereotyped, however, with eight-ball heads and puffy white lips. They quailed with fear or had to be shoved into the ring. But after the loss of his first contest with Max Schmeling, Louis was portrayed in the *Daily News* of August 14, 1936, as an eight-ball figure quailing before his next opponent, Sharkey, saying "Woe is me!" On August 7, 1936, that same newspaper had portrayed him as an eight-ball being smashed by the gloves of his no-longer-overawed sparring partners. But Louis was restored to mulatto "Brown Bomber" status after defeating Baer.

"He's doing more to help our race than any man since Abraham Lincoln," Pastor James Marston was reported to have said of Joe Louis in the *World Telegram* of September 30, 1935. The *Pittsburgh Courier* once credited him with lifting the entire race to "a sense of self-importance"; but the *Chicago Defender*, somewhat more sober, raised the question of how much significance could be placed upon a prize fighter's triumphs as symbols of racial advancement. Equally reserved was New York's *Daily Mirror* with the following observations on June 27, 1935:

SO JOE LOUIS WON

The colored citizens rejoice with singing, dancing, but it is doubtful whether Louis's victory will prove a good thing on the whole for his race. All depends on later happenings. Some suggest that it would have been better for the colored race had it shown excellence in something more important and noble than fist-fighting.

There again, fifty-seven-year-old champion Arthur Johnson might be quoted: "Boy if Joe Louis beat Professor Einstein at his own game, whatever that is, white men would pay no attention. But when he knocks out a white man sixty pounds heavier than he is, white men do pay attention."

If Joe Louis inspired among black Americans a quasi-religious feeling approximating the millennial exuberance that Garvey had inflamed a decade earlier, he stirred the emotions of white Americans as well. The *New York Times* of June 27, 1935, called his victory over Carnera a "boon to boxing . . . catching the public imagination." For some reason the *Times* pointed to him as "leading the way to prosperity." Franklin D. Roosevelt invited him to the White House in the spring of 1938, felt his muscles, and said, "Joe, we're depending on those muscles for America." This was shortly before his second fight with Max Schmeling, billed as a contest between fascism and democracy. Ironically, this was a period when black people were segregated in most public facilities in Washington, D. C.

Joe Louis's first fight with Schmeling had been a fiasco. Marcus Garvey observed caustically that "Joe did not know that he was surrendering the pugilistic dignity of his race to the vanity of a German world." Indeed it was widely felt that Joe, a ten-to-one favorite over Schmeling, had entered the ring cocky and underprepared. "As is customary to us," Garvey remarked, "Joe . . . thought only of himself. . . . Schmeling knew that he had the responsibility of satisfying a watching and waiting Germanic world." Garvey deeply lamented Joe Louis's defeat, of course, but claimed that it could have been predicted. Joe had simply begun to celebrate too early. Flushed with victory following his fourth-round knockout of Max Baer, he had married Marva Trotter. "We hope Mrs. Louis will not think hard of us," said Garvey, "but we think Joe got married too early before securing his world championship."⁹

When Louis defeated Schmeling two years later, sending him to the hospital in less than one round, Garvey took it as a matter of course. Joe had "had time for reflection and for the appreciation of the responsibility our race has placed upon his shoulders." His victory punches represented behavior "typical of our race in true action."¹⁰ The exiled Garvey was not the only Negro to view Joe Louis's triumph as a racial victory. Harlem held its maddest revel yet, according to the *New York Sun* of June 23, 1938. Five thousand or more black people paraded up Seventh Avenue, while others leaned out of windows haranguing white passers-by who had come up to Harlem to witness the victory celebration: "How do you like that, white man?" "Hello, Braddock!" "Come on, white man, go get Schmeling now!" Elliott Arnold, staff writer for the *New York World Telegram*, reported on June 23, 1938, that 500,000 Harlem Negroes addressed one another all night with Nazi salutes and shouts of "Heil Louis!" Apparently, or at least so the story was told, a drunk had bumped into a black woman on the street and, instead of excusing himself, had snapped to attention, thrown up his arm in a Nazi salute, and shouted "Heil Louis!" And that started it, according to Arnold: "One joyous Negro passed it on to another and finally Seventh Avenue looked like a weird burlesque of Wilhelmstrasse in Berlin—staggering, yelling, singing, jumping, dancing, hugging, men and women jutting out their hands to one another in mock Nazi salute." Others took up the cheer "Ethiopia fights on," waving the banner of that nation. Street vendors chanted, "Don't be a Nazi; buy a Joe Louis button."

While the white press (and subsequent popular historical presentations) tended to view Louis's victories over Carnera and Schmeling as triumphs of American democracy over fascism and racism, black America clearly saw them in a somewhat different light. Joe Louis was a symbol of black America, of its own latent nationalism and ethnic chauvinism. For Garvey, Louis symbolized "the Negro of America. . . . He is our international leader and we take the greatest amount of pride in complimenting Joe Louis as the representative of the ring."[11] But Louis was not the only black man to capture the imagination of black Americans and to inspire feelings of racial pride similar to that which Garvey had stirred during the 1920s. Two others of much importance were Haile Selassie and Father Divine, who appealed to both the millennial enthusiasm and the ethnic chauvinism of the black masses.

It is said that when Ras Tafari [Makonnen] ascended the throne of Ethiopia and was crowned Emperor Haile Selassie I, black Americans, "especially the religious and nationalist oriented," viewed the coronation "with immense pride." William R. Scott has argued that the emperor assumed in the mythology of the urban, working-class, black American a place similar to that of the deported Marcus Garvey: "In the early years of the depression Emperor Haile Selassie was being increasingly viewed as the 'Black Messiah'."[12] A long-standing tradition existed among black Americans of regarding Ethiopia as the symbol for black people throughout the world. Since the eighteenth century, the black-nationalist leaders had conjured with the Biblical prophecy, "Princes shall come out of Egypt; Ethiopia shall soon stretch forth her hands unto God." (Psalms 68:31) When in 1896 Emperor Menelik II repulsed an army of Italian invaders at Adowa, black people throughout the world had been heartened and inspired. For the ensuing three decades, the Ethiopian victory had ranked in the minds of the race-conscious along with the triumph of Japan in the Russo–Japanese war as symbolic of the colored world's throwing off of the shackles of European domination. It was therefore profoundly distressing to many black people to hear first reports of Mussolini's invasion of Ethiopia in 1935.

Black newspapers such as the *Baltimore Afro–American, New York Age, Amsterdam News*, and *Pittsburgh Courier* expressed their reaction to the invasion with vehemence. Numerous community-front organizations materialized out of the amorphous black nationalism that had lain dormant since Garvey's deportation. Mass rallies were held in the churches. Itinerant agitators harangued crowds from soapboxes in the dark ghettoes, calling on the crowds for donations to the relief efforts. Several colorful and charismatic leaders appeared, volunteering to lead armies of liberation and boasting that they had collected names of enlistees numbering into the tens of thousands. There was rioting in response to published reports of mass executions of Ethiopian patriots by the Fascist armies. Four hundred insurrectionists led by Garveyite Ira Kemp swarmed through Harlem, attacking Italian-owned stores.[13]

In some quarters there was an obsession with the personality of Haile Selassie, actually a rather unpromising candidate for a black messiah. It is doubtful, despite the role of black messiah incarnate that many black people tried to thrust upon him, whether the emperor ever understood the ideas that he was supposed to symbolize. His autobiography, completed after his flight from Ethiopia in 1937, was a pathetic and vainglorious work in which he unconsciously revealed his delusions of grandeur and his longing for acceptance from the greater nations of the world. Dr. Willis N. Huggins, Executive Secretary of the International Council of Friends of Ethiopia, is said to have remarked that the Ethiopian crisis marked Ethiopia's return to the black race.[14] There is little evidence that Haile Selassie really thought so, or that he made any real attempt to exploit the sympathies of black Americans. Still, Huggins reported after touring Ethiopia in 1935 that "the emperor is very conscious of the fact that he is today the only Black Sovereign in the world, and he considers himself as the natural leader of the (black) Negro race. He is fond of repeating the phrase that 'Ethiopia is the trustee for the future of the black races'."[15]

Marcus Garvey was not impressed. Early in the war, his attitude was optimistic and encouraging. He bravely asserted in *The Black Man* (June 1935) that "the Abyssinian Emperor is quite capable of maintaining the tradition of his fathers, and so there is no scare in Ethiopia, but a united front. . . ." But by late March of 1936, Garvey was expressing his disillusionment in an article entitled "Unpreparedness a Crime": "There is much suspicion that Abyssinia has invited her own trouble, by not adhering to a positive racial nationality." The Ethiopian government had not shouldered its responsibilities as an African imperial power. It had failed to maintain contact through embassies with the black republics of Haiti and Liberia; and it did not have missions to the West Indies and the United States, where it could have maintained contact with millions of black people. Editorials became increasingly bitter. As late as June of 1936, Garvey refrained from blaming the emperor personally for Ethiopia's disgrace; but in July and August of that same year, he accused Haile Selassie of "inconsistency." He should have financed a modern army by issuing a paper currency backed up by the wealth of the empire. If that had not been sufficient, he should have funded his war by more aggressively seeking foreign loans. No one cared any longer about the line of Solomon and Sheba; and, in any case, Solomon was not a Negro, but a Jew. The emperor should have laid aside the outworn trappings of a decadent empire, with its useless references to genealogies: "If Haile Selassie had only the vision, inspired with Negro integrity, he would have still been the resident Emperor in Addis Ababa." But no such vision existed; and, even since coming to England, he showed no evidence of having learned his lesson. He ignored a black delegation known as the Negro Federation. "His first reception in London was to the white people, some of whom refused the invitation. . . . No invitation went to representative Negro institutions, organizations or individuals."[16]

When a Miss Una Brown wrote a letter of protest criticizing the editor for criticizing Haile Selassie, Garvey revealed considerable bitterness:

> It is for me to inform you that whilst I appreciate your enthusiasm I cannot in the same manner compliment your intelligence, because there is no man on earth above criticism. The Emperor of Abyssinia was not only Emperor in himself, but he held a trust as Emperor of the surviving Negro Empire in Africa, and by his behaviour he has betrayed that trust consciously or unconsciously.[17]

Garvey was clearly unsympathetic with those New World Negroes who had raised Ras Tafari (the emperor's name before coronation) to the status of a god. Garvey tended to be contemptuous of the superstitions of uneducated West Indians, and his reaction to the Rastafarian cult, one assumes, would have been violently negative.[18] Be that as it may, the growth of Rastafarianism shows the religious reverence that many black people in the Americas felt for the Lion of Judah, as Selassie styled himself. Ironically, the rise of the Rastafarian cult has been attributed by at least one scholar to the persistence of Garveyist sentiment. A prophetic statement, credited to Garvey, has been seen by Leonard Barrett as one source of the movement: "Look to Africa where a black King shall arise—this will be the day of your deliverance."[19] It is certainly true that Garvey was fond of allusions to the Ethiopian prophecy of Psalms 68:31, and he had even made reference to it in connection with the Ethiopian war; but, as we can see in the following statement, he certainly had no intention of deifying Haile Selassie:

> Probably it is through Italy in Abyssinia that "Ethiopia shall stretch forth her hands unto God and Princes shall come out of Egypt."

> We are not condemning the Emperor. Probably he was only an innocent instrument of God's Will in bringing home to the Abyssinians a consciousness of themselves, and impressing the Negroes of the world with their true responsibility. . . . Let us not curse him, but let us hope that he will spend his days in a monastery. . . . We hope the Emperor will forget that he is from Solomon and realize that the world looks upon him as a Negro. . . .[20]

Garvey's hostility to Haile Selassie reveals a consciousness of a fact that scholars have often observed. The emperor had inherited—without seeking it or particularly caring—much of the black nationalist enthusiasm that had been generated throughout the black world by Marcus Garvey.[21] The energies that had been generated by Garveyism, deprived of their accustomed channel, surged up around the symbolic figure of the emperor and a series of other new idols. Scholars have observed similarities between Marcus Garvey and Father Divine, another black messiah, who was already based in New York when Garvey arrived. That Garvey would not have appreciated such comparisons seems abundantly clear; and yet he felt compelled to draw some comparisons between himself and the new black messiah. He was reluctant to be critical, he maintained, "because I myself suffered from misrepresentation." His enemies had stated that he "claimed to be a Messiah," that he claimed to be "a Moses leading the people back to the Promised Land." But Garvey denied having invited or encouraged such an interpretation of his personality or his movement. If, indeed, Father Divine was calling himself God, he was wrong to do so; and his followers were foolish to believe in him.[22] But Garvey surely could not have escaped an awareness that much of his own support had been from among the very kind of people who were glorifying Ras Tafari and Father Divine.

Although Garvey did not want to admit it, much of his own appeal had been to irrational, escapist emotions. E. Franklin Frazier did well to recognize "the messianic element in this movement," which Garvey, as a matter of fact, did consciously exploit.[23] The "black gods of the metropolis"—Prophet Cherry, Daddy Grace, Father Divine—were flamboyant and egotistical. Their methods of mass hypnotism were similar to those of Garvey. Their appeal was to the easy excitability and love of color that characterized the black-ghetto populations. Although Garvey's movement was ostensibly political, it was emotional, not rational, in its attraction; it was a form of Anabaptist millennialism swelling up irrepressibly in the sweaty bosoms of urban peasants. Like the responses to Father Divine, Joe Louis, and Haile Selassie, it was a wonderful blend of half-formed political idealism, religious feeling, and racial enthusiasm.

Father Divine is particularly suited to the central themes of this study because of his ambiguous status between black nationalism and assimilation. In her biography of Father Divine, Sara Harris observed how racial chauvinism may have played an important part in attracting black followers to the cult. Where Garvey had said that God was black, Father Divine, a black man, had claimed that he was God. He said, interprets Harris, "I am a Negro and God dwells in me. You are a Negro and you are like unto me. Therefore, you are superior to white."[24] He had come to New York about 1915 and founded the Peace Mission Movement. He provided free food and lodging for his followers in those Depression years in various sites called heavens. In some ways, the cult of "Divinism" was a typical example of American enthusiastic religion. The ritual was loose and reminiscent of that of many cults—"Holiness," "Sanctified," "Shoutin' Baptist." Father claimed supernatural powers of healing. Members of the cult were forbidden to use tobacco, alcohol, or drugs; as for sex, that was forbidden even to married couples. White as well as black people could join the cult; and in 1946, at the age of sixty-one, he was to take unto himself a "spotless virgin bride," a voluptuous, young, blonde Canadian. She was called Sweet Angel, Mother Divine, the reincarnation of Peninah (Divine's first wife).

He was arrested and jailed in 1930 for "causing a public nuisance" in the Long Island suburb where he resided. His congregation often met there to engage in joyous celebration, punctuated by cries of "Thank you Father Most Sweet!" As he was sentenced and led away, Father was heard to say: "Pity the Judge, he can't live long. He's offended Almighty God." Four days later, the judge was dead; and it was reported that Father Divine, in his jail cell, was overheard to remark, "I hated to do it." His exploitation of the judge's death led Roger Bastide to comment on the methods of Father Divine as similar to those of Obeah men in the West Indies.[25] Father subtly took credit for the death of anyone who passed away after ridiculing or attacking him. The list included Will Rogers, Huey Long, and Adolph Ochs, publisher of the *New York Times*, who had printed unsympathetic editorials about the Messenger. When the glamorous leader of the Jobs For Negroes Campaign—His Holiness, Bishop Amiru Al-Mu-Minin Sufi A. Hamid, head of the Universal Holy Temple of Tranquility—was killed in an airplane accident, Father took credit. Apparently speaking with good authority, one of his angels, Miss Light-o'-Love, conveyed to another, Faithful Mary, the reason for Sufi's fall:

> Sufi Hamid was crazy. He thought he could drive Father out of New York City. He bought an airplane to show he could go higher than God. Father showed nobody could go higher. He brought Sufi lower than low. He made that plane crash and all the breath went out of Sufi Hamid's body.[26]

The observation of Roger Bastide that Divinism seemed to have cognates among the cults of the West Indies was anticipated by Marcus Garvey. "I was accustomed," he said, "to Jamaica Negroes who had become crazy over local pocomania religions."[27] These, as Garvey maintained, flourished among "ignorant Negroes"; their religious ritual was "barbaric expression. . . . But whilst the Jamaica Negroes are practicing pocomanianism, a certain section of the Negroes of the enlightened State of New York, United States of America, have accepted a Negro 'god,' by the name of Father Divine."[28]

Father Divine's followers were seen as rivaling the simple-mindedness of those who defended Ras Tafari. "The Negro hasn't a long memory on things that are sentimental and emotional," Garvey wrote. The tendency of journalists and false prophets to exploit the ignorance of the Negro "makes him unreal and unfits him for anything competently worthwhile." Now that Ethiopia had been defeated, prognosticated Garvey, black people would probably turn to Father Divine "as the new sensation that attracts a large number of the race."

> It is surprising that this "god" was without sympathy for his race, as to have allowed the Italians to conquer Abyssinia. Father Divine is a wicked "god" to have done this; but he is smart enough to say that he doesn't regard race, so even though he is black he sees a black Kingdom crushed by a white nation without considering it unfair to the people who look like him.[29]

Several Universal Negro Improvement Association affiliates met in Toronto in August 1936, and in addition to other weighty matters passed three resolutions condemning Father Divine as a fake. When a former Garvey supporter wrote to *The Black Man* to defend Father Divine and sing the praises of the new messiah, the editor responded: "Father Divine is known in New York as a Fashion Plate Dresser. He wears flannel pants and dress shoes—God wears pants?" It must have depressed the President General to read a letter from a "Past member of U.N.I.A." that spoke of Father as "UNIVERSAL MIND SUBSTANCE."[30] However, not all of Garvey's former followers moved into the religious cults during the 1930s. Some of them continued to focus on political activities. This was to be seen in their support of Senator Theodore G. Bilbo's Negro-repatriation bill, which was not without its appeal to millenarian black nationalists.

Senator Bilbo, a white supremacist and former governor of Mississippi, was elected to the U. S. Senate in 1934 (and again in 1940 and 1946). He denounced the antilynching bill and advocated the deportation of all Negroes to Africa. He later admitted membership in the Ku Klux Klan. His Negro-repatriation bill was even more racist than nineteenth-century colonization.

It lacked the sentimental, paternalistic, romantic conception of African racial traits that had softened the rhetoric of Hollis Read and Harriet Beecher Stowe. It had certain messianic overtones (the ideas of Manifest Destiny and exportation of American values), but it was thoroughly anti-black and gained no significant support among philanthropic whites.

> I wish every newspaper in America would carry the statement—we can

take our choice; we must either repatriate the Negro to his fatherland, or this country will suffer amalgamation, and we will have a race of mongrels in the years to come. Whether we like it or not, it is true, and all history proves it to be true. . . .

The trouble with the Negro who is guilty of the unthinkable crimes that are sometimes committed is that he is abnormal. He has no reason for committing crime. The sutures of the skull have ossified and the brain has stopped growing. . . .

He is an obstacle; he is in the way; he retards progress; and as the Negroes multiply and become more and more numerous, they will more and more drag down our progress and our civilization to lower levels.[31]

"They are sensual in their nature," he asserted, and therefore inclined through no fault of their own to crimes of passion—that is, murder and rape. He went on to speak of the inferiority of the mulattoes, recalling that Alexander Dumas had fought twenty duels "and he boasted of the fact that he was the father of 500 illegitimate children." Bilbo claimed that he had been able to secure 1,000,000 black signatures for a petition to use WPA money for repatriation. Liberia, he observed, limited citizenship rights to anyone having "Negro blood." How then could the black people complain "if we who own this country [say] that it is ours because we took it away from the Indians?"[32] Bilbo's plan was to create a new republic by annexing French and British territories to Liberia:

> We might conclude a bargain by which we could enable the French people and the English people to pay a part, at least, of their war debts by trading to the United States the English territory and the French territory in Africa, and thus give us a great wilderness, a great country almost as large as the United States, in which we might be able to colonize and to repatriate the unfortunate Negro whom we find in our midst.[33]

He asserted that the Negroes were not and could not be happy in the United States, even though their experience in North America had immeasurably improved their condition over their previous savagery and cannibalism. Two things were certain to occur in the future history of the black people: their condition would deteriorate, and they would become totally amalgamated. As for the white people among whom they lived, Negro slavery had already hurt them more than the black people. He read the following into the *Congressional Record*:

> White sentimentalists and the Negroid writers of America will trace to the institution of slavery the American Negro's cultural incapacity. Unmindful of the truth known to ethnology—that the cultural status of the American Negro has antecedents in Africa—they ignore the fact that in his own country the centuries have rolled away, finding him always in the same condition of dense ignorance and unalleviated savagery. . . .

From the standpoint of our civilization, and we should not be affected by any other consideration, the Negro problem is that of daily contact with a race that has no high material history, and whose spiritual history is not in harmony with our own, not merely the enforced contact with this race, but with its increasing millions. We are bequeathing to posterity the greatest burden that civilization may know—millions upon millions of an alien race whose increase will spread over the United States.[34]

This was the man with whom Garveyite remnant groups in the United States were to urge trustful cooperation.

Bilbo had a superficial knowledge of the history of back-to-Africa movements. In 1939 he cited Henry McNeal Turner and Marcus Garvey as spokesmen for colonization. He defended Garvey, saying that "there was no more reason for penalizing Garvey . . . than there was for penalizing bankers who flooded the country with Peruvian bonds . . . just as worthless."[35] Garvey was a man of vision, said Bilbo; and although he met with some failure because of his forthright statements of reality, and although his efforts were undermined by mulattoes and amalgamationists in New York, he had done much to quicken the racial consciousness and pride of the black American. Bilbo read from a series of letters and telegrams from persons claiming to represent black organizations. Some of them were ostensibly Garveyist groups; all of them favored the repatriation bill.

CLEVELAND, OHIO, *April 24, 1939*

We congratulate you in sponsoring the program for American Negroes returning to their fatherland.

DIVISION NO. 272, U.N.I.A.
John Wiggs, *Secretary*

JACKSONVILLE, FLA., *April 23, 1939*

Your law abiding citizens, followers of the martyred African Princess Laura Adorkor Koffey, assassinated Miami, Fla., March 8, 1928, in hearty accord with your views as published under your name in *Chicago Defender* of April 22, 1939. Prayerful wishes for your continued interest and courageous efforts in this cause so thoroughly misrepresented by an element of our visionless misleaders.

MISSIONARY AFRICAN UNIVERSAL CHURCH, INC.

NEW YORK, N.Y., *April 24, 1939*

Ten thousand Negroes of the Universal Negro Improvement Association, assembled in mass meeting, endorse your proposed repatriation bill. Hoping for the full support of your fellow Senators.

GARVEY CLUB, INC.
G. E. Harris, *President.*
C. A. Wright, *Secretary.*[36]

Bilbo was the last of the American colonizationists; he utilized the old nineteenth-century colonization rhetoric of racism disguised as paternalism. It was a blessing of Providence that the Negro had been brought from the wilds of Africa to these shores, here to be instructed under the benevolent tutelage of slavery in the arts of civilization. It was now up to America to carry forward the manifest destiny of the Negro by returning him to Africa as a leavening agent where he could take up the work of lifting the entire continent from its savage state. The colonists would Christianize the Africans and "teach them the American way of life."[37]

Among the supporters of Bilbo's repatriationism was Ramon A. Martinez, a Detroit black attorney, who had received his legal training at the University of Puerto Rico. He, too, favored the idea of prevailing upon France and England to cede African territories adjacent to Liberia in payment for the war debt. Martinez was interviewed by the *Detroit News*, which identified him as spokesman for "The Negro Nationalist Movement." This, said Martinez, "is a new school of thought in American race relations." The movement was made up of a number of smaller groups, including "The Grand United Order of Knights of the Golden Lions and Daughters of Ethiopian Redemption." They claimed to represent mass sentiment among black people and asserted that those black people who opposed their activities were snobs or contented members of the professional classes or artists and intellectuals. Such persons were only idle dreamers who refused to look at the situation "scientifically."

> The situation of the Negro in America is that of a nation within a nation, with the white people bearing the greater cost and the Negro the greater moral and material suffering. The endeavor to form an American national unit out of heterogeneous individuals who are originally dissimilar in all essentials is not only an absurdity but an impossibility. This is the core of the difficulty in the United States.[38]

"The Peace Movement of Ethiopia," which operated under the slogan "One God, One Country, One People; to Return People of African descent to their Motherland, Africa," communicated with President Roosevelt and Senator Bilbo. They claimed to be appalled by miscegenation and other horrors resulting from racial contacts in the United States. "There are several million of us," asserted the movement's spokesmen, "who will go back to Africa by our own consent." Despite their professed nationalism and their stated belief that black people could not survive in America, the representatives of the movement were willing to trust that "the colonial activity of America has always been one of benevolent paternalism." Unlike the "Nationalist Movement" of Detroit, they did not ask the government to support an elaborate Greater Liberia scheme; they would be contented simply to have the government negotiate with Liberia "for such land as existing treaty rights entitle us to, sufficient to

colonize the entire body of the signatories hereto and finance the movement to the extent desirable for ultimate success."³⁹

Senator Bilbo denied that he favored the forced deportation of black
Americans, but there was an ominous tone in much of what he said. He
reminded the Senate of the refusal of the Daughters of the American
Revolution to allow Marian Anderson to sing in Constitution Hall.
Feigning sympathy, he went on to claim that he was a mere witness to the
growing spirit of race hatred that the D.A.R. refusal symbolized. He
alluded to the racial problems "which we have seen so bitterly
demonstrated in Italy and in Germany."⁴⁰ The situation was lamentably
getting worse in the United States, where there was "a rising tide of
opposition to various races." The Senator displayed a letter which he said
was "penned by the black hand of a descendant of a Zulu tribe in
Zululand, South Africa, represent[ing] the overpowering impulse of an
Afro–American to plead in his simple peculiar way for race nationality."
The letter, from J. Milton Batson, was an attack on "those within our
own racial group represented by the professional doctor and clergy, the
successful businessman, and the one half or three fourths caste mulattoes" who favor the establishment of "a socialist-communist state." The
writer invoked the names of Jefferson, Lincoln, and Warren G. Harding
as men of vision who had acknowledged the "inescapable difference
between the white man and the black man." He found it strange that the
national government was advocating a national homeland for German-
refugee Jews and yet refusing to take action on the repatriationist
proposals of Senator Bilbo.⁴¹

Meanwhile, Marcus Garvey was keeping a close watch on these
proceedings from his London office. "The Senator's desire for carrying
out the purpose of his bill may not be as idealistic as Negroes may want,"
he admitted, "but that is not the point to be considered." This was an
opportunity for the Negro to establish the dreamed-of black empire in
Africa; and no thoughtful Negro, no matter how well situated in the
States, should oppose the bill or counsel their fellows to put all their eggs
in the one basket of integrationism: "Whilst some may seriously fight for
the realization of the Negro's opportunity in America, another group
should fight most strenuously, as the Universal Negro Improvement
Association is doing, for his complete independence nationally, on the
continent of Africa." The UNIA affiliates were encouraged to give their
whole-hearted support to Senator Bilbo's bill.⁴²

Senator Bilbo was certainly not perceived as a messiah by black people,
but he was clever enough to understand that he could gain black support
for even the most racist of proposals by establishing a rhetorical linkage
to the messianic nationalism of the nineteenth century. His success in
gaining black support for his repatriation bill demonstrated that the
coalition between black nationalists and white racialists, established in
the nineteenth century and revived by Garvey, was not yet defunct. The

black deportation movement, as it had been represented by the American Colonization Society, was still alive. The black supporters of Senator Bilbo were "Uncle Tommish" in the classical sense that they lent credence to the doctrine of permanent racial separatism and elitism and supported the old messianic African redemptionist scheme outlined in *Uncle Tom's Cabin.*

Garvey questioned the sincerity of whites who supported Father Divine and he questioned the integrity of Divine for accepting their aid, but he was perfectly willing to trust in the benevolence of whites to pour billions of dollars into an African repatriation scheme with no strings attached. He characterized Bilbo as "the real exponent of the suppressed Negro who is not able in that house to express himself, and who is gradually being misrepresented by a group of Negroes who are directly benefiting from the misrepresentation under a pro-white system of Government." He reminded his readers of the plight of the German Jews who were "a part of German civilization for centuries . . . uppermost in the intellectual, industrial, and financial groups." With the rise of Hitler, they now found themselves once again wandering. The black American should learn from the experience of the Jews, for what had happened to one minority could happen to another, but blacks could not hope for even the small degree of international sympathy that the Jews had received. In the same issue of *The Black Man* that publicized these views, Garvey reprinted a story describing a fascist plot in the United States that would attempt to marshal support behind the "Negro Race Issue." The conspiracy was headed by Major General George Van Horn Mosely, a former Army officer, who had apparently expected the assistance of the American Legion and the Ku Klux Klan in this attack on Negroes, Jews, and the New Deal. Garvey was probably correct in seeing parallels between German anti-Semitism and American racism, but far too trusting in his appeal to American protofascists for deliverance from fascism.[43]

During these years, the Communist Party was making its own millenarian appeal to the nationalist utopianism of black Americans, but with few results. In part, their lack of success was due to the confusing nature of their position. On the one hand, they took the position that the black people were the victims of class oppression and that their problems could be solved through an economic revolution that would eliminate the causes of class and racial conflict. At the same time, they were supporters of a "Black Belt Nationalism." This led to a dual approach by the Communist Party, continuing from the 1930s to the 1950s. It was often stated in declarations of the official Communist position during these decades that

> in the South . . . the main Communist slogan must be: The right of self determination of the Negroes in the Black Belt. The Negroes in the North

are very much interested in winning the right of self determination of the Negro population of the Black Belt and can thereby hope for strong support for the establishment of true equality of the Negroes in the North. . . . One of the Communist slogans is "Death for Negro lynching. . . ." The struggle for the equal rights of the Negroes does not in any way exclude recognition and support for the Negro's right to their own special schools, Government organs, and so forth, wherever the Negro masses put forward such national demands of their own accord.[44]

Here was more grist for Senàtor Bilbo's mill. The Communist Party was clearly committed to the mongrelization of the United States through a policy of black separatism in the South. He read into the *Congressional Record* reports of "girls employed in Washington offices living with male Negroes." He described the meetings of the National Negro Conference in 1937, where, according to the correspondent, "there were many white Jewish girls sent there to live at the same hotels, be seen in the company of Negroes on the streets, at theaters, restaurants, etc., for the purpose of firing the imagination of the Negroes on the question of 'equality' for the colored race under a soviet America."[45]

Simultaneously, there was a growing "National Movement for the Establishment of a 49th State." The Chicago-based office of its National Council issued a pamphlet in 1934 which outlined its aims. The proposal varied somewhat from the International's, in that it was not based upon the idea of simply giving self-determination to a region that was historically and economically tied to the black masses. Rather, the National Council called upon the government to purchase lands to which those who were interested might migrate.[46] The Communists opposed this as a bourgeois movement which did not recognize the Black Belt as the only legitimate basis for a black state.[47] William Z. Foster, a Communist spokesman who had once run for the presidency against Franklin D. Roosevelt, continued to campaign for "Negro National Liberation" as late as 1953. Foster recognized that black migration to the North and to the urban centers of the South was eroding the numerical dominance of blacks in the black counties. A new wave of education was necessary to do away with the "confusions regarding such concepts as 'race' and 'caste'." The Negro question was a national question, according to Foster, whose book was reissued by International Publishers in 1970 in response to "the new upsurge in the black liberation struggle. . . ."[48]

Around the time that the Communist Party began to advocate separatism for the Black Belt, W. E. B. Du Bois was once again emphasizing the messianic black nationalism that had always been an important element in his thought. As Herbert Aptheker has noted, the same forces that led to the rise of black nationalist thinking among other black people during the 1930s affected him. Du Bois was no black messiah, and yet there was a messianic strain in his thinking that has been commented upon by some observers.[49] This had been apparent in his essay *The Conservation of Races* in 1897, written when he was twenty-nine and still "instinctively bowing" before the influence of the elder statesman of Ethiopianism, Alexander Crummell.[50] In an address before the American Negro Academy, he had called upon the black people of the United States and the rest of the world to deliver their own distinctive mission to civilization. The same mystical ethnic chauvinism had been present in *The Souls of Black Folk*, where he had romanticized the black peasantry as the "sole oasis of simple faith and reverence in a dusty desert of dollars." The messianic quality had been present in *Darkwater*, where he had waxed poetic once again, conjuring up visions of black gods and goddesses, portraying the masses of Southern black folk as a mystical body of Christ, bruised and suffering for the sins of America. His next major work, *Dusk of Dawn*, bespoke a reconsideration of Booker T. Washington's temporary compromise with segregation. He even went so far as to pattern the final sentence of the chapter on black separatism after the allusion to Revelations in Washington's closing statement in the Atlanta Exposition Address. Du Bois presented black separatist development as "the economic ladder by which the American Negro, achieving new social institutions, can move pari passu with the modern world into *a new heaven and a new earth.*"[51]

Du Bois, like Garvey, had long envisioned a messianic leadership role for black Americans in the Pan-African movement. He had called or helped to organize a series of conferences between 1900 and 1927. He deliberately made the comparison to another messianic movement, Zionism, taking the position that identification with the universal race problem should not in any way compromise the struggle for full and immediate integration in all aspects of American life. By 1934, however, Du Bois' opinion on how black people should confront the problem at home had changed considerably from what it had been in the earlier part of the century. In 1934, he returned to the position that he had articulated in *The Philadelphia Negro*—that black folk must assume the prime responsibility for their own uplift. The NAACP had over-emphasized integration to the neglect of needed programs for self-help. "The opposition to segregation," he argued, "is an opposition to discrimination." Desegregation had only been a means to an end, not an end in itself. Freedom and equality could be worked for—indeed must, at times, be worked for—through separate black institutions. Segregation was a fact of life and was certain to remain so for the rest of the century. Du Bois had recognized for many years the "curious paradox" that, "unless we had fought segregation with determination, our whole race would have been pushed into an ill-lighted, unpaved, unsewered ghetto. Unless we had built great church organizations and manned our own Southern schools, we should be shepherdless sheep. . . . Here is a dilemma calling for thought and forbearance. Not every builder of racial cooperation and solidarity is a Jim Crow advocate, and a hater of white folk. Not every Negro who fights prejudice and segregation is ashamed of his race."[52] That was in 1919. In 1934 when Du Bois decided to support voluntary segregation, he denounced the integrationists in no uncertain terms. His attack on Walter White was in exceptionally poor taste:

> The arguments of Walter White, George Schuyler, and Kelly Miller have logic, but they seem to me quite beside the point. In the first place, Walter White is white. He has more white companions and friends than colored. He goes where he will in New York City and naturally meets no Color Line, for the simple and sufficient reason that he isn't "colored"; he feels his new freedom in bitter contrast to what he was born to in Georgia. This is perfectly natural and he does what anyone else of his complexion would do.[53]

This was destructive and unfair criticism, as Du Bois was well aware, since Garvey had subjected Du Bois to the same sort of abuse. Du Bois' support for voluntary segregation in 1934 led, of course, to his resignation from the NAACP office he held as editor of *Crisis*. Marcus Garvey noted the move with interest and suspicion. "If Dr. Du Bois has joined our school of thought we welcome him," he wrote, "but it seems so late in his life for him to turn this way with the hope of much good result."[54]

Du Bois' separatist program of the 1930s was considerably different from the program of self-help through separate institutions that he had advocated at the turn of the century. At that time, he had called for a "Talented Tenth," including a black captain of industry, to uplift the masses of his people; now, he was urging a communal effort. In *Dusk of Dawn*, published in 1940, he outlined a plan similar in many respects to that of The Honorable Elijah Muhammad, who was then, of course, virtually unknown.

> Already Negroes can raise their own food, build their own homes, fashion their own clothes, mend their own shoes, do much of their repair work, and raise some raw materials like tobacco and cotton. A simple transfer of Negro workers, with only a few such additional skills as can easily be learned in a few months, would enable them to weave their own cloth, make their own shoes, slaughter their own meat, prepare furniture for their homes, install electrical appliances, make their own cigars and cigarettes.
> Appropriate direction and easily obtainable technique and capital would enable Negroes further to take over the whole of their retail distribution, to raise, cut, mine and manufacture a considerable proportion of the basic raw material, to invent and build machines.[55]

It was not to be an individualistic or an elitist scheme. On the contrary, "all this would be a realization of democracy in industry led by consumers' organizations and extending to planned production." The plan also called for socialized professional services which would "mutualize in reality and not in name, banking and insurance, law and medicine." Black people, he reasoned, might easily constitute the vanguard of a new movement toward complete socialization and democratization of the American economy. It can be seen, then, that he was not conceiving of segregation as an ultimate goal, and, indeed, when the Stalinists proposed their Black Belt scheme, Du Bois was singularly uninterested.

Earl Ofari has rightly seen *Dusk of Dawn* as representing a high point in Du Bois' nationalist expression.[56] It would be wrong, however, to interpret this as an atypical expression, except that it appears to be the only point at which Du Bois openly seemed to advocate that the messianic role of black people would be to lead the rest of America down the road to socialism by quiet example. It is important to understand that Du Bois' approach to race was always messianic in this way. If integration was only a means to the end of equality, then racial consciousness was only a means to the goal of the universal uplift of all humanity. In 1938, Du Bois returned to Fisk University, his alma mater, to address the graduating class on the fiftieth anniversary of his own graduation. Assuming for himself more than the status of mere commencement speaker, he took the roles of prophet, seer, and priest. "I was here speaking a word of benediction," he later said, "not merely to the three surviving members of my own class or to the graduation class of the day; I was speaking to the intelligent colored citizens of 1938 and seeking to express a certain philosophy of life." The speech was called "The Revelation of Saint Orgne, the Damned." Du Bois had received a message from the hand of St. Orgne (an anagram for Negro), and this message was again one of racial messianism.

> The martyrdom of man may be increased and prolonged through primitive, biological racial propaganda, but on the other hand through cooperation, education and understanding the cultural race unit may be the pipe line through which human civilization may extend to wider and wider areas of fertilization of mankind.[57]

The messianic quality is to be detected in Du Bois' concept of the "race unit" as a cultural entity, an idea to which he had subscribed earlier in his career. Each "cultural race unit," or people, was to find the Universal in the Particular—that is, by realizing its own internal potential, it was to contribute to the progress of all humanity. Until the time of his death, Du Bois continued to believe that the black peoples had a special messianic function; thus his vacillation at the end between Pan–Africanism and Communism represented more than the usual ambivalence of American black nationalists. It reflected his belief that all civilization had originated in Africa. Not only could the primeval mythologies of pre-Christian Europe be traced back to African sources, but even the idea of Communism itself—African socialism "blossomed bold on communism, centuries old." The indigenous cultures would "teach mankind what Non-Violence and Courtesy, Literature and Art, Music and Dancing can do for this greedy, selfish, and war-stricken world."[58]

Because Du Bois was temperamentally austere, and isolated by virtue of intellectual and social preferences from the people of the streets, his messianism did not take the form of an enthusiastic movement among the masses. But his thinking—tending as it sometimes did towards black chauvinism—was in many ways similar to that of Marcus Garvey, Noble Drew Ali, and Elijah Muhammad, though somewhat more controlled and couched in respectable scholarly rhetoric. For black intellectuals like Alphaeus Hunton, Lorraine Hansberry, Paul Robeson, and Vincent Harding, "he was an institution in our lives." He provided a black messianism for the educated and, in the words of Horace Mann Bond, "he was the Great Revelator."[59]

During the years upon which we have been focusing, messianic movements combining religious millennialism with nationalistic striving were appearing in parts of the world other than the United States. Vittorio Lanternari has described some of these movements in *The Religions of the Oppressed*. There has been much debate on the question of whether the religion of the enslaved, colonized, or otherwise oppressed peoples may better be described as an "opiate" or as an inspiration to political militancy.[60] Evidence may be found to argue either point, but it seems obvious that even the most passive and otherworldly religion need not necessarily be devoid of political value. The lives of Mahatma Gandhi, Chief Luthuli, and the Reverend Dr. Martin Luther King, Jr., seem to show this. For better or for worse, they wielded tremendous political influence, and although none lived to see his goals realized, each was able to impress upon a large segment of mankind the worthiness of his means and ends.

The similarities between Gandhi, Luthuli, and King are striking. Each professed a spiritual motivation towards action in the affairs of the material world. All three were committed to the use of nonviolent resistance as a means to achieving radical political ends. All three were world-citizens, committed to the pursuit of justice for all peoples and sympathetic to the sufferings of persons outside their own national, racial, and religious communities.

The differences between them are worthy of comment, as well. They represented widely diverse cultures, although each represented a people dominated by an outside group. Their motivations, like their personalities, were different, having been produced by widely differing environments and experiences. Their values and their ultimate goals were widely divergent, as were their attitudes towards the nationalistic strivings of their several communities. They faced different varieties of opposition from within and from without their respective national groups. King and Luthuli were awarded the Nobel Peace Prize, but Gandhi was not. His biographers seem to have found little interest in the question of why. There was no winner of the Nobel Peace Prize in 1948, the year of Gandhi's death.

Gandhi's nationalism, founded as it was in charismatic leadership and social millenarianism, had many characteristics of a messianic movement in the sense that Bertrand Russell used the term. It demonstrated many of the characteristics often grouped by anthropologists under the heading of "Revitalization Movements." It was a movement by a non-Western, largely pre-industrial people to throw off control by outsiders by utilizing the force of ancestral traditions, which had been somewhat modified by exposure to the outside world. It was conservative in that it was based on a revitalization of ancient values, but radical in that it reinterpreted those values in a context of change and future orientation. Gandhi was able to mobilize the dormant revolutionary powers of Hinduism, a religion that had come to be identified with fatalism and otherworldliness, and transform it, through the philosophy of "passive resistance," into a modern revolutionary ideology.[61]

Gandhi spent twenty years in South Africa, during which time he developed the techniques of pacifist nationalism with which he is today identified. Two themes are ascendent in Gandhi's thought throughout the nationalistic phase of his career—civil disobedience and the rejection of material values. Both ideas are found in the works of the American philosopher Henry David Thoreau, which Gandhi read while imprisoned during 1909 for burning the registration card that all Indians in South Africa were required to carry. One should recoil, however, from too hastily attributing Gandhi's political and spiritual philosophy to the influences of New England transcendentalism, especially since transcendentalism itself is loosely related to ancient Hindu philosophy. Gandhi's philosophy was in harmony not only with Thoreau's, but with many "universal" values common to European religion, Asian religion, and much secular thought. The Mahatma's writings reveal that his political activism was a mere offshoot of his religious beliefs. Nationalism was only a means to spiritual perfection. To Gandhi, British imperialism meant cultural slavery, the undermining of traditional spiritual values with the trinkets and gewgaws of a crassly pragmatic and alien civilization. It is not that Gandhi was provincial; on the contrary, he believed that British imperialism, with its tendency to advance material solutions (both the socialistic and the capitalistic brands) for every problem, was contrary to certain eternal verities. "I want the cultures of all the lands to be blown about my house as freely as possible," he once said, "but I refuse to be blown off my feet by any." Gandhi appealed to universal human values to achieve a particularistic goal, nationalism. This goal of nationalism, however, was in turn only a means to an end that Gandhi perceived as universalistic.[62]

Nonetheless, Gandhi's nationalism was an inspiration to black nationalists. He was admired by Marcus Garvey and by Chief Albert Luthuli, the South African civil-rights activist and Zulu patriot. Luthuli, whose philosophy was closer to King's than to Garvey's, was a Christian activist, and is said to have preached every Sunday during the years of his chieftainship. As did Gandhi's, his thinking revealed an interplay between nationalistic and universal values, and he often stated his belief that "African social values and patterns of life [were] not incompatible with Christianity." Late in life, he witnessed, to his dismay, the policies of the South African government which encouraged tribalism in such a way as to undo the work of missionary education, which Luthuli viewed as culturally broadening and politically unifying.[63]

The Gandhi influence came about indirectly through contact with the Indian community in Durban, South Africa. At the turn of the century, Gandhi had already organized Indians in South Africa around the principle of Satyagraha, the use of spiritual force to achieve political goals. But while Gandhi had conceived of his approach to resistance in Hindu terms, Luthuli adopted a rhetoric of Christian messianism and revolutionary martyrdom:

> I have embraced the non-Violent Passive Resistance technique in fighting for freedom because I am convinced it is the only non-revolutionary, legitimate and humane way. . . .
> What the future has in store for me I do not know. It might be ridicule, imprisonment, concentration camp, flogging, banishment and even death. I only pray to the Almighty to strengthen my resolve so that none of these grim possibilities may deter me from striving. . . .
> It is inevitable that in working for Freedom some individuals and some families must take the lead and suffer: The Road to Freedom is via the CROSS.[64]

Clearly, there were similarities between Luthuli's and King's Christian Gandhiism; there were also differences just as striking. Luthuli was influenced by Gandhi indirectly and believed that Gandhi's nonviolence represented a nonrevolutionary approach to social change. King consciously utilized the techniques of Gandhi as a revolutionary method, and it hardly seems likely that he could have been unaware of the nationalistic implications of adopting Gandhian methods. This is not to say that King was a black nationalist, but merely to note his ideological immersion in currents of nationalism that swept over Africa and Asia during his lifetime.

King was only marginally associated with the nationalistic aspects of black messianism. He was not identified with black separatism, nor with the philosophy of self-determination, nor with the antagonism towards outsiders that so often characterized the movement. It would be incorrect, however, to attempt to disassociate him from those traditions of cultural and religious nationalism that have been identified as essential elements of black American consciousness, for the Reverend King shared with the most strident of nationalists a sense of the special mission of black people. "We have been seared in the flames of suffering," he once said. "We have known the agony of the underdog. . . . So in dealing with our particular dilemma, we will challenge the nation to deal with its larger dilemma."[65] A few years earlier, in his "Letter From Birmingham Jail," he had argued that civil-rights activists were above the law because they adhered to a higher law. These beliefs are characteristic of, if not exclusive to, groups who conceive of themselves as messianic peoples.[66]

Such attitudes are not restricted to black nationalists, but black nationalism is imbued with such attitudes. King represented a people whose messianic tradition was inseparable from their system of social organization. The black churches did not undermine the development of art and ideas (as E. Franklin Frazier had maintained); it nurtured them. The black church had only required creative intelligence and courageous leadership to move beyond the level of quaint folk expression and provincial ethnic chauvinism. Under the direction of King's Southern Christian Leadership Conference, the "Negro spirituals" became battle hymns. The traditional black sermon, better known for its rhythms and resonances than for its social relevance, was transformed into stirring political art. It is often said that the civil-rights movement could never have existed without the organizational structure provided by the black church. It is less common to observe the indebtedness of the Reverend King and his movement to the black messianic tradition and to acknowledge that cultural nationalism was one of the ingredients that made for his success.[67]

Martin Luther King, Jr., popularized the slogan "Black is Beautiful," but that did not make him a black nationalist.[68] He utilized the methods of Gandhi, the Indian nationalist, but that did not make him a nationalist. He made clear his opposition to nationalism, disassociating himself from the "pessimistic doctrine" of Elijah Muhammad and describing black nationalism as "a development that would inevitably lead to a frightening racial nightmare."[69] But, almost in the same breath, he was capable of employing a rhetoric that many black nationalists could have cheered. He recognized that the black American "consciously or unconsciously . . . has been caught up by the *Zeitgeist*, and with his black brothers of Africa and his brown and yellow brothers of Asia, South America and the Caribbean, the United States Negro is moving with a sense of urgency toward the promised land of racial justice."[70]

The changes that took place in Martin Luther King's philosophy during the last year of his life are less frequently commented upon than is the spectacular evolution of the philosophy of Malcolm X. In his later speeches, King revealed an increasing sympathy for the concepts of black unity and black consciousness. This is not to say that he was moving in the direction of ethnocentrism, for he simultaneously expressed increasing concern for issues other than American racism. During the years following his acceptance of the Nobel Peace Prize, he seems to have taken seriously the role of international leadership that was thrust upon him. He alluded with greater frequency to the issues of class oppression and the problems of other ethnic minorities, including the poor whites, who outnumbered poor blacks two to one. And, despite much criticism from other civil-rights leaders, he began to speak out against the war in Vietnam.[71]

At the same time, he was also responding to the challenges presented at home by black-power militants, expressing a desire to "work passionately for group identity . . . the kind of group consciousness that Negroes need to participate more meaningfully at all levels in the life of our nation."[72] He was more forceful in stating that ethical appeals "must be undergirded by some form of constructive coercive power."[73] King had once viewed the existence of separate churches for white and black as symbolizing American religious hypocrisy. While never completely abandoning this view, he became more forceful in describing the Negro church and other separate institutions as "the basis for building a powerful united front. . . . This form of group unity can do infinitely more to liberate the Negro than any action of *individuals*."[74] He came to be less passionate in his criticisms of "our Muslim brothers," and expressed his admiration for their community programs.[75] He responded to the cries for "black power" by speaking about the need "to develop a sense of black consciousness and peoplehood."[76] While he could not countenance indiscriminate antagonism towards whites, he rejected the view of his movement "as one that seeks to integrate the Negro into all existing values of American society."[77]

Martin Luther King, Jr., learned his Christianity in an independent black church and refined it in one of the more progressive schools of theology in the United States. He undertook his work in a nation where traditions of religious conservatism were counterbalanced by traditions of a social gospel—a nation in which Protestant revivalism had been associated with perfectionist doctrines, millennial expectations, and self-righteous Christian soldierism, and whose history could easily be interpreted as a series of "Great Awakenings." True, these traditions had often informed the rhetoric of white supremacy, imperialism, and class oppression; but they had also inspired progressive thinkers to undertake humanitarian social reforms. The black Americans whom King mobilized had a tradition of utilizing religion as a means of resistance. Christian messianism and a millennial view of history were fundamental ingredients of American culture, but were experienced with a special keenness by the Reverend King and the black Americans who referred to him affectionately as "De Lawd."[78]

King was a shrewd manipulator of mass opinion. He recognized that black messianism, if stripped of its implications of racial chauvinism, was potentially appealing to whites. Like Booker T. Washington and W. E. B. Du Bois a half century earlier, he projected to white America an image of black folk as the embodiment of simple faith and virtue, the very soul of homely American pietism. Like Joe Louis, he represented at once the militancy of black people and their willingness to get along with whites; he symbolized not only the rising aspirations of blacks, but the democratic ideals that all Americans associated with their national destiny. As Joe Louis, during the Depression, had been seen as "leading the nation" in some mythic way "back to prosperity," so was King viewed as leading the nation towards fulfillment of the American Dream.

He was able to blend the messianic themes in Afro–American thought with the strains of American millenarianism from which they were partially derived. "We will win our freedom," he prophesied, "because the sacred heritage of our nation and the eternal will of God are embodied in our echoing demands."[79] He did not claim that black Americans were a chosen people or a master race, but he did feel that Providence had often made them pioneers in movements essential to the nation's development. "The first man to die in the American Revolution was a Negro Seaman, Crispus Attucks," he once reminded a radio audience. "Before that fateful struggle ended, the institution of absolute monarchy was laid on its death bed."[80] Although few black thinkers had "exerted an influence on the main currents of American thought," the masses of black people had, "by taking to the streets and there giving practical lessons in democracy and its defaults . . . decisively influenced white thought."[81] The messianic role of the black American people was to save the entire nation by illuminating "imperfections in the democratic structure that were formerly only dimly perceived."[82] They would carry all the American people with them towards the once dimly perceived millennium. "In winning rights for ourselves," King declared, "we have produced substantial benefits for the entire nation."[83]

However, the freedom movement was not to limit itself to the American scene. "The American Negro . . . , like Crispus Attucks, may be the vanguard in a prolonged struggle that may change the shape of the world, as millions of deprived shake and transform the earth in their quest for life, freedom, and justice."[84] He gave indications of his concern for international problems from the very beginning when he spoke of the linkage between the struggles of the American Negro and those of African and Asian nations emerging from colonialism. In his first book, *Stride Toward Freedom*, he cited Toynbee—but actually sounded more like Du Bois—when he said: "It may be the Negro who will give the new spiritual dynamic to Western civilization. . . . The Negro may be God's appeal to this age."[85]

The internationalism that characterized Dr. King's outlook from the early days when he met with Nehru and corresponded with Albert Luthuli was intensified after 1964, the year in which he received the Nobel Prize. During that year, he was subjected to intense criticism from black nationalists, the most significant being Malcolm X. If the style of King was reminiscent of fellow-Negro Baptist Joe Louis, that of Malcolm X was similar to the style of fellow-Black Muslim Muhammad Ali. Until his repudiation of the Black Muslims' extreme separatist philosophy, Malcolm X presented no real threat to King; but by 1963, as his speeches became less concerned with constructing a white demonology and more concerned with penetrating to the root causes of racial oppression, he began to present a real challenge to King's formerly unassailable leadership status. He preceded King in coming to an understanding that the new arena for civil-rights activism would be the urban ghettoes. He also came earlier than King to a radical evaluation of American foreign policy and domestic affairs, as they affected both white and black.

The criticisms of King by the black-power advocates, and his responses to them, symbolized the increasing political consciousness of black Americans and their leadership during the 1960s. King once utilized an anecdote to illustrate his awareness of this growing political consciousness. In one of the Southern states, where poison gas was being used for the first time in place of the gallows, a microphone was placed in the chamber with the condemned so that scientific observers could hear his last words.

> The first victim was a young Negro. As the pellet dropped into the container, and the gas curled upward, through the microphone came these words: "Save me, Joe Louis. Save me, Joe Louis. Save me, Joe Louis. . . ."[86]

King rejoiced that this "bizarre and naive cry" had been replaced by "a mighty shout of challenge," and that the "loneliness and profound despair of Negroes in that period" had been "replaced by confidence."[87] King's crusade was not divorced from traditional messianic conceptions of black religious and cultural nationalism. He utilized such traditions, consciously and unconsciously, throughout his career.[88] Much of his success must also be attributed to the transformation that had taken place among black people during the first half of the twentieth century. That they expected a more sophisticated variety of leadership than either doctrinaire integrationists or separatists could give was a mark of their increased sophistication. The significant majority of black Americans seemed to have progressed, at least temporarily, beyond the point of calling on Joe Louis or Haile Selassie to save them.

11
Chosen Peoples of the Metropolis: Black Muslims, Black Jews, and Others

Black messianic mythology in the United States has obviously not been confined to the Christian community. The "Great Migration" of masses of black people to such urban centers as Chicago, Detroit, New York, and Philadelphia during the period of the World Wars was accompanied by the flourishing of numerous urban cults, whose working-class leadership rejected Christianity as the religion of the hypocritical slavemaster. The new religions were often stridently militant, and often preached a doctrine of black supremacy. In some cases, their members identified with Marcus Garvey and rejected their American identity. They refused to call themselves "Negroes," interpreting the word as a badge of shame. They adopted a messianic rhetoric and proclaimed that they were a chosen people with a favored place in history. They would rise to meet a future of unparalleled glory, while the Christian West sank into oblivion.

The many apparent similarities between Black Jews in the United States and the more widely known sect called the Black Muslims have been noted, or at least implied, by a number of students.[1] Between the Ethiopian varieties of Christianity and Judaism, similarities also exist. Indeed, some ties may exist between Falasha Jews in Ethiopia and Black Hebrews in the United States, some of whom have returned to the Holy Land, where they live in uneasy relationship with Israel. Ties certainly exist between the Black Jews and the so-called "Ethiopian Movement," which originated with the tour of Henry McNeal Turner through South Africa in the 1890s and spread by the 1930s to East Africa, West Africa, and the United States. Rastafarianism in the West Indies is akin to this same Ethiopian movement.[2] The fact that messianic religiosity among the black people of the United States has expressed itself in Jewish and Islamic, as well as in Christian, forms indicates underlying strains of similarity between Pan–Africanism, Pan–Islamism, and Zionism.

The fact that there are similarities between these admittedly diverse phenomena should not be misinterpreted as meaning that they are all the same phenomenon. Nonetheless, the points of comparison between the Nation of Islam and the Black Jews represent similar responses by black Americans to an environment that has frustrated the aspirations of both groups in similar ways. It is ironic that while Pan–Islamism and Zionism find themselves in bitter conflict in the Middle East, both religious systems have legitimate offspring in black America whose practitioners share much of the same ideology. The various sects of Black Muslims and Black Jews in America would bitterly deny that their religions are both expressions of the same phenomenon, mere social movements assuming a messianic rhetoric and religious trappings that are purely accidental or metaphorical expressions of temporal aspirations. Pan–Islamists and Zionists would make similarly bitter denials. All would probably be justified in doing so; but students of religion as well as students of nationalism have long recognized that religion and nationalism are similar phenomena.[3] It would seem possible to discuss the similarities between the aforementioned movements without perforce denying or approving the validity of any or overlooking their individuality.

There is reason to believe that the black Jews of Ethiopia may be able to trace their Jewishness back farther than can some European Jews. During the ninth century, obscure accounts by Jewish travelers (like Eldad Haddani) began referring to the existence of a lost tribe of black Jews in Abyssinia. Medieval accounts of Ethiopia, written by outsiders, are notoriously unreliable. Stories abound of men with their heads in the middle of their chests, one-footed men, cannibals (anthropophagi), and demi-god rulers like Prester John, the legendery Christian king. Nothing definite was known of these black Jews, or Falashas, by the outside world until James Bruce mentioned them in his *Travels to Discover the Sources of the Nile* (Edinburgh, 1790). During the mid-nineteenth century, a number of reports by missionaries and other investigators confirmed the existence of Falasha communities. In 1949, Wolf Leslau reawakened interest in the Falashas with an article in *Commentary* describing the findings of his research in progress, based upon travels to Ethiopia in 1947.[4] Leslau returned to Ethiopia for additional research work in 1950, and in 1951 he published *Falasha Anthology: The Black Jews of Ethiopia*. Leslau's work has made Falasha writings, originally set down in the Geez language, available to English readers for the first time.

The Falashas, who refer to themselves as *beta Israel* or simply as *Israel*, trace their ancestry—as do the Christian royal family of Ethiopia—to the fruits of a liaison between King Solomon and the Queen of Sheba. Their name is believed to derive from the Ethiopic word fälläsä, meaning "to emigrate," which may suggest an origin outside Ethiopia. Some Falashas believe that they became separated from the main body of Judaism at the time of the exodus from Egypt; others believe that they came to Ethiopia with the first or second Diaspora. No one is certain whether the Falashas were originally Jewish immigrants or an indigenous people converted to Judaism. Wolf Leslau suggests, in any case, that their form of Judaism is "very primitive" and "might date from a time when the Mishnah and Talmud were not yet compiled."[5] An American group called the Ethiopian Hebrews claims descent from the Falashas, but scholars are uncertain of their origins.

The Black Jews in the United States were first studied by Raymond Jones, who focused his attention on Bishop Plummer of Washington, D.C., organizer of the Church of God and Saints in Christ.[6] The members of this group identified themselves as the "lost tribe of Israel," asserting that the Biblical Hebrews were originally black. Arthur H. Fauset described a similar group in Philadelphia during the early forties. Under the leadership of Prophet Cherry, they were organized as the Church of God and known popularly as "Black Jews" or "Black Hebrews."[7] This group was notable for its disdain of swine flesh, keeping of the Sabbath, opposition to all pictures or "graven images," tithing of members, and contempt for Christianity, especially black storefront religion. The Church of God was open only to black people, the original inhabitants of the earth. The first white man was named Gehazi; he received his color as a result of a curse for his sinfulness. This was an adaptation of the American Protestant myths identifying the origins of the black race with the curse of Cain or Noah's curse of Canaan. Black Jews and Black Muslims alike have been angered by these myths and have countered with myths of their own.

There are apparently numerous uncharted groups of Black Jews throughout the United States. One is tempted to believe that its adherents have gravitated to black Jewish sects more because of an aversion for mainstream American Protestantism than because of attraction to the religious and ethnic traditions of white Jews. A central idea and common trait of black American Jewish separatist groups has been a belief that all black people are the chosen people of God and that Biblical Hebrews—or at least the more faithful among them—were black. Numerous elaborate rationalizations have been worked out in support of this position. The following, taken from a statement by Rabbi Wentworth A. Matthew, leader of the central congregation in Harlem, is illustrative:

When Rebecca . . . after many years conceived, she brought forth twins, one red and hairy all over like a hairy garment, while the other was plain and smooth as the black man invariably is. The first, the red and hairy one, was called Esau; the plain and smooth brother was called Jacob. This same Jacob, by four wives, begot twelve sons. After twenty years his name was changed from Jacob to Israel, and automatically his sons became the sons of Israel.[8]

Howard Brotz has studied the Black Jews of Harlem, who refer to themselves as the Commandment Keepers and once refused an invitation for closer cooperation with their white counterparts. The Commandment Keepers refuse to be called Negroes, as do the Black Muslims; they conform strictly to Orthodox Jewish religious practices and observe all holidays. Like black Christians, they are fond of comparing the bondage of the Hebrews in Egypt with the plight of black people in America. The Black Jews of Harlem are aware of the existence of the Falasha Jews in Ethiopia. The organizer of the Harlem group was an officer of the Garvey movement named J. Arnold Ford, sometimes wrongly confused with W. D. Fard, the first prophet of the Nation of Islam. Ford emigrated to Ethiopia in 1930.[9]

Vying with Ford to assume the role of spiritual leader among black nationalists was one Noble Drew Ali, leader of the Moorish Science Temple of America. This group was founded around 1914 in Chicago, Illinois. It had a highly secret character and encouraged, as did the Black Jews, ideas of racial supremacy. Membership was open to all "Asiatics," that is to say, dark-skinned people. A number of members of the Moorish Science Temple were also Garveyites. With the decline of the movement, many of its adherents found their way into the Nation of Islam, which was organized by Elijah Muhammad during the 1930s.

Howard Brotz commented upon similarities in doctrine and political ideology between the Nation of Islam and the Commandment Keepers of Harlem. He was incorrect in attributing to them a common organizer in the person of J. Arnold Ford, whom he confused with W. D. Fard, but he was correct in attributing to both of them a messianic conception of black history in the United States, resulting in a chosen-people doctrine and religious black nationalism.[10]

Somewhat more is known of J. Arnold Ford than was available at the time of Brotz's mention of him. He was a native of Barbados, born around 1876, the son of an evangelical preacher. He arrived in the United States shortly after the First World War and identified with the Harlem branch of the UNIA shortly after its founding. In 1924, Ford was forced out of the Garvey organization, in which he had served as music director and choirmaster, and became affiliated with an organization known as the Moorish Zionist Temple. A year later he moved out of that group, taking the choir with him to form Beth B'nai congregation.

Despite an apparent conflict with Garvey, which may have resulted from Garvey's preference for the Christian strain in Ethiopianism, Ford continued to preach Garveyist ideas. His nationalism and his commitment to repatriation were evident in his decision of 1930 to travel to Ethiopia in response to an invitation from an Ethiopian diplomat. The official purpose of the visit was to represent his congregation at the coronation of Ras Tafari and to work for the founding of an Afro–American settlement in the area near Lake Tana. Ford was followed by a small number of other Black Jews, who joined him in establishing a small colony in Addis Ababa.

Ford died in Ethiopia in 1935, and this, of course, invalidates Brotz's conjecture that he was the same person as W. D. Fard, the Detroit peddler who inspired Elijah Poole to assume the name of Elijah Muhammad and establish the Nation of Islam. As late as 1976, Wallace Muhammad, who succeeded his father to leadership of the sect, asserted that Fard was still alive and that he could dial him on the telephone any time he desired.[11]

The group once known as the Nation of Islam, but now called the World Community of Al-Islam in the West, was once the most vigorous black separatist sect. It has undergone dramatic changes since the death of Elijah Muhammad in 1975. The reasons for these changes are shrouded in secrecy, but the old militant, black nationalistic rhetoric that characterized the Nation and all Black Muslim separatism since the First World War has apparently been modified almost out of existence. Under the leadership of Noble Drew Ali and Elijah Muhammad, however, the Black Muslims in America, like the Black Jews, associated themselves with a chosen-people doctrine and a theory of black supremacy. Mr. Muhammad once acknowledged "a very high opinion" of Noble Drew Ali, and indeed many of his teachings were in conformity with those of the Moorish Science Temple.

At the core of Black Islam until 1975 was religious mysticism calculated to counteract doctrines of white supremacy with which most followers were familiar. Whites were viewed as devils, a cursed race brought into existence by the machinations of the mad scientist, Yakub. Total isolation from a white race, doomed by its own sinfulness to oblivion, was the goal of the Nation of Islam. The Black Muslims, like the Black Jews, viewed black Christians with absolute contempt, and they were not particularly concerned about relations with whites of their own religious persuasions. They did not seek acceptance from other Muslims, because their chief concern was with a spiritual jihad against white supremacy, rather than with the authentication of their movement in the eyes of outsiders.

Since the death of Muhammad, the Black Muslims have become less concerned with traditional black nationalistic goals and have focused their efforts on collectivist capitalism. Whites have been invited to join and even to address the congregations. The official weekly newspaper was assuming a "third world" as opposed to a traditional black-nationalist stance even before the death of Muhammad. By the mid-1970s, it had supported such disparate movements as Pan–Africanism, Pan–Islamism, Puerto Rican nationalism, and international socialism. Mr. Muhammad's much-emphasized goal of an all-black homeland for Afro–Americans was being downplayed considerably. The Black Muslims seemed to be abandoning, at least temporarily, territorial black nationalism for a more broadly conceived and conventional variety of Pan–Islamism.[12]

It is not to be expected that the entire Black Muslim community would turn and march in unison down the path to integration at the command of its new leadership. Wallace Muhammad leads the community only by virtue of his father's name and a few legal documents. By attempting to convert the organization from a nationalistic expression of mystical messianism into a pure business enterprise, Mr. Muhammad has, in the eyes of many, stripped the community of its reason for being. The doctrine that "blackness" is a state of mind, and that anyone can be black so long as he or she is willing to fight against the forces of racial oppression, will hardly seem acceptable to the die-hard separatists in the community. Already there have been defectors, among them the charismatic Minister Farrakhan, one-time spokesman for the Nation.[13] Now known as Abdul Haleem, he has broken with the World Community of Al-Islam in the West and has begun to work to revive the Nation of Islam in accordance with the principles of Elijah Muhammad.[14]

In 1967 some 190 Black Jews from Chicago migrated to Liberia, where they attempted to set up kibbutzim in the hinterland. Within two years, half of them had returned to Chicago or found occupations off the kibbutz in Liberia. In 1969 about 40 of this group emigrated to Israel, where they demanded the right to entry under the law of return. Remarkably, some of the "Black Israelites" brought with them their own variety of black-supremacist Zionism. One was quoted as saying: "This is our country—not yours. We will not accept your law." A spokesman back in Chicago added: "We are Israelites claiming our land to establish a kingdom of God. . . . Israel will be a country run totally by black men."[15]

Prince Asiel Ben–Israel, international ambassador for the Original Hebrew Israelite Nation, believes that his group is "genetically connected with the seed of Israel." He contends that the Orthodox Jews "have sent down their wise men and their soothsayers and their astrologists to talk with us, and they know that we are the people . . . , the Messianic people whom the prophecies have foretold would return to the land." Unlike many black nationalists, they do not acknowledge the claims of Palestinian Arabs to the Holy Land—they cannot have a claim on the land, since they have no claim on being Hebrews. Indeed, the Arab nations are enemies of the black world, for they attempt to convert African nations to the Muslim faith. Arabs are not Africans, but Caucasians, cousins of the Israelis, who have usurped the Holy Land. Like the Christians, they spread dissension by converting black people away from the ancestral Hebrew faith.[16]

Prince Asiel Ben–Israel cites Genesis 15:13 to prove his claims: "Know of a surety that thy seed shall be a stranger in a land that is not theirs; and shall serve them; and they shall afflict them 400 years." He also cites the next verse, or his own version of it: "And afterwards I will bring them up out of that land of captivity into the land which I gave unto their fathers for everlasting possession." The manner in which he interprets these words reveals a common characteristic of messianic leaders, including white Zionists. Ben–Israel sees his people as the victims of particularly severe predicaments of a kind unknown to the rest of humanity. Black Americans fulfill the prophecy, says the Prince, because they are "the only people who have been sold and who went into slavery in ships . . . , the only ones who are not being represented on the international scene."[17] So much for the Biblical argument. By way of scholarly support, Ben–Israel cites the work of Father Joseph Williams, *Hebrewisms of West Africa*, which argues that the cultures of West Africa are Hebrew in origin. Ironically, a version of the "Hamitic hypothesis," a myth much scorned by most black nationalists in America, becomes a fundamental belief of this particular sect.

The Hamitic hypothesis was a creation of C. G. Seligman, who argued that all worthwhile culture had been brought to Africa by a mysterious Semitic group of his own invention, whom he named the Hamites. Seligman found it necessary to create this imaginary people because of his belief that Africans were incapable of creating culture. The hypothesis argued not only for the drift of Semitic culture, but implied that only those Africans who were descended from the Hamitic stock were capable of producing civilization. Those black peoples in Africa who had shown any signs of cultural progress, or any ability to dominate less advanced tribes, were really not true Negroes; they were Hamites, a black race of Semitic origin.[18] The Ethiopian Hebrew Nation's insistence that West African culture is Judaic betrays a contempt for indigenous African culture and leaves them with strange bedfellows.

As one might expect, the Ethiopian Hebrew Nation is out of step with the majority of Pan–Africanist groups. Indeed, Prince Ben–Israel came away from the Sixth Pan–African Congress, held in Dar es Salaam, June 1974, thoroughly disenchanted:

> I felt the Congress was a vanity for Africans from America; for again, I witnessed a people who was divided with everybody else's doctrines. Some brothers got up speaking about Marxism; I saw another group of Africans

> from America talking about the Chinese doctrine of socialism; and I saw a group who said they were the intellectuals. . . . But what was really hurting was when the conference was opened, and the president of an African government walked on the stage with a white secretary and told the conference that it wasn't about race, that it was about social issues.[19]

The African unity that Prince Ben–Israel conceives will occur, he believes, only when ideological unity has been achieved. So long as Africans continue "talking about scientific socialism, Marxism, capitalism—all the isms that have been imported into Africa that are not African, Africa can never be unified." The way to African redemption is, of course, through the Hebrew faith. "We in Jerusalem are the unifiers," says the Prince, "because we have a pure, truly African doctrine, first of all, before the whole world; for we are truly the saviors of the world."[20]

Prince Ben–Israel claims that during his travels on the continent, especially in the bush, he has encountered numerous people who "want to come right now up to Jerusalem and be instructed and be taught so that they can go back and redeem their people." He maintains that the Sinai peninsula and the Holy Land are parts of Africa, separated only by the man-made ditch which is the Suez Canal. Africa will be united only when the political fallacy that separates Israel from the rest of the black world is obliterated. Once Jerusalem has been delivered, the rest of Africa will be united under its rightful capital, with the Hebrew faith its proper creed.[21]

Clarke Jenkins, an independent, self-trained scholar in Detroit, has privately published a study called *The Black Hebrews*, in which he argues that:

> The BLACKS of America, Called Negroes, or Negroid, are the descendents of Jacob, of the Tribe of Judah, Benjamin and Levi; forming the other tribes of the nation of Israel, who are among ALL nations of the earth, and being persecuted like their BLACK BROTHERS are, everywhere.[22]

Jenkins argues his point from the Biblical fact that Adam was made of earth, which is always black or dark, but never white. Until the time of Moses, there is no mention made in the Bible of white people. The white race originated with the disease of leprosy, as described in Leviticus, chapter 13. Jesus was not of this white or leprous stock, but of the true line of God's black or chosen people:

> Scripture record [sic] men as having both saw and talked with JESUS; and all accounts recorded were that HE had BROWN REDDISH EYES, SHORT HAIR LIKE THE LAMBS WOOL, and in those days wearing only sandals, or barefooted; the account describing His feet were that they were dark and ashy; as if they were burnt in a BRASS OR COPPER smelting furnace.[23]

Jenkins' facile interpretation of Scripture is reminiscent of that of other Black Hebrews, and it also shares similarities with the doctrines of black Islamic sects. All such groups are concerned primarily with demonstrating that they are a chosen people and that their blackness symbolizes their elect status. Thus, the central doctrines of Hebrew and Muslim sects are essentially the same.

However, the fact that urban messianic movements share basic similarities in origin and ideology does not mean that a spirit of good fellowship exists among them. Hostilities between Hanafi Black Muslims and the Nation of Islam have led to bloodshed.[24] Black Jews in the United States have a history of schism and disunity. Both the Hebraic and the Islamic sects view storefront Christian nationalism with contempt; they view one another as lost sheep, who may have grasped the accidentals of the messianic vision but remain deluded on certain essential points. An example of this attitude can be seen very well in the Ansaru Allah Community of Brooklyn, New York, formerly known as the Nubian Islamic Hebrew Mission, a singularly eclectic sect.

The Ansars are readily identifiable by their white robes and turbans. They are conspicuous in the streets and subways of New York, where they distribute pamphlets, take up collections, and are ever eager to discuss their movement with interested black people. The masses of black people seem to respond positively to them, although there is little likelihood that the Ansars will soon amass the 144,000 dedicated members whose enlistment is seen as a precondition for the millennium. The community is presided over by an elderly patriarch, Shaykh Dau'wd. Occasionally, they are visited by the community's founder, Al Hajj Al Imam Isa Abd'Allah Muhammad Al Mahdi, usually referred to as Imam Isa. "Because he is the spiritual Head and Director of an INTERNATIONAL community, it is very rare that he is able to spend time with us." The Imam is accepted by his community as the great-grandson of Al Imam Muhammad Ahmad Al Mahdi, who led the jihad (or holy war) against British colonialism in the Sudan during the 1880s. The Mahdi is reputed to have said, "I'll have a descendant who will rise in the West, that my name will be heard there." The Ansars attach great significance to the fact that Imam Isa was born one hundred years after the Mahdi and that he organized the community in 1970, thirty years before the turn of the century. The Imam is believed to fulfill the prophecy of Revelation 14:1: "And I looked and lo, a Lamb stood on the Mount Zion, and with him an hundred and forty four thousand having his father's name written on their foreheads." The Imam's followers believe that he is this sacrificial lamb, destined to suffer for the sins of his people, the 144,000, who will be ushered into paradise in the year 2000.[25]

Ansars accept the Old Testament, the New Testament, and the Qur'an as divine revelations, and their publications are filled with quotations from all three. Their symbols represent the eclecticism of their belief and include the seal of Ibrahim, a six-point star within a crescent, the horns of which point upward. The symbol of the Moorish Science Temple is a five-point star within a crescent, with horns pointing right; and that of the Nation of Islam is a five-point star within a crescent, with horns pointing left. According to Ansar literature, both of these Muslim symbols, like the Jewish Shield of David, represent their respective sect's *partial* knowledge of the truth, for the true symbol of the chosen is a six-point star. Ansar iconography also makes use of the ankh, a cross with a loop at the top, which is an ancient Egyptian symbol. They carry the flag of the Mahdi, which bears a crescent transfixed by a spear.[26] They wear white robes in fulfillment of a prophecy:[27]

> And one of the Elders answered, saying unto me, what are these which are arrayed in white robes? and whence came they? And I said unto him, Sir, thou knowest. And he said unto me, These are they which came out of great tribulation, and have washed their robes, and made them white in the blood of the Lamb. (Revelation 7:13–14)

His eminence, Imam Isa, carries a staff, as does a Christian bishop. He is sometimes depicted with a halo surrounding his head and shoulders.

Ansars accept, as do other Black Muslims, the prohibition on eating pork. They accept a mythology common among black cultists that the swine is a cross between the rat, the cat, and the dog.[28] White people are lepers, hence the color of their skin. They are referred to as Amorites, or as Canaan and his offspring, driven to total savagery by the curse of Noah. They retreated in ancient times into the Caucasus mountains, where "they (mainly the women) had sexual intercourse with the jackal (the original dog), and, through this intercourse, the offspring that was brought forth was an ape-like man. This is also how and where venereal diseases came about."[29] Whites are referred to as "Mankind" (man's kind) or as the pale man "that has evolved out of the Black man, through leprosy, to the ape, and back to a kind of man (man's kind)." Their bestial origins, say the Ansars, can still be easily observed in the texture and the quantity of their hair. One Ansar pamphlet is profusely illustrated with pictures of white sideshow freaks, afflicted with extreme hirsuitism.[30]

Despite the complexity of their religious ideology and their system of symbols, which draw upon materials from numerous doctrines, the Ansars' overriding loyalty is to Islam. They are Islamic Hebrews and guard their identity jealously. Their literature is full of contempt for the numerous other black sects that claim a messianic mission, as well as for the figures who have emerged in messianic roles in recent years. There is especial contempt for those groups who claim to be descendants of the original Israelites—Black Jews in the United States and persons claiming to be Falashas. They also reject the claim of Haile Selassie that he was descended from the Israelites. They accept the Ethiopian Falashas as descended from Israel, but they assert that Falashas are Muslims who never leave their Ethiopian sanctuaries.[31]

The Ansars consider themselves Nubians, and feel that it is a disgrace for a black man to allow himself to be referred to by any other name. All Nubians are Ishmaelites and, along with the Bedouins, constitute the only pure, unadulterated human stock on earth; they are the only direct and unadulterated descendants of Abraham and Noah. They must now assert their claims as the chosen people, by reclaiming their heritage which was stolen from them by other nations. They must return to Arabic, the original tongue of original man; although now that language is monopolized by the Arabs living under the five-point star, which symbolizes their corruption. The Ansars support their contentions with inventive interpretations of the Torah, the Gospel, and the Qur'an. They also have a startlingly sophisticated knowledge of scientific jargon, enough to completely exasperate anyone who foolishly attempts to debate the phylogeny of the swine. Imam Isa and his community seem to have some potential for increasing their numbers; they may even be able to muster their 144,000 and fill the vacuum left by the Nation of Islam's defection from its own brand of orthodoxy.

During the black studies renaissance of the late sixties, students of black nationalism focused more attention on the Black Muslims than on the Black Jews. The siege of B'nai B'rith headquarters in Washington, D.C., by Hanafi Muslims in 1977 and the hijacking of an Israeli airliner to Entebbe Airport in Uganda in 1976 have tended to fix some false associations in the public mind. There seems to have been a journalistic tendency to link the Pan–African movement and all black nationalism with anti-Jewish feeling.[32] The fact that Uganda, nominally a Muslim nation, was led at the time by a pseudo-Pan–Africanist, Idi Amin, led many to construe a link between Pan–Africanism and Pan–Islamism. The public imagination was further confused by a tendency to draw parallels between the plight of Uganda's Asians and that of Germany's Jews. Of course, there is not necessarily a link between Pan–Africanism and Pan–Islamism; the Pan–African movement has been predominantly Christian since its founding in the late eighteenth century. In the twentieth century, Pan–Africanism and black nationalism have taken on some Islamic forms, but they have also taken on Judaic forms. Indeed, those black nationalists who are presently most hostile to the Jewish state are not Moslems, but Black Hebrews.

The claims of some black nationalists that they are the chosen people of the Bible and that they should possess the Holy Land are no more bizarre than the designs that some Zionists formerly had on East Africa. The proposal to establish a Jewish homeland in East Africa originated with the British government, and led to bitter dispute among Jewish nationalists.[33] Of course, those who stood firm for Palestinian resettlement won out in the end; but one wonders what would have been the consequences if the state of Israel had been founded in Kenya or Uganda. Would East Africans, rather than Palestinian Arabs, see themselves as the principal foes of the Jewish state? Edward Wilmot Blyden, one of the founders of the Pan–African movement, saw blacks and Jews as kindred peoples. He linked his movement to Zionism and invited the Jewish people to come to Africa and help with the uplift of the continent.[34] It seems unlikely, however, that contemporary Pan–Africanists would consider the offer still valid.

Stateless nationalisms attempt to justify their territorial aspirations in terms of moral, legal, or historical arguments. As the pamphlet literature of the various black sects and cults illustrates, an active imagination can easily manufacture a rationale to support claims of title to various desirable lands. In the long run, however, the claims of a national group to Palestine, Ethiopia, Liberia, or any other territory have nothing to do with moral rightness, Biblical authority, historical argument, or anything other than force of arms. No one really believes that Ugandan Asians would have fared any better under Zionist nationalism than they did under black nationalism. Israel is no more and no less moral than most other nations of the world. It owes its existence to economic and military power, not to its real or imagined messianic mission or historical ties to the Israelites of the Old Testament.

Black messianic sects provide a rich and colorful rhetoric, but have so far failed to endow their adherents with anything resembling economic or military power. Their adaptations of the chosen-people myth are perhaps useful for counteracting the attempts of Western society to impress black people with a sense of inferiority, but they serve no other function than to replace one set of irrationalities with another. It should not be surprising that such myths are appealing to urban-ghetto blacks, however. The Judeo–Christian tradition and American civil religion are eminently messianic. Black messianism, in its urban cultic forms, originated in the black American masses' sense of alienation from the great myth of American moral and spiritual superiority. The chosen peoples of the metropolis counter their sense of exclusion with the rationalization that they are the truly chosen ones. Still, they are dependent on the old Judeo–Christian idea that oppression endows the oppressed with a morally superior status over the oppressors.[35]

The militant rhetoric of black messianic cults and the racist character of many of their beliefs should not be seen as peculiar to black nationalism. There are many precedents for Biblically based racism in American religion that predate the rise of the black cults. Messianic doctrines are usually hostile to outsiders and ruthless in their dealings with them, for messianic doctrines have certain aspects that are not pretty. Every religious doctrine teaches its adherents to think of themselves as superior to the outsider. The ugly similarities shared by all messianic movements are not the exclusive property of Africans, of Asians, of Europeans, nor of any religious group. The "chosen people" doctrine was certainly not invented in America's black ghettoes, and black messianism can hardly be described as singularly racist or bloodthirsty in comparison to other such movements throughout the world.

12
Messianic Oratory and the Theme of "Ethiopianism" in Ralph Ellison's Invisible Man

"I'm a student of history, sir," says a minor character in Ralph Ellison's *Invisible Man.* "The world moves in a circle like a roulette wheel. In the beginning, black is on top, in the middle epochs, white holds the odds, but soon Ethiopia shall stretch forth her noble wings!"[1] Students of Afro–American and African literatures will have little difficulty recognizing in this scene Ralph Ellison's indebtedness to a tradition known as "Ethiopianism," which appears repeatedly in the writings of black authors since the late eighteenth century. The central idea of Ethiopianism is the belief that a reversal in the status of nations is bound to occur at some point in the not-too-distant future, at which time "Ethiopia shall . . . stretch forth her hands unto God." The theme dominates much of the writing of black Americans and, as we have seen in earlier chapters, it is strong in David Walker's *Appeal*, the *Philosophy and Opinions of Marcus Garvey*, and other works. It is not surprising to find this tradition present in *Invisible Man*, one of the best examples of what is meant by black literary traditionalism, although Ellison is reluctant to admit his dependency on any such tradition.[2]

Ellison's attitude is understandable, for *Invisible Man* is concerned with a host of other ideas—some of them seemingly inconsistent with Ethiopianism; some more readily perceived as congruent. On the one hand, the prophetic quality of Afro–American life is clearly consistent with the Emersonian ideals that dominate the story. But *Invisible Man* is just as close in theme and mood to the cynicism of Joseph Heller and Edward Albee as it is to the prophetic idealism of Richard Niebuhr and Martin Luther King—as close to the ethnic iconoclasm of Philip Roth and Bruce Jay Friedman as it is to the classical Ethiopianism of Garvey and Du

Bois. In the *Invisible Man*, Ellison is concerned with several versions of the Ethiopianism theme, including classical Ethiopianism, the view of the world stated by the veteran at the Golden Day (quoted in the opening sentence of this chapter). There are allusions to Ras Tafari and the modern nation of Ethiopia, symbolized by the Ethiopian flag among the possessions of the elderly couple who are evicted in Chapter 12. Another version of the theme is West Indian Ethiopianism, represented by Marcus Garvey, whose career is alluded to directly and indirectly.

Then, of course, there is Ras the Exhorter, symbol of archaic racial romanticism, a black knight upon a great black horse. His several appearances leave little doubt of the author's intentional linking of his novel to the Ethiopian tradition and to Garvey. In the final apocalyptic scenes of the novel, Ras appears "dressed in the costume of an Abyssinian chieftain; a fur cap upon his head, his arm bearing a shield, a cape made of the skin of some wild animal around his shoulders."[3] Although Ellison and the protagonist of *Invisible Man* are clearly unsympathetic to Ras the Exhorter and the variety of black messianism that he represents, the Ethiopian tradition is one of the strongest elements in the novel.

The novel also contains other elements of black messianism, for the narrator himself, though in a different way than Ras, is caught up in millennial myths concerning his sense of duty and racial mission. He visualizes himself at the novel's onset as "a potential Booker T. Washington." He gives a speech to a group of Southerners that is based on Washington's Atlanta Exposition Address. His real ideal is, of course, not Booker T. Washington, but The Founder of the Negro College he attends. This shadowy figure, towering above even Booker T. Washington, looms throughout the first half of the book, a Mosaic figure, "shouting LET MY PEOPLE GO! when it was necessary, whispering it during those times when whispering was wisest." The Mosaic theme is reintroduced at a cocktail party in Chapter 14, where a drunken member of the Brotherhood attempts to make the narrator sing, "Go down Moses. . . . Tell dat ole Pharaoh to let ma colored folks sing."[4]

From earliest childhood, the narrator has been imbued with a sense of racial mission; and he has never questioned the idea that his destiny is to become a "Negro leader." The role is forced upon him in part by the deathbed confession of his grandfather:

> On his deathbed he called my father to him and said, "Son, after I'm gone I want you to keep up the good fight. I never told you, but our life is a war and I have been a traitor all my born days, a spy in the enemy's country ever since I give up my gun back in the Reconstruction. Live with your head in the Lion's mouth. I want you to overcome 'em with yeses, undermine 'em with grins, agree 'em to death and destruction, let 'em swoller you till they vomit or bust wide open."[5]

The injunction is even more cryptic than it appears to be, and one can only guess about whether the ambiguities are fully intentional. To whom has the grandfather been a traitor? To blacks? To whites? To both? Is he speaking as a black man revolting against the constraints of white society, or is he simply an individual reacting against the constraints of society as a whole? We cannot disregard the latter possibility, since this is perhaps the most important theme in the story. The grandfather never said that he was in a war against the whites—he simply said that he was at war. It is the narrator who fixes the racial interpretation on his grandfather's confession. Then it hangs over him like a curse, for he must somehow reconcile his desire to gain the approval of whites with his suspicion that by so doing he is involved in treachery. Only in the story's epilogue does the narrator begin to sense the possibility that his grandfather's message may have gone deeper than race. Until that time he has been a victim of illusions, not the least of which is his conception of his duty to become a black messiah.

Because he conforms to what is expected from him by society during childhood, he is praised by the white men of his home town and elevated to the status of "an example." So long as he is dedicated to the ideal of "social responsibility," the city fathers are willing to sustain him. "We mean to do right by you," says their spokesman, "but you've got to know your place at all times." When he finishes his speech before the town's leading white citizens, he receives thunderous applause, and the spokesman says, "He makes a good speech and some day he'll lead his people in the proper paths." Throughout the novel, he is encouraged by black and white alike to assume a leadership role. Mary Rambo, his good-hearted benefactress, lectures him constantly on "leadership and responsibility" (225). She has a simple faith in educated Negro youth, every one of whom she must encourage to become "a credit to the race" (222). But the greatest pressure comes from within the protagonist himself. He has an "urge to make speeches" (226) that, unbidden, asserts itself. Interestingly, he seems to equate leadership with speechmaking and sermonizing. This is not surprising in a representative of a group whose leadership has traditionally been associated with the ministry.

The narrator has provided us with the texts of three of his major speeches as well as the audiences' reactions. The first speech occurs several months after he arrives in New York. The scene is the eviction of an elderly couple on a cold and windy afternoon. A crowd has begun to form and to murmur resentfully. "We ought to beat the hell out of those paddies," remarks one spectator.

> "Sho, we ought to stop 'em," another man said, "but ain't that much nerve in the whole bunch."
> "There's plenty nerve," the slender man said. "All they need is someone to set it off. All they need is a leader . . ." (233).

The narrator has never seen an eviction before. As he looks over the clutter of household objects piled up on the walk, he sees a number of strangely familiar and symbolic objects: a breast pump, a faded tintype of Lincoln, an Ethiopian flag, a baby shoe, a hair-straightening comb, and a curling iron. Gazing at the old couple huddled on the pavement, he is affected by the old woman's sobbing, "as when a child, seeing the tears of its parents, is moved by both fear and sympathy to cry" (235). He feels himself drawn into "a warm, dark, rising whirlpool of emotion" (235). Then the old couple, armed with a tattered Bible, rush up the steps demanding that they be allowed a few moments to pray in their vacant apartment. The crowd becomes more vociferous; a scuffle ensues; there is pushing at the top of the stairs; the old woman falls backwards; and the crowd explodes. With cries of "Get that paddie sonofabitch!" and "Rush that bastard!" the mob surges forward spontaneously (238–39). Outraged, angered, and afraid of the violence that is about to be released within himself, the narrator feels conflicting emotions welling up inside:

> And beneath it all there boiled up all the shock-absorbing phrases that I had learned all my life. I seemed to totter on the edge of a great dark hole. "No, no," I heard myself yelling. "Black men! Brothers! Black Brothers! That's not the way. We're law-abiding. We're a law-abiding people and a slow-to-anger people" (239).

The people obviously do not need a leader in order to take action. The crowd is moving forward under its own steam and, interestingly, it is the instinctive impulse of the narrator, as "leader," to soothe the crowd, to render them once again inactive. His advice is to follow a leader like "that wise leader down in Alabama . . . , who when that fugitive escaped from the mob and ran to his school for protection . . . was strong enough to do the legal thing, the law-abiding thing, to turn him over to the forces of law and order. . . ." The crowd is unimpressed. They denounce the Alabama educator as "a handkerchief-headed rat" (240). As the crowd becomes increasingly angry and continues to yell, the narrator laughs in response, "as though hypnotized," so that by degrees it is the crowd who is leading the narrator. His words become downright insurrectionary, and yet neither the reader, nor the crowd, nor the narrator himself, can be certain whether he is trying to incite a riot or prevent one.

In the beginning, the speech is abstract and irrelevant; but, in response to the audience's promptings, it soon becomes specific and immediate. It is reminiscent of the traditional black sermon, because the narrator, like a traditional preacher, is interacting with his audience. The audience, by either giving or withholding approval, guides the speaker in what to say. While they are turned off by the irrelevancy of his references to the Alabama educator, they respond positively to the greater body of the speech, which focuses on the old couple themselves and the meaning of their lives and the things they have worked for, now strewn carelessly in the street. In spite of himself, the speechmaker becomes increasingly provocative, but, strangely, as the crowd strains forward, he attempts to hold them back. He works on their sentiments, reminding them of their own parents, of their own poverty and their own helplessness. But when a voice in the crowd cries angrily, "Hell, they been dispossessed, you crazy sonofabitch, get out the way," he cries, "No wait!" (242). Is there an intentional irony here, or some subtle element of sarcasm in the narrator's apparent doctrine of patience? Is it his intention to furtively counsel violence, while only pretending to restrain the crowd? Or is he under the power of some force that compels him to incite violence that even he does not want?

The crowd does not really know how to take the preaching of the narrator, although they are inclined towards tolerance because of his obviously intimate knowledge of ordinary black life and his sympathy for the elderly Rambos. But the onlookers quickly lose their patience with him and, shoving him out of the way, storm the stairway to the apartment building. The marshal is beaten and chased down the street, while a West Indian woman chants, "Give it back to him unto the third and fourth generations" and "Repay the brute a thousandfold" (244). Then the narrator leads the people in carrying the couple's possessions back into the apartment; and while they are thus engaged, they are joined by a group of whites who identify themselves as "friends of all the common people," saying "we believe in brotherhood." One of these newcomers suggests that they stage a march and, without thinking, the speechmaker yells out, "Why don't we march?" (245). By this time, he has completely surrendered his will to the events that are swirling around him.

When the police arrive and call for reinforcements, he escapes by running across the rooftops, guided by the instructions of a white girl, presumably one of the "Brotherhood." When he descends to the street, he is joined by Brother Jack, a member of that same group, who has followed him in his flight. Brother Jack has been impressed by the speech at the eviction, but for what reason? Has he been blind to the speechmaker's ambivalence and to the crowd's impatience with his attempts at pacification? Or has he recognized that the narrator has an instinctive desire to try to keep the lid on the emotions of the people? He is certainly not unaware of the vacillation of the speaker, who first insists that he "just felt like making a speech," and then confesses his real feelings of compassion for the Rambos (252). Both motivations are real, of course, but the reader ought not to forget that the narrator has already confessed in the preceding chapter to an uncontrollable "urge to make speeches" (226). Perhaps this is what Brother Jack sees and identifies as the makings of a Negro leader.

After joining the Brotherhood at Brother Jack's behest, the narrator is brought to a large public meeting in an old sporting arena, where he is told to make another speech. This is his most perplexing performance in the entire story. It is divided into three sections. In the first of these, he fumbles with the theme of dispossession and the audience's reaction is difficult to judge. They are polite, perhaps too polite, and one faceless voice shouts out ambiguous comments of such a nature that the speaker is forced to ask himself, "Is he with me or against me?" (297). Then the speaker drifts into a second theme—the theme of insight, which is, of course, a major concern of the novel.

"We're a nation of one-eyed mice," he tells the audience. "Let's get together, uncommon people. With both our eyes, we can see what makes us so uncommon" (298). It is ironic that he has chosen to characterize himself and the audience as one-eyed, for Brother Jack, the man from whom he takes orders, is missing an eye. The narrator does not discover Brother Jack's affliction until the end of the novel, nor does he realize until then that the Brotherhood, taken as a whole, is half-blind. They have obviously arrived at some degree of insight, and their world view is more profound than that prevailing at The Founder's college. Nonetheless, the narrator's unpremeditated remark that the Brotherhood is only partially sighted is ingenuously perceptive. The audience responds more warmly to this section of the speech, bursting into applause, not because they admit their half-blindness, but simply in response to the speaker's warming up to his subject.

The third section of the speech is totally lacking in insight or rational content, and yet it is an overwhelming success. It is a purely emotional outburst in which the speaker confesses his need for the approval of the crowd:

"I feel your eyes upon me. I hear the pulse of your breathing. And now at this moment with your black and white eyes upon me, I feel . . . I feel . . . suddenly that I have become more human" (300).

The ritual that the speaker is enacting is, of course, the familiar religious ceremony of public confession. By standing before the audience and admitting that they have the power to endow him with his humanity, the convert proves his right to membership in the religious brotherhood. The crowd signals its acceptance, bursting into thunderous applause. When the speaker displays his gratitude with unashamed tears, the audience becomes even more demonstrative. They are far more impressed by the sincerity of his conversion, the fact that he has been born again in their sight, than by the content of his homily. The doctrinarian brothers, who confront him as he is leaving the arena, are not interested in homilies. They criticize the speech as "unscientific." They recognize that he knows little and cares less about the theoretical aspects of the Brotherhood. Brother Jack recognizes this as well, but sees in the Invisible Man a vitality of spirit that is worthy of exploitation. There is nothing wrong with the new brother that cannot be straightened out by a few sessions with party theoretician, Brother Hambro, he reasons. In Brother Jack's estimation, the narrator has passed his test with flying colors, and he is duly appointed "chief spokesman of the Harlem District" (312).

The Invisible Man is now achieving his life's ambition by becoming a recognized Negro leader. The work goes well; he stages demonstrations, organizes parades, gives speeches. There are drill teams, flags and banners, cards bearing slogans, drum majorettes, and much sheer corn. He has no mean ability as a community organizer but, still, it is speechmaking that is winning him his place. It is a speech that gets him his college scholarship and another speech that brings him to the attention of the Brotherhood. His new position—although he is only dimly aware of it—is analogous to that of Dr. Bledsoe. The narrator has become an appointed spokesman of the black community, but there is growing resentment, both within and without the organization. Jealousies within the Brotherhood lead to his being abruptly transferred out of Harlem and sent downtown to lecture on "the Woman Question."

The narrator gives us only one report on his speechmaking on "the Woman Question," and although he does not furnish us with a text, he does tell us something about the audience reaction. By this time, he is becoming aware that what a speaker has to say in any context is of relatively little importance. As he heads for his first lecture downtown, he finds himself wishing for the awesome physical proportions and sexual magnetism of a Paul Robeson. As usual, his audience makes him a success by their own enthusiasm, and afterwards he is approached by an attractive matron who invites him to her apartment to "discuss ideology." Has anyone ever told him, she asks, "that at times you have tom-toms beating in your voice?" "My God," he responds, "I thought that was the beat of profound ideas." His hostess is determined; his voice sounds "so—so primitive! . . . it has so much naked power that it goes straight through one" (357). Naturally, she seduces him; and later that evening, when her husband returns and stares into the darkness, he is oblivious to the Invisible Man lying next to his wife in her separate bedroom.

Throughout this sequence, the narrator is discovering not only a literal invisibility—the blackness that allows him to blend into the darkness of a lady's boudoir—but on a symbolic level he is discovering the invisibility of his own humanity, for the persons he encounters react to their own impressions of him, rather than to the personality behind the various roles he assumes. He has no one but himself to blame for this, however, for he has allowed his surroundings to determine the roles he plays. It is in the events surrounding his final—and most disastrously effective—speech that he moves towards personal responsibility and takes the fateful step towards self-definition, rejecting the externally imposed messianic role.

Brother Jack orders the Invisible Man back to Harlem to discover the whereabouts of Tod Clifton, who has unaccountably vanished. Brother Tod, erstwhile organizer of the Harlem youth for the Brotherhood, has taken to the life of a street huckster; and the narrator soon discovers him at Forty-third Street and Fifth Avenue, vending his wares—little, black, dancing puppets. The narrator is appalled, for he sees this as a degrading way to make a living—worse than selling apples or shining shoes. He wanders away in a state of shock but, on circling the block, he encounters Clifton again—this time in the custody of a policeman. Provoked by the policeman's manner, Clifton resists arrest and is killed on the spot. The narrator wanders back to the Harlem district, blaming himself. Although he is increasingly doubtful about the Brotherhood and their work in the black community, he continues to think of himself as a leader and, as he says, "although I knew no one man could do much about it, I felt responsible" (384).

Unable to get in touch with headquarters, the Invisible Man assumes "personal responsibility" for organizing a public funeral for Brother Tod, and this is the setting for his third recorded speech. So far, he has been most successful as a speaker when forging his orations from materials immediately at hand. In the first instance, he is inspired by the possessions of the Rambos which are piled up on the sidewalk. In the second, he is inspired by the much-desired applause of the audience. In Clifton's eulogy, he is inspired by the body itself; he has nothing to say about the personality of the youth leader, nor does he seek to exploit his martyrdom for its ideological potential. He simply describes the body and reminds the crowd that Tod Clifton is dead. The speech is not "scientific" or "doctrinally correct," but that is not what is ultimately upsetting to the Brotherhood. What disturbs and frightens them is that, once more, the speechmaker has moved a crowd to action, although unintentionally. It is not the funeral oration that causes Harlem to erupt into a riot, perhaps not even the spectacle of the funeral which the narrator has organized on his "personal responsibility." As in the case of every urban disorder, there are conflicting tales of how the violence originates; but the death of Clifton seems to be one factor, and the Brotherhood feels that the Invisible Man has been an irresponsible leader.

When the apocalypse comes, it takes everyone by surprise. Summoned back to Harlem by an abruptly terminated phone call, the narrator witnesses the activities of a citizen named Dupre, who has a knack for spontaneous community organization of a destructive variety. When first encountered, Dupre and his friend Scofield are organizing the looting of a series of stores. They make certain to obtain buckets of gasoline; then, seeing to it that all the sick and elderly have been evacuated, they thoroughly douse the apartment building in which Dupre resides and set fire to it. The community has begun to protest its dissatisfaction in a manner that is absolutely unequivocal, and without any leadership except that which springs up spontaneously in the un-structured situation. At this point, Ras the Exhorter proclaims to a cynically amused Harlem that he has become Ras the Destroyer.

Ras, a self-consciously messianic leader, has made several appearances in the course of the story. He represents the one variety of black leadership with which the narrator never experiments. The Invisible Man has adhered to the Booker T. Washington doctrine of patience, humility, cleanliness, and hard work. He has then shifted to the W. E. B. Du Bois variety of leadership, characterized by proletarian ideology and cooperation with white, armchair radicals. The Marcus Garvey variety of leadership, which is marked by a hatred of all things white, is represented by Ras. This is not to say that Ras is a parody of Marcus Garvey, although, like Garvey, he is clearly influenced by the Ethiopian tradition, as his title "Ras" implies; nor, for all his similarity to Perigua in *Dark Princess*, is there any evidence that he is at all influenced by that character. He is Ralph Ellison's own creation, which is interesting, for he gives a good account of himself and the philosophy he represents. Indeed, the one example of his speechmaking that is recorded is more sophisticated, rational, and issue-oriented than anything the narrator has to say throughout the book.

The Invisible Man first becomes aware of Ras when, like some modern Jonah, he is deposited in the sinful city, "feeling like something regurgitated from the belly of a frantic whale."[6] Unlike ancient Ninevah, Harlem already has its preacher of salvation; and he is extremely possessive about his territory. "We gine chase 'em out" is the first statement the narrator hears him make (142). We soon learn that Ras intends to chase out not only the whites, but any rivals for leadership of the Harlem community. When the narrator first encounters Brother Tod, he bears the marks of a violent confrontation with "Ras the Ex-horter's boys." Brother Tod has a certain grudging respect for Ras and also for Marcus Garvey. He remarks "with sudden passion" shortly after he enters the story that Garvey "*must* have had something to move all those people! Our people are hell to move. He must have had plenty" (318).

Tod Clifton's latent sympathy for black nationalism and his am-bivalence towards the Brotherhood become evident on the occasion of a later confrontation with Ras. One evening, while the narrator is up on a stepladder holding forth to an all-black crowd, his gathering is disrupted by Ras and about twenty of his supporters. In the general melee that ensues, Ras outmaneuvers Clifton, knocks him down, and draws his knife—but cannot use it. With angry tears running down his face, he stands sobbing over his adversary. How can a good boy like Tod Clifton go wrong? How can he call the white man *brother*? Brothers are the same color! "We sons of Mama Africa, you done forgot? You black, BLACK!" The narrator sneaks up and strikes the knife from the Exhorter's hand with a length of pipe; but Ras stands his ground and turns to the Invisible Man, "I been hearing your rabble rousing. Why you go over to the enslaver? What kind of black mahn is that who betray his own mama?" Although both younger men, filled with hatred and fear, command him to shut up, Ras continues to preach: "By God, you listen to the Exhorter!" He urges them to throw in with him, not to sell out for money—"That's *bahd* shit!"; not to sell out for the embraces of white women—"These women dregs, mahn." Perhaps the narrator, who is contaminated, will sell out; but certainly not Clifton, for he is of unadulterated stock: "In Africa this mahn be a chief, a black king." Clifton is not unaffected by this harangue, although he tries to quip:

> "It's a wonder he didn't say something about 'Ethiopia stretching forth her wings. . . .' He makes it sound like the hood of a cobra fluttering . . . I don't know . . . I don't know . . ." (327).

In a sense, Tod Clifton is a more interesting case of black leadership than the narrator himself, for he has depth, sensitivity, and ambiguity—indeed, invisibility—greater than that of the central character. Not that the narrator is so single-minded as to be immune to Ras's rhetoric, for even he is relieved to get "away from that exhorting voice" (326), which does touch a sensitive nerve. Tod starts out as a noble and heroic Uncle Tom. His loyalty to the Brotherhood is so strong that he accepts the narrator's imposed spokesmanship without jealousy or question, even though he is far more experienced in the affairs of Harlem. His reversion to the role of Harlem huckster symbolizes the fact of his penetrating to the central irony of black leadership before it dawns upon the novel's protagonist. Every black leader must live with the suspicion that he may be just a little dancing doll, unaware of who is pulling his strings.

One final example of the black messiah is portrayed in *Invisible Man*, by the thoroughly cynical Rinehart. He is the least visible character in the book, although—ironically—one of the best-known, with his unvarying attire—a wide-brimmed hat and a pair of dark sunglasses, which he wears even at night. In crass monetary terms, Rinehart is the most successful black leader. Pimp, racketeer, corrupter of the police, storefront preacher, he moves from one arena of public action to another without difficulty. The narrator is fascinated by this character (whom he never meets), who is at home in a world "without boundaries. A vast, seething, hot world of fluidity." Perhaps, the narrator muses, Rinehart has the answer; "perhaps the truth is always a lie" (430).

Invisible Man is the story of how one man is divested of the burden of race leadership. Step by step, he discards the expectations of society that he become a black Moses, a messiah, or a credit to his race. Now, freed of his illusions, he realizes that all along he has been a sort of Rinehart, although unaware. He has been an amoebic Proteus, flowing to fit the shape of various social containers, a series of changing forms with no skeletal substance. His concept of race·leadership has been chimerical, an abstraction without any real body; his pursuit in life, the pursuit of a myth. Little by little, he has realized that he has been possessed by words, symbols, generalities. But he has steadily moved from the general to the specific, even as his speeches have been most successful when he has moved from ideology to the subject matter that lies at hand. At one point in the novel, he is reminded of his English professor at the College who says in a commentary on Joyce:

> "Stephen's problem, like ours, was not actually one of creating the un-created conscience of his race, but of creating the uncreated features of his face. . . . We create the race by creating ourselves" (307).

In the end, neither the narrator nor the novelist has rejected racial responsibility; what they have rejected is a mythical racial messianism. They have tried to bring the reader to an understanding of the fact that the messianic brand of leadership is often based on abstracted forms— ideas with no founding in reality. The would-be leader is often blind to the people for whom he attempts to speak. When Brother Tobbitt sneeringly accuses the narrator of believing that he is "in touch with the black God" (78), the shaft strikes a sensitive nerve. The narrator has begun to question the validity of black messianic ideals. Yet, he cannot entirely reject these ideals, for it is painful to live without illusions— painful and empty (492).

It is as true today as it was almost thirty years ago when the novel was first published that the Invisible Man speaks on the lower levels, not only for black Americans but for the whole nation, when he attempts to describe an age of broken ideals. He has discarded his illusions, as he says in the closing pages, but not his sense of social responsibility. It is only the old traditional patterns of black messianism that he has rejected. However, if the Invisible Man had cast aside these patterns, there were others who were not doing so. Black leadership of the late fifties and the sixties would reassert messianic ideals with eloquence, vigor, and force.

13
Racial Messianism
and Political Revivalism
in the 1960s

The ambiguity of the terms "accommodationism" and "militancy," when applied to black messianism in the United States, are well illustrated in the leadership of Martin Luther King, Jr., and Elijah Muhammad. It would be overly simplistic to characterize either as unqualifiedly accommodating or militant, for there were elements of both approaches in the styles of both men. They conformed well to the prediction of Oliver Cox that any great leader of the black population in the United States would necessarily be forced to enlist the support of whites while maintaining a posture of defiance and aggressiveness.[1]

Martin Luther King, Jr., was associated with confrontationist politics that often employed illegal techniques similar to those of nationalist militants in Africa and Asia. At the same time, he was committed to nonviolence, and he believed in the eventual withering away of racial oppression from American life.

Elijah Muhammad, on the other hand, was a racial chauvinist, committed to a belief in the inevitability of racial conflict, yet totally opposed to political agitation. Hostility towards whites became an emotional substitute for political activism and a perfect excuse for avoiding confrontation with segregationist forces. Since whites were devils, unclean eaters of swine flesh, it was foolish to push for integration. Black people could only be corrupted by association with whites. The only hope for black Americans was extreme separatism, for inevitably—and soon—God would rain down destruction upon the Christian West. Race hatred makes strange bedfellows. While extreme tribalists in South Africa were finding support for their myopic values among white supremacists, Muhammad was gaining the attention and support of segregationists in the United States.

Louis Lomax, a black journalist, reported a rumor that H. L. Hunt, a Dallas millionaire, was covertly funding a publicity campaign that bestowed upon the Black Muslims an unaccustomed notoriety.[2] Certainly, Lomax was conscious of a historical pattern when he noted the tendency of white separatists cynically to exploit the publicity given to black separatist movements. By so doing, they gave segregation a legitimacy with militant blacks, countering the image of black separatists as meek, compliant lackeys of the whites. Indeed, they painted a picture of integrationists as people ashamed of their race and willing to suffer any indignity in order to be tolerated by white people. Of course, the irony of such a view is that both separatists and integrationists seek alliances with sympathetic whites and are dependent upon them for the funding and publicity without which a mass movement must be severely handicapped in an electronic civilization.

Thus, although the rhetoric of Mr. Muhammad was steadfastly opposed to any cooperation with whites, it is not altogether clear that he came to prominence without the sympathy and support of some sectors of white opinion. Although Muhammad talked incessantly about the necessity for hostility towards whites, the Nation of Islam under his leadership was notable for its commitment to law-abiding behavior, support for the local police, and hostility to the confrontationism associated with the militant civil-rights movement.[3] His programs were essentially conservative, although his rhetoric was militant. The Nation of Islam attempted to withdraw from American society on a symbolic level, while accommodating bourgeois values on a practical level. It was never strident in its attempt to modify the environment or make it more hospitable to black Americans. Talk of creating a racially open society was usually met with cynical sneers; talk of open agitation for civil rights was viewed as suicidal.

The most prominent exponent of the Black Muslim philosophy during the early 1960s was Malcolm X, Mr. Muhammad's official spokesman and heir apparent. His father had been a militant and a follower of Marcus Garvey; thus we may assume that the early childhood experiences of Malcolm Little (his original name) were touched, at least indirectly, by the influence of Christian black nationalism. As a teenager and as a young man, Malcolm seemed compelled to act out the white-held stereotype of the black-ghetto hipster. Then, through his discovery of the Muslims, the black nationalist fires were rekindled after smoldering in his sub-conscious for many years. When he first came to the attention of American television audiences, he was held up as an example of "the hate that hate produced." As the official representative of the Black Muslims, he openly invited comparison with Martin Luther King, Jr., and the civil-rights advocates with policies of direct but nonviolent confrontation of Jim Crow laws. Malcolm pointed out with a certain undeniable logic that one could not hope to win acceptance through confrontation, since confrontation tends to worsen antagonisms rather than to alleviate them. If blacks were going to intentionally engage in behavior that was certain to make whites antagonistic, and then refuse to defend themselves once passions had been inflamed, they must be exposed as fools.[4]

Malcolm's words did not fall on deaf ears; there were a number of younger blacks, artists, students, and intellectuals, who found his militant stance attractive. Some of these had lived in the South and were veterans of the sit-ins and voter-registration drives. They had seen women and children beaten by psychotic policemen, set upon with cattle prods and vicious dogs, and sent bowling down the streets by streams from fire hoses. They had seen friends killed or maimed and many had been jailed and tortured. They were frustrated and embittered with the slow pace of integration, and they were beginning to ask themselves if they really wanted to be integrated into a society that so obviously did not want them. There were also the Northern youth, many of whom had never been south of Chicago or Newark. They had never confronted blatant segregation, although they knew what it was to be discriminated against. They resented white people and were keenly aware of their power, but they had never been forced to submit to the day-to-day indignities of Jim Crow. They had heard their parents' and their grandparents' horror stories of the South. The sound of a white Southern drawl inspired mingled feelings of hatred, fear, and contempt. They were proud of the integration movement and of King, but they found both the man and the movement difficult to understand. They did not see how it would be possible for any self-respecting black man to live in the South without carrying a gun and using it at least once a day.

While the young blacks liked to hear Malcolm X speak, they found it difficult to accept either his or Mr. Muhammad's religious beliefs. The mysticism of the Black Muslims was amusing and exhilarating, but the young urban intellectuals found it difficult to take seriously the myth of Yakub, the mad scientist who had created the white race in ancient times and was driven out of the Garden for his crime.[5] The artists were not willing to give up pot smoking; the students were not willing to give up their beer busts; nor were many in either category prepared to sacrifice barbecued pork in order to join the Nation. The Black Muslims' appeal was that they provided an ego-restoring rhetoric for blacks who had no intention of participating in Alabama sit-ins and who were, at least verbally, opposed to nonviolence. They attracted much support even among those who would never think of entering one of the mosques.

Just as the young urban blacks were influenced by Malcolm X, so was he influenced by them. He judged correctly that the basis of his appeal to persons outside the Black Muslims was only partially derived from his status as a Muslim minister. It was based more on the self-assertiveness that his position represented and his hostility to the idea that the rights and privileges of black people existed solely on the sufferance of whites.

When relations between Malcolm and Elijah Muhammad became strained, Malcolm grew increasingly interested in Old World varieties of Islam.[6] He made his celebrated trips to Africa and to Mecca, which some observers interpreted as a complete renunciation of black nationalism.[7] During the last year of his life, Malcolm seemed to be developing an interest in Pan–African socialism. Albert Cleage is certainly correct when he argues that Malcolm never accepted the simplistic notion that social assimilation, in and of itself, was a desirable or even a possible solution to the problem of American racial oppression.[8] On the other hand, it cannot be denied that he was increasingly committed to the idea that the specific concerns of black people could best be addressed within the wider context of a world social revolution. By the time of his death, he seems to have been won over to the position that race conflict is inextricably bonded to class conflict.[9]

Malcolm X was not an integrationist in the sense of believing that the random dispersal of blacks throughout American society was the ultimate solution to the racial problem. At the same time, there is ample evidence that from late 1963 until his death in 1965 he was less and less concerned with the wickedness of individual "white devils" and increasingly inclined to look upon the problem in terms of its economic causes. Albert Cleage is perhaps correct in faulting Alex Haley for having overly dramatized the effects of Malcolm's conversion to "Orthodox Islam." He seems to be in agreement with George Breitman that there are important elements of continuity linking together the nationalist and the internationalist phases of Malcolm's life.[10] Of course, once the man was dead, it became possible to attribute all sorts of ideas to him. A dead messiah is often more appealing than a live one, since it is possible for proponents of widely diverse philosophies to claim successorship to the mantle of his ideology.

Malcolm X may be expediently characterized as a sort of "apostle to the Gentiles," because he expended an appreciable amount of energy during his last years addressing predominantly white audiences. His speeches at Harvard, Oxford, the London School of Economics, and the Socialist Workers' Forum consisted largely of attempts to explain the position of black nationalists to white students and intellectuals. They also consisted of attempts to make his audiences think more critically about contemporary revolutionary movements that were being reported in the newspapers—specifically, those in the Congo and Indochina. The spirit of skepticism that he represented was balanced by an idealism that kept him from becoming a Marxist in the truest sense. His awareness of corruption in American politics and duplicity in American foreign policy did not lead him to cynicism. At the time of his death, he was calling for a revolutionary reconstruction of American society; and he placed great hope in the younger generation of whites, whom he viewed, perhaps too optimistically, as potential allies.[11]

At the same time, Malcolm seems never to have abandoned his role as evangelist for black nationalism. His principal talents, as Milton Henry and George Breitman agree, were those of a "teacher and inspirer."[12] His aim was the spiritual regeneration of black Americans, a heightening of their consciousness of themselves as an African people. Separatism was no more to be seen as an end in itself than integration had been; hence, he no longer insisted on a migrationist strategy. Afro–Americans were urged to go "back to Africa culturally, philosophically, and psychologically, while remaining here physically."[13] Thus would a spiritual bond grow up between the kindred peoples of the black ghettoes and Mother Africa, which would strengthen the position of the former in dealing with their problems in America. Despite his increasing interest in Marxism and in the economic roots of racism, Malcolm never gave up this interest in spiritual regeneration. His speeches retained their evangelical quality until the end; and despite the fact that he was forced out of his role as a Muslim minister, he never completely abandoned his revivalistic style. He had the ability to control an audience, to make them feel his own emotions, to carry them along with his rhetoric, and to get them to accept the burden of his argument, even when he was in error on minor facts.

Yet, despite the consistent quality of religious exhortation in his performances, his appeal was not purely emotional. Malcolm X was able to broaden the appeal of black nationalist thought by moving away from the mystical racism of the Black Muslims. He explained its common-sense basis and universal concerns to those who were put off by the Yakub myth. Once he left the Muslims, Malcolm was never able to reestablish an organizational base; nonetheless, he was more important than anyone since Marcus Garvey in making black nationalism a topic of serious discussion in intellectual circles.

It may well be, as Louis Lomax has suggested, that the Black Muslim creed gave comfort to white separatists during the late 1950s. The existence of a separatist "hate movement" among black nationalists certainly lent validity to the old Southern racist argument that the civil-rights leaders did not speak for the black masses and that they were content with segregation. But Malcolm X did not allow himself to be interpreted in this way. No sooner did he gain the attention of the national media than he began to veer away from the simplistic idea that separatism was a race-relations panacea. True, he continued to scorn the idea that desegregation would provide a solution to the problems of black Americans; but he spoke increasingly of the economic origins of racism in America, and he put forth a view of black people in the Northern ghettoes as undergoing trials similar to those of colonial subjects in Africa and Asia.[14]

This graduation to a higher level of analysis on the part of Malcolm X stimulated the increasing sophistication of Martin Luther King, Jr. The black nationalist position had indeed pointed out a weak spot in the program of the Southern civil-rights movement, which addressed itself only to some of the more easily resolved questions of visible racism in that part of the country where it was most virulent. Integrationism did not confront the lack of economic and educational opportunity for blacks in the North. In response to Malcolm's challenge, King was forced to abandon the idea of integration as a panacea. Although he continued to reject separatism or extreme black nationalism as a cure for racial problems, King was becoming increasingly impatient with those who felt that desegregation of public facilities should be the sole objective of the civil-rights movement. He became less cautious about making references to black power and, like Malcolm, insisted on the importance of black groups presenting a united front. He became increasingly critical of the black middle class and of bourgeois organizations, and urged them to take a more aggressive role in political life.

As a result of their confrontations, Malcolm and Martin both became more radical and each added a dimension to his philosophy. But, as a result of their reciprocally stimulated growth, each began to present a greater threat to American conservatives—black and white—and each experienced some erosion of his power base. This was particularly true as the two of them moved towards solidarity on an issue on which they could both agree, the war in Vietnam.[15]

The Black Muslim movement had internationalist implications all along, of course. Not only is Islam outside the mainstream tradition of American religious history, it is a religion of the so-called "Third World." The Black Muslims, with their constant criticism of American values, were naturally interpreted as seeking an alliance with those African and Asian nations that were hostile to Western values. The Black Muslims encouraged such an interpretation of their position, although on close examination it could be seen that they were somewhat more ambivalent about American bourgeois values than they admitted. Despite their having adopted certain elements of Islam, and despite their increasing vociferousness against American foreign policy, they reiterated certain characteristic themes of black messianic Christianity. They were traditional in their criticism of American democracy, in their condemnation of Christian hypocrisy, and in their sense of common cause with the anti-imperialists of the African and Asian worlds. During the 1940s and 1950s, while the movement was under the direct leadership of Elijah Muhammad, there was little more than mysticism in the rhetoric of unity with Africans and Asians. In the early 1960s, however, as Malcolm X assumed the prime spokesmanship role, the Black Muslims became increasingly political in both domestic and foreign affairs.

In 1959 Malcolm visited several Muslim countries, preparing the way for a tour later that year by Elijah Muhammad and two of his sons. The fact that Mr. Muhammad was then allowed into "forbidden areas of Arabia" and accepted as a bona fide Muslim on his pilgrimage to Mecca, "welcomed and honored by [Islam's] most respected religious leaders," did much to legitimize the Black Muslim movement.[16] Clearly, the acceptance of Mr. Muhammad—aside from demonstrating the ability of Islam to absorb heretical sects—showed the political shrewdness of leaders in the Muslim countries who no doubt delighted in publicizing racial antagonisms in the United States. Saudi Arabia, in particular, had an ambiguous relationship with America. While welcoming trade with the United States and sympathizing fully with America's sense of holy war against Godless communism, the Arabs resented her supporting Zionism. Encouraging the Black Muslims in America was a way of giving the United States a taste of its own medicine, in a manner symbolically provocative but unlikely to lead to diplomatic misunderstanding. The claims of Muslims in North America were similar to those of Zionists in the Middle East. The message of the Arabs who supported Elijah Muhammad was subtly conveyed, yet unmistakable: "Let the Americans attend to the claims of nationalists in their own backyard before supporting the claims of nationalist groups in other parts of the world."

In its early stages, the "foreign policy" of the Nation of Islam was limited to establishing ties with Muslim states as a means of asserting its own religious and political legitimacy. By 1962, however, Malcolm was expressing his opinion on numerous issues that seemed remotely connected, if at all, to the world of Islam. Speaking at Yale University in that year, he referred to "crucial blunders" in American foreign policy. These included the U-2 spy-plane incident that had led to President Eisenhower's being "tricked, trapped and exposed before the whole world as a liar."[17] He made passing reference to student unrest and anti-American protest in Korea, Turkey, and Japan; he alluded to anti-American feeling in Latin America; he compared the anti-colonial struggle in the Congo, Kenya, and Algeria to the nationalistic aspirations of the Black Muslims—but the "so-called American Negro" was the most important of all these nations. Fate had placed black Americans in a vital position:

> Mr. Muhammad says that only after the American Negro's condition is "corrected" will Uncle Sam's health improve . . . for only then will Uncle Sam look "healthy" in the eyes of the fast-awakening dark world.[18]

There was an intentional ambiguity in this 1962 speech, however; for while Malcolm asserted that "the handwriting is on the wall for America," he left the audience in some doubt as to how he interpreted its message.

> What will God's price be? What will God's solution be? Can America pay God's price? And, if not, what will be the alternative . . . ? Will America blindly reject God's Messenger, and in so doing bring on her own Divine Destruction?[19]

What was this "Divine Destruction" of which he spoke? Would it be a direct act of God? Would it be a revolt among the masses of black Americans? Would it be a cosmic revolution of the world's darker peoples against Western imperialism? Malcolm's prophecy was similar to David Walker's, 130 years earlier, which had predicted an apocalyptic bloodbath for America in retribution for crimes against the African race. Of course, David Walker, who wrote in 1829, could not have anticipated Malcolm X's optimism at the very real prospects of a decline in Western supremacy.

The jeremiadic theme became more pronounced in the next few years. In 1963, Malcolm offered an enthusiastic but unrealistic analysis of the Bandung Conference held in Indonesia in 1954.[20] At this conference, representatives of the African and Asian nations attempted to hammer out their differences and to come together as a united bloc against a commonly perceived European threat.[21] With the wisdom of the past twenty-five years, one easily observes that the lesson of Bandung is not the viability of Afro–Asian unity, but the impossibility of uniting vast groups of people simply on the basis of hostility to Europe. A resentment of white domination was naturally the key ingredient of black nationalism in the United States; but most of the "Third World" countries had never experienced white dominance in the extreme form known to black Americans. While racial consciousness was certainly a factor in the African and Asian nationalist movements of the mid-twentieth century, it was not the one issue of overwhelming importance that it was for black Americans.

However, if Malcolm was overly optimistic concerning the prospects for Afro–Asian unity, he did judge accurately the propaganda effects of exposing to the court of world opinion American guilt in the area of human rights. He used that term, "human rights," repeatedly in his speeches during the 1960s, openly showing his contempt for those who felt that the concern of black Americans should be restricted to the struggle for civil rights in the United States. With his characteristic appreciation for the subtleties of semantics, he urged a Cleveland audience in 1964 to cease to approach the problems of American racialism in terms of "civil rights" and expand "to a higher level . . . the level of human rights." He advised black Americans to take their case "into the United Nations where our African . . . , Asian [and] Latin–American brothers can throw their weight on our side, and where 800 million Chinamen are sitting there waiting to throw their weight on our side." He reminded a New York audience later that year that "on the world stage the white man is just a microscopic minority." Black people should not go to court begging the United States government for their civil rights; they should take the government to court, "before that body of men who represent international law, and let them know that the human rights of black people are being violated in a country that professes to be the moral leader of the free world."[22]

Long before Malcolm X suggested it, the civil-rights movement had already dragged the United States before the court of world opinion. It has been observed that Martin Luther King's success was due in part to "international pressures generated by the publicity arising from mass arrests and incidents of violence."[23] Although King never intentionally led his people into violent confrontations and even retreated from situations that might have led to violence, his movement benefited from the world-wide publicity given to racial violence in America. The distinction that Malcolm X attempted to draw between civil rights as a purely domestic concern and human rights as an international concern was a false one. King clearly conceived of the struggle for civil rights as a struggle for human dignity going far beyond the claims of black Americans for their heritage as American citizens. King suffered a loss of prestige among more conservative black leaders as a result of this shift; Malcolm X's punishment for his shift to the left was banishment from the Nation of Islam.

The hour of parting was on the evening of December 4, 1963, less than a week after the assassination of President Kennedy. Malcolm gave a speech in the Manhattan Center called "God's Judgement on White America." This was another of his topical jeremiads, reminiscent of David Walker's *Appeal*. He cited the Scriptures to show how ancient wicked civilizations had been destroyed in the time of Lot, in the time of Noah, and in the time of Moses. After preaching for some minutes on the doom of white America, he began to compare the black moderate leaders to Pharaoh's magicians and the late President Kennedy to Pharaoh himself. In the question-and-answer period that followed, Malcolm was asked to comment on the death of the President, and was reported to have said that it was only a case of "chickens coming home to roost."[24] Shortly thereafter, Malcolm was summoned to Chicago, where Mr. Muhammad suspended him from the Nation—ostensibly for having made such an injudicious remark.[25] There were, of course, those who felt that Muhammad simply used this as an excuse to clip Malcolm's wings. Others attributed the action to Muhammad's political conservatism.

At the time of Malcolm's split with Muhammad, Eldridge Cleaver, a black Muslim inmate of San Quentin Prison, became involved in debate with other Muslim prisoners over whether to follow Malcolm out of the Nation or to remain loyal to Muhammad. Cleaver went along with Malcolm, and a few years later published his reasons for doing so in *Soul on Ice*.[26] Shortly after his release from prison, Cleaver, having severed all ties with the Black Muslims, became a member of the Black Panthers, where he held the office of Minister of Information. The Panthers were a purely secular group, although they seemed to be spiritually in the tradition of the Nation of Islam. The list of ten demands that they issued to white America are reminiscent, in some particulars, of the ten-point manifesto, "What the Muslims Want."[27] Like the Muslims, they insisted on self-determination for the black community.

During these years, the Black Panthers were attracting not only refugees from the Nation, but veterans of the civil-rights movement. They adopted as their symbol the black panther of the Lowndes County Freedom Organization. They sought a secular movement and a freedom from the racial mysticism on which the Nation had insisted. Nonetheless, they clung to the jeremiadic tradition of referring to the United States as Babylon, and it was certainly no accident that the Panthers retained the Muslim habit of referring to whites as pigs.

The veterans of the civil-rights movement were represented best by Stokely Carmichael, former head of the Student Nonviolent Coordinating Committee (SNCC). Carmichael and Cleaver quarreled violently and eventually both were forced out of the Panthers. Carmichael began to commute between Africa and the United States, organizing a Pan–African political party based loosely on the idea of the Organization for Afro–American Unity that Malcolm X had proposed. Cleaver went into exile in Algeria, where things went well for a while. After a few years, a more subdued Cleaver turned up in Paris, attempting to earn a living as a writer. In 1976, he announced that he had been "born again." He had become a Christian and was now ready to confess the folly of his past career and avow that America was the seat of justice, the citadel of opportunity, and the best place imaginable for a born-again Negro to live.[28]

Although the angry children of Malcolm X seem at first glance to have renounced the messianic religiosity of both the Nation of Islam and the Southern Christian Leadership Conference, closer inspection shows that they have clung to elements of religious traditionalism. Eldridge Cleaver, like many black writers and would-be race leaders, has understood well that the Christian biases and superstitions of white Americans can be manipulated in ways that serve the good of blacks, as a whole, and sometimes in ways that serve the selfish interests of individuals who just incidentally happen to be black. Stokely Carmichael has understood well that the Christian heritage of black Americans can be exploited. I saw him in action a few years ago, and it was interesting to observe that he assumed the manner of the authoritarian storefront preacher. Indeed, he seemed to be a case in point of the theory advanced by E. Franklin Frazier in *The Negro Church*, that the authoritarian pattern of black leadership that evolved in black religious institutions has left its mark on all black social institutions. And, says Frazier, black Americans respond to authoritarian leadership, because that is the only kind of leadership they have ever known.

Attending one of the rallies that Stokely Carmichael gives on college campuses is very much like going to church, as I learned on attending a workshop at the University of Iowa in the spring of 1975. Most of the students in attendance were less than twelve years old when Carmichael first began to popularize the term, "black power." He co-authored a book by that name which was published in 1967, of course; but, with the exception of those few students in the audience who had been enrolled in my courses, few had read it. I have often used *Black Power* in my courses. It is a systematic, rational appraisal of the position occupied by black Americans during the late 1960s, and some of its advice, had it been followed, could have prevented our experiencing many of the disappointments of the 1970s. I have never given much credence to those who assert that Charles V. Hamilton wrote the book by himself and only shared credit with Carmichael in order to sell copies. At the very least, Carmichael must have been aware of the book's contents, and he must have endorsed its central thesis since he did not, at the time, deny responsibility for it. In *Black Power*, Carmichael and Hamilton said that the black people of the United States constitute a *domestic colony*, and that this makes them a subject people rather than citizens in the proper sense.[29] The Negroes of the United States, they argued, can liberate themselves only by following a policy of internal cohesion and engaging in ethnic politics. Integration was a premature policy; blacks must learn to function independently for the present, although at some time in the future a coalition with the white working class might become feasible.

In his second book, *Stokely Carmichael Speaks*, the author departed dramatically from the position that he had earlier shared with Hamilton. Here he was no longer inclined to think in terms of ethnic politics, and there was no talk of possible cooperation with whites, even in the remote future. Carmichael had become a neo-Garveyite, an extreme Pan–Africanist, arguing that there was no future for black people in the United States.[30] This book was simply a collection of speeches and did not have the rational, systematic quality that had characterized the first. Nonetheless, it was clearly the product of a forceful and imaginative mind. Of course, there was much hostile reaction among black Marxists to the contents of *Stokely Carmichael Speaks*. Henry Winston, for example, called him a reactionary and denounced his ideology as a bogus nationalism, comparable to that of South Korea, Taiwan, and pre-1975 Saigon.[31] Angela Davis, in her *Autobiography*, accused Carmichael of egotism and demagoguery. Describing a typical harangue, she said: "Because he knew how to turn a phrase, he had the audience applauding, not so much what he said as his way of saying it." As for the content of his speech, Davis claims to have been so put off that she would have left SNCC on the spot if Carmichael had still been chairman at the time.[32]

When Stokely Carmichael spoke at the University of Iowa, he began his remarks with a denunciation of messianism. He asserted that revolution comes from the people, not from bourgeois leaders, heroes, or great men. It was not necessary to wait for any Black Moses to lead us to the promised land. This drew applause from the audience and shouts of "Teach!" and "Right on!" It became apparent from the outset that Stokely could say anything he wanted to say (so long as he went through the usual radical posturings), and the crowd was going to back him up. It was exactly as Angela Davis had said; he knew all the buttons to push and just when to push each button. He knew how to milk that audience and get from it those last few spasms of response left over from the once-thriving movement of the sixties. But while his method was essentially an appeal to the emotions, Carmichael found it necessary to give his presentation the trappings of social scientific respectability.

First of all, he said, a philosophy of liberation for black people "must be scientific" (shouts of "Right on!" "Yeh!"). Secondly, "it must be socialistic" ("That's right!" "Teach!"). And what did he mean by scientific? Very simple. Science deals in truth. Every statement that can be made is either true or false. We can determine by empirical methods whether or not something is true. He provided several demonstrations of his point. For example, the piece of chalk that he held in his hand was not a piece of chicken. This produced a few chuckles. He argued, reasonably enough, that a glass of water was not a glass of hydrochloric acid, and that the consequences of denying the difference could be disastrous for anyone who took a drink. Having demonstrated these weighty points, Carmichael began to advance down the aisle, shaking his finger just like a Baptist preacher, until he stood directly in front of me; and, then, leaning into my face, he said: "I'll bet that if you study history, they tell you that you have to study both sides of a question."[33]

Stokely Carmichael is a perfect argument for the validity of E. Franklin Frazier's central thesis in *The Negro Church*. Frazier, of course, asserted with some conviction that the authoritarian pattern of leadership that originated in the black church was carried over into secular institutions in the post-Reconstruction period. Frazier's thesis is somewhat overstated; the black church has not been anti-democratic, nor has it been responsible for stifling the political and artistic traditions of black people. On the contrary, as C. Eric Lincoln and other scholars have demonstrated, the black church since Frazier's death in 1961 has clearly vindicated itself as a source of social activism.[34] It is nonetheless tempting to view Carmichael as representing the revival of absolutist and dogmatic traditions that Frazier associated with black institutional life.

There is also something clearly reminiscent of religious absolutism in Carmichael's desire to return to an eighteenth-century universe of Lockean and Newtonian absolutes. Stokely does not care to argue whether or not the means to black liberation must be scientific. He accepts this as a given, and yet his technique is to appeal to the emotions and utilize crowd sympathies to discredit dissenters. It would be incorrect to attribute demagogic techniques utilized by black leaders solely to the influence of the black church. On the other hand, American demagoguery has historically been associated with the evangelical tradition. The paranoid tendencies of American society, which were so well described by Richard Hofstadter, have not been confined to any racial, religious, or ethnic group.[35] Most persons who aspire to political leadership in America find it useful to resort to revivalistic techniques. If this is particularly true of black leaders, it is probably due to their awareness that Afro–Americans have time and again given evidence of their susceptibility to messianic leadership and millennial thought.

Stokely Carmichael *is* a revivalist. His present-day function seems to be traveling about the country visiting college campuses, attempting to resuscitate the spirit of activism that flourished in his youth. To his credit, Carmichael often visits black student groups free of charge. Unfortunately, his attempts to organize local cadres or to inspire self-motivated study groups have not been successful so far. Yet he was a popular speaker even in the late 1970s and seemed able to kindle, at least momentarily, some of the old crusading zeal and sense of racial mission that prevailed during the decades of civil-rights and black-power activism.

If he could be persuaded to make the most of his skills as a revivalist, Carmichael could be of great usefulness to the cause of black unity. There is much that he could learn from other American evangelists—like Billy Graham, for instance, who, notwithstanding his international fame, remains a loyal parishioner in a fashionable Baptist congregation in Dallas, Texas. As Malcolm X once observed, Graham knows better than to organize his own independent church or to present himself as a rival to local Southern Baptist leaders.[36] On the contrary, he works to strengthen the power of local leaders so that they welcome his coming into their communities and are even eager to turn their pulpits over to him for a day or two. Needless to say, if Billy Graham were to behave as Stokely Carmichael does and attempt to undercut or ignore the activities of local leaders, he would not enjoy the success that is currently his.

It is ironic that Carmichael, who is a revivalist and who sees himself as following in the tradition of Marcus Garvey, is so opposed to religion. I have heard him assert that all religion tends to thwart political action and leads to passive submission. This is, of course, historically inaccurate; and the works of Vincent Harding, Joseph Washington, and Gayraud Wilmore point up the irresponsibility of such an assertion.[37] Early in his career, Carmichael expressed some admiration for the Black Muslims and encouraged black people to "go to their mosque to find out what they are talking about first hand." He insisted that their leader be addressed as "the Honorable Elijah Muhammad," and reminded his audience that "he represents a great section of the black community. Honor him."[38] Speaking at the University of Iowa in 1975, however, Carmichael asserted that all religions—without exception—are evil, because they teach that mankind is evil. When I asked him if he intended to include the Nation of Islam in this indictment, he said: "Yes, the Muslims, too; if Allah is so bad, let him come down here and get the man off my back."

Carmichael's attacks on religion have not gone unanswered. The most interesting response has been that of the Rev. Albert B. Cleage of the Shrine of the Black Madonna in Detroit, Michigan. In an epistle to Stokely Carmichael, Cleage called for the ordination of "the young men who make up SNICK's organization throughout the country." This would be legitimate because "the Movement is the Christian church in the 20th century and . . . the Christian Church cannot truly be the church until it also becomes the Movement." Cleage asserted that the young militants of the sixties knew nothing whatsoever of true Christianity and that the "otherworldly" religion that they were rejecting bore no relation to the true teaching of Jesus Christ, the Black Messiah.[39]

The Reverend Cleage follows in the tradition of Bishop Turner, Marcus Garvey, and Archbishop McGuire in asserting that God is black; and, like the Black Muslims and Black Jews, he has developed ethnological and biblical arguments for his assertions. He gives his endorsement to the historical writings of Rabbi Hilu Paris, a native of Ethiopia and a graduate of Yeshiva University. Rabbi Paris asserts that the central core of Hebrew teaching, including the concept of monotheism, derives from predynastic Egypt, which makes it African. The rite of circumcision, the prohibition of certain foods, certain mathematical concepts borrowed from the Egyptians—all serve to show that "the Israelites were never far away from their roots, the roots that lie in Africa."[40] Cleage endorses, as well, the writings of Josef Ben Jochannan, the author of several works of dubious originality. Ben Jochannan is ecumenical in his preaching and urges African people to "come together for the purpose of recapturing a common theological basis." Judaism, Christianity, Islam, Yoruba, Voodooism, and Spiritualism are all African religions. Sons and daughters of Africa should "recognize one another's right to hold separate, although basically similar, religious theories."[41] Cleage, Paris, and Ben Jochannan are all indebted to the later writings of Du Bois, who traced the origins of the great world religions and philosophies to African sources. Ironically, Cleage sees Du Bois as an "integrationist" and is apparently oblivious to the contributions of Du Bois to the tradition of messianic Ethiopianism.[42]

Cleage reiterates the familiar argument that the biblical Hebrews were a black nation: "Present day white Jews were converted to Judaism in Europe and Asia following the fall of Jerusalem in A.D. 70." Joseph was married to an African woman. His descendants, and the descendants of his brothers, likewise intermarried with Africans during their sojourn in Egypt. Moses was an African, driven into exile for killing an Egyptian. He married a black woman and sat at the foot of his African father-in-law, who revealed to him the ancient truths of the African religion. "The Israelites and the Egyptians were all black people," but, as Mediterranean Africans, the Egyptians had a less pure form of the African religion than that which Moses learned from Jethro. When the Israelites left Egypt, they were a black people with an African religion.[43] Jesus was a black nationalist fighting against colonial oppression. He was opposed by Uncle Toms within the black nation; that is to say, the Pharisees and other official leaders:

> Jesus was black and he was speaking to a Black Nation. He was always telling black people how to fight white people. So there wasn't any way in the world that a white man could read Jesus and know what he was talking about.[44]

Paul was the great distorter of the Christian message; in his capacity as self-appointed apostle to the Gentile world, he was responsible for adulterating the Christian message with primitive paganism. He borrowed ideas from Greek and Roman philosophy in order to make the Christian teaching palatable for whites. He preached that circumcision and other Jewish rituals were no longer important:

> The Epistles of Paul are in direct contradiction to the teachings of the Old Testament. Slave Christianity emphasizes these distortions of the Apostle Paul and denies and repudiates the basic teachings of Jesus Christ and the Black Nation Israel.[45]

Although Cleage presents his message as seeking "to rediscover the original teachings of Jesus and the Nation Israel," it is obviously only a reaction to an American context—and a traditional reaction at that. For the past three hundred years, black Americans have been reacting to the hypocrisy of white Christians either by rejecting Christianity or by adapting its message to suit their own spiritual needs. But Cleage's reaction is not only a response to white racists, it is an attempt to beat the Black Muslims at their own game. It is a transparent attempt to appeal to emotional black militants by distorting the essential message of the Gospels. Needless to say, Cleage's version of Christianity has not attracted large numbers of followers.

I first met the Reverend Cleage when I was about fourteen years old, and he impressed me as a calm, rational, and sensitive man. He would open his home on one of Detroit's fashionable boulevards to teenagers from all over the city for "junior fellowship" on Sunday afternoons and for "senior fellowship" later in the evening. I remember an occasion when some members of the junior fellowship were gathered in his basement recreation room for a discussion, and somehow the subject of Mariolatry came up. I remember how patiently and fairly the Reverend Cleage explained that Catholics do not worship Mary, although some less educated Catholics may fail to recognize the difference between reverence and worship. Years later, I attended senior fellowship meetings at Central Congregational Church; again, I was impressed by his calm manner and his obvious affection for the young people with whom he worked. His congregation was stable working class or middle class, but not, as some of his detractors have attempted to convey, a black elite. He spoke slowly and with a middle-class accent. He was fair-skinned, almost ruddy, with grey eyes and sandy hair; but he had unmistakably Negro features. According to that strange American logic that classifies the Reverend Cleage as black, it may be justifiable to refer to the ancient Egyptians and Mosaic Hebrews as black, too. During the late sixties, when he changed the name of his church to the Shrine of the Black Madonna, I remembered his attempt to clarify the Catholic doctrine on the veneration of Mary and wondered if his desire to be fair had not stemmed from a latent sympathy for the doctrine.

The veneration of the Black Madonna is linked to a blend of scholarly and pseudo-scholarly speculations having to do with certain paintings and sculptures located throughout Europe and the Middle East that depict the mother of Christ as a dark or black woman. Joseph Ben Jochannan hardly departs from conventional anthropology when he says:

> The Black Madonna, the Mother of Jesus Christ, is nothing more than an adaptation of the African's *symbol of fertility*, as depicted by the Egyptian statue of Isis and Osiris—the god and goddess of fertility of the Nile Valley high-culture that predated Mary and Jesus by thousands of years.[46]

Many scholars believe that the Black Madonna's coloring reveals her pre-

Christian origins as an earth goddess, or as a soot-blackened goddess of the hearth. Leonard Moss has suggested that some of the Black Madonnas venerated today in European communities are ancient statues of pre-Christian goddesses whose functions were redefined in early Christian times.[47] Cleage rejects the "soft, childishly pretty Madonna of the Roman Church" in favor of the strong, dark Earth Mother of the East. He does not view the coloring of the Black Madonnas as mystical, but prefers a more anthropomorphic view. He observes that the Black Madonnas were created by Byzantine artists before the rise of Western Europe in the fifteenth century. The peoples of the Eastern Empire were darker than those of the Western Empire and, thus, less inclined to distort images of Mary and her son. The large chancel mural in the Shrine of the Black Madonna is meant to represent

> the Black women of the ages, who have made it possible for the black nation to survive in the midst of oppression, exploitation, and brutality. She resembles the Madonnas of the Orthodox churches that have retained a closer kinship to their African beginnings.[48]

Unlike Ben Jochannan, who rejects the doctrine of the "virgin birth" and attributes it to St. Augustine's tampering with the text of the Vulgate Bible, Cleage finds the dogma useful in his own system, where Jesus was the Son of God and Jesus was black. "Then don't tell me God doesn't have any color," he concludes. "There had to be a seed there."[49] Cleage has moved beyond the metaphors of Turner and Garvey, who only asserted the black man's right to view God through his own spectacles and to depict him accordingly. He insists on a literal interpretation of the phrase "God is Black." But although he believes in a black God, Cleage does not find it necessary to construct a white demonology. He is most emphatic in rejecting Mr. Muhammad's Yakub myth, not because it departs from Christian doctrine, but because he feels that to think of the white man as a devil is to endow him with superhuman powers. Still, he sees the Yakub myth as containing "elements of truth."[50]

The Reverend Cleage's black messianic Christianity is, in large part, a response to Malcolm X, who he claims once said: "I am going to tell the brothers and sisters who live in Detroit to join the Shrine of the Black Madonna." Cleage admits that he "cannot resist the temptation to compare Brother Malcolm to Jesus, Jesus whom we worship, the black Messiah." He expresses his sorrow that Malcolm died when he did, before he could fully develop his philosophy; but in a contradictory vein, he asserts that "he knew when to die, because dead he has more followers than he could ever have had alive."[51] Cleage is not the only person to have made this observation, nor is he the only black clergyman to have assigned a messianic or prophetic role to him. Dr. James H. Cone, a professor at Union Theological Seminary, cites Malcolm X repeatedly, implicitly endowing the latter's opinions with the status of major theological pronouncements. C. Eric Lincoln, another black professor at Union Theological Seminary, described Malcolm X—even before his assassination—as, "at this point the symbol rather than the leader of an important new dimension of the black revolution." After the assassination, Lincoln wrote of the "Malcolm X cult [that] sprang up immediately after his death." Gayraud S. Wilmore has referred to Malcolm as a prophet, and apparently endorses a view that he attributes to "many black churchmen" who are saying: "The God who spoke by the prophets and in the fullness of time by his Son, *now in this present time, speaks to us through Brother Malcolm.*"[52]

Cleage's attitude towards Malcolm is possessive; he fails to recognize that he is not the only black Christian minister to have responded to Malcolm's challenge. Gayraud S. Wilmore has intelligently borne witness to the fact that the black revolution of the 1960s cannot be understood without an understanding of the "interdependence between Malcolm and Martin which bound them together in a dialectic of social action. . . ." But Cleage is inclined to damn King with faint praise. He admits that "Dr. King made a genuine contribution. . . . No one would have listened to Brother Malcolm until Dr. King had created the confrontation situations in which we began to learn step by step, that black people can unite, black people can fight, black people can die for the things they believe in."[53] What Cleage does not admit is that King, during his last years, moved steadily towards a greater tolerance for the black-power ideology advanced by Malcolm. Cleage, Malcolm, and King were all part of a general movement of the black church towards a reclamation of its messianic political heritage. Within such a context it is absurd for Cleage to maintain that "Brother Malcolm didn't come to a people who were waiting for a messiah [but] to a people who were tired of being a separate people."[54]

Martin Luther King, who moved away from his conception of integration as a panacea, owed his success all along to his ability to appeal to the millennial element in the thinking of black people. His skillful manipulation of their sense of messianic mission was also basic to his success. The same was obviously true of Elijah Muhammad and Malcolm X. That the three leaders were similar with respect to their exploitation of black American messianic traditions is increasingly recognized.[55] It is also coming to be accepted that, if traditional black religion in the United States had been as devoid of political culture as Cleage and others have maintained, Martin Luther King would have had no base from which to work. The Southern Christian Leadership Conference was not so far removed from the black Christian nationalism of the Reverend Cleage as he likes to pretend. Nor would either movement have evolved as it did without the stimulus of the Black Muslims.

In the city of Detroit, where W. D. Fard, Elijah Muhammad, and Malcolm X all began their ministerial careers, the distance from Muslim Temple No. 1 to the Shrine of the Black Madonna is not too far to walk. The ideological proximity of Christian, Islamic, Hebraic, and atheistic black nationalism; the messianic rhetoric characteristic of the movements; and the great potential for a unified front—although ignored by the various factions—have not gone ignored by the enemies of black power. Secret memos, recently released by the FBI as a result of a lawsuit filed by NBC reporter Carl Stern under the Freedom of Information Act, reveal an awareness of latent subconscious sympathies among rival organizations. Agents were once directed to

> 1. Prevent the *coalition* of militant black nationalist groups. In unity there is strength; a truism that is no less valid for all its triteness. An effective coalition of black nationalist groups might be the first step toward a real "Mau Mau" in America, the beginning of a true black revolution.[56]

Even more revealing is the following directive with its recognition of an underlying religious tone in militant black nationalism. The names of individuals were deleted with a heavy marker from the photocopies released by the government.

> 2. Prevent the rise of a "messiah" who could unify, and electrify, the militant black nationalist movement. [name deleted] might have been such a "messiah"; he is the martyr of the movement today. [several names deleted] all aspire to this position. [name deleted] is less of a threat because of his age. [name deleted] could be a very real contender for this position should he abandon his supposed "obedience" to "white liberal doctrines" (nonviolence) and embrace black nationalism. [name deleted] has the necessary charisma to be a real threat in this way.[57]

It is obvious that the religious and ideological barriers that have been perceived by some black nationalists as adamantine have been perceived by others as flimsy and ephemeral. The FBI official who dictated this secret memorandum in 1967 clearly perceived black messianism as a substantial threat. No doubt he sensed, as well, that there was little ideological distance from Muhammad's mosque to the Shrine of the Black Madonna.

14
Black Messianism
and American Destiny

Throughout this study, I have treated messianism primarily as a group concept. Thus I have minimized the importance of individual messiahs and have accepted the definition of "messiah" entertained by Bertrand Russell, Martin Buber, and standard reference works, which view messianism as the belief in a chosen people's destiny to bring about the Kingdom of God on earth—that is, the millennium or messianic era. Black messianism in the United States has derived from the tendency of both white and black Americans to assume that the tribulations of black Americans have endowed them with a special righteousness. Black Christian tradition has tended to identify the black race with such Biblical motifs as the "Man of Sorrows" and the "Suffering Servant." The messianic myths that came to have the most importance in the pre-Civil War history of the American Negro people were the jeremiadic prophecies of Thomas Jefferson and the Christian perfectionism of Harriet Beecher Stowe.

I have seen the origins of black messianism in the United States as being essentially American and Christian. A search for African roots of the tradition has not been altogether fruitless, but African messianism would seem to be a cognate, rather than a source, of such expressions in the New World. Messianism is undoubtedly an almost universal phenomenon. It is not the special province of the wretched of the earth, for even prosperous and powerful nations have often revealed a penchant for describing themselves as lonely and abused benefactors of mankind. Stalinist Russia, Nazi Germany, and Imperial America have all assumed a messianic self-concept, as Bertrand Russell and others have observed. Black messianism is subtly influenced by the American chauvinistic tradition. The strident Christian-soldierism of an expansionist social gospel has strongly influenced Afro–American millenarianism.

There is a certain cosmic self-esteem, if not a worldly pride, involved in coming to think of one's nation or race as a "chosen people." David Walker's *Appeal*, which was treated in Chapter 3, revealed its author's vacillation between the concepts of brotherly love and Christian self-righteousness. The document was a jeremiad, inspired by Thomas Jefferson's passing observation in *Notes on the State of Virginia* that "I tremble for my country when I reflect that God is just."[1] Walker's argument in the *Appeal* used this statement as the point of departure for an entire theory of history in which a series of chosen peoples, most recently the Americans, had abused their covenantal responsibilities and thus lost their special blessings. Black Americans, by virtue of their suffering, had become a chosen people of God. White America would retain the favor of Providence only insofar as it linked its destiny with the uplift of the black population. The messianism of David Walker, and later that of Henry Highland Garnet, was filled with the rhetoric of violence; but by the mid-nineteenth century, a much milder version of black messianism seemed to have become dominant.

This variety of the myth centered on the Christian heroism in Harriet Beecher Stowe's *Uncle Tom's Cabin*. Uncle Tom represented the supposed characteristics of the black race—gentleness, loyalty, and the enduring power of unshakable faith. The African race was thus assumed to have a natural predisposition to the acceptance of Christian principles. Stowe believed that the millennium would be ushered in by Christianized Africans leading their race into the messianic era. When Ethiopia stretched forth her hand unto God, the entire human race would be uplifted.

Contrasting with the fatalism of Uncle Tom was the fiery prophetism of Nat Turner. The fictional suffering servant was no more a product of America's myth-making propensity than was the historical slave revolutionary. As Vincent Harding has observed, a mythical Nat Turner has existed side by side with the historical one. Even the historical Nat Turner is a product of myth-making. The county clerk, who first recorded Turner's confessions, imbued the narrative with his own feelings of guilt and superstitious dread. The tradition that places Turner within the context of messianism is conveyed to us through one single source —the account of a white man who was himself totally immersed in the backwoods evangelical traditions of nineteenth-century America.

Messianic millenarianism, like other varieties of human experience, harbors the fatalist side by side with the activist. By the late nineteenth century, the black church was involved in a controversy between those who urged passive acceptance of the will of God and those who believed that God helps those who help themselves. This was the time when the perfectionist strain in American Christianity found its voice in a social gospel, whose adherents hoped to attain a worldly millennium through Christian activism. Social gospelers hoped to give Providence a little assistance in bringing about the Kingdom of God on earth. This was the point at which Booker T. Washington emerged as black America's most powerful leader, to be hailed repeatedly in the press as a "Black Moses." Booker T. Washington made use of millenarian rhetoric in his Atlanta Exposition address and in other speeches. He sided with the social gospelers, never losing an opportunity to attack religious fatalism and otherworldly ideology. Like the other social gospelers, he hoped that an enlightened and pragmatic Christianity would lead the nation to the building of "a new heaven and a new earth."

Throughout the nineteenth century, black leaders and friends of the Afro–American people exploited the messianic myth which black and white Americans held in common. Most of them seemed to agree with Booker T. Washington that America was a chosen nation and that black Americans were a specially chosen people within that nation. As the twentieth century dawned, the United States began to adjust to its emerging role as a world leader. Black Americans were quick to seize this opportunity to formulate an appeal to the conscience of the United States. The nation could fulfill its mission in the larger cosmos only if it fulfilled its destiny at home by guaranteeing the God-given inalienable rights to its own citizenry.

America's sense of mission in the first half of the twentieth century was heightened by participation in the World Wars and by competition with the rising power of Russia. The contradiction between egalitarian ideals and the realities of racial segregation was a source of embarrassment to many Americans; and as the United States attempted to assert international leadership in the post-war world, considerable attention was focused on what Gunnar Myrdal called "An American Dilemma"— the contradiction between a liberal tradition and a caste system. The American people were by no means wholeheartedly committed to the eradication of racism, but they were certainly embarrassed by de jure segregation and racial limitations on voting rights. These were hardly good advertisements for a nation self-consciously cultivating an image as "Leader of the Free World." It was a combination of liberal guilt, missionary ideals, and political expediency that led to the success of the civil-rights movement—none of these factors would have been sufficient in itself to have brought about the changes in American race relations that characterized the period from 1954 to 1964. American race relations were inextricably bound up with foreign policy.

As the civil-rights movement began to take shape during the 1940s and early 1950s, black leaders continued to exploit the American sense of mission and revolutionary zeal to redeem the world. This they had done during the years of the abolition movement and, although the tradition subsided during the segregation era, it was resuscitated by the Second World War and its aftermath, the "Cold War."

In 1944, a coalition of black organizations, led by such spokespersons as Walter White and Mary McLeod Bethune, declared that their conception of the war effort demanded victory over the "Hitler-like forces within our own country" as well as those abroad. Victory must mean the triumph of "political and economic democracy . . . in Africa, the West Indies, India, and all other colonial areas." America must "formulate a foreign policy [that would] resolutely and unequivocally oppose either perpetuation or extension of exploitation based upon white superiority." In dealing with racial matters, "the United States must point the way . . . in international post-war reconstruction." Black leaders were clearly attempting to manipulate the nation's post-war, self-righteous messianic impulse.[2]

Black Marxists, like William L. Patterson, Paul Robeson, and Benjamin Davis, were naturally inclined to the approach that linked American civil rights to post-war foreign policy. In 1951, the Civil Rights Congress, a Marxist-influenced organization, delivered a petition, *We Charge Genocide, The Historic Petition to the United Nations for Relief from a Crime of the United States Government Against the Negro People.*[3] The document was endorsed by a number of black American communists. It appears that the purpose of the petitioners was to embarrass American missionary liberals by questioning the sincerity of American democratic ideals. The presentation of such a charge was not a disavowal of American ideals but rather a statement of faith in them. The petitioners revealed a belief in the conscience of the American people and its susceptibility to moral pressure.

When, in 1964, Malcolm X urged black Americans to stop talking about civil rights and to start talking about human rights and called for protests to the United Nations, he was following in the tradition of the numerous black leaders since the nineteenth century who had internationalized their struggle by lecturing abroad on the defects of American democracy. Followers of this tradition had hoped to profit from the moral vulnerability of a nation self-conscious of its destiny as a "City on a Hill." It is remarkable that black Americans preserved such faith in America's concern for its international image at a time when the nation was showing flagrant disregard for international opinion by continuing its war in Vietnam. Shortly before his death, Malcolm had begun to insist that there was a connection between the mentality that waged war abroad and that which oppressed black Americans at home. Shortly thereafter, the embattled Martin Luther King, Jr., announced that he had "left the realm of constitutional rights" and was "entering the area of human rights."[4]

A Congregationalist minister, who literally felt the last heartbeat of the dying Reverend King, eventually came to play a highly visible role in America's messianic diplomacy.[5] One may easily identify those elements of Andrew Young's style that derived from a two-hundred-year tradition of black Christian messianism. And, his concern with the human-rights issue was not isolated from his earlier activism in the civil-rights movement. Indeed, Young's critics from New York to Nigeria often commented that he was far too eager to draw parallels between the international human-rights movement and the civil-rights movement at home.

The pattern of Young's opposition to South African apartheid was symbolic of this attitude. His views on the role of business in that Republic were based on a questionable interpretation of the history of desegregation in the United States. In May of 1977, he addressed an audience of South African businessmen, attempting to persuade them with economic arguments against racial oppression:

> ". . . when in Atlanta, Georgia, five banks decided that it was bad business to have racial turmoil, racial turmoil ceased."[6]

In October 1978, he told a television audience that "the key to change in South Africa is going to be a more responsible, more aggressive role by business."[7] It was statements such as these, no doubt, that led Edgar Lockwood to describe Young's United Nations career as an "apostleship for capitalism."[8]

Young's approach to fighting apartheid was based on a missionary concept. He encouraged blacks and other Americans to make pilgrimages to South Africa. He argued, for example, that black athletes ought to compete in South Africa. "My political education and sense of selfhood really came from people like Joe Louis," he once said. "When Joe Louis knocked out Max Schmeling, that was freedom day; when Jesse Owens won the 1936 Olympics, I was only four years old, but I knew what that was about, and my consciousness as a black person came almost entirely from sport."[9] Young clearly envisioned a policy in which black athletes might work hand in hand with the State Department to spread the gospel of American egalitarianism. Thus would America be placed in the position of perfecting civil rights at home in order to fulfill its mission of encouraging human rights universally.

Andrew Young's linking together of international capitalism and human rights symbolized an attempt to smooth over conflicting interpretations of America's messianic destiny. Among his critics were those who opposed any sort of formal cooperation between the United States and South Africa, and those who felt the United States should openly and actively support the white-supremacist regime. Young attempted to appease the former and to ignore the latter. This involved keeping up the pretense that there had never been any conflict between the two views of America's role as a world power. He assumed, perhaps too hastily, that American business, whether at home or abroad, necessarily viewed a crusade against racism as being in its best interest.

If Young's foreign policy was somewhat optimistically conceived, it was hardly as ahistorical and unrealistic as the view presented by Martin Weil, arguing in *Foreign Policy*. Weil contended that black Americans ought to associate their interests with American chauvinism, as other ethnic groups presumably have done. In his view, American Poles and Zionist Jews have been "exporters of the American tradition to a familiar overseas market. And from this derived their powerful appeal to a proud and morally supercilious citizenry, glorying in the magnificence of the American way of life." He argued that the Poles and the Jews had channeled "this chauvinistic enthusiasm into their own causes." Thus, they had been "wise enough to flow with the current of American nationalism, not against it." Their causes had profited from "the traditional American missionary zeal to transform the world in its own image."[10]

A blind commitment to American "chauvinism" and "missionary zeal" would be inconsistent with the commitment of black Americans to perfecting American democracy. Black Americans have never viewed the United States as a perfect society, and it is unfair to imply that American Poles or Jews or any other group have consistently viewed it in that way. The views of those who suggest that black Americans can or should align themselves with the jingoistic version of American destiny betray an ahistorical perception of the black experience. The chauvinistic conception of American destiny has frequently been hostile to black-American aspirations, as blacks have well perceived, and it is by challenging this view with an alternative sense of mission that they have made their most important contributions to American values.

In 1977, Jimmy Carter came to the Presidency of the United States with significant support from the black population, which he had acquired during the years of his governorship of Georgia. It has been suggested that his evangelical Christianity may have had something to do with his appeal to black Americans. During the campaign of 1976, Michael Novak wrote for the *Washington Post*: "Blacks more than Catholics and Jews are familiar with the Carter symbolic style; they too are Evangelical, Protestant and Southern in their tradition."[11] Novak must have felt that his views were vindicated later that year when the aged Martin Luther King, Sr., said, in the process of offering the closing benediction at the Democratic National Convention, "Surely the Lord sent Jimmy Carter to come out and bring America back where she belongs."[12]

The messianic role that "Daddy" King prophesied for Jimmy Carter—that of a good shepherd bringing Americans back to the garden—was not to materialize. Carter's evangelicalism was perceived as old-fashioned and naive in an age when America (in the view of youthful, progressive, and liberated people) needed to be learning to "look out for Number One." His unquestionably appropriate words in an address delivered on July 15, 1979, fell on deaf ears. There were few who would have disagreed with him that the nation was experiencing a "crisis of confidence . . . , that strikes at the very heart and soul of our national will."[13] There were few, however, who were willing to entertain his explanation of the causes. Carter suggested that the fault was somewhere in ourselves; that Americans were being punished for having abandoned the virtues that originally brought them to greatness; that conditions would improve only if the nation underwent moral reform.

Behind President Carter's jeremiad was the disquieting specter of "intolerable dependence on foreign oil [which] threatens our economic independence and the very security of our nation." But in Carter's view and in the view of many others, the problem did not originate with any desire on the part of oil-supplying nations to exert a stranglehold on the United States. American oil dependency stemmed from the behavior of Americans themselves. It derived from self-indulgence and the "mistaken idea of freedom [as] the right to grasp for ourselves some advantage over others."

> Human identity is no longer defined by what one does, but what one owns. But we've discovered that owning things, and consuming things, does not satisfy our longing for meaning. We've learned that piling up material goods cannot fill the emptiness of lives which have no confidence or purpose.[14]

The problems that Carter identified in his jeremiad were similar to those of which Christopher Lasch has spoken in The Culture of Narcissism.[15] There has been a recent tendency in American life to think of self-indulgence as a virtue, to think of dedication or sense of duty as an "erroneous zone," to rationalize that anarchy is a desirable state.[16] Ironically, some of those who are readiest to defend the spirit of anarchy are most appalled by the social and environmental disasters that it produces. While shedding tears for murdered seal pups, they gyrate to the electronic vibrations of godless freedom. Their sincerity is questionable because to face the reality of an ecological crisis requires habits of self-denial that cannot be cultivated in an environment of affable moral plasticity. It is difficult to believe that a society that has come to define mental health in terms of divesting itself of inhibitions can exert the qualities of discipline necessary to save itself from an ecological disaster or a nightmare in human relations. The slick "New Wave" mentality has no interest in a social gospel, and the rising "Moral Majority" do not concern themselves with it. Indeed the social gospel, in its traditional sense, is rejected as decisively by the Moral Majority as it is by the secularists whom they oppose.

The present hostility towards the values of a social gospel does not bode well for the struggle for racial equality. The battle for the rights of black Americans has traditionally been a part of the campaign for moral reform. It was in Boston's churches, not New Orleans' brothels, that reformers linked together temperance, antislavery, and the struggle for women's rights before the Civil War. The key figures in the American civil-rights struggle have all borne the mark of puritan discipline and self-denial. This is not to suggest that either America's black population or its leaders may be characterized as "puritanical." It is simply to illustrate that the black liberation tradition has never been libertine.

Black leadership in America continues to preach conservatism in lifestyles and liberalism in politics. It maintains the religious authoritarianism and messianic traditions that have been attributed to it by E. Franklin Frazier, C. Eric Lincoln, Joseph Washington, and other historians. The recent career of the Reverend Jesse Jackson exemplifies the persistence of these tendencies, as Barbara Reynolds has noted in her biography of him.[17] Jackson announced during the late 1970's that his organization, People United to Save Humanity (PUSH), would no longer be committed primarily to protest. It would concern itself with self-help at the grass-roots level and would emphasize laboring within the black community to encourage respect for authority and the work ethic. Jackson declared war on teenage drinking, drug abuse, sexual promiscuity, and excessive television viewing. He called on parents, schools, youth groups, and civic organizations to work together in efforts to strengthen public morality.[18] Although he finds himself treading the folkways in company with the Moral Majority, he still advocates decisive action by government in such areas as equal opportunity, housing programs, health, education, and welfare. Thus he takes issue with the Reagan administration's welfare and employment policies, while agreeing with some of its moral concerns.[19]

The black liberation tradition has been inextricably interwoven with the American traditions of evangelical reform, perfectionism, and the social gospel. It has been bound up historically with the quest for moral excellence and discipline. It is, therefore, difficult to imagine what forms the struggle against racism might take in a society where religious rhetoric has been appropriated by a "Moral Majority" oblivious to the horrors of Malthusian economics.

Should the religion-based myths of American mission and destiny disappear with their admittedly mixed blessings, what would rise to take their places? Ronald Reagan's pietism notwithstanding, America's crusading spirit is being challenged by a narcissistic anarchism that wafts through supermarket aisles, university seminars, suburban patios, and ghetto streets. Regardless of race or class, we are all being affected. The bunny may soon become our national totem as we become a nation of bunnies—cute and sexy, clever and fast, with an ideology that never rises above the level of a nightshow comic's monologue. A "redeemer nation" must have something to offer the world besides plastic gadgets, pot-smoking children, and chic pornography. The question confronting black Americans at the end of the twentieth century is whether we can remain separate enough from American culture to assume the role that Martin Luther King, Jr., envisioned—a conscience and a soul for the nation. Alas, I fear this is too heavy a cross for black Americans to be asked to bear.

Notes

Short-form references are used for works listed in the Selected Bibliography, where complete publishing information is given.

Preface

1. *Newsweek*, January 27, 1969; and October 18, 1971.
2. *'Id With the Ansars*, tabloid publication of the Ansaru Allah Community, undated, p. 19.
3. H. N. Smith, *Virgin Land*, p. xi.
4. Ibid., p. x.
5. See Chapter 1 text and note 20.
6. M. L. King, Jr., *Stride Toward Freedom*, p. 201.
7. Louis Jacobs and Sergio J. Sierra, "Messiah: In Modern Jewish Thought," in *Encyclopedia Judaica*, Vol. 11 (New York: Macmillan, 1971), p. 1415.
8. These points are argued and documented at length in Chapter 1. For Buber, see *Encyclopedia Judaica*, Vol. 11, p. 1427; and for Russell, see his *History of Western Philosophy*, p. 364.
9. Ward, *Andrew Jackson*, pp. 432–38.
10. Levine, *Black Culture and Black Consciousness*, pp. 432–38.
11. A creative interpretation of the Uncle Tom myth can be found in Furnas, *Goodbye to Uncle Tom*. While Furnas is rightly concerned with the hostility of black Americans to the Uncle Tom stereotype, my own interpretation pays more attention to the ambivalence of black Americans and the complexity of their sometimes unwitting responses to it.
12. Stowe, *Uncle Tom's Cabin*.
13. The literary methodology of these scholars is treated in Tate, *Search for a Method in American Studies*, p. 26.
14. Fishman, *The Disinherited of Art*, p. 61.
15. Vincent Harding on Du Bois' messianism, in Clarke et al., *Black Titan*, pp. 52–69; Ellison, *Invisible Man*.
16. Moses, "The Poetics of Ethiopianism."

Chapter 1

1. The problems of definition can best be appreciated after a survey of the literature. Readers may wish to peruse the article by R. J. Zwi Werblowski, "Messiah and Messianic Movements," in *Encyclopedia Britannica* (1979). Cf. with the article cited in Preface, note 7; and Harold Walter Turner, "Tribal Religious Movements," in *Encyclopedia Britannica* (1979). A

useful pioneering study is Lanternari, *Religions of the Oppressed*; see also A. J. F. Köblen, "Prophetic Movements as an Expression of Protest," *International Archives of Ethnography* (1960); W. La Barre, "Materials for a History of Studies of Crisis Cults: A Bibliographic Essay," *Current Anthropology* (1971): 3–44; Linton, "Nativistic Movements"; Mair, "Independent Religious Movements on Three Continents"; and A. F. C. Wallace, "Revitalization Movements: Some Theoretical Considerations for Their Comparative Study," *American Anthropologist* (1956): 266.

2. For additional information about the Columbus meeting, see the article by Jacobs and Sierra in the *Encyclopedia Judaica* (see Preface, note 7). References for Martin Buber's and Bertrand Russell's arguments can be found in Preface, note 8.

3. Tuveson, *Redeemer Nation*; Marty, *Righteous Empire*; Bellah, *The Broken Covenant*; H. Niebuhr, *Kingdom of God in America*.

4. McLoughlin, *The American Evangelicals*, p. 28; cf. Wilson, *Patriotic Gore*, p. 97.

5. Fredrickson, *The Black Image in the White Mind*, pp. 97–129; Fullinwider, *Mind and Mood of Black America*, pp. 72–73. See the index references to Theodore Parker in Tuveson, *Redeemer Nation*; and Harding's reference to Du Bois' messianism cited in Preface, note 15. August Meier has identified "efforts made to invest King with the qualities of a Messiah" in his "On the Role of Martin Luther King," *New Politics*, 4 (Winter 1965): 52–59; reprinted as "The Conservative Militant," in Lincoln, *Martin Luther King, Jr.*, p. 153.

6. Bracey describes religious black nationalism in the introduction to Bracey et al., *Black Nationalism in America*; Kohn sees religion as an ingredient of nationalism, rather than as a variety, in his *The Idea of Nationalism*, p. 36.

7. H. W. Turner (see note 1, above).

8. A more extensive etymology for the term "messiah" is given by Werblowski in his article in the *Encyclopedia Judaica* (see note 1, above).

9. Bastide, *African Civilizations in the New World*, pp. 164–65, 217.

10. S. Walker, *Ceremonial Spirit Possession in Africa and Afro-America*. Cf. Gluckman, *Rituals of Rebellion in South East Africa*; and Kuper, *An African Aristocracy*. A. J. F. Köblen, in "Prophetic Movements," considers the possibility that prophetic movements may antedate the crisis of confronting Westernization and Christianity. Also see I. M. Lewis, *Ecstatic Religion*, pp. 32–33, for observations on the political implications of spirit possession.

11. Oosthuizen, *Theology of a South African Messiah*.

12. Leslau, *Falasha Anthology*.

13. Ibid., p. xxxv.

14. Black nationalists, in particular the Black Jews, are fond of citing Father Joseph Williams, *Hebrewisms of West Africa*.

15. George Shepperson, "Ethiopianism: Past and Present," in Baeta, *Christianity in Tropical Africa*, p. 249; cf. D. Barrett, *Schism and Renewal in Africa*, p. 25.

16. D. Barrett, *Schism and Renewal*, pp. 25, 52.

17. Ibid., pp. 18–36.

18. Shepperson, "Ethiopianism: Past and Present," p. 251; Oosthuizen, *Post Christianity in Africa*, p. 32.

19. Oosthuizen, in *Post Christianity* (p. 7), does not view "Ethiopianism" as nationalistic; but Shepperson attributes a protonationalistic meaning to the movement in "Ethiopianism: Past and Present," as does E. Anderson in *Messianic Popular Movements in the Lower Congo*. D. Barrett, in *Schism and Renewal*, also acknowledges the importance of a political element in Ethiopianism.

20. S. Walker, *Ceremonial Spirit Possession*, p. 163.

21. L. Barrett, *The Rastafarians*, pp. 65–67. Garvey's editorials in *The Black Man* are discussed in Chapter 10.

22. For an overview, see Lanternari, *Religions of the Oppressed*; Worsley, *The Trumpet Shall Sound*, also discusses cargo cults.

23. Tuveson, *Redeemer Nation*; Cherry, *God's New Israel*.

24. Cults and utopias in the United States before the Civil War are discussed in Tyler, *Freedom's Ferment*, pp. 46–224.

25. Kilson's observations are recorded in Robinson, *Black Studies in the University*, p. 14.

26. T. Smith, *Revivalism and Social Reform*, notes the rise of millenarian feeling and its relation to Christian social movements including abolitionism; see especially pp. 178–224.

See McLoughlin's comments on "The Battle Hymn of the Republic" in *American Evangelicals*. Strout, in *New Heavens and New Earth*, discusses millenarian interpretations of the Civil War, pp. 189–205. Also see Hudson, *Nationalism and Religion in America*, and a recent full-length treatment by Moorhead, *American Apocalypse*.

27. Discussions of caste with reference to black Americans no longer seem to be fashionable. The most often cited studies include Lloyd Warner's introduction to Allison Davis et al., *Deep South*, which also uses the caste approach. Other examples include Dollard, *Caste and Class in a Southern Town*. For a critique of the caste approach, see Cox, *Caste, Class, and Race*.

28. The discussion of slavery as a moral issue is a principal theme in Elkins, *Slavery*. Also see David B. Davis, "Slavery and Sin," in Duberman, *The Antislavery Vanguard*; and Kraditor, *Means and Ends in American Abolitionism*.

29. Novak, "Black and White in Catholic Eyes," reprinted in Dinnerstein and Jaher, *Uncertain Americans*, p. 320.

30. Fauset, *Black Gods of the Metropolis*.

31. Ibid., p. 23.

32. J. R. Washington, Jr., *Black Sects and Cults*, pp. 11–12, 127.

33. Indeed, this is the central theme of Fullinwider's *Mind and Mood of Black America*; also see J. R. Washington, Jr., *Politics of God*.

34. Durkheim, *Suicide*. It should be remembered, however, that Durkheim uses the terms "egoism" and "altruism" in a somewhat idiosyncratic way.

35. Frazier, *Negro Church in America*, p. 86.

36. Russell, *History of Western Philosophy*.

37. Botkin, *Lay My Burden Down*, pp. 16–19.

38. Shortly after the death of Elijah Muhammad, *Bilalian News* printed a photograph of a man who appeared to be white, identified as W. D. Fard; see *Bilalian News* (February 20, 1976), p. 12, and the photograph in *Newsweek* (March 15, 1976), p. 33. Lincoln, in *Black Muslims in America*, reports a number of rumors as to Fard's national background but expresses no clear preference for any of these; the same is true of Essien–Udom, *Black Nationalism*. Both of these studies contain index references to W. D. Fard.

39. *Time*, December 4, 1978. A number of books have appeared on the Jonesville cult including: Marshall Kilduff and Ron Javers, *The Suicide Cult: The Inside Story of the People's Temple Sect and the Massacre in Guyana* (New York: Bantam, 1979); Charles A. Krause, *Guyana Massacre: The Eyewitness Account* (New York: Berkley, 1979); John Maguire and Mary Lee Dunn, *Hold Hands and Die: The Incredibly True Story of the People's Temple and the Reverend Jim Jones* (New York: Dale Books, 1979); Jeannie Mills, *Six Years With God: Life Inside Reverend Jim Jones' People's Temple* (New York: A & W Publishers, 1979); U. S. Congress, House Committee on Foreign Affairs, *The Assassination of Representative Leo J. Ryan and the Jonestown Guyana Tragedy: Report of a Staff Investigative Group to the Committee on Foreign Affairs, U. S. House of Representatives* (Washington, D. C.: U. S. Government Printing Office, 1979).

40. James Lampley, Letter to the Editor, *Africa* (February 1979): 68–69.

41. Ellison, *Invisible Man*, p. 493.

42. J. R. Washington, Jr.'s, *Politics of God* views black Americans as "the black hope of mankind" (pp. 166–67); see also Part III of same, "God's Humanizing Agents."

Chapter 2

1. See Turner's article, "Tribal Religious Movements"; Sundkler, *Bantu Prophets in South Africa*; and Du Bois, *The Negro Church*, p. 5.

2. The idea of a transcending unity among African religions superseding various ethnic peculiarities is associated with the writings of Davidson, *The African Genius*, and Parrinder, *African Traditional Religion*. Also see Mbiti, *African Religions and Philosophy*. A more recent study and an exercise in advocacy scholarship is Diop, *Cultural Unity of Black Africa*. The concept of a "Negro Church" is traceable to Du Bois' *The Negro Church*; in *Souls of Black Folk*, pp. 193–94, he sees the church as the core of national consciousness. Compare to Frazier, *Negro Church in America*, especially pp. 29–46, in which it is argued that the church constitutes "a nation within a nation." Also see Frazier and Lincoln, *The Negro Church in America and The Black Church Since Frazier*. In this work, Lincoln seems to be attempting a revision of his own and Frazier's

earlier views which attacked the Negro Church as an obstacle to political progress. J. R. Washington, Jr., is critical of the concept of "the Negro Church" in *Black Religion*, pp. 292–97.

3. Du Bois, *The Negro Church*, p. 5. Quotations of Du Bois in the discussion following are from this source.

4. Park, "The Conflict and Fusion of Cultures with Special Reference to the Negro," p. 116; L. Turner, *Africanisms in the Gullah Dialect*; Herskovits, *The Myth of the Negro Past*, p. 30; and Herskovits, *The New World Negro*, p. 121.

5. Malinowski, "The Pan–African Problem of Culture Contact."

6. Frazier, *Negro Church in America*, pp. 71–86, argues that the "Negro Church" has lost its past relevancy in the lives of black Americans and functions mainly as a refuge from bitter realities. G. Johnson sees black religious music, for example, as mainly derivative; see his *Folk Culture on St. Helena Island, South Carolina*. Myrdal's pejorative treatment is in *An American Dilemma*, Vol. 2, Chapter 40.

7. Blassingame, *Slave Community*, pp. 17–18, 32–35. Genovese argues that elements of Christian–pagan syncretism were present in both the Afro–American and the Euro–American communities; see his *Roll, Jordan, Roll*, pp. 229–32. Great emphasis is placed on African retentionism in slave culture in Gutman, *The Black Family in Slavery and Freedom*; religious syncretism is alluded to on p. 71. Levine, *Black Culture and Black Consciousness*, is concerned with culture fusion throughout.

8. Davidson, *The African Genius*, Part Three: "Structures of Belief," especially pp. 121–30; also see the pictorial essay between pp. 176 and 177.

9. Ibid., pp. 36–40.

10. Mbiti, *African Religions and Philosophy*, pp. 15–28. This fundamental chapter tends to extrapolate from Gikuyu and Akamba concepts, although it should be noted that Mbiti's study includes numerous peoples from every major geographical area of the continent.

11. Parrinder, *West African Religion*, presents a fairly unified picture of West African religion. These patterns of unity are extended in his *African Traditional Religion*. In a similar vein, see Jahn, *Muntu*.

12. Herskovits, *Myth of the Negro Past*, p. 85.

13. Ibid., p. 207.

14. Ibid., p. 207.

15. Raboteau, *Slave Religion*, pp. 7–16.

16. Ibid., p. 86.

17. Ibid., p. 85.

18. Ibid., p. 86.

19. Bastide, *African Civilizations*, p. 100. Also see Herskovits, "Problem, Method, and Theory in Afroamerican Studies," *Afroamericana*, 1 (1945): 5–24 (reprinted in Herskovits, *New World Negro*), where he comments: ". . . the progression of Guiana, Haiti, Brazil, Jamaica, Trinidad, Cuba, Virgin Islands, the Gullah Islands, and southern and northern United States comprise a series wherein a decreasing intensity of Africanisms is manifest" (p. 54).

20. Bastide, *African Civilizations*; see the chapter on "Syncretism and Amalgamation Between Religions," pp. 153–69, and especially the chart on p. 158.

21. O. Patterson, *Sociology of Slavery*, p. 183.

22. Ibid., pp. 185–86, 192, 193.

23. The emotionalism of ceremonial spirit possession associated with baptism by total immersion and the existence of African cognates is discussed in Herskovits, *Myth of the Negro Past*, pp. 232–35.

24. Frazier, *The Negro in the United States*, pp. 338–39.

25. Herskovits, *Myth of the Negro Past*, p. 208.

26. Rawick, *From Sundown to Sunup*, p. 33.

27. Ibid., p. 40.

28. References to Herskovits, Bascom, Courlander, and Mintz, and discussion of the significance of the "iron pot," are in Rawick, *From Sundown to Sunup*, pp. 35–45; conversion experiences and their African analogues, pp. 45–48.

29. Levine, *Black Culture and Black Consciousness*, pp. 24, 63–67.

30. Blassingame, *Slave Community*, p. 33.

31. Huggins, *Black Odyssey*, pp. 173–82.

32. Owens, *This Species of Property*, pp. 155–60.
33. A recent study published since the completion of this chapter is Handler and Lange, *Plantation Slavery in Barbados*, which is based on archeological methodologies and contributes new data and methods of research.
34. Genovese, *Roll, Jordan, Roll*, pp. 280–84.
35. Ibid., p. 283.
36. Boas, *The Mind of Primitive Man*; the 1965 edition of this book includes a foreword by Melville Herskovits, who identifies one of Boas' contributions as the demonstration of "the unities which exist in the endowments, needs and aspirations of all men" (p. 11). Levy–Bruhl's *Primitive Mentality* and *How Natives Think* are somewhat dated, but were advanced for the time, as Evans–Pritchard has observed in *Theories of Primitive Religion*. Levi-Strauss, in *The Savage Mind*, sees the mind of the primitive with its reliance on the concept of magic as being in some ways more rigorous and more advanced than the scientific mind. Only in its higher stages does science realize some of the "methods or results" of magical thinking (p. 11).
37. Hayford, *Ethiopia Unbound*, pp. 199–205.
38. Fadumah, *Defects of the Negro Church*, pp. 15–16.
39. Davidson, *The African Genius*, p. 125.
40. Duff and Mitchell, *The Nat Turner Rebellion*, pp. 17–18.
41. Crummell, *Africa and America*, p. 94.
42. Bellah, *The Broken Covenant*.

Chapter 3

1. P. Miller, *New England Mind: Seventeenth Century*, p. 472; Bercovitch's *American Jeremiad* is a variation on Miller's theme; Moorhead, *American Apocalypse*, p. 44. See also Jordan's description of the jeremiad on slavery in *White Over Black*, pp. 297–301.
2. P. Miller, *New England Mind: From Colony to Province*, pp. 27–39.
3. Ahlstrom, *Religious History of the American People*, pp. 130–32, 135–50.
4. Bellah comments on the imagery of Israel in Egypt in Jefferson's second inaugural address in "Civil Religion in America," pp. 9–10.
5. Cherry, *God's New Israel*, Introduction.
6. P. Miller, in *New England Mind: Seventeenth Century*, says that "among New England sermons, those at the end of the century rather than at the beginning contain the more confident descriptions of God as tied by the agreement with the nation" (p. 490).
7. P. Miller, "From the Covenant to the Revival," in Smith and Jamison, *Religion in American Life*, Vol. 1, p. 349.
8. Jefferson, *Notes on the State of Virginia*, p. 156. [Hereafter cited as *Notes*.]
9. The suggestion is offered by Ducas and Van Doren in *Great Documents in Black American History*, in which Othello's letter is reprinted (p. 30).
10. Benjamin Banneker, *Copy of a Letter from Benjamin Banneker to the Secretary of State, with his Answer* (Philadelphia, 1792).
11. Richard Allen and Absolom Jones, *A Narrative of the Proceedings of the Black People During the Late Awful Calamity in Philadelphia. . . .* (Philadelphia: Printed for the Authors, 1794), p. 20.
12. Ibid., pp. 21–22.
13. Prince Hall, "A Charge Delivered to the African Lodge, June 24, 1797, at Menotomy," reprinted in Brawley, *Early American Negro Writers*, pp. 103–8.
14. Foner, *History of Black Americans*, p. 449.
15. Hall, "A Charge Delivered . . . at Menotomy," p. 108.
16. Foner, *History of Black Americans*, pp. 443–61. See also Aptheker, *American Negro Slave Revolts*, pp. 27, 42f., 96ff.; Johnston, *Race Relations in Virginia*; and Jordan, *White Over Black*, pp. 375–403.
17. Aptheker, *American Negro Slave Revolts*, pp. 42–47.
18. Foner, *History of Black Americans*, p. 449.
19. Ibid., pp. 443–44; and Aptheker, *American Negro Slave Revolts*, pp. 96–98.
20. Foner, *History of Black Americans*, discusses boisterousness (pp. 448–49) and mentions Sedition Act (p. 446).
21. Brodie, *Thomas Jefferson*, pp. 342–43; Foner, *History of Black Americans*, p. 446; Jordan, *White Over Black*, p. 396.

22. Mullin, *Flight and Rebellion*, pp. 158–60.

23. Levine, *Black Culture and Black Consciousness*, p. 75.

24. H. W. Flournoy, ed., *Calendar of Virginia State Papers and Other Manuscripts*, Vol. 9 (Richmond, 1890), p. 151.

25. Starobin, *Denmark Vesey*; Starobin comments on the rich ideology (p. 5) and biblical arguments for slavery (p. 56).

26. Wade, "The Vesey Plot," pp. 148–61.

27. Reverend Richard Furman to Governor Thomas Bennett; from the *Furman Papers* at the University of South Carolina Library in Columbia. Reprinted in Starobin, *Denmark Vesey*, pp. 120–23.

28. "Productions of Mrs. Maria W. Stewart," originally published in Boston in 1835 by the Friends of Freedom and Virtue; reprinted in Porter, *Early Negro Writing*, pp. 134–35. The Porter anthology contains several documents in the jeremiadic mode.

29. "*The Sons of Africans: An Essay on Freedom with Observations on the Origin of Slavery, by a Member of the African Society in Boston*," printed for the Members of the Society in Boston in 1808; reprinted in Porter, *Early Negro Writing*, pp. 25, 27.

30. David Walker and Henry Highland Garnet, *Walker's Appeal and Garnet's Address to the Slaves of the United States of America* (New York: Arno Press, 1969). Nationalistic elements in *Walker's Appeal* have been commented on by Bracey et al., in *Black Nationalism in America*, p. xxxiii. Stuckey also treats the *Appeal* as a nationalistic document in *Ideological Origins of Black Nationalism*, pp. 8–13. Quotations of Walker in the following discussion are from this source with page numbers in parentheses following each quotation.

31. Jefferson, *Notes*, p. 139.

32. William Hamilton, "An Address to the New York African Society for Mutual Relief" (New York, 1809); reprinted in Porter, *Early Negro Writing*, pp. 33–41.

33. Persons discusses this and other views of history in the early republic in "The Cyclical Theory of History in Eighteenth-Century America." Persons distinguishes between the cyclical and the millennial views of history, but Walker's *Appeal* is an instance in which the distinction is not clear-cut.

34. Jefferson, *Notes*, p. 133.

35. Jefferson, in his *Notes*, referred to color as "unfortunate" (p. 138) and shared aesthetic judgments (p. 133).

36. Franklin refers to the non-slave black population as "quasi-free" in *The Free Negro in North Carolina*, p. 223. The term "slaves of the community" was used by ante-bellum black Americans at their conventions; see Bell, *Minutes of the Proceedings of the National Negro Conventions*.

37. Compare Walker's prediction with that of Robert Alexander Young in *Ethiopian Manifesto* (1829), reprinted in Stuckey, *Ideological Origins of Black Nationalism*.

38. Douglass, *Life and Times of Frederick Douglass*, p. 85.

39. Winks, *Autobiography of Josiah Henson*.

40. Mehlinger, "Attitude of the Free Negro Toward African Colonization." This article, despite its early date of publication, provides a relevant illustration of the distaste for colonization on the part of most of the United States' black population. For some alternative views, see Uya, *Black Brotherhood*—a collection of contemporary documents and scholarly articles, including Mehlinger's.

41. Staudenraus, *African Colonization Movement*, pp. 27–29.

42. Jefferson, *Notes*, p. 157.

43. Mullin, *Flight and Rebellion*, p. 158.

44. Letter from "A Colored Female of Philadelphia," in *The Liberator*, 2, 4 (January 28, 1832): 14; reprinted in Porter, *Early Negro Writing*, pp. 292–93.

45. Sweet, *Black Images of America*, p. 5.

46. Garnet, *Address to the Slaves* . . . ; D. B. Davis, *The Slave Power Conspiracy and the Paranoid Style*, p. 77.

47. Daniel A. Payne, cited in W. W. Brown, *The Black Man*, pp. 209–10.

48. Fladeland, *Men and Brothers*.

49. Abraham Lincoln, *Second Inaugural Address*; reprinted in Hofstadter, *Great Issues in American History*, pp. 416–17.

50. Bellah, "Civil Religion in America," p. 9.

51. Stowe's comments for the *Watchman and Reflector* of Boston are quoted in Sandburg, *Abraham Lincoln*, Vol. 2: *The War Years*, pp. 592–93; and in Oates, *With Malice Toward None*, p. 389.

52. The idea of Lincoln giving himself up to be crucified is discussed with sneering vivacity in L. Lewis, *Myths After Lincoln*. Also see Moorhead, *American Apocalypse*, pp. 174–76, 180; Emanuel Hertz, *The Religion of Abraham Lincoln*, a speech delivered before the Forum of the Jewish Center on the afternoon of February 7, 1930 (n.p., n.d.; copy in the John Hay Library, Brown University); Wolf, *The Almost Chosen People*.

53. Joel Augustus Rogers, *The Five Negro Presidents: According to What White People Said They Were* (New York: The Author, 1965), pp. 8–9.

54. Quoted from Bellah, "Civil Religion in America," pp. 11–12.

Chapter 4

1. Stowe, *Uncle Tom's Cabin*, p. 428.

2. Robert Breckinridge, "Speech before the Maryland State Colonization Society," 2 February, 1838, *African Repository*, 14: 141.

3. Marcus Garvey, "Can The Negro Find His Place?" *The Black Man* (August 1938): 10–13. Reprinted in A. Garvey and Essien–Udom, *More Philosophy and Opinions of Marcus Garvey*, p. 37.

4. Delany, *Condition of the Colored People*, p. 37.

5. Young, *Ethiopian Manifesto*, in Stuckey, *Ideological Origins*, p. 33.

6. Alexander Crummell to Reverend Irving, August 26, 1854; in *Domestic and Foreign Missionary Society Papers*, Episcopal Seminary of the Southwest, Austin, Texas.

7. Edward Wilmot Blyden, "The Call of Providence to the Descendants of Africa in America" (1862); in Brotz, *Negro Social and Political Thought*, p. 133.

8. Stuckey, *Ideological Origins*, p. 11.

9. Walker's *Appeal*, in Stuckey, *Ideological Origins*, p. 60. The cruelty of blacks toward blacks has received minimal attention in recent scholarship. That black slavedrivers occasionally practiced cruelty has been acknowledged by Owens in *This Species of Property*, pp. 123–24. Genovese also believes that such cruelty existed but feels that the state of the evidence prevents determining how widespread it was; *Roll, Jordan, Roll*, pp. 371–72. Similar conclusions are drawn in Van Deburg, *The Slave Drivers*.

10. Blassingame, *Slave Community*; Genovese, *Roll, Jordan, Roll*; and Fogel and Engerman, *Time on the Cross*, have all been admirably motivated by a desire to counteract the image of the cringing, subservient Negro slave, totally brainwashed by the brutal institution. However, their obsession with the healthiness of slave culture has caused them to dismiss contemporary opinions of widespread mental and cultural degradation under slavery. Such opinions are expressed in Walker's *Appeal*, pp. 62–72; and by Delany, Crummell, and Blyden, as cited in notes 4, 6, and 7, above.

11. Vincent Harding, "You've Taken My Nat and Gone," in Clarke, *William Styron's Nat Turner*; and Harding and Genovese, "An Exchange on 'Nat Turner'."

12. The Duff and Mitchell book, *The Nat Turner Rebellion*, is a handy collection of documents which includes the text of the *Confessions* as published by Thomas R. Gray (Baltimore, 1831).

13. A discussion of the Uncle Tom myth is provided by Fredrickson, *The Black Imge in the White Mind*, pp. 97–129. In *Autobiography of Josiah Henson*, Winks refers to the blurring of distinctions between Uncle Tom and his supposed prototype, Josiah Henson, during Henson's lifetime. Fullinwider, in *Mind and Mood of Black America*, pp. 72–73, sees little negative reaction to the "Uncle Tom" stereotype before 1930; but Furnas, in *Goodbye to Uncle Tom*, sees negative reactions appearing much earlier. The earliest expression of hostility towards "Uncle Tom" that I have been able to locate is that of the Reverend J. B. Smith early in 1852, the year in which *Uncle Tom's Cabin* appeared. Smith's reaction is reported by William Cooper Nell in a letter to William Lloyd Garrison, *The Liberator* (March 5, 1852).

14. H. N. Smith, *Virgin Land*, p. xi; R. F. Berkhofer, Jr., *A Behavioral Approach to Historical Analysis*, pp. 123–24.

15. Wells, *Crusade for Justice*, p. 152; Frederick Douglass, "The Lesson of the Hour," in Foner, *The Life and Writings of Frederick Douglass*, Vol. 4, pp. 498–99; B. T. Washington, *Up From*

Slavery, in Harlan, *The Booker T. Washington Papers,* Vol. 1: *The Autobiographical Writings,* ed. by John Blassingame, p. 332. For the use of the myth by Joel Chandler Harris and Sutton Griggs, see Moses, "Literary Garveyism."

16. Cone, *Black Theology and Black Power;* J. R. Washington, Jr., *Politics of God.*

17. Fullinwider does not quote these lines from the well-known spiritual, but they might provide evidence to illustrate his point; see his *Mind and Mood of Black America,* pp. 27–28.

18. A point often lost on interpreters of slave religion is that self-righteous Puritanism and evangelical expansionism—essential ingredients of American Protestantism—indirectly affected the slaves. It is impossible to conceive of uprooted Africans learning their Christianity in North America, yet remaining blind to such concepts as "righteous wrath" and the idea of a God who expects his faithful to behave as instruments of his wrath. Howe's "Battle Hymn of the Republic" is alluded to in Chapter 1 (see note 4). For Edward Taylor (1645?–1729), see R. H. Pearce, "Edward Taylor: The Poet as Puritan," *New England Quarterly,* (1950). Edward Hicks (1780–1849), American folk artist and Quaker minister, is known for his charming painting "The Peaceable Kingdom," of which he painted more than fifty versions; it shows the lion, the lamb, the wolf, the goat, the ox and the tiger existing together in peaceful harmony, while angelic children play among them. In the background William Penn signs a treaty with trusting Indians.

19. Walker's *Appeal,* in Stuckey, *Ideological Origins,* p. 108.

20. Stowe, *The Key to Uncle Tom's Cabin.*

21. Mays, *The Negro's God,* pp. 96, 156. Frederick Douglass also attested to the fact that many slaves believed that God desired submission to slavery; *Life and Times of Frederick Douglass,* p. 85. Nichols describes the submission of black Christian slaves in *Many Thousand Gone,* pp. 73–87. The present state of the discipline and dominant concerns of researchers have so far provided only occasional glimpses of the relationship between religious fatalism and the submissive behavior that led slaves to identify excessively with the welfare of their owners. The conversion experiences published under the title *God Struck Me Dead* (Nashville: Social Science Institute, Fisk University, 1945)—and reprinted as Vol. 19 of *The American Slave* series, edited by George Rawick—are uniformly otherworldly and escapist—a far cry from the revelations attributed to Nat Turner.

22. Du Bois was clearly ambivalent about the black church. On the one hand, he noted its importance as the central institution of black political life; but he also felt that it represented only a primitive level of struggle towards full political consciousness. In *The Negro Church,* he was sympathetic to the church, tracing its traditions of cultural and political resistance; but in his fictional writing, hostility is often expressed—see the short story "Of the Coming of John," in *Souls of Black Folk,* especially page 241; and *The Quest of the Silver Fleece,* pp. 370–74. In these works, the good and the ill effects of black religion are described, but it is clear that Du Bois views the militant religion as a survival of the old African social institutions, which he describes in *Negro Church.*

23. Cone, *Black Theology and Black Power;* Wilmore, *Black Religion and Black Radicalism.*

24. Osofsky makes the distinction between the type of religion encouraged by slaveowners and what was actually accepted by the slaves in *Puttin' on Ole Massa,* pp. 31–39. Albanese describes in *The Plantation School,* pp. 168–74, the distorted variety of Christianity that slaveholders encouraged.

25. Notably, Blassingame, *Slave Community;* Genovese, *Roll, Jordan, Roll;* Gutman, *The Black Family in Slavery and Freedom;* Rawick, *From Sundown to Sunup;* and Webber, *Deep Like the Rivers.*

26. Stowe, *Uncle Tom's Cabin,* p. 332.

27. Douglass, *Life and Times of Frederick Douglass,* p. 85.

28. Stowe, *Uncle Tom's Cabin,* p. 38.

29. Ibid., p. 352.

30. Ibid., p. 388.

31. Ibid., pp. 374, 375.

32. Ibid., p. 388.

33. Ibid., pp. 388–89.

34. Ibid., pp. 407–8.

35. An excellent introduction to the concepts of sadism and masochism within a literary context is Gilles Deleuze, *Masochism: An Interpretation of Coldness and Cruelty* (New York: George Braziller, 1971). In my opinion, the views of Sigmund Freud in *Beyond the Pleasure Principle* and

Theodore Reik in *Masochism in Modern Man* are useful speculations whose primary service is the insight they have provided into works of nineteenth-century art.

36. Stowe, *Uncle Tom's Cabin*, p. 21.

37. Ibid., p. 349.

38. The question of whether or not Henson was the model for Uncle Tom is discussed in Winks, *Autobiography of Josiah Henson*, pp. xviii–xxii; cf. Stowe, *Key to Uncle Tom's Cabin*, pp. 42–45.

39. Winks, *Autobiography of Josiah Henson*, pp. 27–28.

40. For example, one often encounters a contempt for "pencil pushers" expressed by the unskilled laborer, who professes, "I work for my money!"

41. Alexander Crummell attributed the Negro's survival to his trait of imitativeness, and argued that this trait was the source of all advanced civilization. See "The Destined Superiority of the Negro," in *The Greatness of Christ and Other Sermons*.

42. John S. Rock delivered these remarks to a meeting in Boston's Faneuil Hall; they were printed in *The Liberator* (March 12, 1858).

43. Aldous Huxley observed the tendency of the working classes, despite hunger and privation, to identify with the upper classes and to derive pleasure from viewing displays of wealth, pomp, and circumstance. See his "Waterworks and Kings," widely anthologized.

44. *Narrative of the Life of Frederick Douglass*, pp. 12–13.

45. The stereotype of natural docility in the African personality is discussed throughout Fredrickson's *The Black Image in the White Mind*, where the reader may consult the index entry under "Stereotypes."

46. Phillips, *American Negro Slavery*.

47. Ibid., p. ix.

48. Ibid., p. viii.

49. The classic study is, of course, Adorno et al., *Authoritarian Personality*.

50. Elkins, *Slavery*—a study that has been subjected to the most intense criticism during the past fifteen years and often faulted for minor inaccuracies. Critics, however, have found it difficult to invalidate Elkins' central contention that *under certain conditions* slaves were forced to play a role of subservience that was internalized in many instances, and that the habitual playing of this role led to some acceptance of it and a corresponding deterioration of self-esteem. In other words, the grinning, infantile mask of "Sambo" became an iron mask that could not be removed at will.

51. Adorno et al., *Authoritarian Personality*, provides extended discussion on various authoritarian institutions and the process of socialization that the individual experiences within them.

52. These lines from Stowe's *Uncle Tom's Cabin* were quoted by Hollis Read in *Negro Problem Solved*, pp. 387–88:

53. Ibid., p. 388.

54. Read, *Negro Problem Solved*, pp. 372–73.

55. Ibid., p. 375.

56. I do not subscribe to such theories, although I describe them in *Golden Age of Black Nationalism, 1850–1925*. Leopold Senghor, a black-cultural nationalist and prophet of *negritude*, does subscribe to such a theory in his essay, "African-Negro Aesthetics." He approvingly quotes Gobineau's description of the Negro as "the most energetic creature seized with artistic emotion."

57. Crummell, *Future of Africa*, p. 274.

58. Delany, *Condition of the Colored People*, p. 37.

59. For example, see Blyden's "Call of Providence."

60. See Garvey's "God as a War Lord" and "The Image of God" in A. Garvey, *Philosophy and Opinions of Marcus Garvey*, Vol. 1, pp. 43–44.

61. Reprinted in Harlan et al., *The Booker T. Washington Papers*, 3:585. [Hereafter cited as *BTW Papers*; I also adhere to the convention of referring to Washington himself as BTW.]

62. Du Bois, *Souls of Black Folk*, p. 80.

63. Ibid., p. 199.

64. Du Bois, "The Servant in the House," in *Darkwater*; he speaks of "domestic service at its best" and "the ancient high estate of Service, now pitifully fallen, yet gasping for breath . . . ," p. 117.

65. Moses, *Golden Age of Black Nationalism*; index entry for "Protestantism" and Chapter 5. [Also see Chapter 6 of this manuscript.]

66. Walker's *Appeal*, in Stuckey, *Ideological Origins*, p. 108; Henry Highland Garnet, "The Past and Present Condition, and the Destiny of the Colored Race," in Brotz, *Negro Social and Political Thought*, pp. 199–202.

67. This point was made by Aptheker in *American Negro Slave Revolts*, a book more often criticized than read. Aptheker defines a slave revolt in terms of the definition offered by the state of Texas: "By 'insurrection of slaves' is meant an assemblage of three or more, with arms, with intent to obtain their liberty by force." For the purpose of his study, however, Aptheker is more rigorous in defining "slave revolt" and will accept no less than a minimum of ten slaves involved. More important than the cataloguing of slave revolts is Aptheker's telling argument that the fear of rebellion was a principal influence on the cultural, social, and political institutions of the "Old South."

68. Marion D. Kilson, "Towards Freedom: An Analysis of Slave Revolts in the United States," in Meier and Rudwick, *The Making of Black America*, Vol. 1, pp. 165–78.

69. Tyson offers a sketch of his life in *Toussaint L'Ouverture*, pp. 1–23.

70. Clarke's *William Styron's Nat Turner*, pp. 28–29, contains Vincent Harding's relevant criticism that Styron has extracted from the personality of Turner most elements of religious radicalism and replaced them with a fabricated homosexuality. Like most black readers, I too found this offensive, since there is no evidence to support the allegation. At the same time, if one accepts the credibility of Nat Turner's confession, one must ponder the elements of religious fatalism in it, as well as the "martyr complex" that seems to reveal itself. Styron's emphasis on these latter concerns is not without validity.

71. Thomas R. Gray claimed that he recorded the *Confessions* "with little or no variation, from his [Turner's] own words" and produced six witnesses to verify that Turner acknowledged their accuracy. It seems unlikely that, if six white men had conspired to create a false confession, they would have created one so darkly brooding and filled with sinister majesty. It simply was not customary to portray Negroes in such a way.

72. Since the *Confessions* is relatively short, and since several editions are readily accessible, I shall trust to the reader's familiarity with the text and refrain from specific note references.

73. William Lloyd Garrison, "Editorial on Nat Turner's Insurrection," *The Liberator* (September 3, 1831); reprinted in Duff and Mitchell, *The Nat Turner Rebellion*, p. 41.

74. Thomas Wentworth Higginson, "Nat Turner's Insurrection," *Atlantic Monthly*, 8 (August 1861): 173–86; reprinted in Duff and Mitchell, *The Nat Turner Rebellion*. Higginson observes that Gray "rises into a sort of bewildered enthusiasm" before Turner (p. 65).

Chapter 5

1. This influx is described by McPherson in *The Abolitionist Legacy*, pp. 184–202.

2. Du Bois, *Souls of Black Folk*, pp. 199–201, contains these observations, as well as the verses quoted from the spirituals in the following two paragraphs.

3. Durkheim, *Suicide*, pp. 217–40.

4. Du Bois, *Souls of Black Folk*, p. 201.

5. "Go Down Moses," quoted from the first standard printed edition; reproduced in Epstein, *Sinful Tunes and Spirituals*.

6. McLoughlin, in his introduction to *The American Evangelicals* (pp. 1–27), emphasizes the movement's progressive and reformist strains. Also see his *Revivals, Awakenings, and Reform* for amplification of this thesis.

7. Franklin, *From Slavery to Freedom*, p. 199; see also Raboteau, *Slave Religion*, pp. 152–210, especially pp. 178–81.

8. Genovese, *Roll, Jordan, Roll*, pp. 190–91.

9. Osofsky's introduction to *Puttin' on Ole Massa* (pp. 236–39) describes the slaves' cynical view of the masters' religion; Genovese, *Roll, Jordan, Roll* (pp. 161–68), describes the complexity of the religion to which the slaves were exposed.

10. T. Smith, *Revivalism and Social Reform*, pp. 15–44; also see McLoughlin, *Revivals, Awakenings, and Reform*, pp. 128–29.

11. McLoughlin notes the political quietism and aversion to reform of Southern Evangelicalism in *Revivals, Awakenings, and Reform*, pp. 137–38.

12. Kucharsky, *The Man From Plains*, pp. 50–66.

13. Harlan et al., *BTW Papers*, 4:194, 2:516, 3:73.

14. C. S. Johnson, *Shadow of the Plantation*, pp. 80–83, and Powdermaker, *After Freedom*, p. 272, agree that religiosity and respectability did not necessarily imply adherence to Protestant sexual morality. Gutman, *Black Family in Slavery and Freedom*, p. 559, disputes Frazier's contention regarding the impossibility of sexual misconduct between two Christians; see Frazier, "Sex Life of the African and the Afro–American Negro," in Ellis and Abarbanel, *Encyclopedia of Sexual Behavior*.

15. Rawick has edited slave narratives under the series title, *The American Slave: A Composite Autobiography*, 19 vols. (Westport, Conn.: Greenwood, 1972), and *The American Slave: A Composite Autobiography, Supplement Series 1*, 12 vols. (Westport, Conn.: Greenwood, 1978). [Hereafter, references to *The American Slave* series will be abbreviated *AS*; those to *Supplement Series 1* will be abbreviated *AS, Suppl.*]

16. *AS*, 18:68.

17. *AS*, 7:356.

18. *AS*, 18:299.

19. *AS*, 18:211

20. One of the Fisk University slave narrative volumes is entitled, *God Struck Me Dead: Religious Conversion Experiences and Autobiographies of Negro Ex-Slaves*; reprinted as Vol. 19 of *The American Slave* series.

21. *AS*, 18:223.

22. *AS*, 7:356.

23. *AS*, 7:675.

24. *AS*, 7:515, 523.

25. See Stowe, *Uncle Tom's Cabin*, Chapter 38, for a treatment of suppression of religion in the fields; see Delany's treatment of religious frenzy as a means of legitimizing protest in *Blake*, p. 45.

26. *AS*, 18:125.

27. *AS*, 7:439.

28. *AS*, 18:117.

29. *AS*, 18:136.

30. *AS*, 7:515.

31. *AS*, 18:308.

32. *AS*, 18:111.

33. *AS*, 18:167.

34. *AS*, 7:443.

35. *AS*, 18:107.

36. *AS*, 18:177.

37. *AS*, 7:446.

38. *AS*, 18:121.

39. *AS*, 7:772.

40. *AS*, 7:562. Other Lincoln myths are in *AS*, 7:587, and in *AS, Suppl.*, 5:49.

41. *AS, Suppl.*, 5:45.

42. *AS*, 7:567.

43. *AS*, 18:259.

44. Ibid.

45. *AS*, 18:46.

46. *AS*, 18:47.

47. Ibid.

48. Ibid.

49. Sheldon Harris, *Paul Cuffe*, p. 244.

50. Bragg, *History of the African Group of the Episcopal Church*, p. 55.

51. Payne, *Recollections of Seventy Years*.

52. Ibid., p. 50.

53. Sermon quoted in W. W. Brown, *The Black Man*, pp. 209–10.

54. Payne, *Welcome to the Ransomed*, p. 11.

55. Ofari, *"Let Your Motto Be Resistance"*; Schorr, *Henry Highland Garnet*.

56. T. L. Smith, *Revivalism and Social Reform*, pp. 204–24.

57. Garnet, *Address to the Slaves*; reprinted in Ofari, *"Let Your Motto Be Resistance,"* p. 149.

58. Garnet's *Address to the Slaves*, published in 1848, was first delivered in 1843, thus predating by five years the miscegenationist views of "Past and Present Condition" (1848); reprinted in Ofari, "*Let Your Motto Be Resistance*," p. 180.

59. Ibid., p. 182.

60. Ibid., p. 179.

61. Ibid., pp. 179–80.

62. *North Star* (January 26, 1849); reprinted in Ofari, "*Let Your Motto Be Resistance*," p. 72.

63. *Weekly Anglo-African*, December 22, 1860, and April 6, 1861; *Douglass Monthly*, February 1859, p. 19.

64. *Douglass Monthly*, February 1859, pp. 19–20; ibid., October 1859, p. 151.

65. Garnet, "Discourse Delivered in the House of Representatives" (Washington, D. C., 1865); reprinted in Ofari, "*Let Your Motto Be Resistance*."

66. Ibid., p. 114.

67. Ibid., p. 198.

68. Ibid., p. 203.

69. The literature on the effects of religion on slave revolts indicates that the relationship was complex. Slave revolts were caused by a variety of factors and religion was sometimes among them, but religion in and of itself could neither enkindle nor suppress the spirit of revolt. See Genovese, *Roll, Jordan, Roll*, pp. 280–84, and *From Rebellion to Revolution*.

70. There is still no comprehensive treatment of the effects of the social gospel movement on the Afro–American clergy. The chapter on "Racial Christianity" in Fullinwider's *Mind and Mood of Black America*, pp. 26–44, is the best effort so far. Although Fullinwider is aware that the social concerns in the theology of Channing, the Beechers, Horace Bushnell, and Walter Rauschenbusch had little direct impact on the thought of typical black preachers, he shows how the intellectual leaders among the clergy were affected by "mission ideology" and "Social Gospel" to "set the Negro up as the moral arbiter of American Civilization."

71. Fullinwider, *Mind and Mood of Black America*, pp. 230–39; D. Lewis, *King*, p. 29.

72. Fullinwider, *Mind and Mood of Black America*, p. 46.

Chapter 6

1. Max Weber, in defining "the spirit of capitalism," turns to the writings of Benjamin Franklin for examples of that spirit "in almost classical purity"; see *The Protestant Ethic and the Spirit of Capitalism*, pp. 48–51.

2. William J. Cansler to BTW, September 26, 1895, in Harlan et al., *BTW Papers*, 4:30. Additional Mosaic references in *BTW Papers*, 4:3, 8, 30, 34, 55, 73, 351, 550–51; 6:468, 480, 492.

3. Others include Harriet Tubman, Joe Louis, and Marcus Garvey; but Washington himself referred to General Samuel C. Armstrong as "a savior, a Moses, under whose leadership there could be no back steps"; quoted in V. Matthews, *Black Belt Diamonds*. The same tribute was paid to Lincoln by Elizabeth Keckley: "The Moses of my people had fallen in the hour of his triumph"; *Behind the Scenes*, p. 191. Characterization of BTW as a Moses is protested in an editorial in the *Cleveland Gazette*, July 20, 1901, p. 2; reprinted in *BTW Papers*, 6:179.

4. Frances E. Leupp, "Why Booker T. Washington Has Succeeded in His Life Work," *Outlook*, 71 (May 31, 1902):326–33; in *BTW Papers*, 6:480.

5. BTW, *Up From Slavery*: "In the early days of the school I think my most trying experience was in the matter of brickmaking. . . . I had always sympathized with the 'children of Israel,' in their task of 'making bricks without straw,' but ours was the task of making bricks with no money and no experience"; reprinted in *BTW Papers*, 1:295.

6. BTW, "The Standard Printed Version of the Atlanta Exposition Address"; reprinted in *BTW Papers*, 3:583–87.

7. V. Matthews, *Black Belt Diamonds*, p. 5. Alexander Crummell also used the term "new people," in *Africa and America*, pp. 18, 379. In a recent study, this term has been interpreted as applying to the mulatto population. Charles Waddell Chesnutt did indeed use it in this way; see Williamson, *New People*.

8. In *The Broken Covenant*, Bellah traces the idea of Americanization within the context of

the "state religion." For further discussion of this philosophy, see Gordon, *Assimilation in American Life*; and Higham, *Strangers in the Land*.

9. BTW, "Atlanta Exposition Address"; in *BTW Papers*, 3:87.

10. Novak, "Black and White in Catholic Eyes," *New York Times Magazine*, November 16, 1975.

11. *BTW Papers*, 1:224.

12. Du Bois, *Souls of Black Folk*, p. 43.

13. *BTW Papers*, 1:244.

14. Bellah, *The Broken Covenant*, p. 70.

15. BTW, *Character Building*.

16. An excerpt from the journal of Florence Ledyard Cross Kitchelt, dated April 3, 1901; in *BTW Papers*, 6:84.

17. Rischin, *American Gospel of Success*; Tebbell, *From Rags to Riches;* Cawelti, *Apostles of the Self-Made Man;* and Wylie, *The Self-Made Man in America*. Also see Bellah, *The Broken Covenant*.

18. BTW, *Character Building*, p. 93.

19. *BTW Papers*, 5:322.

20. *BTW Papers*, 5:345.

21. BTW, *Future of the American Negro* (Boston: Small, Maynard & Co., 1899); reprinted in *BTW Papers*, 5:351.

22. Ibid., p. 347.

23. Ibid., p. 365.

24. Ibid., p. 391.

25. BTW, "Address at the Dexter Avenue Baptist Church" (Montgomery, Alabama, May 19, 1901); in *BTW Papers*, 6:113.

26. Du Bois, "The Servant in the House," in *Darkwater;* BTW, "Address at the Dexter Avenue Baptist Church."

27. *BTW Papers*, 6:115.

28. Du Bois, *Souls of Black Folk*, p. 12.

29. BTW to John Gale, April 14, 1896; *BTW Papers*, 4:160–61.

30. B. Matthews, *Booker T. Washington*, p. 123.

31. BTW, *The Story of My Life and Work*, (1900); reprinted in *BTW Papers*, 1:178.

32. BTW to Nathalie Lord, April 21, 1904; in *BTW Papers*, 7:485. Also see B. Matthews, *Booker T. Washington*, p. 190.

33. BTW, *Character Building*.

34. Dunbar to BTW, January 23, 1902; in *BTW Papers*, 6:300.

35. Extracts from BTW's address before the National Baptist Convention in 1903 are reprinted in *BTW Papers*, 7:287–91.

36. Meier, *Negro Thought in America*, pp. 218–22.

37. Reverdy C. Ransom's socialism has been remarked by Meier in *Negro Thought*, p. 185. Also mildly influenced by Christian socialism were Richard R. Wright, Jr., and Francis J. Grimke.

38. *BTW Papers*, 5:526.

39. Walters, *My Life and Work*, p. 260.

40. *BTW Papers*, 5:122.

41. Walters to BTW, June 27, 1901, in *BTW Papers*, 6:160; Meier, *Negro Thought*, p. 181.

42. Meier, *Negro Thought*, p. 223.

43. Grimke to BTW, September 20, 1895; in *BTW Papers*, 4:25.

44. Du Bois to BTW, September 24, 1895; in *BTW Papers*, 4:26.

45. Woodson, *Works of Francis J. Grimke*, 1:360. [Hereafter cited as Grimke, *Works*.]

46. Grimke to BTW, November 7, 1895, in *BTW Papers*, 4:74–75; BTW to Grimke, November 27, 1895, in *BTW Papers*, 4:85–86; Grimke to BTW, December 12, 1895, in *BTW Papers*, 4:95–96.

47. Meier, *Negro Thought*, p. 223; Grimke, *Works*, 1:237–39, 2:379–80, and 3:7–8.

48. Charles S. Morris, "The Wilmington Massacre," and C. S. Smith, "The Fallacy of Industrial Education as the Solution of the Race Problem"; both are in Foner, *Voice of Black America*, pp. 604–11.

49. *The First Mohonk Conference on the Negro Question, June 4–6, 1890* (Boston: George H. Ellis, 1890), pp. 108–14.

50. BTW to George W. Cable, April 7, 1890; in *BTW Papers*, 3:45.

51. Speech of Andrew H. White, in *First Mohonk Conference*, p. 118.

52. Speech of John Glenn of Baltimore, in *First Mohonk Conference*, pp. 121–23.

53. BTW, *Character Building*, p. 61.

54. BTW, *Up From Slavery*; in *BTW Papers*, 1:244.

55. Jefferson, *Notes*, p. 133.

56. BTW, "Reading, a Means of Growth," *Tuskegee Student*, 2 (October 31, 1890): 1–2; reprinted in *BTW Papers*, 3:94.

57. BTW, *Up From Slavery*, Chapter 5; in *BTW Papers*, 1:257.

58. *Christian Union*, 42 (August 14, 1890): 199–200; reprinted in *BTW Papers*, 3:71–75.

59. Daniel A. Payne to BTW, November 3, 1890; in *BTW Papers*, 3:97.

60. Payne, *Recollection of Seventy Years*, pp. 173ff., 253. *The Constitution of the African Civilization Society* (New Haven, 1861) lists Payne among its vice presidents.

61. Delany, *Condition of the Colored People*, Chapter 4; and Blyden, *Christianity, Islam, and the Negro Race*, pp. 33–39. The most detailed of these discussions of black religion is by Crummell in *Africa and America*, p. 274.

62. Fadumah, *Defects of the Negro Church*, pp. 15–16.

63. *Indianapolis Freeman*, November 29, 1890, p. 4; reprinted in *BTW Papers*, 3:101–3.

64. See Stephen R. Fox, *The Guardian of Boston* (New York: Atheneum, 1970), pp. 47–48, 108–9; and *BTW Papers*, 6:384–86.

65. Crummell, *Africa and America*, pp. 325–41.

66. Alexander Crummell, "The Prime Need of the Negro Race," *Independent*, 49 (August 19, 1897): 1–2, 14; excerpted in Richardson, *Liberia's Past and Present*, pp. 77–78.

67. Alexander Crummell to John W. Cromwell, October 5, 1897; Alexander Crummell letters from the Bruce Collection in the New York Public Library, Schomburg Collection.

68. R. C. Bedford to BTW, August 26, 1897; in *BTW Papers*, 4:321.

69. Crummell, *Civilization: The Primal Need of the Race*.

70. Reprinted in *BTW Papers*, 4:367.

71. BTW, *Future of the American Negro*; in *BTW Papers*, 5:351. Crummell's reference to "the Gradgrinds" is in *The Attitude of the American Mind Toward the Negro Intellect*, Occasional Papers, No. 3 (Washington, D.C.: American Negro Academy, 1898), p. 16. Thomas Gradgrind was a character in Charles Dickens' *Hard Times*, who prided himself on being eminently practical but blighted his children by his hard ways.

72. Harlan, "Booker T. Washington and the White Man's Burden," pp. 441–67.

73. Shepperson and Price, *Independent African*, p. 91.

74. Hayford, *Ethiopia Unbound*, p. 163.

75. Harlan, "Booker T. Washington and the White Man's Burden," pp. 441–67.

76. *BTW Papers*, 4:262–63, 327.

77. J. W. E. Bowen to BTW, November 12, 1895; in *BTW Papers*, 4:78.

78. Heli Chatelain to BTW, October 5, 1896; in *BTW Papers*, 4:223–24; and Bowen, *Africa and the American Negro*.

79. Lynch, *Edward Wilmot Blyden*, p. 137; and Drachler, *Black Homeland/Black Diaspora*, p. 53.

80. Blyden to BTW, September 24, 1895; in *BTW Papers*, 4:26–28.

81. Henry McNeal Turner, in *The Voice of the Missions* (October 1895); reprinted in Redkey, *Respect Black*, pp. 165–66.

82. *Chicago Inter-Ocean*, September 28, 1895; reprinted in *BTW Papers*, 4:40–42.

83. Bowen, *Africa and the American Negro*, pp. 195–98.

84. Moses, *Golden Age of Black Nationalism*, pp. 32, 44, 274.

85. Ferris, *The African Abroad*, 1:308, 405.

86. This is one of the themes of Crummell's *Future of Africa*; see Chapters 1 and 3.

87. BTW, "Christianizing Africa," *Our Day* (December 1896); reprinted in *BTW Papers*, 4:251.

88. Harlan, "Booker T. Washington and the White Man's Burden."

89. Josiah Strong's affinities to Lyman Beecher are suggested in *Our Country*, p. 8. For Philafrican League, see *BTW Papers*, 4:225.

90. Strong, *Our Country*, Chapter 14, especially p. 202. BTW quoted Strong (*BTW Papers*, 2:435) and rejoiced in the Anglo–Saxon tongue in a speech entitled "Our New Citizen,"

delivered in Chicago, December 11, 1895; reprinted in Brotz, *Negro Social and Political Thought.*
Also seen V. Matthews, *Black Belt Diamonds*, p. 9.

91. Strong, *Expansionism Under New World Conditions*, p. 36.

92. V. Matthews, *Black Belt Diamonds*, pp. 13–14; cf. with BTW, *Future of the American Negro*, in *BTW Papers*, 5:345.

93. Strong, *Expansionism*, pp. 36–37.

94. BTW, "Extracts from an Address in New York City"; reprinted in *BTW Papers*, 7:117.

95. William H. Ferris to BTW; reprinted in *BTW Papers*, 6:384–86. Also see Ferris, *The African Abroad*, 1:296–311.

96. Strong, *Expansionism*, pp. 187–95; and Griggs, *The Hindered Hand*, pp. 203–4.

97. BTW, "Atlanta Exposition Address"; in *BTW Papers*, 3:584–85.

98. Brotz, *Negro Social and Political Thought*, p. 361.

99. BTW, *Future of the American Negro*; in *BTW Papers*, 5:387.

100. BTW, quoted in *Atlanta Constitution* (April 22, 1901); reprinted in *BTW Papers*, 6:93.

101. BTW, quoted in *Chicago Times Herald* (December 12, 1895); reprinted in *BTW Papers*, 4:93.

102. V. Matthews, *Black Belt Diamonds*, p. 111.

103. BTW, "On Making our Race Life Count in the Life of the Nation"; in Brotz, *Negro Social and Political Thought*, pp. 379–80.

Chapter 7

1. Robert Russa Moton, "The Negro's Debt to Lincoln," in Woodson, *Negro Orators and their Orations*, p. 577.

2. See the letter of George Harris to a friend in Stowe, *Uncle Tom's Cabin*, Chapter 43, any edition. Black acceptance of Stowe's stereotypes is illustrated in Chapter 4 of this manuscript.

3. W. A. Williams, "The Legend of Isolationism in the 1920's," pp. 1–20.

4. Reinhold Niebuhr, "Awkward Imperialists," quoted in Dulles, *America's Rise to World Power*, p. 143. See also Noggle, *Into the Twenties*, p. 131; Levin, *Woodrow Wilson and World Politics*; and Thompson, *Russia, Bolshevism, and the Versailles Peace*, p. 17.

5. The best-known introductions to the Harlem Renaissance and the New Negro Movement include: Locke, *The New Negro*; Cruse, *Crisis of the Negro Intellectual*; and Huggins, *Harlem Renaissance*.

6. Henri, *Black Migration*; and J. Scott, *Negro Migration During the War*.

7. Locke, *The New Negro*, p. 7.

8. Gosnell, *Negro Politicians*; Cayton and Drake, *Black Metropolis*; Osofsky, *Harlem*; and Spear, *Black Chicago*.

9. Waskow, *From Race Riot to Sit In*; and Chicago Commission on Race Relations, *The Negro in Chicago*.

10. Woodrow Wilson, Address to Congress, April 2, 1917. That there was a reaction to Wilson's messianism and an isolationist backlash during the 1920s is undeniable, but it is equally undeniable that America during the 1920s was, in one scholar's words, "a nation of enormous influence in world affairs and had acquired the position held by England during the century that followed Waterloo"; Graebner, *Ideas and Diplomacy*, p. 547.

11. Dulles, *America's Rise to World Power*, pp. 9–15.

12. Ibid., pp. 21–86.

13. Mordecai Johnson, "The Faith of the American Negro," an address delivered at Harvard University commencement, June 22, 1922; reprinted in Woodson, *Negro Orators*, pp. 659–60.

14. Ibid., pp. 661–62.

15. Ibid., p. 663.

16. From James Weldon Johnson's "Address delivered at a dinner for Congressman La Guardia, March 10, 1923"; reprinted in Woodson, *Negro Orators*, p. 670.

17. Ibid., p. 670.

18. Ibid., p. 671.

19. Reverdy C. Ransom. "William Lloyd Garrison: A Centennial Oration"; in Woodson, *Negro Orators*, p. 541.

20. William H. Lewis, "Address before the Massachusetts House of Representatives, February 12, 1913"; in Woodson, *Negro Orators*, p. 570.

21. Ibid., p. 572.

22. Du Bois, *Souls of Black Folk*, p. 4.

23. Ibid., p. 13.

24. Du Bois, "Worlds of Color," in Locke, *The New Negro*, p. 414: "And thus again in 1924 as in 1899, I see the problem of the 20th century as the Problem of the Color Line."

25. Du Bois, *The Gift of Black Folk*, p. 188.

26. Ibid., pp. 188–89.

27. Du Bois, "The Prayers of God," in *Darkwater*, pp. 249–52.

28. Du Bois, "Credo," in *Darkwater*, pp. 3–4.

29. Garvey and Essien–Udom, *More Philosophy and Opinions of Marcus Garvey*, p. 9.

30. Francis J. Grimke, "Victory for the Allies and the United States: A Ground for Rejoicing and Thanksgiving"; in Woodson, *Negro Orators*, pp. 690–707.

31. Fullinwider, *Mind and Mood of Black America*, p. 17.

32. Grimke, "Victory for the Allies," in Woodson, *Negro Orators*, p. 697.

33. Ibid., pp. 704, 707.

34. W. E. B. Du Bois, "Close Ranks," *Crisis*, XVI, 3 (1918): 111; and Harrison, "The Descent of Dr. Du Bois," in his *When Africa Awakes*, pp. 66–73.

35. Grimke, "Victory for the Allies," in Woodson, *Negro Orators*, p. 702.

36. Grimke, *Works*, 1:448.

37. Bracey, Meier, and Rudwick, *Black Nationalism in America*, contains examples of accommodationist black nationalism from the speeches of Booker T. Washington and William Hooper Councill.

38. Grimke, *Works*, 2:552.

39. Ibid., 1:360.

40. Locke, *The New Negro*, p. 16.

41. S. Brown, "Negro Character as Seen by White Authors."

42. Levine, *Black Culture and Black Consciousness*, p. 295.

43. Jordan, *White Over Black*, pp. 3–40.

44. Sypher, *Guinea's Captive Kings*.

45. S. Brown, "Negro Character," p. 197.

46. Melville Herskovits, "The Negro's Americanism"; in Locke, *The New Negro*, pp. 353–60.

47. Herskovits, "The Ancestry of the American Negro."

48. Albert C. Barnes, "Negro Art and America"; in Locke, *The New Negro*, pp. 19–25.

49. Statements on the strengths and weaknesses of black art from a nationalistic perspective are to be found in Ferris, *The African Abroad*, 1:255–78. Also see Griggs, *Life's Demands*, pp. 26, 51–52, 98; and Levine, *Black Culture and Black Consciousness*, pp. 293–98.

50. W. E. B. Du Bois, "Criteria of Negro Art," *Crisis* (October 1926): 290–97. Garvey's attitudes on the functions of the arts may be deduced from such speeches as "Discussion on Formulating of Plans to Unify the Religious Beliefs and Practices of the Entire Negro Race," *The Black Man* (August 31, 1929).

51. Du Bois' rhapsody on *Lohengrin* is in *Souls of Black Folk*, pp. 236–37; and he mentions the beauties of Schubert in his *Autobiography*, p. 170. One should also see his essay on Samuel Coleridge Taylor in *Darkwater*, pp. 193–218.

52. Garvey's anthems and marching songs were often printed in *The Black Man*. In January 2, 1930, he called for the building of a national opera house in Jamaica; see Editorial, *The Black Man* (April 4, 1929).

53. Van Vechten, *Nigger Heaven*; McKay, *Home to Harlem*. Du Bois' attitudes on these two books have been documented in his "Review of Van Vechten's *Nigger Heaven*," *Crisis*, 33 (1926); and in his article *"Home to Harlem* and *Quicksand*," *Crisis* (June 1928).

54. Garvey's reaction to *Home to Harlem* can be found in *Negro World* (September 29, 1928). Also see Levine, *Black Culture and Black Consciousness*, pp. 270–97.

55. Locke, *The New Negro*, p. 15.

56. Locke, "The Legacy of the Ancestral Arts"; in *The New Negro*, pp. 254–67.

57. Alain Locke, "A Retrospective Review," *Opportunity* (January 1929).

58. Brawley, "The Negro Genius," pp. 305–8.

59. Schuyler, "The Negro Art Hokum," pp. 662–63.
60. Robert Hayden in the preface to the 1970 edition of Locke, *The New Negro*.
61. Locke, *The New Negro*, p. 12.
62. Ibid., p. 15.
63. Ibid., p. 14.
64. Du Bois describes his Liberian mission in *Crisis* (April 1924): 247–51.
65. R. R. Porter, "Garveyism: A Religion," *Negro World* (November 22, 1920).

Chapter 8

1. Burkett, *Garveyism as a Religious Movement*.
2. E. Franklin Frazier, "Garvey: A Mass Leader," *Nation*, 123 (August 18, 1926): 147–48.
3. Both Prophet Jones and Father Divine are discussed in J. R. Washington, Jr., *Black Sects and Cults*, pp. 15–16, 77, 116–18, 127, 149, 158–59.
4. Bracey, Meier, and Rudwick, in *Black Nationalism in America*, observe that there was "a thirty-year period in which nationalism as a theme in black thought was virtually non-existent" (p. xiv). They do not, however, attribute this to Garvey but to the effects of the Depression and consequent reliance on the New Deal. Amiri Baraka laments the swelling of integrationist sentiment during World War II in *Blues People*, pp. 177–91. An example of the tendency to ridicule Garveyism is in Ottley, *New World A-Coming*, pp. 68–81, although Ottley is not overtly hostile. Du Bois attributed the decline of Pan–Africanism to Garveyite excesses in *Dusk of Dawn*, p. 278. John Henrik Clarke says that "the decline of his [Garvey's] movement left a multitude of people stunned and suspicious of other leaders and their promises"; see his introduction to Sara Harris, *Father Divine*, revised edition. For a convincing discussion of the influence of Garveyism on African leadership, see Jabez Ayodele Langley, "Marcus Garvey and African Nationalism," in Mezu and Desai, *Black Leaders of the Centuries*, pp. 185–202.
5. I have preferred to accept Garvey's statements concerning his father's prosperity, although Rogers says in his *World's Great Men of Color* that the senior Garvey was a breaker of stones on the roadway (p. 602). Garvey's autobiographical statement, "The Negro's Greatest Enemy," appeared in *Current History* (September 1923), and was reprinted in A. Garvey, *Philosophy and Opinions of Marcus Garvey*, Vol. 2. Early book-length treatments of the movement include A. Garvey, *Garvey and Garveyism*; Cronon, *Black Moses*; and Edwards, *Marcus Garvey, 1887–1940*.
6. M. Garvey, "The Negro's Greatest Enemy," pp. 124–34; and Du Bois, *Souls of Black Folk*, p. 2.
7. Significant research on Garvey's early years has been performed by Robert Hill; see "The First England Years and After, 1912–1916," in Clarke, *Marcus Garvey and the Vision of Africa*, a collection of recent essays and useful primary sources. Another important book is Martin, *Race First*.
8. Bellah, "Civil Religion in America."
9. Fleming, "Pap Singleton, The Moses of the Colored Exodus"; also see Garvin, "Benjamin or 'Pap' Singleton and His Followers." Aptheker's objections are in *A Documentary History of the Negro People in the United States*, pp. 713, 715–21. More recent discussions of the "Kansas Exodus" are Painter, *Exodusters*; and Athearn, *In Search of Canaan*.
10. M. Hill, "The All-Negro Communities of Oklahoma."
11. Tindall, "The Liberian Exodus of 1878"; Bittle and Geis, *The Longest Way Home*; and Redkey, *Black Exodus*.
12. Lynch, in *Edward Wilmot Blyden*, sees little enthusiasm on Blyden's part for Turner's repatriationism (p. 108).
13. Fadumah's association with Sam and other Pan–Africanists is treated in Moses, *Golden Age of Black Nationalism*, pp. 203–4, 212, 231, 234.
14. See Osofsky, *Harlem*; and Henri, *Black Migration*.
15. Moses, *Golden Age of Black Nationalism*, is a treatment of "romantic racialism"; see especially the chapters on Du Bois and Crummell.
16. For details on the life of Blyden, see Lynch, *Edward Wilmot Blyden*. Alexander Crummell is treated in Moses, *Golden Age of Black Nationalism*. Other figures are discussed in F. Miller, *Search for a Black Nationality*.

17. Redkey, *Black Exodus*, pp. 47–72.

18. Ibid., pp. 110–11.

19. Locke, *The New Negro*, p. 3; McKay, *Home to Harlem*, p. 131. Locke's discussion of contemporary trends in *The New Negro* is perhaps too close for objectivity. He failed to recognize the continuity between nineteenth-century patterns and those of his own era. This was symbolized by his almost complete neglect of Garveyism in *The New Negro*. Fullinwider recognizes the shifting conception of the black personality in *Mind and Mood of Black America*, a study that makes at least two important contributions: the author sees the significance of social science in encouraging the Harlem Renaissance mythology; and he recognizes the importance of the "Uncle Tom" image in black messianism, although he overstresses it to the neglect of militant messianism.

20. A. Garvey, *Philosophy and Opinions of Marcus Garvey*, 2:84. Du Bois wrote an editorial for the *Crisis* of May 1924 entitled "A Lunatic or a Traitor," saying: "One of his [Garvey's] former trusted officials, after being put out of the Garvey organization, brought the long concealed cash account of the organization to this office and we published it. Within two weeks the man was shot in the back in New Orleans and killed" (pp. 8–9).

21. A. Garvey, *Philosophy and Opinions of Marcus Garvey*, 2:84.

22. W. E. B. Du Bois, "Intermarriage," *Crisis* (February 1913): 180–81. Du Bois told the story of an embarrassing incident on the street in Nashville, after which he "never knowingly raised my hat to a Southern white woman"; see *Darkwater*, p. 14.

23. Cruse, *Crisis of the Negro Intellectual*, p. 6.

24. Du Bois' description of Garvey is in *Crisis*, December 1920; January 1921; May 1924; reprinted in Lester, *The Seventh Son*, 2:173–86.

25. William H. Ferris to Francis J. Grimke; in Grimke, *Works*, 3:298.

26. Crummell's hatred for mulattoes becomes apparent in his correspondence with the Trustees of Donations of Liberia College; see especially his letter of 24 August 1866 in the papers pertaining to Liberia College in the Massachusetts Historical Society. The theme of mulatto hatred is strong in his later correspondence, as well. See Crummell to John E. Bruce, 7 April 1896, August 1897, and 5 November 1897; in John E. Bruce Papers, Schomburg Collection, New York Public Library.

27. In *Black Nationalism in America*, p. 321, Bracey, Meier, and Rudwick attribute these words to Monroe Work. These words are reprinted from an article under Work's name in the *Journal of Negro History* (January 1916): 34–41. However, these same words were attributed to the South African writer P. K. I. Seme by William H. Ferris in *The African Abroad*, p. 439, published three years earlier.

28. Photographs of Garvey in regalia reminiscent of the European military elite are widely reprinted; see Cronon, *Black Moses*.

29. A. Garvey, *Philosophy and Opinions of Marcus Garvey*, 2:120, 126.

30. Ferris, *The African Abroad*, 1:405. Ferris was Assistant President General of the UNIA and literary editor of *Negro World*, where his function was to polish up the writing of less articulate contributors. See Grimke, *Works*, 3:298. Ferris seems to have been a man of some integrity, despite the unfavorable comments included in his obituary in the *Journal of Negro History*, 24 (1941): 550. The writing of Ferris provides us with excellent insights into the peculiar variety of racism inflicted upon black intellectuals. Ferris' offense was being a black man and attempting to live the life of the mind in America. Men of his type were ridiculed by Tuskegee and jeered in the popular literature of the day. Ferris was well-read in literature, history, and the social sciences, and earned M.A. degrees from Harvard and Yale. Whatever the shortcomings of his masterwork, *The African Abroad*, it is the product of an above-average mind. For details on Ferris, see Burkett, *Black Redemption*. Other bourgeois intellectual Garveyites were John E. Bruce and T. Thomas Fortune. Bruce, like Ferris, was a protégé of Alexander Crummell; but blond, blue-eyed Fortune was denounced by Crummell as a mulatto bastard.

31. Ferris, *The African Abroad*; see especially Chapter 24, "Africa, the Dark Continent."

32. Du Bois, "What is Civilization? Africa's Answer," *Forum* (February 1925); reprinted in Weinberg and Clark, *W. E. B. Du Bois*, pp. 374–81.

33. See the biographical sketch of Lott Carey in Simmons, *Men of Mark*.

34. A. Garvey, *Philosophy and Opinions of Marcus Garvey*, 2:38.

35. Antebellum religious protest is well treated by Vincent Harding, "Religion and Resistance Among Ante-Bellum Negroes, 1800–1860," in Meier and Rudwick, *The Making of*

Black America, Vol. 1. Other sources for the study of Christian militancy are provided in the notes for Chapter 1 of this manuscript.

36. Henry M. Turner, in *Voice of the Missions* (February 1, 1898); reprinted in Redkey, *Respect Black.*

37. A. Garvey, *Philosophy and Opinions of Marcus Garvey,* 1:44.

38. Terry–Thompson, *History of the African Orthodox Church,* p. 4.

39. Burkett, *Black Redemption,* p. 9.

40. Quoted in Burkett, *Black Redemption,* pp. 106, 110–11.

41. Ibid., pp. 144, 145, 147.

42. Ibid., pp. 4–6.

43. In addition to the cited works by Terry-Thompson and Burkett, the reader should see Rushing, "A Note on the Origin of the African Orthodox Church."

44. African Orthodox Church, *The Negro Churchman,* 2, 2 (February 1927): 2.

45. Osofsky, *Harlem,* p. 14.

46. J. Arnold Ford is discussed in Vincent, *Black Power and the Garvey Movement,* which also includes a picture of him with his musical ensemble. Regarding his migration to Ethiopia, see W. R. Scott, *Going to the Promised Land.*

47. Essien–Udom, *Black Nationalism,* p. 34.

48. Fauset, *Black Gods,* p. 47.

49. Indeed, Burkett argues that the pronounced sectarianism of the African Orthodox Church led to a temporary feud between Garvey and Archbishop McGuire during which "*Negro World* explicitly disavowed any special relationship between the AOC and the UNIA"; *Black Redemption,* p. 163. Also see Rushing, "A Note on the African Orthodox Church."

50. Bellah, "Civil Religion in America."

51. Crummell, "The Destined Superiority of the Negro," in his *Greatness of Christ.*

52. A. Garvey and Essien–Udom, *More Philosophy and Opinions of Marcus Garvey,* 3:37.

53. Ibid., 3:134–42.

54. Rogers, *World's Great Men of Color,* p. 602. Rogers says that he was a friend of Garvey's from boyhood, but he did not become a member of the UNIA. He says he attempted to restrain Garvey from financial recklessness. Rogers did write for *Negro World,* and he attended some UNIA meetings. Garvey never expressed any admiration for Mussolini, although he did praise the extreme nationalism of Hitler. He also praised those Jews who were Zionistic and wished to return to Palestine. He praised nationalism in most cases, so long as it did not violate the principle of "Divine Apportionment of Earth."

55. A. Garvey, *Philosophy and Opinions of Marcus Garvey,* 2:74ff.

56. Ibid., 2:279. According to Garvey's own testimony, with the exceptions of Bishop McGuire and Lady Henrietta Vinton Davis, "not one of the elected officers was worth more than $1200 a year as an office boy or a lackey. The men were lazy, incompetent, treacherous, and visionless." Since not all of these men were incompetent, they were probably not all treacherous and visionless either. Garvey was, nonetheless, unfortunate in his selection of Captain Joshua Cockbourne as maritime advisor; see Cronon, *Black Moses,* pp. 53–54, and Ottley, *New World A-Coming,* p. 72.

57. A. Garvey, *Philosophy and Opinions of Marcus Garvey,* 2:76.

58. Ibid. He called Du Bois a monstrosity because of his mixed blood (2:310) and demanded inbreeding (2:86).

59. Ibid., 2:76.

60. Burkett, *Black Redemption,* p. 183.

61. Photograph in D. L. Lewis, *King,* following page 148.

62. Breitman, *Malcolm X Speaks,* p. 201.

Chapter 9

1. Du Bois' attitudes on service are revealed in his *Darkwater,* especially the sections entitled "Credo" and "The Servant in the House." The German quotation appears more than once in his work; for example, see *Souls of Black Folk,* p. 83, and the *Autobiography,* p. 212.

2. "Jesus Christ in Texas" is contained in *Darkwater;* "Of Alexander Crummell" is in *Souls of Black Folk.*

3. Du Bois alluded to this case in "The Dilemma of the Negro," *American Mercury,* 3 (October 1924).

4. Hostilities between Du Bois and Randolph are described in Cruse, *Crisis of the Negro Intellectual*; also see Anderson and Stone, *A. Philip Randolph*. The fictional presentations of life on the railways that come instantly to mind are J. W. Johnson, *Autobiography of an Ex-Colored Man*; McKay, *Home to Harlem*; Rogers, *From Superman to Man*; and McPherson, *Hue and Cry*.

5. Frazier, *Black Bourgeoisie*, describes the spurious culture of the black middle class; and Gosnell, *Negro Politicians*, gives the background for the political action of the novel.

6. Du Bois, *Dark Princess*, p. 4.

7. Some examples are McKay, *Banjo*; Smith, *The Stone Face*; Yerby, *Speak Now*; C. Brown, *The Life and Loves of Mr. Jiveass Nigger*; and John A. Williams, *The Man Who Cried I Am*.

8. Du Bois, *Dark Princess*, p. 8. In the remainder of this chapter, page numbers for citations from this source are given in parentheses immediately following the reference.

9. Haygood, *Negro Liberation*, p. 205.

10. See Du Bois' letter of application for membership in the Communist Party, published on page 1 of the *Baltimore Afro-American* (October 21, 1961); reprinted in the *Autobiography*. Du Bois mentions visiting the Soviet Union in 1926, 1936, 1949, and 1959.

11. Stoddard, *Rising Tide of Color*; Spengler, *Hour of Decision*; and V. I. Lenin, *Imperialism: The Highest Stage of Capitalism* (Peking: Foreign Languages Press, 1970).

12. Du Bois' description of Garvey is in *Century* (February 1923).

13. This idea is recurrent in Du Bois' writings—see his *Conservation of Races; Souls of Black Folk* is an extended treatment of this theme.

Chapter 10

1. Cox, *Caste, Class, and Race*, p. 572; and Reid, "Negro Movements and Messiahs, 1900–1949," p. 362.

2. Du Bois' aloofness is described in Yancy, "William Edward Burghardt Du Bois' Atlanta Years: The Human Side." John Hope Franklin's reminiscences on Du Bois' aloofness are in Star, "Above All, A Scholar." The extent of Du Bois' influence is estimated by Lorraine Hansberry in Clarke et al., *Black Titan*, p. 17: "I believe that his personality and thought have colored generations of Negro intellectuals far greater, I think, than some of those intellectuals know. And without a doubt, his ideas have influenced a multitude who do not even know his name."

3. Reid, "Negro Movements and Messiahs," p. 362; and Dalfiume, "The 'Forgotten Years' of the Negro Rebellion," pp. 90–106.

4. W. R. Scott, "Black Nationalism and the Italo–Ethiopian Conflict, 1934–1936," p. 124.

5. Ottley, *New World A-Coming*, p. 188; and Joe Louis, *My Life*, p. 58.

6. Joe Louis, *My Life*, p. 63.

7. Wright, "Joe Louis Uncovers Dynamite," p. 18.

8. *New York Sun*, June 27, 1935. All newspaper reports of the Louis fights are taken from the *Joe Louis Scrapbook* (microfilm), in the Schomburg Collection, New York Public Library.

9. Marcus Garvey, "Schmeling and Joe Louis," *The Black Man*, 2, 2 (July–August 1936): 19; cf. Garvey's articles on the unpreparedness of Haile Selassie in that same issue and in those of March 1936 and May–June 1936.

10. Garvey, in *The Black Man*, 3, 10 (July 1938): 1.

11. Ibid.

12. W. R. Scott, *Going to the Promised Land*, p. 2.

13. Black reactions to the Ethiopian crisis are described in W. R. Scott, "Black Nationalism," as cited above; Ottley, *New World A-Coming*, pp. 106–12; Weisbord, *Ebony Kinship*; and Ross, "Black Americans and the Italo–Ethiopian Relief, 1935–1936," pp. 123–31.

14. See Ottley, *New World A-Coming*, p. 111.

15. Ibid., p. 112.

16. Garvey, in *The Black Man*, 2, 2 (July–August 1936): 6.

17. Ibid., 2, 3 (September–October 1936): 15.

18. Rastafarians are described in L. E. Barrett, *Soul Force*, Chapter 7; also see L. E. Barrett, *The Rastafarians*.

19. L. E. Barrett, *Soul Force*, p. 158.

20. Garvey, in *The Black Man*, 2, 2 (July–August 1936): 6.

21. W. R. Scott, "Black Nationalism," p. 119, and *Going to the Promised Land*, p. 2.
22. Garvey, in *The Black Man*, 1, 8 (July 1935): 11–13.
23. Frazier, "Garvey: A Mass Leader," pp. 147–48. Also see the introduction to Burkett, *Black Redemption*.
24. Sara Harris, *Father Divine*, p. 15. The text contains several references to Garvey, as does the introduction by John Henrik Clarke.
25. Bastide, *African Civilizations*, pp. 164–65. Bastide interpreted Divinism as representing African cultural retentionism.
26. Sara Harris, *Father Divine*, p. 80.
27. Garvey, in *The Black Man*, 1, 8 (Late July 1935): 12.
28. Ibid., 1, 12 (Late March 1936): 16.
29. Ibid., 2, 1 (May–June 1936): 1.
30. Ibid., 2, 3 (September–October 1936): 9–13.
31. U. S. Congress, Senate, *Congressional Record*, 75th Cong., 3rd Sess., February 1, 1938, Vol. 83, pt. 2: 1345.
32. Ibid., p. 1341.
33. Ibid., p. 1342.
34. Bilbo did not divulge the source of this material, which he read into the [Senate] *Congressional Record*; 75th Cong., 3rd Sess., April 24, 1938, Vol. 83, pt. 2:1342, 1344.
35. Ibid., 76th Cong., 1st Sess., April 24, 1939, Vol. 84, pt. 5: 4665.
36. Ibid., p. 4651.
37. Ibid., p. 4671.
38. Martinez's plan as described in the *Detroit News* is reprinted in Senate, *Appendix to the Congressional Record*, 75th Cong., 3rd Sess., April 5–6, 1938, Vol. 83, pt. 10: 1345–47.
39. The Peace Movement of Ethiopia was a rival to the UNIA. See Robert Hill's introduction to *The Black Man*, pp. 26–27; Senate, *Congressional Record*, 75th Cong., 3rd Sess., February 7, 1938, Vol. 83, pt. 2: 1533–35; and ibid., 76th Cong., 1st Sess., April 24, 1939, Vol. 84, pt. 5: 4666–67.
40. Senate, *Congressional Record*, 76th Cong., 1st Sess., April 24, 1939, Vol. 84, pt. 5: 4671.
41. Ibid., July 14, 1939, Vol. 84, pt. 9: 9112.
42. Garvey, in *The Black Man*, 4, 1 (June 1939): 6–8.
43. Ibid., p. 19.
44. Reprinted in Senate, *Congressional Record*, 75th Cong., 3rd Sess., February 7, 1938, Vol. 83, pt. 2: 1550.
45. Ibid., p. 1549.
46. The "National Movement for the Establishment of a 49th State"; reprinted in Aptheker, *Documentary History of the Negro People in the United States*, pp. 84–89.
47. Record, *The Negro and the Communist Party*, p. 96.
48. Foster, *The Negro People in American History*, pp. 555–66.
49. Vincent Harding, "W. E. B. Du Bois and the Black Messianic Vision," *Freedomways*, 9, 1 (1969): 44–58; reprinted in Clarke et al., *Black Titan*. Also see Moses, "The Evolution of Black National-Socialist Thought: A Study of W. E. B. Du Bois," in Richards, *Topics in Afro-American Studies*, pp. 77–99.
50. Du Bois, *Souls of Black Folk*, p. 216.
51. Du Bois, *Dusk of Dawn*, pp. 11–12; italics provided.
52. W. E. B. Du Bois, "Jim Crow," *Crisis* (January 1919): 112–13. After the First World War, Du Bois insisted that his Pan–Africanism did not imply a lessened interest in integrationism; see his "Reconstruction and Africa," *Crisis* (February 1919): 165–66.
53. W. E. B. Du Bois, "Segregation in the North," *Crisis* (April, 1934): 115.
54. Garvey, in *The Black Man*, 1, 5 (May–June 1934): 1–2.
55. Du Bois, *Dusk of Dawn*, Chapter 7: "The Colored World Within."
56. Earl Ofari, "W. E. B. Du Bois and Black Power," *Black World* (August 1970): 26–28.
57. W. E. B. Du Bois, "The Revelation of St. Orgne, the Damned"; reprinted in Aptheker, *The Education of Black People*, pp. 103–26.
58. Clarke et al., *Black Titan*, pp. 299–302; Du Bois, *Autobiography*, pp. 400–401.
59. Clarke et al., *Black Titan*, contains these tributes to W. E. B. Du Bois.
60. Gary T. Marx is concerned with this question; see "Religion: Opiate or Inspiration of Civil Rights Militancy?" in his *Protest and Prejudice*.

61. Russell's extension of the messianic construct to phenomena outside the Judeo–Christian context is in his *History of Western Philosophy*, pp. 363–64.

62. Duncan, *Selected Writings of Mahatma Gandhi*, p. 168.

63. Luthuli, *Let My People Go*, pp. 20, 22.

64. Ibid., p. 238.

65. M. L. King, Jr., *Where Do We Go From Here?*, p. 134.

66. M. L. King, Jr., "Letter From Birmingham Jail," in his *Why We Can't Wait*.

67. August Meier does make this connection in Lincoln, *Martin Luther King, Jr.*; Meier's essay was originally published as "On the Role of Martin Luther King," *New Politics*, 4 (Winter 1965): 52–59.

68. The slogan was attributed to King by Turner Brown, Jr., in *Black Is* (pages are not numbered).

69. M. L. King, Jr., *Why We Can't Wait*, p. 87.

70. Ibid.

71. David Halberstram, "The Second Coming of Martin Luther King," *Harper's Magazine* (August 1967); and Carl Rowan, "Martin Luther King's Tragic Mistake," *Reader's Digest* (September 1967). Both articles, which are reprinted in Lincoln, *Martin Luther King, Jr.*, treat on King's Vietnam involvement.

72. M. L. King, Jr., *Where Do We Go From Here?*, p. 12.

73. Ibid., p. 129; the uses of power are discussed on pp. 129–161.

74. Ibid., p. 125.

75. Ibid.

76. M. L. King, Jr., *The Triumpet of Conscience*, p. 16.

77. M. L. King, Jr., *Where Do We Go From Here?*, p. 133.

78. August Meier mentions this agnomen; see Lincoln, *Martin Luther King, Jr.*, p. 153. Also see Lomax, *To Kill a Black Man*, p. 112.

79. M. L. King, Jr., *Why We Can't Wait*, p. 93.

80. M. L. King, Jr., *The Trumpet of Conscience*, p. 25.

81. M. L. King, Jr., *Where Do We Go From Here?*, p. 138.

82. Ibid.

83. Ibid., p. 133.

84. M. L. King, Jr., *The Trumpet of Conscience*, p. 26.

85. M. L. King, Jr., *Stride Toward Freedom*, p. 201.

86. M. L. King, Jr., *Why We Can't Wait*, p. 110.

87. Ibid.

88. Efforts made by Ralph Abernathy "to invest King with the qualities of a Messiah" are noted by August Meier in Lincoln, *Martin Luther King, Jr.*, p. 153.

Chapter 11

1. Brotz makes this comparison in *The Black Jews of Harlem*, pp. 12, 57, 58. This should be supplemented by Gerber, *The Heritage Seekers*. Also see Fauset, *Black Gods*, p. 99; and J. R. Washington, Jr., *Black Sects and Cults*, p. 155. During the 1960s, the Black Muslims preferred to be referred to as the Nation of Islam, and most scholars respected their wishes. After the death of Elijah Muhammad in 1975, the Nation changed its name to the World Community of Al Islam in the West, a matter that was widely unnoticed due to the declining effectiveness of the organization's publicity and the drabness of its new leadership. For the sake of convenience, I refer to the organization by its best-known name—the Black Muslims.

2. For an introduction to the traditions of Ethiopianism, see Shepperson, "Ethiopianism and African Nationalism," pp. 9–18. Further discussion of the tradition is in Drake, *The Redemption of Africa and Black Religion*; Kenyatta, *Facing Mt. Kenya*; and Thwaite, *The Seething African Pot*. The influence of Ethiopianism on the Black Jews is discussed by Deanne Shapiro in "Factors in the Development of Black Judaism," in Lincoln, *The Black Experience in Religion*, pp. 254–72.

3. For example, see Kohn, *The Idea of Nationalism*. Kohn argues not only that nationalism and religion are related concepts, but that the very idea of nationalism grew out of the Jewish tradition: "Three essential traits of nationalism originated with the ancient Jews: the idea of the chosen people, the consciousness of national history, and national Messianism.

The act by which Jews became a people and at the same time a chosen people occurred at the beginning of Jewish history . . . [when] the people received the mission to live and to act in history according to God's will" (pp. 36–37).

4. Leslau, "The Black Jews of Ethiopia."

5. Leslau, *Falasha Anthology*, p. x.

6. Jones, *A Comparative Study of Religious Cult Behavior Among Negroes*, p. 103. Cf. J. R. Washington, Jr., *Black Sects and Cults*, pp. 132–33. Washington follows after Clark, *The Small Sects in America*, p. 151, in attributing this group's founding to Prophet William S. Crowdy.

7. Fauset, *Black Gods*, pp. 31–40.

8. Quoted in Brotz, *Black Jews of Harlem*, p. 20.

9. Brotz, *Black Jews of Harlem*, pp. 11, 49, 57; Vincent, *Black Power and the Garvey Movement*, p. 222; J. R. Washington, Jr., *Black Sects and Cults*, p. 134; and Ottley, *New World A-Coming*, p. 144. Vincent says that Ford studied Judaism in Ethiopia; but the most authoritative source on Ford's Ethiopia years is W. R. Scott's *Going to the Promised Land*, which makes no mention of Ford's studying Judaism in Ethiopia, but does mention a meeting between him and Falasha scholar Taamarat Emanuel in Manhattan in 1928 or 1929.

10. Fauset, *Black Gods*, p. 48; and Vincent, *Black Power and the Garvey Movement*, pp. 134–35. Essien–Udom, *Black Nationalism*, p. 47, mentions the drifting of Moorish templars into the Nation. Brotz, *Black Jews of Harlem*, p. 12, contains the mistake concerning the identicality of Ford and Fard.

11. W. R. Scott, *Going to the Promised Land*, pp. 4–6; K. J. King, "Some Notes on Arnold Ford and New World Black Attitudes to Ethiopia," pp. 81–87; and Shapiro, "Factors in the Development of Black Judaism," pp. 266–70. Wallace Muhammad, quoted in *Newsweek*, March 15, 1976, p. 33, says: "I can go to the telephone and dial his [W. D. Fard's] number anytime I want to."

12. *Newsweek*, March 15, 1976, p. 33, notes the abrupt shift in Muslim philosophy from the separatism shared by Mr. Muhammad and Noble Drew Ali that was described in Essien–Udom, *Black Nationalism*. The doctrine of Yakubism is outlined in Elijah Muhammad, *Message to the Blackman in America* (Chicago: Muhammad Mosque of Islam No. 2, 1965), pp. 110–22. The principal revisionist text is Wallace Dean Muhammad, *As the Light Shineth From the East* (Chicago: WDM Publishing Co., 1980).

13. The most accessible summary of the Black Muslims' abandonment of their central doctrine is in Pinkney, *Red, Black, and Green*.

14. Minister Farrakhan expressed his views in an interview in *First World* (Spring 1978): 11.

15. *Newsweek*, January 27, 1969; and October 18, 1971. The author visited the Black Hebrew community in Liberia during February 1980.

16. Fuller, "Original Hebrew Israelite Nation," pp. 62–85.

17. Ibid., p. 64.

18. Seligman, *Races of Africa*.

19. Fuller, "Original Hebrew Israelite Nation," p. 84.

20. Ibid., p. 83.

21. Ibid., pp. 67, 76, 79, 83.

22. Clarke Jenkins, *The Black Hebrews of the Seed of Abraham, Isaac, and Jacob, of the Tribe of Judah, Benjamin, and Levi, After 430 Years in America* (Detroit: The Author, 1969), p. 142.

23. Ibid., p. 113.

24. "Muslim Rivalry," *Christianity Today*, 17 (February 16, 1973): 53–54; and "Holy War?" *Newsweek*, February 5, 1973, p. 41.

25. *'Id With the Ansars*, an undated tabloid publication of the Ansaru Allah Community distributed in New York during the summer of 1978, contains a sampling of doctrine.

26. Isa Muhammad, *Our Symbol* (New York: Ansaru Allah Community, 1977). The six-point star represents the six members of man, including the head, arms, legs, and penis. The five-point star represents the incompleteness of woman, and is believed to be Satanic.

27. *'Id With the Ansars*, p. 3.

28. Al Hajj Imam Isa Abd'Allah Muhammad Al Mahdi, *Did the Hog Come for Mankind?* (New York: Ansaru Allah Community, n.d.).

29. Ibid., p. 7. Elijah Muhammad also makes much of the friendship between the white man and the dog in *Message to the Blackman*, pp. 119–20.

30. Ibid., pp. 7–12.
31. Al Hajj Imam Isa Abd'Allah Muhammad Al Mahdi, *The Tribe of Israel Is No More* (New York: Ansaru Allah Community, n.d.), contains arguments against veneration of Haile Selassie and other false prophets, and rejects the claims of black nationalists in the United States that they represent true Judaism or Islam.
32. Weisbord, *Ebony Kinship*.
33. The best summary of this aspect of the history of Zionism is Weisbord, *African Zion*.
34. Drachler, *Black Homeland/Black Diaspora*, p. 3, observes Blyden's interest; also see Edward W. Blyden, "The Jewish Question" (1898; reprinted in Lynch, *Black Spokesman*).
35. Elijah Muhammad, *Message to the Blackman*, pp. 133–34, attacks "The White Race's False Claim to be Divine Chosen People."

Chapter 12

1. Ellison, *Invisible Man*, p. 75.
2. However, Ellison does not actually deny the influence of black tradition in literature, song, and folklore. See, for example, "The Art of Fiction: An Interview," in *Paris Review* (Spring 1955); and "Some Questions and Some Answers," in *Prevues* (May 1958). Both essays are reprinted in Ellison, *Shadow and Act*. Also see Allen Geller, "An Interview with Ralph Ellison," *Tamarack Review*, 32: 3–24; and Stanley Edgar Hyman, "The Negro Writer in America: An Exchange," *Partisan Review*, 25 (1958).
3. Ellison, *Invisible Man*.
4. Ibid. Examples of the linkage between Moses, The Founder, and Booker T. Washington are on pp. 21, 109, 265–72.
5. Ibid., pp. 19–20. Further page references in this chapter to *Invisible Man* are cited in the text following the quotation.
6. Rudolph Fisher, "City of Refuge"—anthologized in Brown, Davis, and Lee, *The Negro Caravan*—contains a similar scene with a reference to the story of Jonah, pp. 57–58.

Chapter 13

1. Cox, *Caste, Class and Race*, p. 572.
2. Lomax, *To Kill a Black Man*, p. 108.
3. Official lapses occurred but confrontations with the authorities never seemed to be officially authorized. Shortly before the death of Mr. Muhammad, Mayor Daley of Chicago even set aside a special day in honor of the Messenger.
4. *The Autobiography of Malcolm X*, p. 3: "My father bought a house, and soon, as had been his pattern, he was doing free-lance Christian preaching in local Negro Baptist churches and during the week he was roaming about spreading word of Marcus Garvey." Louis Lomax—who collaborated with Mike Wallace on a five-part television series for New York's Channel 13, "The Hate That Hate Produced"—reprints the text of the section dealing with the Black Muslims in *To Kill a Black Man*, pp. 65–76.
5. Elijah Muhammad, *Message to the Black Man*, pp. 111–19.
6. *Autobiography of Malcolm X*, pp. 336–42.
7. George Breitman denies that there was a complete renunciation of black nationalism in his *The Last Year of Malcolm X*, p. 65. Compare to *Autobiography of Malcolm X*, pp. 374–76, where Malcolm still refers to himself as a black nationalist in 1965, but also see Breitman, *Malcolm X Speaks*, where in a late speech he asks, "Can we sum up the solution to the problems confronting our people as black nationalism? And, if you notice, I haven't been using the expression for several months" (p. 212).
8. Albert B. Cleage, Jr., "Myths About Malcolm X," in Clarke, *Malcolm X*.
9. Breitman, *Malcolm X Speaks*, pp. 121, 199, 217.
10. Cleage, *Black Christian Nationalism*, p. 113; compare to George Breitman in Breitman et al., *Assassination of Malcolm X*, p. 114.
11. Malcolm X, "The *Young Socialist* Interview (New York, January 18, 1965)," in Breitman, *By Any Means Necessary*, p. 114.
12. Breitman, *The Last Year of Malcolm X*, p. 71.
13. Breitman, *Malcolm X Speaks*, p. 210.
14. Ibid., pp. 143, 168–69.

15. Lomax, *To Kill a Black Man*, p. 9, recognizes the similarities between Malcolm X and Martin Luther King, Jr. The dialogue and mutual influence between Malcolm X and King is mentioned by Wilmore in *Black Religion and Black Radicalism*, p. 260.

16. Lomax, *When the Word is Given*, p. 122; *Autobiography of Malcolm X*, p. 238; Lincoln, *Black Muslims in America*, p. 246.

17. Malcolm X's Yale speech is printed in Lomax, *When the Word is Given*, pp. 153–67; the quotation is on p. 156.

18. Ibid., p. 160.

19. Ibid., pp. 165–67.

20. Malcolm X, "Message to the Grass Roots," in Breitman, *Malcolm X Speaks*, p. 6.

21. An interesting discussion of the Bandung Conference by a black American is Richard Wright's *The Color Curtain*.

22. References to human rights are numerous. See, for example, Lomax, *When the Word is Given*, p. 159; and Breitman, *Malcolm X Speaks*, pp. 35, 52–53.

23. August Meier, in Lincoln, *Martin Luther King Jr.*, p. 146.

24. Lomax, *To Kill a Black Man*, pp. 124, 125, 126; *Autobiography of Malcolm X*, pp. 300–301.

25. *Autobiography of Malcolm X*, pp. 301–2.

26. Cleaver, *Soul on Ice*, pp. 54–58.

27. Both the Black Muslim and the Black Panther manifestoes are reprinted in Bracey, Meier, and Rudwick, *Black Nationalism in America*; they differ in such important respects as the Muslim ban on intermarriage which goes unmentioned in the Panther demands.

28. Cleaver, *Soul on Fire*, contains the story of his conversion experience.

29. Carmichael and Hamilton, *Black Power*, pp. 2–32. The colonial analogy had already been drawn, albeit in a misleading way, by Silberman in *Crisis in Black and White*, pp. 309–55; cf. *Black Power*, p. 183.

30. Carmichael, *Stokely Carmichael Speaks*, pp. 201–6.

31. Winston, *Strategy for a Black Agenda*, pp. 20–23.

32. Angela Davis, *An Autobiography*, pp. 167–68.

33. My position, as I attempted to tell Carmichael, is that the post-Einstein questioning of scientific absolutism has led to a questioning of social absolutism, including the doctrine of white supremacy. Bertrand Russell, *The ABC of Relativity* (1925; repr. New York: Mentor, 1959) is an explication of Einstein's theories and a discussion of some of its implications for practical life.

34. Lincoln, *The Black Church Since Frazier*.

35. Hofstadter, *The Paranoid Style in American Politics*.

36. Breitman, *Malcolm X Speaks*, pp. 40–41; and *The Last Year of Malcolm X*, pp. 75–76.

37. Harding, "Religion and Resistance Among Ante-Bellum Negroes, 1800–1860," in Meier and Rudwick, *The Making of Black America*, Vol. 1, pp. 179–97; J. R. Washington, Jr., *Black Religion*; and Wilmore, *Black Religion and Black Radicalism*.

38. Stokely Carmichael's Chicago speech, July 28, 1966, in "Notes and Comment" (Chicago: Student Nonviolent Coordinating Committee, 1966), mimeographed; reprinted in Bracey, Meier, and Rudwick, *Black Nationalism in America*, p. 474.

39. Cleage, *The Black Messiah*, p. 37.

40. Quoted in Cleage, *Black Christian Nationalism*, pp. 265–74.

41. Ibid., p. 283.

42. Ibid., p. 13; and yet Cleage is clearly aware of Du Bois' Pan–Africanist work, *The World and Africa*, which he mentions in *The Black Messiah*, p. 98.

43. Cleage, *Black Christian Nationalism*, pp. 4–7.

44. Ibid., p. 156.

45. Ibid., p. 44.

46. Ibid., p. 305.

47. Leonard Moss, "In Quest of the Black Virgin: She is Black Because She Is Black," xeroxed typescript (Detroit: Wayne State University, Department of Sociology and Anthropology, 1979).

48. Cleage, *Black Christian Nationalism*, p. 136.

49. Cleage, *The Black Messiah*, p. 86.

50. Cleage, *Black Christian Nationalism*, pp. 101–2, 113.

51. Cleage's essays on Malcolm X are to be found in his works cited above, and in Clarke, *Malcolm X*.

52. Cone, *Black Theology and Black Power*, pp. 18, 21, 130; Lincoln, *My Face Is Black*, p. 114; Lincoln, *Black Muslims in America*, pp. 211–13; and Wilmore, *Black Religion and Black Radicalism*, p. 256.

53. Wilmore, *Black Religion and Black Radicalism*, p. 260; Cleage, *The Black Messiah*, pp. 210–12.

54. Cleage, *The Black Messiah*, p. 188.

55. Wilmore, *Black Religion and Black Radicalism*; and August Meier, "The Conservative Militant," in Lincoln, *Martin Luther King, Jr.*, pp. 147, 153. Meier refers to King's use of religious traditions and "efforts made to invest King with the qualities of a Messiah."

56. The FBI memos are reprinted in Breitman et al., *Assassination of Malcolm X*, pp. 178–90.

57. Ibid.

Chapter 14

1. Jefferson, *Notes*, p. 156.

2. Walter White et al., "A Declaration by Negro Voters," *Crisis*, 51, 1 (January 1944): 16–177.

3. W. L. Patterson, *We Charge Genocide*.

4. Breitman, *Malcolm X Speaks*, p. 83; M. L. King, Jr., *Where Do We Go From Here?*, p. 130.

5. D. L. Lewis, *King*, p. 389.

6. Quoted by Edgar Lockwood, "The Future of the Carter Policy Toward Southern Africa," in Lemarchand, *American Policy in Southern Africa*, p. 439.

7. Roy Harvey, "Young Says Business Key to Change in S. A.," *Chicago Defender*, October 2, 1978. An attack on Young's policy in another black newspaper is Franklin H. Williams, "U. S. Business: A Partner in Apartheid," *Amsterdam N. Y. News*, October 21, 1978.

8. Lockwood, "Future of Carter Policy Toward Southern Africa," p. 439.

9. "Ambassador Young at USIS, Johannesburg," May 27, 1977, official text (Washington, D. C.: United States Information Service, 1977), p. 10.

10. Martin Weil, "Can the Blacks Do for Africa What the Jews Did for Israel?" *Foreign Policy*, 15 (Summer 1974); reprinted in Lemarchand, *American Policy in Southern Africa*, pp. 315–22.

11. Quoted in Kucharsky, *The Man From Plains*, p. 96.

12. Ibid., p. 135.

13. "Text of Carter's White House Speech, July 15, 1979," in *International Herald Tribune*, Tuesday, July 17, 1979.

14. Ibid.

15. Christopher Lasch, *The Culture of Narcissism* (New York: W. W. Norton, 1979).

16. Wayne W. Dyer, *Your Erroneous Zones* (New York: Funk & Wagnalls, 1976); Robert Ringer, *Looking Out for Number One* (New York: Fawcett, 1977).

17. Barbara Reynolds, *Jesse Jackson: The Man, the Movement, the Myth* (Chicago: Nelson Hall, 1975). This book, written by "one of the new breed of black reporters of the seventies," is a critical biography that dwells on Jackson's messianic traits. See the index citation, "Jackson, Jessie Louis . . . , as Messiah," and note especially page 411.

18. See the printed circular, "Jesse Jackson's Message to Today's Students," distributed by Push to Excel, 930 East 50th Street, Chicago, Illinois 60615. The circular quotes Jackson as saying, "Students must stop seeking excuses and blaming others for their failure to learn. . . . The general rebellion against all authority must cease. We must distinguish between the authority that is tyrannical and authority which is moral and noble." The flyer also calls on students to "form 'peace corps' to monitor hallways," on educators to emphasize "hand skill careers," and on the media "to actively fight 'mind pollution' by curbing the manufacture, promotion and proliferation of phonograph records which advocate drugs and promiscuity."

19. Jackson is quoted in the article "Putting the Poor to Work," *Time* (March 23, 1981), p. 10.

Selected Bibliography

Adorno, T. W., et al. *The Authoritarian Personality*. New York: Norton, 1969.
Ahlstrom, Sidney. *A Religious History of the American People*. New Haven: Yale University Press, 1972.
Albanese, Anthony G. *The Plantation School*. New York: Vantage Press, 1976.
Anderson, E. *Messianic Popular Movements in the Lower Congo*. Uppsala: Almquist & Wiskell, 1958.
Anderson, Jervis; and Stone, Peter. *A. Philip Randolph: A Biographical Portrait*. New York: Harcourt Brace Jovanovich, 1974.
Aptheker, Herbert. *American Negro Slave Revolts*. 1943; repr. New York: International Publishers, 1969.
———, ed. *A Documentary History of the Negro People in the United States, 1933–1945*. Secaucus, N.J.: Citadel Press, 1974.
———, ed. *The Education of Black People: Ten Critiques, 1906–1960*. Amherst: University of Massachusetts Press, 1973.
Athearn, Robert G. *In Search of Canaan: Black Migration to Kansas, 1879–80*. Lawrence: Regents Press of Kansas, 1978.
Baeta, C. G., ed. *Christianity in Tropical Africa*. London: Oxford University Press, 1968.
Baraka, Amiri. *Blues People*. New York: Morrow, 1963.
Barrett, David B. *Schism and Renewal in Africa*. London: Oxford University Press, 1968.
Barrett, Leonard E. *The Rastafarians*. London: Heinemann, 1977.
———. *Soul Force: African Heritage in Afro–American Religion*. Garden City, N.Y.: Anchor Books, 1974.
Bastide, Roger. *African Civilizations in the New World*. New York: Harper & Row, 1971.
Bell, Howard Holman, ed. *Minutes of the Proceedings of the National Negro Conventions, 1830–1864*. New York: Arno Press, 1969.
Bellah, Robert. *The Broken Covenant*. New York: Seabury Press, 1975.
———. "Civil Religion in America." *Daedalus*, 96 (Winter 1967): 1–21.
Bercovitch, Sacvan. *The American Jeremiad*. Madison: University of Wisconsin Press, 1978.
Berlin, Ira. *Slaves Without Masters: The Free Negro in the Antebellum South*. New York: Vintage Books, 1974.
Bittle, William E.; and Geis, Gilbert. *The Longest Way Home: Chief Alfred C. Sam's Back to Africa Movement*. Detroit: Wayne State University Press, 1964.
Blassingame, John. *The Slave Community*. New York: Oxford University Press, 1972.
Blyden, Edward W. *Christianity, Islam, and the Negro Race*. 1887; repr. Edinburgh: Edinburgh University Press, 1967.

Boas, Franz. *The Mind of Primitive Man*. 1938; rev. ed. New York: Free Press, 1965.

Botkin, B. A. *Lay My Burden Down: A Folk History of Slavery*. Chicago: University of Chicago Press, 1945.

Bowen, J. W. E., ed. *Africa and the American Negro*. Atlanta: Gannon Theological Seminary, 1896.

Bracey, John H.; Meier, August; and Rudwick, Elliott M., eds. *Black Nationalism in America*. Indianapolis: Bobbs–Merrill, 1970.

Bragg, George F. *History of the African Group of the Episcopal Church*. Baltimore: Church Advocate Press, 1972.

Brawley, Benjamin. "The Negro Genius." *Southern Workman*, 44 (May 1915): 305–8.

——, ed. *Early American Negro Writers*. Chapel Hill: University of North Carolina Press, 1935.

Breitman, George. *The Last Year of Malcolm X*. New York: Pathfinder Press, 1970.

——, ed. *By Any Means Necessary: Speeches, Interviews, and a Letter by Malcolm X*. New York: Pathfinder Press, 1970.

——, ed. *Malcolm X Speaks*. New York: Grove Press, 1965.

——, et al. *The Assassination of Malcolm X*. New York: Pathfinder Press, 1976.

Brodie, Fawn. *Thomas Jefferson: An Intimate History*. New York: Norton, 1974.

Brotz, Howard. *The Black Jews of Harlem*. New York: Schocken, 1970.

——, ed. *Negro Social and Political Thought, 1850–1920*. New York: Basic Books, 1966.

Brown, Claude. *The Life and Loves of Mr. Jiveass Nigger*. New York: Farrar, Strauss & Giroux, 1969.

Brown, Sterling. "Negro Character as Seen by White Authors." *Journal of Negro Education* (April 1933): 198.

——; Davis, Arthur P.; and Lee, Ulysses, eds. *The Negro Caravan*. 1941; repr. New York: Arno Press, 1969.

Brown, Turner, Jr. *Black Is*. New York: Grove Press, 1969.

Brown, William Wells. *The Black Man*. 1863; repr. New York: Arno Press, 1969.

Burkett, Randall K. *Black Redemption: Churchmen Speak for the Garvey Movement*. Philadelphia: Temple University Press, 1978.

——. *Garveyism as a Religious Movement*. Metuchen, N.J.: Scarecrow Press, 1979.

Carmichael, Stokely. *Stokely Carmichael Speaks*. New York: Vintage Books, 1971.

——; and Hamilton, Charles V. *Black Power*. New York: Vintage Books, 1967.

Cawelti, John W. *Apostles of the Self-Made Man*. Chicago: University of Chicago Press, 1965.

Cayton, Horace; and Drake, St. Clair. *Black Metropolis*. New York: Harper Torchbook, 1962.

Cherry, Conrad, ed. *God's New Israel: Religious Interpretations of American Destiny*. Englewood Cliffs, N.J.: Prentice–Hall, 1971.

Chicago Commission on Race Relations. *The Negro in Chicago*. Chicago: University of Chicago Press, 1922.

Clark, Elmer T. *The Small Sects in America*. Nashville: Abingdon Press, 1965.

Clarke, John Henrik, ed. *Malcolm X: The Man and His Times*. New York: Macmillan, 1969.

——, ed. *Marcus Garvey and the Vision of Africa*. New York: Vintage Books, 1974.

——, ed. *William Styron's Nat Turner: Ten Black Writers Respond*. Boston: Beacon Press, 1968.

——, et al. *Black Titan: W. E. B. Du Bois*. Boston: Beacon Press, 1970.

Cleage, Albert B., Jr. *Black Christian Nationalism*. New York: Morrow, 1972.

——. *The Black Messiah*. New York: Sheed & Ward, 1969.

Cleaver, Eldridge. *Soul on Fire*. Waco, Tex.: Word Books, 1978.

——. *Soul on Ice*. New York: McGraw–Hill, 1967.

Cone, James H. *Black Theology and Black Power*. New York: Seabury Press, 1969.

——. *A Black Theology of Liberation*. Philadelphia: Lippencott, 1970.

Cox, Oliver C. *Caste, Class, and Race: A Study in Social Dynamics*. Garden City, N. Y.: Doubleday, 1948.

Cromwell, John W. *The Negro in American History*. Washington, D. C.: American Negro Academy, 1914.

Cronon, Edmund David. *Black Moses*. Madison: University of Wisconsin Press, 1966.

Crummell, Alexander. *Africa and America: Addresses and Discourses*. Springfield, Mass.: Wiley Co., 1891.

——. *Civilization: The Primal Need of the Race*. Washington, D. C.: American Negro Academy, 1898.

———. *The Future of Africa.* New York: Charles Scribner, 1862.
———. *The Greatness of Christ and Other Sermons.* New York: T. Whittaker, 1882.
Cruse, Harold. *The Crisis of the Negro Intellectual.* New York: Morrow, 1967.
Dalfiume, Roger. "The 'Forgotten Years' of the Negro Rebellion." *Journal of American History,* 55 (June 1968): 90–106.
Davidson, Basil. *The African Genius.* Boston: Little, Brown, 1969.
Davis, Allison, et al. *Deep South.* Chicago: University of Chicago Press, 1941.
Davis, Angela. *An Autobiography.* New York: Random House, 1974.
Davis, David B. *The Slave Power Conspiracy and the Paranoid Style.* Baton Rouge: Louisiana State University Press, 1969.
Delany, Martin. *Blake.* Boston: Beacon Press, 1970.
———. *'The Condition, Elevation, Emigration, and Destiny of the Colored People of the United States.'* 1852; repr. New York: Arno Press, 1969.
Dinnerstein, Leonard; and Jaher, Frederick Cople, eds. *Uncertain Americans.* New York: Oxford University Press, 1977.
Diop, Cheikh Anta. *The Cultural Unity of Black Africa.* Chicago: Third World Press, 1977.
Dollard, John. *Caste and Class in a Southern Town.* New York: Harper & Brothers, 1937.
Douglass, Frederick. *The Life and Times of Frederick Douglass: The Complete Autobiography.* New York: Collier Books, 1962.
———. *Narrative of the Life of Frederick Douglass, Written by Himself.* Boston: At the Antislavery Office, 1845.
Drachler, Jacob. *Black Homeland/Black Diaspora.* Port Washington, N.Y.: Kennikat, 1975.
Drake, St. Clair. *The Redemption of Africa and Black Religion.* Chicago: Third World Press, 1970.
Duberman, Martin, ed. *The Antislavery Vanguard.* Princeton: Princeton University Press, 1965.
Du Bois, W. E. B. *The Autobiography of W. E. B. Du Bois.* New York: International Publishers, 1968.
———. *The Conservation of Races.* Washington, D. C.: American Negro Academy, 1897.
———. *Dark Princess: A Romance.* New York: Harcourt, Brace, 1928.
———. *Darkwater: Voices from Within the Veil.* New York: Harcourt, Brace & Howe, 1920.
———. *Dusk of Dawn.* New York: Harcourt, Brace, 1940.
———. *The Gift of Black Folk.* 1924; repr. New York: Washington Square Press, 1970.
———. *The Negro Church.* Atlanta: Atlanta University Publications, 1903.
———. *The Quest of the Silver Fleece.* Chicago: McClurg, 1911.
———. *The Souls of Black Folk.* Chicago: McClurg, 1903.
Ducas, George; and Van Doren, Charles, eds. *Great Documents in Black American History.* New York: Praeger, 1970.
Duff, John B.; and Mitchell, Peter M. *The Nat Turner Rebellion: The Historical Event and the Modern Controversy.* New York: Harper & Row, 1971.
Dulles, Foster Rhea. *America's Rise to World Power.* New York: Harper & Row, 1963.
Duncan, Robert, ed. *Selected Writings of Mahatma Gandhi.* London: Faber & Faber, 1951.
Durkheim, Emile. *Suicide: A Study in Sociology.* Translated by John A. Spaulding and George Simpson. London: Routledge & Kegan Paul, 1952.
Edwards, Adolph. *Marcus Garvey, 1887–1940.* London: New Beacon Publications, 1967.
Einstein, Albert. *Relativity.* 1916; repr. New York: Crown, 1961.
Elkins, Stanley M. *Slavery: A Problem in American Institutional and Intellectual Life.* Chicago: University of Chicago Press, 1959.
Ellis, Albert; and Abarbanel, Albert, eds. *Encyclopedia of Sexual Behavior.* New York: Hawthorn Books, 1961.
Ellison, Ralph. *Invisible Man.* New York: Signet, 1952.
———. *Shadow and Act.* New York: Signet, 1966.
Epstein, Dena J. *Sinful Tunes and Spirituals.* Urbana: University of Illinois Press, 1977.
Essien–Udom, E. U. *Black Nationalism: A Search for an Identity in America.* Chicago: University of Chicago Press, 1962.
Evans–Pritchard, E. E. *Theories of Primitive Religion.* Oxford: Clarendon Press, 1965.
Fadumah, Orishatukeh. *The Defects of the Negro Church.* Washington, D. C.: American Negro Academy, 1904.
Fauset, Arthur Huff. *Black Gods of the Metropolis.* 1944; repr. Philadelphia: University of Pennsylvania Press, 1971.

Ferris, William H. *The African Abroad*. 2 vols. New Haven: Tuttle, Morehouse & Taylor, 1913.
Fishman, Solomon. *The Disinherited of Art*. Berkeley: University of California Press, 1953.
Fladeland, Betty. *Men and Brothers: Anglo-American Antislavery Cooperation*. Urbana: University of Illinois Press, 1972.
Fleming, Walter L. "Pap Singleton, The Moses of the Colored Exodus." *American Journal of Sociology*, 15 (July 1909): 61–82.
Fogel, Robert W.; and Engerman, Stanley L. *Time on the Cross: The Economics of Negro Slavery*. Boston: Little, Brown, 1974.
Foner, Philip S. *History of Black Americans: From Africa to the Emergence of the Cotton Kingdom*. Westport, Conn.: Greenwood, 1975.
———, ed. *The Life and Writings of Frederick Douglass*. 4 vols. New York: International Publishers, 1955.
———, ed. *The Voice of Black America*. New York: Simon & Schuster, 1972.
Foster, William Z. *The Negro People in American History*. 1954; repr. New York: International Publishers, 1970.
Franklin, John Hope. *The Free Negro in North Carolina, 1790–1860*. New York: Norton, 1971.
———. *From Slavery to Freedom*. New York: Knopf, 1961.
Frazier, E. Franklin. *Black Bourgeoisie*. Glencoe, Ill.: Free Press, 1957.
———. *The Negro Church in America*. New York: Schocken, 1964.
———. *The Negro in the United States*. New York: Macmillan, 1957.
———; and Lincoln, C. Eric. *The Negro Church in America and The Black Church Since Frazier*. New York: Schocken, 1973.
Fredrickson, George M. *The Black Image in the White Mind*. New York: Harper & Row, 1971.
Freud, Sigmund. *Beyond the Pleasure Principle*. London: Hogarth Press, 1942.
Fuller, Hoyt. "An Interview: The Original Hebrew Israelite Nation." *Black World* (May 1975): 62–85.
Fullinwider, S. P. *The Mind and Mood of Black America: Twentieth Century Thought*. Homewood, Ill.: Dorsey Press, 1969.
Furnas, J. C. *Goodbye to Uncle Tom*. New York: William Sloane Associates, 1956.
Gandhi, Mohandas (Mahatma). *An Autobiography: The Story of My Experiments with Truth*. Translated from the Gujarati by Mahadev Desai. London: Phoenix Press, 1949.
Garnet, Henry Highland. *An Address to the Slaves of the United States*. [*See* Walker, David; and Garnet, Henry H. *Walker's Appeal and Garnet's Address. . . .*]
Garvey, Amy Jacques. *Garvey and Garveyism*. New York: Collier Books, 1970.
———, ed. *Philosophy and Opinions of Marcus Garvey*. 2 vols. 1923–25; repr. New York: Atheneum, 1969.
———; and Essien-Udom, E. U., eds. *More Philosophy and Opinions of Marcus Garvey*. Vol. 3. London: Frank Cass, 1977.
Garvey, Marcus. *Speech Presenting the Case of the Negro for International Racial Adjustment*. London: Universal Negro Improvement Association, 1928.
Garvin, Roy. "Benjamin or 'Pap' Singleton and His Followers." *Journal of Negro History*, 33 (January 1948): 7–23.
Genovese, Eugene D. *From Rebellion to Revolution: Afro-American Slave Revolts in the Making of the Modern World*. Baton Rouge: Louisiana State University Press, 1980.
———. *Roll, Jordan, Roll: The World the Slaves Made*. New York: Vintage Books, 1976.
George, Carol V. R. *Segregated Sabbaths: Richard Allen and the Rise of Independent Black Churches, 1760–1840*. New York: Oxford University Press, 1973.
Gerber, Israel J. *The Heritage Seekers: American Blacks in Search of a Jewish Identity*. Middle Village, N. Y.: Jonathan David Publishers, 1977.
Gluckman, Max. *Rituals of Rebellion in South East Africa*. Manchester: University of Manchester Press, 1954.
Gordon, Milton M. *Assimilation in American Life*. New York: Oxford University Press, 1964.
Gosnell, Harold Foote. *Negro Politicians*. Chicago: University of Chicago Press, 1935.
Graebner, Norman, ed. *Ideas and Diplomacy*. New York: Oxford University Press, 1964.
Griggs, Sutton E. *The Hindered Hand*. Nashville: Orion, 1905.
———. *Life's Demands, or According to Law*. Memphis: National Public Welfare League, 1924.
Grimke, Francis J. *Works*. [*See* Carter G. Woodson, ed., *Works of Francis J. Grimke*.]
Gutman, Herbert G. *The Black Family in Slavery and Freedom, 1750–1925*. New York: Pantheon Books, 1976.

Hamilton, Charles V. *The Black Preacher in America*. New York: Morrow, 1972.

Handler, Jerome S.; and Lange, Frederick W. *Plantation Slavery in Barbados*. Cambridge: Harvard University Press, 1978.

Harding, Vincent. "W. E. B. Du Bois and the Black Messianic Vision." *Freedomways*, 9 (1969): 44–58.

———; and Genovese, Eugene. "An Exchange on 'Nat Turner'." *New York Review of Books* (November 7, 1968): 35–37.

Harlan, Louis. "Booker T. Washington and the White Man's Burden." *American Historical Review*, 71 (January 1966): 441–67.

———, et al., eds. *The Booker T. Washington Papers*. 8 vols. Urbana: University of Illinois Press, 1972–.

Harris, Sara. *Father Divine*. Rev. ed., with introduction by John Henrik Clarke. New York: Macmillan, 1971.

Harris, Sheldon, ed. *Paul Cuffe: Black Americans and the African Return*. New York: Simon & Schuster, 1972.

Harrison, Hubert. *When Africa Awakes*. New York: Porro Press, 1920.

Hayford, J. E. Casely. *Ethiopia Unbound: Studies in Race Emancipation*. 1911; repr. London: Frank Cass, 1969.

Haygood, Harry. *Negro Liberation*. New York: Liberator Press, 1976.

Henri, Florette. *Black Migration: Movement North, 1900–1920*. Garden City, N.Y.: Doubleday, 1975.

Herskovits, Melville J. "The Ancestry of the American Negro." *American Scholar*, 8 (1938–39): 84–94.

———. *The Myth of the Negro Past*. 1941; repr. Boston: Beacon Press, 1958.

———. *The New World Negro*. New York: Minerva Press, 1969.

Higham, John. *Strangers in the Land*. New Brunswick, N. J.: Rutgers University Press, 1955.

Hill, Mozell C. "The All-Negro Communities of Oklahoma: The Natural History of a Social Movement." *Journal of Negro History*, 31 (July 1946): 254–68.

Hill, Robert. *The Black Man*. Millwood, N.Y.: Kraus Thompson, 1975.

Hofstadter, Richard. *The Paranoid Style in American Politics*. New York: Knopf, 1965.

———, ed. *Great Issues in American History: From the Revolution to the Civil War, 1765–1865*. New York: Vintage Books, 1958.

Hudson, Winthrop S. *Nationalism and Religion in America*. New York: Harper & Row, 1970.

Huggins, Nathan. *Black Odyssey: The Afro-American Ordeal in Slavery*. New York: Pantheon Books, 1977.

———. *Harlem Renaissance*. New York: Oxford University Press, 1971.

Jahn, Janheinz. *Muntu: The New African Culture*. New York: Grove Press, 1961.

Jefferson, Thomas. *Notes on the State of Virginia*. New York: Harper & Row, 1964. [Reprinted from H. A. Washington, ed., *The Writings of Thomas Jefferson*, Vol. 8; New York, 1861.]

Johnson, Charles S. *Shadow of the Plantation*. Chicago: Phoenix, 1966.

Johnson, Guy B. *Folk Culture on St. Helena Island, South Carolina*. Chapel Hill: University of North Carolina Press, 1930.

Johnson, James W. *The Autobiography of an Ex-Colored Man*. New York: Knopf, 1927.

Johnston, James H. *Race Relations in Virginia and Miscegenation in the South, 1776–1860*. Amherst: University of Massachusetts Press, 1970.

Jones, Raymond Julius. *A Comparative Study of Religious Cult Behavior Among Negroes with ꝑecial Reference to Emotional Group Conditioning Factors*. Washington, D. C., 1939.

Jordan, Winthrop. *White Over Black*. Chapel Hill: University of North Carolina Press, 1968.

Keckley, Elizabeth. *Behind the Scenes, or Thirty Years a Slave and Four Years in the White House*. 1868; repr. New York: Arno Press, 1968.

Kenyatta, Jomo. *Facing Mt. Kenya*. London: Secker & Warburg, 1953.

Killiam, Charles, ed. *Sermons and Addresses, 1853–1891: Bishop Daniel A. Payne*. New York: Arno Press, 1972.

King, K. J. "Some Notes on Arnold Ford and New World Black Attitudes to Ethiopia." *Journal of Ethiopian Studies*, 10 (January 1972): 81–87.

King, Martin Luther, Jr. *Stride Toward Freedom: The Montgomery Story*. New York: Harper & Row, 1958.

———. *The Trumpet of Conscience*. London: Hodder & Stoughton, 1968.

———. *Where Do We Go From Here?* New York: Harper & Row, 1967.

——. *Why We Can't Wait.* New York: Signet Books, 1964.

Kohn, Hans. *The Idea of Nationalism.* New York: Macmillan, 1944.

Kraditor, Aileen S. *Means and Ends in American Abolitionism.* New York: Vintage Books, 1967.

Kucharsky, David. *The Man From Plains: The Mind and Spirit of Jimmy Carter.* New York: Harper & Row, 1977.

Kuper, Hilda. *An African Aristocracy.* London: Oxford University Press, 1947.

Lanternari, Vittorio. *The Religions of the Oppressed.* New York: Knopf, 1963.

Lemarchand, Rene, ed. *American Policy in Southern Africa.* Washington, D. C.: University Press of America, 1978.

Leslau, Wolf. "The Black Jews of Ethiopia." *Commentary,* 7 (1949): 216–24.

——, trans. *Falasha Anthology: The Black Jews of Ethiopia.* New Haven: Yale University Press, 1951; repr. New York: Schocken, 1969.

Lester, Julius. *The Seventh Son.* 2 vols. New York: Random House, 1971.

Levin, Gordon. *Woodrow Wilson and World Politics.* New York: Oxford University Press, 1968.

Levine, Lawrence. *Black Culture and Black Consciousness.* New York: Oxford University Press, 1977.

Levi–Strauss, Claude. *The Savage Mind.* Chicago: University of Chicago Press, 1966.

Levy–Bruhl, Lucien. *How Natives Think.* London: George, Allen & Unwin, 1926.

——. *Primitive Mentality.* New York: Macmillan, 1923.

Lewis, David L. *King: A Critical Biography.* New York: Praeger, 1970.

Lewis, I. M. *Ecstatic Religion.* Baltimore: Penguin, 1971.

Lewis, Lloyd. *Myths After Lincoln.* London: Harper & Brothers, 1933.

Lincoln, C. Eric. *The Black Church Since Frazier.* New York: Schocken, 1974.

——. *The Black Muslims in America.* Boston: Beacon Press, 1973.

——. *My Face Is Black.* Boston: Beacon Press, 1964.

——, ed. *The Black Experience in Religion.* New York: Doubleday, 1974.

——, ed. *Martin Luther King, Jr.: A Profile.* New York: Hill & Wang, 1970.

Linton, R. "Nativistic Movements." *American Anthropologist* (1943): 230–40.

Locke, Alain, ed. *The New Negro: An Interpretation.* Preface by Robert Hayden. 1925; repr. New York: Atheneum, 1970.

Lomax, Louis. *To Kill a Black Man.* Los Angeles: Holloway House, 1968.

——. *When the Word Is Given.* New York: Signet, 1963.

Louis, Joe. *My Life.* New York: Harcourt Brace Jovanovich, 1978.

Luthuli, Albert. *Let My People Go.* New York: New American Library, 1962.

Lynch, Hollis R. *Edward Wilmot Blyden: Pan–Negro Patriot, 1832–1912.* London: Oxford University Press, 1967.

——, ed. *Black Spokesman: Selected Published Writings of Edward Wilmot Blyden.* New York: Humanities Press, 1971.

McKay, Claude. *Banjo.* New York: Harper Brothers, 1929.

——. *Home to Harlem.* New York: Harper Brothers, 1928.

McLoughlin, William G. *The American Evangelicals, 1800–1900.* New York: Harper & Row, 1968.

——. *Revivals, Awakenings, and Reform.* Chicago: University of Chicago Press, 1978.

McPherson, James A. *The Abolitionist Legacy: From Reconstruction to the NAACP.* Princeton: Princeton University Press, 1975.

——. *Hue and Cry.* Greenwich, Conn., 1969.

Mair, Lucy P. "Independent Religious Movements on Three Continents." *Comparative Studies in Society and History* (January 1959): 113–36.

Malcolm X. *The Autobiography of Malcolm X.* New York: Grove Press, 1965.

Malinowski, Bronislaw. "The Pan–African Problem of Culture Contact." *American Journal of Sociology,* 43 (1943): 649–66.

Martin, Tony. *Race First.* Westport, Conn.: Greenwood, 1976.

Marty, Martin E. *Righteous Empire.* New York: Dial Press, 1970.

Marx, Gary T. *Protest and Prejudice.* New York: Harper Torchbook, 1969.

Matthews, Basil. *Booker T. Washington.* Cambridge: Harvard University Press, 1948.

Matthews, Victoria Earle, ed. *Black Belt Diamonds.* New York: Fortune & Scott, 1898.

Mays, Benjamin. *The Negro's God: As Reflected in His Literature.* 1938; repr. New York: Atheneum, 1968.

Mbiti, John S. *African Religions and Philosophy.* London: Heinemann, 1969.
Mehlinger, Louis. "Attitude of the Free Negro Toward African Colonization." *Journal of Negro History,* 1 (July 1916): 217–301.
Meier, August. *Negro Thought in America, 1880–1915.* Ann Arbor: University of Michigan Press, 1963.
———; and Rudwick, Elliott, eds. *The Making of Black America.* 2 vols. New York: Atheneum, 1971.
Mezu, S. Okechukwu; and Desai, Ram, eds. *Black Leaders of the Centuries.* Buffalo, N.Y.: Black Academy Press, 1970.
Miller, Floyd. *The Search for a Black Nationality: Black Colonization and Emigration, 1787–1863.* Urbana: University of Illinois Press, 1975.
Miller, Perry. *The New England Mind: From Colony to Province.* Cambridge: Harvard University Press, 1953.
———. *The New England Mind: The Seventeenth Century.* New York: Macmillan, 1939.
Moorhead, James H. *American Apocalypse: Yankee Protestants and the Civil War, 1860–1869.* New Haven: Yale University Press, 1978.
Moses, Wilson J. *The Golden Age of Black Nationalism, 1850–1925.* Hamden, Conn.: Archon, 1978.
———. "Literary Garveyism: The Novels of Reverend Sutton E. Griggs." *Phylon,* 40 (Fall 1979): 213–14.
———. "The Poetics of Ethiopianism: W. E. B. Du Bois and Literary Black Nationalism." *American Literature,* 47 (1975): 411–26.
Mullin, Gerald. *Flight and Rebellion: Slave Resistance in the Eighteenth Century.* New York: Oxford University Press, 1972.
Myrdal, Gunnar. *An American Dilemma.* 2 vols. New York: Harper & Brothers, 1944.
Nichols, Charles H. *Many Thousand Gone.* Bloomington: Indiana University Press, 1963.
Niebuhr, Helmut Richard. *The Kingdom of God in America.* New York: Harper & Brothers, 1937.
Niebuhr, Reinhold. "Awkward Imperialists." *Atlantic Monthly,* 145 (May 1930): 670–75.
Noggle, Burl. *Into the Twenties.* Urbana: University of Illinois Press, 1974.
Novak, Michael. "Black and White in Catholic Eyes." *New York Times Magazine,* November 16, 1975.
Nozick, Robert. *Anarchy State and Utopia.* New York: Basic Books, 1975.
Oates, Stephen B. *With Malice Toward None: The Life of Abraham Lincoln.* New York: Harper & Row, 1977.
Ofari, Earl. *"Let Your Motto Be Resistance": The Life and Thought of Henry Highland Garnet.* Boston: Beacon Press, 1972.
Oosthuizen, Gerhardus Cornelius. *Post Christianity in Africa.* London: C. Hurst, 1968.
———. *The Theology of a South African Messiah.* Leiden: E. J. Brill, 1967.
Osofsky, Gilbert. *Harlem: The Making of a Ghetto.* New York: Harper Torchbook, 1968.
———. *Puttin' on Ole Massa.* New York: Harper & Row, 1969.
Ottley, Roi. *New World A-Coming: Inside Black America.* 1943; repr. New York: Arno Press, 1968.
Owens, Leslie. *This Species of Property: Slave Life and Culture in the Old South.* New York: Oxford University Press, 1976.
Painter, Nell Irvin. *Exodusters: Black Migration to Kansas After Reconstruction.* New York: Knopf, 1977.
Park, Robert E. "The Conflict and Fusion of Cultures with Special Reference to the Negro." *Journal of Negro History,* 4 (1919): 111–33.
Parrinder, Geoffrey. *African Traditional Religion.* Westport, Conn.: Greenwood, 1970.
———. *West African Religion: A Study of the Beliefs and Practices of Akan, Ewe, Yoruba, Ibo, and Kindred Peoples.* London: Epworth Press, 1969.
Patterson, Orlando. *The Sociology of Slavery.* London: Fairleigh Dickinson University Press, 1970.
Patterson, William L., ed. *We Charge Genocide.* New York: Civil Rights Congress, 1951.
Payne, Daniel A. *Recollections of Seventy Years.* Nashville: AME Sunday School Union, 1888.
———. *Welcome to the Ransomed; or Duties of the Colored Inhabitants of the District of Columbia.* Baltimore: Bull & Tuttle, Clipper Office, 1862.

Persons, Stow. "The Cyclical Theory of History in Eighteenth-Century America." *American Quarterly*, 6 (Summer 1954): 147–63.

Phillips, Ulrich Bonnell. *American Negro Slavery*. New York: D. Appleton, 1918.

Pinkney, Alphonso. *Red, Black, and Green*. New York: Cambridge University Press, 1976.

Porter, Dorothy, ed. *Early Negro Writing, 1760–1837*. Boston: Beacon Press, 1971.

Powdermaker, Hortense. *After Freedom*. New York: Russell & Russell, 1968.

Raboteau, Albert J. *Slave Religion*. New York: Oxford University Press, 1978.

Rawick, George P. *From Sundown to Sunup: The Making of the Black Community*. Westport, Conn.: Greenwood, 1972.

———, ed. *The American Slave: A Composite Autobiography*. 19 vols. Westport, Conn.: Greenwood, 1972–.

———, ed. *The American Slave: A Composite Autobiography, Supplement Series 1*. 12 vols. Westport, Conn.: Greenwood, 1978.

Read, Hollis. *The Negro Problem Solved: or Africa As She Was, As She Is, and As She Shall Be, Her Curse and Her Cure*. New York: A. A. Constine, 1864.

Record, Wilson. *The Negro and the Communist Party*. Chapel Hill: University of North Carolina Press, 1951.

Redkey, Edwin S. *Black Exodus: Black Nationalist and Back to Africa Movements, 1890–1910*. New Haven: Yale University Press, 1969.

———, ed. *Respect Black*. New York: Arno Press, 1971.

Reid, Ira D. "Negro Movements and Messiahs, 1900–1949." *Phylon*, 9 (1949): 362.

Reik, Theodore. *Masochism in Modern Man*. New York: Grove Press, 1941.

Reynolds, Barbara A. *Jesse Jackson: The Man, the Movement, and the Myth*. Chicago: Nelson Hall, 1975.

Richards, Henry J., ed. *Topics in Afro-American Studies*. Buffalo, N.Y.: Black Academy Press, 1970.

Richardson, N. R. *Liberia's Past and Present*. London: Diplomatic Press & Publishing Co., 1959.

Rischin, Moses, ed. *The American Gospel of Success*. Chicago: Quadrangle Books, 1965.

Robinson, Armstead L., ed. *Black Studies in the University*. New Haven: Yale University Press, 1969.

Rogers, Joel Augustus. *From Superman to Man*. New York: The Author, 1941.

———. *World's Great Men of Color*. New York: The Author, 1947.

Ross, Red. "Black Americans and the Italo–Ethiopian Relief, 1935–1936." *Ethiopia Observer*, 15 (1972): 123–31.

Rushing, Byron. "A Note on the Origin of the African Orthodox Church." *Journal of Negro History* (January 1972): 37–39.

Russell, Bertrand. *A History of Western Philosophy*. New York: Simon & Schuster, 1945.

Sandburg, Carl. *Abraham Lincoln*, Vol. 2: *The War Years*. New York: Harcourt, Brace, 1939.

Schorr, Joel. *Henry Highland Garnet: A Voice of Black Radicalism in the Nineteenth Century*. Westport, Conn.: Greenwood, 1977.

Schuyler, George S. "The Negro Art Hokum." *Nation* (June 16, 1926): 662–63.

Scott, Emmett J. *Negro Migration During the War*. London: Oxford University Press, 1920.

Scott, William R. "Black Nationalism and the Italo–Ethiopian Conflict, 1934–1936." *Journal of Negro History*, 63 (April 1978): 124.

———. *Going to the Promised Land: Afro-American Immigrants in Ethiopia, 1930–1935*. Atlanta: Institute of the Black World, 1975.

Seligman, C. G. *Races of Africa*. 1930; repr. New York: Oxford University Press, 1966.

Senghor, Leopold. "African–Negro Aesthetics." *Diogenes*, 16 (Winter 1956): 23–28.

Shepperson, George. "Ethiopianism and African Nationalism." *Phylon*, 14 (1953): 9–18.

———; and Price, Thomas. *Independent African*. Edinburgh: Edinburgh University Press, 1958.

Silberman, Charles. *Crisis in Black and White*. New York: Random House, 1964.

Simmons, William J. *Men of Mark*. Cleveland: Geo. M. Rewell, 1887.

Smith, Henry Nash. *Virgin Land: The American West as Symbol and Myth*. Cambridge: Harvard University Press, 1950.

Smith, James W.; and Jamison, A. Leland, eds. *Religion in American Life*. 4 vols. Princeton: Princeton University Press, 1961.

Smith, Timothy L. *Revivalism and Social Reform*. New York: Harper & Row, 1965.

Smith, William Gardner. *The Stone Face*. New York: Farrar, Strauss, 1963.

Spear, Allan H. *Black Chicago: The Making of a Negro Ghetto.* Chicago: University of Chicago Press, 1967.

Spengler, Oswald. *The Hour of Decision.* New York: Knopf, 1934.

Star, Jack. "Above All, a Scholar." *Change* (February 1977): 30.

Starobin, Robert, ed. *Denmark Vesey: The Slave Conspiracy of 1822.* Englewood Cliffs, N.J.: Prentice–Hall, 1970.

Staudenraus, P. J. *The African Colonization Movement, 1816–1865.* New York: Columbia University Press, 1961.

Stoddard, Lothrop. *The Rising Tide of Color.* New York: Charles Scribner's Sons, 1920.

Stowe, Harriet Beecher. *The Key to Uncle Tom's Cabin: Presenting the Original Facts and Documents upon Which the Story is Founded, Together with Corroborative Statements Verifying the Truth of the Work.* 1854; repr. New York: Arno Press, 1968.

——. *Uncle Tom's Cabin.* 1852; repr. New York: Dodd, Mead, 1952.

Strong, Josiah. *Expansionism Under New World Conditions.* 1900; repr. New York: Garland, 1971.

——. *Our Country.* 1891; repr. Cambridge: Harvard University Press, 1963.

Strout, Cushing. *The New Heavens and New Earth.* New York: Harper & Row, 1974.

Stuckey, Sterling, ed. *The Ideological Origins of Black Nationalism.* Boston: Beacon Press, 1972.

Sundkler, Bengt. *Bantu Prophets in South Africa.* London: International African Institute, 1948.

Sweet, Henry F. *Black Images of America, 1784–1870.* New York: Norton, 1976.

Sypher, Wylie. *Guinea's Captive Kings.* Chapel Hill: University of North Carolina Press, 1942.

Tate, Cecil F. *The Search for a Method in American Studies.* Minneapolis: University of Minnesota Press, 1973.

Tebbell, John W. *From Rags to Riches: Horatio Alger, Jr., and the American Dream.* New York: Macmillan, 1963.

Terry–Thompson, A[rthur] C[ornelius]. *The History of the African Orthodox Church.* New York: n.p., 1956.

Thompson, John M. *Russia, Bolshevism, and the Versailles Peace.* Princeton: Princeton University Press, 1966.

Thwaite, Daniel. *The Seething African Pot.* London: Constable & Co., 1936.

Tindall, George B. "The Liberian Exodus of 1878." *South Carolina Historical Magazine,* 53 (July 1952): 133–45.

Tuveson, Ernest L. *Redeemer Nation: The Idea of America's Millennial Role.* Chicago: University of Chicago Press, 1968.

Turner, Lorenzo D. *Africanisms in the Gullah Dialect.* Chicago: University of Chicago Press, 1949.

Tyler, Alice Felt. *Freedom's Ferment.* New York: Harper & Row, 1962.

Tyson, George F., Jr., ed. *Toussaint L'Ouverture.* Englewood Cliffs, N.J.: Prentice–Hall, 1973.

United States Congress, Senate. *Congressional Record.* 75th Congress, 3rd Session, Volume 83; and 76th Congress, 1st Session, Vol. 84.

Uya, Okon Edet, ed. *Black Brotherhood: Afro–Americans and Africa.* Lexington, Mass.: D. C. Heath, 1971.

Van Deburg, William L. *The Slave Drivers: Black Agricultural Labor Supervisors in the Antebellum South.* Westport, Conn.: Greenwood, 1979.

Van Vechten, Carl. *Nigger Heaven.* New York: Knopf, 1926.

Vincent, Theodore. *Black Power and the Garvey Movement.* Berkeley, Calif.: Ramparts Press, 1971.

Wade, Richard C. "The Vesey Plot: A Reconsideration." *Journal of Southern History,* 30 (May 1964): 148–61.

Walker, David; and Garnet, Henry H. *Walker's Appeal and Garnet's Address to the Slaves of the United States of America.* 1848; repr. New York: Arno Press, 1969.

Walker, Sheila S. *Ceremonial Spirit Possession in Africa and Afro–America.* Leiden: E. J. Brill, 1972.

Walters, Alexander. *My Life and Work.* New York: Fleming H. Revel, 1917.

Ward, John William. *Andrew Jackson: Symbol for an Age.* New York: Oxford University Press, 1962.

Washington, Booker T. *Character Building.* New York: Doubleday, Page & Co., 1902.

Washington, Joseph R., Jr. *Black Religion.* Boston: Beacon Press, 1964.

——. *Black Sects and Cults.* Garden City, N.Y.: Doubleday, 1972.

——. *The Politics of God.* Boston: Beacon Press, 1967.

Waskow, Arthur I. *From Race Riot to Sit In.* Garden City, N.Y.: Doubleday, 1966.
Webber, Thomas L. *Deep Like the Rivers: Education in the Slave Quarter Community, 1831–1865.* New York: Norton, 1978.
Weber, Max. *The Protestant Ethic and the Spirit of Capitalism.* New York: Scribner, 1958.
Weinberg, Meyer; and Clark, Kenneth B., eds. *W. E. B. Du Bois: A Reader.* New York: Harper & Row, 1970.
Weisbord, Robert G. *African Zion: The Attempt to Establish a Jewish Colony in the East African Protectorate, 1903–1905.* Philadelphia: Jewish Publication Society of America, 1968.
———. *Ebony Kinship: Africa, Africans, and the Afro–American.* Westport, Conn.: Greenwood, 1973.
Wells, Ida B. *Crusade for Justice: The Autobiography of Ida B. Wells.* Edited by Alfreda M. Barnett Duster. Chicago: University of Chicago Press, 1970.
Williams, John A. *The Man Who Cried I Am.* New York: Signet, 1968.
Williams, Joseph J. *Hebrewisms of West Africa.* New York: Bilbo & Tannen, 1967.
Williams, William Appleman. "The Legend of Isolationism in the 1920's." *Science and Society,* 18 (Winter 1954): 1–20.
Williamson, Joel. *New People.* New York: Free Press, 1980.
Wilmore, Gayraud S. *Black Religion and Black Radicalism: An Examination of the Black Experience in Religion.* Garden City, N.Y.: Doubleday, 1972.
Wilson, Edmund. *Patriotic Gore: Studies in the Literature of the American Civil War.* New York: Oxford University Press, 1962.
Winks, Robin, ed. *An Autobiography of the Reverend Josiah Henson.* Reading, Mass.: Addison-Wesley, 1969.
Winston, Henry. *Strategy for a Black Agenda.* New York: International Publishers, 1973.
Wolf, William J. *The Almost Chosen People.* Garden City, N.Y.: Doubleday, 1959.
Woodson, Carter G. *History of the Negro Church.* Washington, D. C.: Associated Publishers, 1921.
———, ed. *Negro Orators and Their Orations.* Washington, D.C.: Associated Publishers, 1925.
———, ed. *Works of Francis J. Grimke.* Washington, D. C.: Associated Publishers, 1942.
Worsley, Peter. *The Trumpet Shall Sound.* London: MacGibbon & Kee, 1968.
Wright, Richard. *The Color Curtain: A Report on the Bandung Conference.* Cleveland: World Publishing Co., 1956.
———. "Joe Louis Uncovers Dynamite." *New Masses,* 17 (October 8, 1935): 18.
Wylie, Irvin G. *The Self-Made Man in America: The Myth of Rags to Riches.* New York: Free Press, 1966.
Yancy, Dorothy C. "William Edward Burghardt Du Bois' Atlanta Years: The Human Side— A Study Based upon Oral Sources." *Journal of Negro History,* 63 (January 1978): 59–67.
Yerby, Frank. *Speak Now.* New York: Dial Press, 1969.

Index

Abernathy, Ralph, 256 n.88
Abolition, 10, 46–47, 236 n.26
Abysinnian Baptist Church, 137, 156
Accommodation: and Christianity, 55; of BTW, 87–88, 94, 98, 106; of King, 180, 207; of Elijah Muhammad, 207–8
Adams, Henry, 127
African Civilization Society, 80–81, 83
African Orthodox Church: organized, 136–37; related to Garvey and UNIA, 133–37, 253 n.49
Afro–American League, 93
Al Hajj al Imam Isa Abd'Allah Muhammad al Mahdi. *See* Imam Isa
Al Imam Muhammad Ahmad al Mahdi, 6, 191, 192
Albee, Edward, 196
Ali, Duse Muhammad, 126, 133
Ali, Muhammad, 181
Ali, Noble Drew, 137, 175, 186, 187
Allen, Richard, 34, 37, 45, 78–79, 134
AME Zion Church, 93
American Negro Academy, 27, 98, 128
American Studies method: and Henry Nash Smith, x, 53; and John William Ward, xi; in literary criticism, xii
Amin, Idi, 193
Anderson, Marion, 169
Ansaru Allah Community, ix, 191, 192, 193, 257 nn.25, 26, 27. *See also* Imam Isa

Aptheker, Herbert, 35, 127, 171
Armstrong, Samuel C. (General): and Hampton Institute, 89; as Mosaic figure, 246 n.3
Arnold, Elliott, 159
Atlanta compromise: "Uncle Tom" in, 62, 87–88; lauded by Grimke and Du Bois, 94, by Blyden, 101; Grimke, critical of, 94; Henry McNeal Turner, critical of, 101; exploited fear of foreigners, 105
Attucks, Crispus, 180

Baer, Max, 158, 159
Baldwin, James, 145
Bancroft, George, 112–13
Bandung Conference, 214, 259 n.21
Banneker, Benjamin, 33–34
Barnes, Albert C., 120, 121, 122
Barrett, Leonard, 7
Bascom, William, 25
Bastide, Roger, 5, 7, 23–24, 164
Batson, J. Milton, 169
Beatrice (prophetess), 6
Bedford, Robert Charles, 98
Beecher, Henry Ward, 49, 103
Beecher, Lyman, 3, 49, 103, 248 n.89
Bell, William Yancy, 135
Bellah, Robert, 3, 29, 89, 138
Ben–Israel, Prince Asiel, 188–90
Ben Jochannan, Josef, 220–21, 222, 223

Bercovitch, Sacvan, 30
Bergson, Henri, x
Berkhofer, Robert, Jr., 53
Bethel Literary and Historical Association, 94
Bethune, Mary McLeod, 229
Bilbo, Theodore G.: Negro repatriation bill of, 165–70; supported by Garveyites, 167; praises Garvey, 167
"Black Belt Nationalism," 170–71
Black Jews, 5, 183–93, 256 nn.2,3. See also Commandment Keepers; Ethiopian Hebrews; Falasha Jews; Jews
Black Madonna, 220, 222–23, 259 n.47
Black messianism. See Messianism
Black Muslims, 183–88 passim; 209, 220, 256 n.1, 259 n.27; Hanafi sect, 191, 193; and Malcolm X, 208–16 passim
Black nationalism. See Nationalism
Black Panthers, 216, 259 n.27
Black preachers, 71, 78–80, 84; and "Old Time Religion," 72–78; attacked by BTW, 96–97, 99, by Crummell, 99
Blassingame, John, 20, 26, 52
Blyden, Edward Wilmot, 51, 62, 66, 97; admires BTW, 101, 102; a romantic racialist, 129; hostile to mulattoes, 128; saw blacks and Jews as kindred people, 194
Boas, Franz, 27
Bond, Horace Mann, 175
Booth, Joseph, 100
Botkin, B. A., 13
Bowen, J. W. E., 100
Bowen, T. J., 61
Bracey, John H., 3
Brawley, Benjamin, 122
Breckinridge, Robert, 50
Breitman, George, 210, 211
Brotz, Howard, 186, 187
Brown, John, 13, 46
Brown, Sterling, 118, 119
Brown, Una, 162
Bruce, James, 184
Bruce, John E., 252 nn.26, 30
Buber, Martin, xi, 2, 226
Bunyan, John, 89
Burgess, Ebeneezer, 66
Burkett, Randall K., 124, 126, 135, 138

Cable, George Washington, 95
Cargo cults, 7

Carmichael, Stokely, 13, 216–20 passim; as Garveyite, 220; opposed to religion, 220; admires Black Muslims, 220
Carnera, Primo, 156, 160
Carter, Jimmy, 231–32
Channing, William Ellery, 83
Channing, Willaim H., 83, 246 n.70
Chatelain, Heli, 100, 103
Chesnutt, Charles Waddell: mulattoes described as "new people," 246 n.7
Chiliasm. See Millenarianism
Christian Industrial Education: at Tuskegee, 90–93, 94–95, 104; criticized, 94–95; Crummell and, 97–98
Christianity: Black church, 17; African survivals and, 22–29; and ideal of submission, 54–55, 242 n.21; natural to African race, 60–62, 65; Du Bois on, 67ff.; Northern and Southern, 71; slaves and, 72–78, 242 nn.21, 24; practical morality of BTW, 90–91; BTW attacks "colored ministry," 96; false, denounced by Grimke, 116; and Martin Luther King, 177–80. See also Evangelicalism
Church of God, 185
Church of God and Saints in Christ, 185
Civil Rights Congress, 229
Civil rights movement, 125, 178, 212, 214–15, 216, 219, 228–29, 230, 233
Clarke, John Henrik, 125, 251 n.4
Clay, Henry, 44
Cleage, Albert J., 1, 12, 210, 220, 221–23; distorts Christianity, 220–22; and black Jesus, 220, 223; admires Malcolm X, 223, 224; and Black Madonna, 220, 222–23
Cleaver, Eldridge, 13, 216, 259 nn.26, 28
Coleman, J. E., 144
Colonization: David Walker opposed to, 44–45; Mrs. Stowe favors, 49–50; Robert Breckinridge favors, 50; Bilbo's repatriation bill, 165–70
Commandment Keepers, 186. See also Black Jews
Communism: and "Black Belt Nationalism," 170–71; and black Marxists, 229; and Du Bois, 254 n.10
Cone, James H., 54, 223–24
Congo Reform Movement, 100
Congress on Africa, 100–102
Councill, William Hooper, 117, 250 n.37

Courlander, Harold, 25
Cox, Oliver, 10, 155, 156
Cromwell, John W., 54, 98
Crummell, Alexander, 27, 31, 51, 61–62, 66, 81; critical of Tuskegee, 97, and BTW, 98–99; extols Anglo–Saxon culture, 102; romantic racialist, 129; hostile to mulattoes, 130, 132, 138, 252 nn.26, 30; Ethiopian millennialist, 132; used term "new people," 246 n.7
Cruse, Harold, 131
Cuffe, Paul, 78

Dalfiume, Roger, 156
Dark Princess (Du Bois) 1, 144–54
Davidson, Basil, 21, 27
Davis, Allison, 10
Davis, Angela, 218
Davis, Benjamin, 229
Davis, David Brion, 46
Delany, Martin, 51, 52, 65–66, 97, 129, 140
Dessalines, 7
Diggs, James Robert Lincoln, 135
Divine. *See* Father Divine
Divinism. *See* Father Divine
Dollard, John, 10
Douglass, Frederick, 42, 53, 55, 59
Dubé, John Langalibalele, 100
Du Bois, W. E. B., xii, 3, 10, 89, 108, 113; and religion, 17–20, 55, 237 n.2, 242 n.22; on nobility of servitude, 62, 115, 120, 253 n.1; and Pan–Africanism, 93, 140–41, 221, 255 n.52; and Garvey, 129–31; dislikes *Home to Harlem* (McKay) and *Nigger Heaven* (Van Vechten), 121, 123, 250 n.53; supports voluntary segregation, 172–74; nationalism in *Dusk of Dawn*, 172–74; and "Crises," 173; and communism, 254 n.10; discussion of works of, 143–54, 185
Dumas, Alexander, 166
Dunbar, Paul Lawrence, 93
Durkheim, Emile, 68
Duvalier, Francois, 7, 140
Dwight, Timothy, 3, 106, 108

Elkins, Stanley M., 59, 60
Ellison, Ralph, xii, 15–16, 144, 196, 258 nn.1–5
Emerson, Ralph Waldo, 196

Essien–Udom, E. U., 137
Ethiopian Hebrews, 185. *See also* Black Jews; Commandment Keepers; Falasha Jews
"Ethiopian Movement," 183. *See also* Black Jews; Commandment Keepers; Ethiopian Hebrews; Falasha Jews
Ethiopianism, 17, 160; defined, 6–7; and Rastafarians, 7; of Garvey, 118, 162, 196; of William Yancy Bell, 135–36; in *Invisible Man* (Ellison), 196–97; and Black Jews, 256 n.2
Evangelicalism, 69–70, 71, 89, 219, 231–32. *See also* Christianity
Evans–Pritchard, E. E., 27

Fadumah, Orishatukeh, 27, 97, 128, 251 n.13
Falasha Jews, 5–6, 183, 184–85, 186, 192, 193. *See also* Black Jews; Ethiopian Hebrews; Jews
Fard, W. D., 13, 186, 187, 225, 237 n. 38
Father Divine, 11–12, 124, 160, 163
Fauset, Arthur H., 11
Federal Writers' Project: interviews with blacks on "Old Time Religion," 72–78
Ferris, William H., 97, 102, 105, 129, 140, 252 n.30
Fishman, Solomon, xii
Fiske, John, 110
Foner, Philip, 35
Ford, J. Arnold, 134, 253 n.46; and Garvey, 137, 186–87; in Ethiopia, 187; forms Beth B'nai, 186; study of Judaism, 257 n.9
Forten, James, 78
Fortune, Timothy Thomas, 93, 252 n.30
Foster, William Z., 171
Franklin, Benjamin, 89–90, 246 n.1
Frazier, E. Franklin, 13, 20, 23, 145, 217, 233; critical of black religion, 55, 178, 218–19, 238 n.6; and Garvey, 124, 163
Fredrickson, George M., 3, 50
Free African Society, 78
Freeman, Frederick, 66
Fullinwider, S. P., 3, 48, 54, 65, 85, 116, 252 n.19

Gabriel, 36, 45
Gandhi, Mahatma, 175, 176–77

Garnet, Henry Highland, 46, 65, 66, 81; and
    racial Christianity, 81; and "Address
    to the Slaves of the United States,"
    81–85; messianism of, 227
Garrison, William Lloyd, 66
Garvey, Marcus, 7, 10, 31, 51, 62, 66, 108,
    118, 120, 139, 156, 251 nn.4, 5; and
    "Uncle Tom" myth, 51, 115; dislikes
    Home to Harlem (McKay) 121, 123; ro-
    mantic racialist, 129; dislike for mu-
    lattoes, 130, 135, 140; conflict with
    Du Bois, 130–32, 253 n.58; and reli-
    gion, 133–39, 164–65; as fascist, 139,
    253 n.54; on Joe Louis, 159, 160; dis-
    likes Haile Selassie, 161–63; and Fa-
    ther Divine, 165, 170; and Bilbo, 167,
    169–70; and *Invisible Man* (Ellison),
    196, 197; and black Jesus, 220, 223
Genovese, Eugene D., 20, 26
Gibbon, Edward, 54
Gladden, Washington, 84 ·
Gobineau, Arthur Joseph de, 22
Grace, Charles Emanual (Daddy Grace), 11,
    125, 163
Graham, Billy, 219
Grand United Order of Knights of the
    Golden Lions and Daughters of Ethi-
    opian Redemption, 168
Gray, Thomas R.: and Nat Turner "Confes-
    sions," 52, 64–65, 66, 241 n.12, 244
    n.71
Griggs, Sutton, 53, 105, 130
Grimke, Francis J., 94, 115–18 passim, 247
    n.37
Gullah, Jack, 28
Gutman, Herbert G., 20

Haddani, Eldad, 184
Haile Selassie, 7; black Messiah, 160, 161;
    Garvey unsympathetic to, 161–63;
    ancestral claims, 192–93; alluded to
    in *Invisible Man* (Ellison), 197
Haleem, Abdul. *See* Minister Farrakhan
Haley, Alex, 210
Hall, Prince, 34–36
Hamid, Sufi A., 164
Hamilton, Charles V., 217
Hamilton, William, 39
Hamitic hypothesis, 189
Hansberry, Lorraine: on Du Bois, 175, 254
    n.2
Harding, Vincent, xii, 3, 175, 220, 227

Harding, Warren G., 169
Harlan, Louis, 100
Harlem Renaissance, 108, 118–19, 129,
    249 n.5. *See also* New Negro Move-
    ment
Harris, James Dennis, 66, 102
Harris, Joel Chandler, 53
Harris, Sara, 163
Harrison, Hubert, 117
Hayden, Robert, 122
Hayford, J. E. Casely, 27, 100, 101
Hayford, Mark, 100
Haygood, Atticus, 95
Heller, Joseph, 196
Henry, Milton, 211
Henson, Josiah, 42–43; related to "Uncle
    Tom," 52, 243 n.38; felt superior to
    master, 57, 134
Herskovits, Melville J., 20, 22–25, 119–20
Herzl, Theodore, 101
Hicks, Edward, 54, 242 n.18
Hofstadter, Richard, 219
Holly, James T., 66, 102, 129
Hopkins, Samuel, 66
Howe, Julia Ward, 3, 54
Huggins, Nathan, 26
Huggins, Willis N., 161
Hunt, H. L., 208
Hunton, Alphaeus, 175

Imam Isa, ix, 191, 192, 257 n.28, 258 n.31. *See*
    also Ansaru Allah Community
Integration, 117, 131, 180, 209, 212, 224
International Council of Friends of Ethio-
    pia, 161
Interracial marriage, 40, 82, 125–26, 130–
    31, 259 n.27
Invisible Man (Ellison), 196–206

Jackson, Jesse, 233, 260 nn.17–19
Jazz, 119–20
Jefferson, Thomas: Jeremiadic prophecies in
    "Notes on the State of Virginia,"
    31–39 passim, 108, 226, 227
Jenkins, Clarke, 190–91
Jeremiad: defined, 30–31; as black messian-
    ism, 29–32; and slavery, 30–46; in
    David Walker's "Appeal," 38–46; of
    Jefferson, 31–39 passim; of Malcolm
    X, 214, 215, 258 nn.4, 7
Jews: and messianism, xi, 2, 3; Garvey sees
    slavery as punishment for Egypt's

sin, 138, and compares black Americans with, 170. *See also* Black Jews; Falasha Jews; Ethiopian Hebrews; Zionism

Jobs for Negroes Campaign, 164
Johnson, Guy B., 20
Johnson, James Weldon, 111–12, 115, 121, 144
Johnson, Mordecai, 110–11
Jones, Absolom, 34, 37, 78
Jones, James Warren, 14. *See also* People's Temple
Jones, Raymond Julius, 185

Kemp, Ira, 161
Kilson, Marion D., 63
Kilson, Martin, x, 9
King, Martin Luther, Jr.: accommodation and militancy, 207, 215; compared with Gandhi and Luthuli, 175–76; and human rights, 229, 234; and Malcolm X, 212, 224, 259n.15; and messianism, 224; millenarian integrationism, ix–xi, 3, 12, 15, 156; opposed to nationalism, 178; on Vietnam War, 256n.71. *See also* Civil rights movement
King, Martin Luther, Sr., 231–32
Kohn, Hans, 3
Ku Klux Klan, 109

Lampley, James, 14
Lanternari, Vittorio, 175
Las Casas, Bartolomew, 43, 58
Lasch, Christopher, 232
Leslau, Wolf, 184, 185
Levi–Strauss, Claude, 27
Levine, Lawrence, 20, 26, 36, 120
Levy–Bruhl, Lucien, x, 27
Lewis, R. W. B., xii
Lewis, William H., 112–13
Lincoln, Abraham, 13, 47–48, 158, 241n.52
Lincoln, C. Eric, 224, 233
Lindsay, Vachel, 119
Locke, Alain; 109, 119–20, 121–23, 252n.19
Lomax, Louis, 208, 211
Long, Huey P., 164
Louis, Joe, xi, 13, 163; as messianic figure, 156–58, 181, 182; represents Ethiopia, 156; King and, 180, 230
L'Ouverture, Toussaint, 7, 36, 63
Luthuli, Albert, 175, 176, 177

McCabe, Edwin P.: and migration to Oklahoma, 127
McGuire, George Alexander, 133–37, 220
McKay, Claude: Du Bois and Garvey reject *Home to Harlem*, 121, 122, 250nn.53, 54; and concepts of black nationalism, 130, 144, 145
Mackie, Mary F., 89
McLoughlin, William G., 3
Mahan, Alfred T., 110
Mahdism, ix, 6, 191. *See also* Ansaru Allah Community; Imam Isa
Malcolm X, 15, 141, 179, 181; Black Muslim spokesman, 208–10; and Martin Luther King, 212, 224, 259n.15; breaks with Elijah Muhammad, 211, 215, 216; and messianism, 224, 225; and human rights, 229; and black nationalism, 209–12 passim. *See also* Black Muslims; Nation of Islam
Malinowski, Bronislaw, 20
Manning, William T., 136–37
Marston, J. H., 156–57, 158
Martin (brother of Gabriel), 36
Martinez, Ramon A.: supports Bilbo, 168
Marty, Martin E., 3
Marxism, 13, 211, 229. *See also* "Black Belt Nationalism"; Communism
Mather, Cotton, 89
Matthew, Wentworth A., 185–86
Matthiessen, F. O., xii
Mays, Benjamin, 55
Mbiti, John, 21
Meier, August, 3, 93
Messiah, 1, 4–5, 54, 210, 226, 236n.8. *See also* Messianism
Messianism: defined, xi, 1–2, 4; of America, 2–3, 8; black: defined, x–xii, 2, 226; and redemptive mission of black race, x–xi, xii, 1, 3, 66; and Christianity, 4, 9, 15; African cognates of, 5–8; manifestations of, 9–13, 110, 119, 123, 125, 142, 171–72, 177–78, 191, 194–95, 211, 224, 227
Migration: to the North, 109, 128–29, 183; westward, 127–28; back to Africa, 125, 127
Millenarianism: defined, 4, 226; and "Uncle Tom" myth, 66; and Garnet, 83–85; and BTW, 85; Gandhi's social, 176; and Civil War, 236–37n.26
Miller, Perry, 30–31

Mills, Samuel, 66
Milton, John, 54
Minister Farrakhan: splits from Messenger's sons, ix; revives Nation of Islam, 188
Mintz, Sidney, 25
Mohonk Conference, 95
Moody, William Vaughn, 84
Moorhead, James H., 30
Morris, Charles S., 94
Moorish Science Temple: attracts Garveyites, 137, 186; symbol of, 192; members join Nation of Islam, 257 n.10
Moorish Zionist Temple, 186
Moral Majority, 233
Mosaic theme: examples of, 13, 246 n.3; and BTW, 86–87, 228
Mosely, George Van Horn, 170
Moss, Leonard, 223
Moton, Robert Russa, 107–8, 116, 123
Muhammad, Elijah, 175, 178, 224, 225; founds Nation of Islam, 186, 187; preaches black supremacy, 187, 188, 207; death of, 187; opposed to political activism, 207, 208; and Malcolm X, 208–16 passim
Muhammad, Wallace, 188
Mullin, Gerald, 36
Myal Man (Good Enchanter), 24
Myrdal, Gunnar, 20, 228
Myth, x–xii

Nation of Islam, 186, 187, 188; symbol of, 192; conservatism of, 207, 208, 212; name, 256 n.1. See also Malcolm X; Muhammad, Elijah
National Association for the Advancement of Colored People (NAACP), 130–31, 172, 173
National Movement for the Establishment of a 49th State, 171
National Negro Business League, 93
National Negro Conference, 171
Nationalism: defined, 3–4, 32; black nationalism: defined, 3; and black messianism, 3–4; religious, 3, 24, 26, 28–29, 236 n.6; of Nat Turner and Uncle Tom, 55, 66; of Walker's "Appeal," 38ff., 240 n.30; of Grimke, 117; of Garvey, 132ff., of Du Bois, 171–75; of Gandhi, 176–77; of Malcolm X,

209–12 passim; at low ebb, 251 n.4; and Jewish tradition, 256–57 n.3
Nell, William Cooper, 102
New Negro Movement, 108, 118–19, 129, 249 n.5. See also Harlem Renaissance
Newton, Huey, xi
Niebuhr, H. Richard, 3, 108, 196
Nobel Peace Prize: awarded Lithuli and King, 176; Martin Luther King assumes international role after receiving, 179, 181
Novak, Michael, 10, 231
Nubian Islamic Hebrew Mission. See Ansaru Allah Community

Obeah man (Evil Enchanter), 24; Father Divine as, 164
Obi, 19, 133. See also Obeah man
Ochs, Adolph S., 164
Ofari, Earl, 174
Original Hebrew Israelite Nation, 188–90
"Othello," 33
Ottley, Roi, 156
Owens, Jesse, 230
Owens, Leslie, 26

Painter, Nell, 127
Pan-Africanism, 17, 128, 129, 189; in Dark Princess (Du Bois), 146–48, 153–54, 189; and Malcolm X, 210–14 passim; of Carmichael, 217; decline of, 251 n.4; and Fadumah, 251 n.13. See also Pan-Islamism
Pan-Islamism, 184; of Black Muslims, 188; and Pan-Africanism, 193
Paris, Hilu, 220, 221
Park, Robert E., 20, 100
Parker, Theodore, 58
Parrinder, Geoffrey, 21, 27
Patterson, Orlando, 24
Patterson, William L., 229
Payne, Daniel Alexander, 79–80, 84; shares BTW's contempt for black clergy, 96–97
Peace Mission Movement, 163
Peace Movement of Ethiopia: rival to UNIA, 168, 255 n.39
Pearce, Roy Harvey, xii
Pegler, Westbrook, 157
Penney, Edgar James, 92–93
Pennington, J. W. C., 84

People United to Save Humanity (PUSH), 233; Push to Excel, 260 n.18
People's Temple, 14, 237 n.39. *See also* Jones, James Warren
Philafrican Liberator's League, 103
Phillips, Ulrich Bonnell, 59–60
Poole, Elijah. *See* Muhammad, Elijah
Porter, R. R., 123
Powell, Adam Clayton, Sr., 84, 137, 156
Prophet Cherry, 163, 185
Prophet Jones, 11
Prophetic movements, 1, 17, 236 n.10. *See also* Messianism
Prosser, Gabriel. *See* Gabriel

Raboteau, Albert J., 22–23
Randolph, John, 35
Ransom, Reverdy C., 84, 112
Ras Tafari Makonnen. *See* Haile Selassie
Rastafarianism, 7, 162, 183
Rauschenbusch, Walter, 84, 246 n.70
Rawick, George P., 25–26
Ray, C. B., 84
Read, Hollis, 61, 66
Reagan, Ronald, 223, 224
Redkey, Edwin S., 129
Reid, Ira D., 155, 156
Reynolds, Barbara, 233
Robeson, Paul, 175, 229
Rock, John S., 58
Rogers, J. A., 139, 144, 253 n.54
Rogers, Will, 164
Romantic racialism, 243 n.56, 251 n.15; of Africans, xi; and Lincoln, 48; and "Uncle Tom," 49, 66; and black moral superiority, 50–51, 57, 60–61, 66; in *Souls of Black Folk* (Du Bois), 172; in *Invisible Man* (Ellison), 197
Roosevelt, Franklin D., 159, 168, 171
Ruffner, Viola, 89
Russell, Bertrand, xi, 13, 176, 226

Sado-masochism: in *Uncle Tom's Cabin* (Stowe), 56–58; in *Dark Princess* (Du Bois), 152
Sam, Alfred C., 27, 125, 128, 140
Satyagraha, 177
Schmeling, Max, 158, 159, 160, 230
Schuyler, George S., 122
Scott, William R., 160
Seligman, C. G., 189

Separatism, 129, 171–74, 186, 187, 207, 208, 211, 217
Shaykh Dau'wd, 191
Shembe, Isaiah, 5
Shepperson, George, 6, 100
Singleton, Benjamin "Pap," 127–28
Slave revolts, 24, 63, 244 n.67; L'Ouverture, 35–36, 63; Vesey, 36–37; Nat Turner, 63–66
Slavery, 51, 56–60, 237 n.28, 241 nn.9,10; and black jeremiad, 30–34. *See also* Chapters 2, 3, 4, 5
Smith, C. S., 94
Smith, Henry Nash, x, 53
Smith, J. B., 51
Social Gospel, 8, 86, 227–28, 236 n.26, 246 n.70
Southern Christian Leadership Conference (SCLC), 178, 216, 224
Starobin, Robert, 36–37
Stern, Carl, 225
Stewart, Maria, 39
Stowe, Harriet Beecher, xi, 47, 49, 107, 108, 115, 119–20, 226. *See also* "Uncle Tom" myth; *Uncle Tom's Cabin*
Strong, Josiah, 3, 8, 103–6, 110, 126–27, 248 nn.89,90
Stuckey, Sterling, 52
Student Nonviolent Coordinating Committee (SNCC), 216
Styron, William, 63, 244 n.70
Suffering servant motif: messianic people as, x, 5, 16, 54, 60–61, 234; and "Uncle Tom" myth, xi, 55–57; Lincoln as, 47–48; Garvey and, 51, 115; in *Dark Princess* (Du Bois), 152, 153. *See also* "Uncle Tom" myth
Sunday, Billy, 126
Sweet, Henry F., 46
Syncretism, 17, 24, 26, 238 n.7

Taylor, Edward, 54
Thoreau, Henry David: works read by Gandhi, 176
Tourgee, Albion W., 95
Toynbee, Arnold, 9, 181
Trotter, Marva, 159
Turner, Harold W., 4
Turner, Henry McNeal, 101–2, 128; romantic racialist, 129; and Bilbo, 169; God is black, 220, 223

Turner, Lorenzo, 20
Turner, Nat, 28, 36, 46, 63, 64–66, 227, 244
  nn.70,71
Tuveson, E. L., 2, 48, 50
Twain, Mark, 100

"Uncle Tom" myth: Christian heroism as
  misguided altruism, xi–xii, 3; mod-
  eled on Josiah Henson, 43, 243 n.38;
  Lincoln as, 47–48; BTW and, 62, 66;
  Du Bois and, 66–67, 142, 143; Gar-
  vey and, 51, 115; Grimke and, 115.
  See also Suffering servant motif
Uncle Tom's Cabin (Stowe), 49–50, 55–58,
  227, 245 n.25
Universal Holy Temple of Tranquility, 164
Universal Negro Improvement Association
  (UNIA), 133–41 passim; flag of, used
  by Rastamen, 7; condemns Father
  Divine, 165; and J. Arnold Ford, 186

Vaihinger, Hans, x
Van Vechten, Carl, 121
Vesey, Denmark, 28, 36, 63. See also Slave
  revolts
Vilatte, Bishop Pere, 137

Wade, Richard C., 37
Waldrond, Eric, 121
Walker, David, 1, 61, 63, 66, 196, 214, 215;
  "Appeal," 38–46, 55, 81–82, 227
Walker, Sheila S., 5
Walters, Alexander, 93–94
Ward, John William, xi
Ward, Samuel Ringgold, 84
Warner, Lloyd, 10

Washington, Booker T., 172, 197, 228, 246
  nn.3 and 5, 250 n.37; "Uncle Tom"
  stereotype, 62; and Payne, 96–97;
  feuds with Ferris, 97; and Pan–Afri-
  canism, 100–101, 117, 120, 129;
  American blacks as chosen people,
  106–8, 115; and Garvey, 140–41. See
  also Atlanta compromise
Washington, Joseph R., 12, 54, 220, 233
Weil, Martin, 231
Wells, Ida B., 53
White, Walter, 121, 131, 229; attacked by
  Du Bois, 173
Williams, Henry Sylvester, 93
Williams, John A., 144, 145
Williams, Joseph J., 189
Williams, Peter, 78, 81
Wilmore, Gayraud S., 220, 224
Wilson, Woodrow, 109, 249 n.10
Winston, Henry, 217–18
Winthrop, John, 50, 108
Woodson, Carter G., 126
Woolfolk, Ben, 36
World Community of Al-Islam in the West,
  187, 188, 256 n.1. See also Nation of
  Islam
World War I, 108–10, 116–17
Wright, Richard, 144
Wright, Richard R., Jr., 84, 247 n.37

Yakubism, 187, 209, 211, 223, 257 n.12
Yerby, Frank, 145
Young, Andrew, 13, 15, 230–31
Young, Robert Alexander, 51

Zangwill, Israel, 112
Zionism, 184, 188, 194–98, 213, 253 n.53.
  See also Jews

To The Next Messiah

Plan to arrive and recognize that they
Who plot your proddings—Gods goading to the good
Have ordered all—will give you strength today
Where yesterday they proffered cups of blood.

Your tenuous water-walking on the face
Of tepid shallows fails to impress.
Veronica won't bother to erase
The stains of wasted tears. You will not bless
Your foes . . . for, standing on the blunted peak
Of Calvary, you'll find you are alone.

Now surely they have struck the other cheek,
For friends and enemies alike have flown
And none on earth can spare a speck of spit,
For your salvation or their loss of it.

W.J.M.

Wilson Jeremiah Moses was born in 1942 in Detroit, Michigan, where he was educated in the
Nativity of Our Lord Parochial School from 1952 to 1960. He attended Wayne State University,
where he received the A.B. in 1965 and the M.A. in 1967, writing his thesis on Percy B. Shelley's
"The Witch of Atlas." He holds the Ph.D. in American Civilization from Brown University
(1975). After teaching at the University of Iowa (1971–1976) and Southern Methodist University (1976–1978) and living in Cambridge, England (1978–1980), he returned to Brown
University as Associate Professor of American Civilization and Afro-American Studies. His
articles have been published in numerous scholarly periodicals including Journal of Negro History, American Literature, and Phylon. He is the author of The Golden Age of Black
Nationalism, 1850–1925 (Hamden, Conn.: Archon Books, 1978). He is working on a biography of Alexander Crummell.